Olympiad Champs

LOGICAL REASONING

Class 4

with **Chapter-wise Previous** **5 Year** (2018 - 2022) Questions

DISHA™
Publication Inc

DISHA Publications Inc.

45, 2nd Floor, Maharishi Dayanand Marg,
Corner Market, Malviya Nagar, new Delhi –110017
Tel: 49842349/ 49842350

Typeset By

DISHA DTP Team

Buying books from DISHA

Just Got A Lot More Rewarding!!!

We at DISHA Publication, value your feedback immensely and to show our apperciation of our reviewers, we have launched a review contest.

To participate in this reward scheme, just follow these quick and simple steps:
- Write a review of the product you purchase on Amazon/Flipkart.
- Take a screenshot/photo of your review.
- Mail it to *disha-rewards@aiets.co.in*, along with all your details.

Each month, selected reviewers will win exciting gifts from DISHA Publication. Note that the rewards for each month will be declared in the first week of next month on our website.

https://bit.ly/review-reward-disha.

Write To Us At

feedback_disha@aiets.co.in

Preface

We are pleased to launch the 2nd edition of **Olympiad Champs Logical Reasoning Class 4** which is the first of its kind book on Olympiad in many ways.

The Unique Selling Proposition of this new edition is the inclusion of past year questions till 2022 of different Olympiad exams held in schools.

The book is aimed at achieving not only success but deep rooted learning in children. It is prepared on content based on National Curriculum Framework prescribed by NCERT. All the text books, syllabi and teaching practices within the education programme in India must follow NCF. Hence, Olympiad Champs become an ideal book not only for the Olympiad Exams but also for strengthening the concepts for Class 4.

There is an exhaustive range of thought provoking questions in MCQ format to test the student's knowledge thoroughly. The questions are designed so as to test the knowledge, comprehension, evaluation, analytical and application skills. Solutions and explanations are provided for all questions. The questions are divided into two levels - Level 1 and Level 2. The first level, Level 1, is the beginner's level which comprises of questions like fillers, analogy and odd one out. When the child covers Level 1, it means his basic knowledge about the subject is clear and now it is ready for Level 2. The second level is the advanced level. Level 2 comprises of techniques like matching, chronological sequencing, picture, passage and feature based, statement correct/ incorrect, integer based, puzzle, grid based, crossword, venn diagram, table/ chart based and much more.

The first concern which each parent faces is how to make their children read a book especially when it is based on academics. Keeping this in mind interesting facts, real life examples, historical preview, short cut to problem solving, charts, diagrams, illustrations and poems are added. In addition to this, we have introduced comic strip which increases the readability quotient and make the reading experience for the children more exciting.

With the vision to remove all the misconception a child may have pertaining to the subject, to relate his knowledge to the real world and to develop a deeper understanding of the subject this book will cater all the requirements of the students who are going to appear in Olympiads.

While preparing this book, some errors might have crept in. We request our readers to identify those errors and send it across on **feedback_disha@aiets.co.in.**

We wish you all the best for your Olympiads and happy reading.......

Team Disha

For feedback : **feedback_disha@aiets.co.in.**

CONTENTS

10 Principles to CRACK ANY EXAM

1. Chase consistency, not intensity.

Doing intensive study makes your day. But it also exhausts you in the long run, leading to lesser output and added pressure. Toppers always focus on doing consistent work daily, for consistency is far more valuable than intensity.

Remember consistent study of 4 hours every day is more important and powerful than studying 12 hours a day and then not studying at all for next 2 days.

2. Go beyond the surface.

Most students only see a few reasons (teacher, coaching, books, etc) behind Toppers' success, which is only the tip of the iceberg. What they donot see is Toppers Mindset, self belief, habits and discipline and that is where the real problem is.

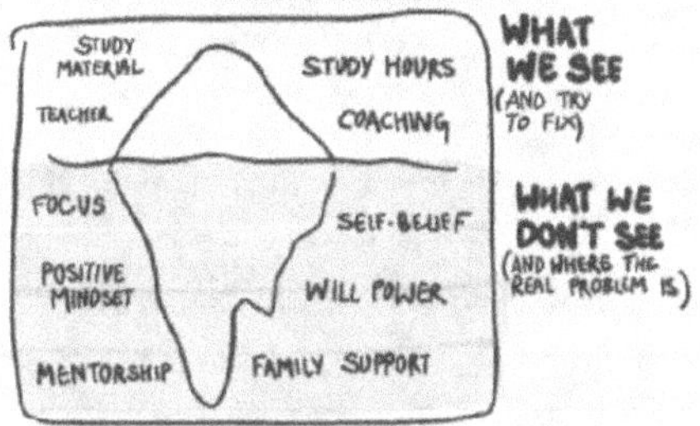

3. Focus on giving your best, not chasing the best.

We want the best coaching, the best teacher, best batch and the best books but we are not ready to give our BEST. Success comes only when we are ready to give our best. We must focus on giving our best than chasing excuses to cover up our failures.

4. Clarity of concept is the key

Concept clarity is critical. If you cannot solve a question, you must go back to the theory and thoroughly examine the concept instead of referring to the solutions. Remember question is one of the chehra(face) of the concept. When toppers get stuck in a problem, they go back and refer the theory(read the concept again and again on which the question is based)

5. Every failure should be a lesson learned.

Most students do not learn from their failures and repeat their mistakes. Toppers also face failures, but they learn from mistakes and elevate themselves. Making mistakes and learning from them is the key to success.

6. Choosing the quality of resources is more important than quantity.

More than 90% of the questions in most books are the same as their substitutes. Instead of practicing from four books and failing to complete them, it is best to prepare from two books and complete them with thorough revisions.

7.

Difficult things become easy by taking it one day at a time.

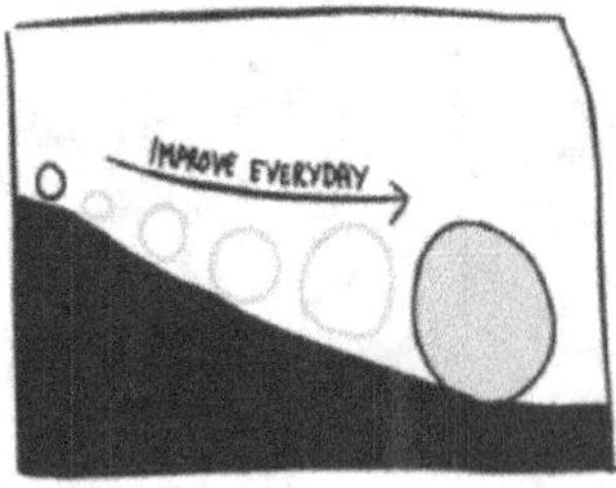

The best way to take any preparation forward is by taking it one day at a time. It makes the impossible possible by taking small steps every day.

Starting a difficult subject. No worries. Keep on working session by session, day by day and week by week and one day you will become unstoppable force.

8. Everything is easy

Before starting everything looks difficult. Once you take a first step, it slowly starts looking easy and over a period of time you become master in the activity. This is toppers secret to become master in any subject.

9. Nobody is gifted

We think toppers are god gifted. We think toppers have high IQ. We think toppers are special/lucky. But the truth is every topper was once an average student(no body is born topper). What makes them different is their consistent and focused efforts.

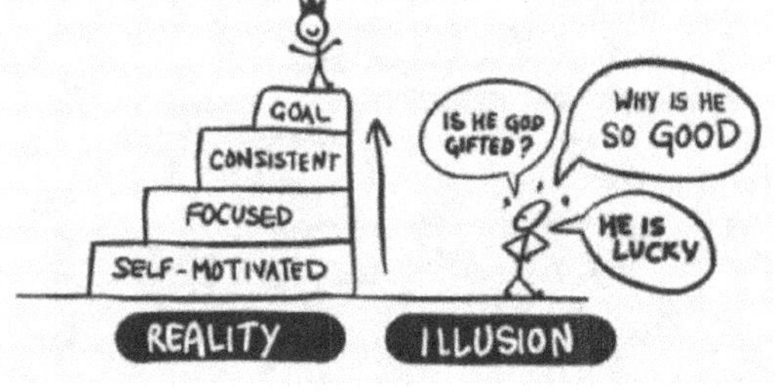

10. Believe in your journey and success will come to you.

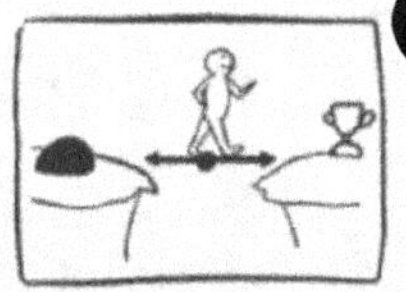

There is never a straight path to success; hard work & patience is required for the results to show up. Keep on working hard without thinking too much about the results and success will come to you eventually.

Analogy

OBJECTIVES

- Students will be able to study the similar patterns.
- They will be able to sort out objects on the basis of similarity.

INTRODUCTION

In 'analogy', a pair of figures/letters/words/numbers is provided and a similar relationship is followed by another pair of figures/letters/words/numbers. This is also known as 'Similarity' or 'Matching pairs'.

Types of Analogy

1. **Word Analogy**

   In word analogy, a group of three words is given, followed by four alternatives. The student is required to choose the alternative, which is similar to the given group of words.

Example 1

Paw: Cat :: Hoof: ?

    (a) Horse   (b) Lion   (c) Lamb   (d) Elephant

Ans. (a)

Explanation: First is the name given to the foot of the second.

Example 2

Moon is related to satellite in the same way as Earth is related to ..... ?

    (a) Sun   (b) Planet   (c) Solar system   (d) Asteroid

Ans. (b)

Explanation: Moon is a satellite and earth is a planet.

2. Letter Analogy

In letter analogy, a group of letters is given, followed by four alternatives. The student is required to choose the alternative, which is similar to the given group of letters.

Example 3

Complete the second pair in the same way as first pair.

AT is to CV, as LR is to

(a) MS   (b) NT   (c) KQ   (d) RL

Ans. (b)

Explanation: As,

As,	A	T	Similarly,	L	R
	+2↓	+2↓		+2↓	+2↓
	C	V		N	T

So, NT will complete the second pair.

Example 4

COME is related to EOMC, in the same way HOME is related to

(a) EMOH   (b) IPNF   (c) EOMH   (d) FNPI

Ans. (c)

Explanation: As,

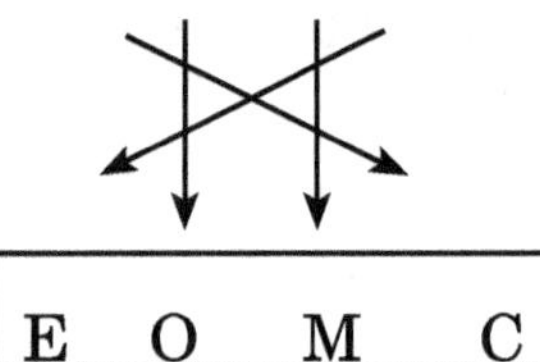

Similarly,

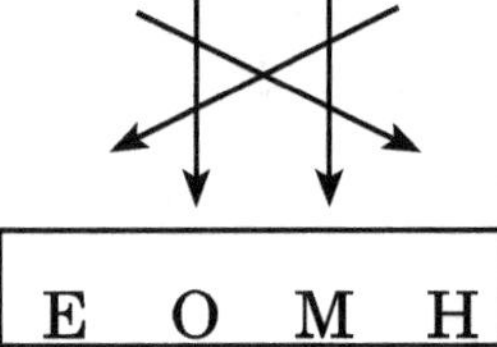

So, HOME is related to EOMH.

3. Number Analogy

In number analogy, a group of numbers is given, followed by four alternatives. The student is required to choose the alternative, which is similar to the given group of numbers.

63 is related to 3, in the same way as 96 is related to...............?

   (a) 15   (b) 3   (c) 9   (d) 5

Ans. (d)

Explanation: As, $\qquad 63 = 6 + 3 = 9$ and $9 \div 3 = 3$

$\qquad\qquad$ Similarly, $\quad 96 = 9 + 6 = 15$ and $15 \div 3 = 5$

So, 96 is related to 5.

4. **Mixed Analogy**

In mixed analogy, a group of combination of numbers/letters/words is given, followed by four alternatives. The student is required to choose the alternative, which is similar to the given group of combination of numbers/letters/words.

Example 6

A : 1 :: C : ?

   (a) 2   (b) 4   (c) 6   (d) 9

Ans. (d)

Explanation: As, $\qquad A \rightarrow (1)^2 = 1$ (the positional value of A is 1)

$\qquad\qquad$ Similarly, $\quad C \rightarrow (3)^2 = 9$ (the positional value of C is 3).

So, C is related to 9.

5. **Figure Analogy**

In figure analogy, a group of figures is given, followed by four alternatives. The student is required to choose the alternative, which is similar to the given group of figures.

Example 7

Which figure will complete the second pair in the same way as first pair.

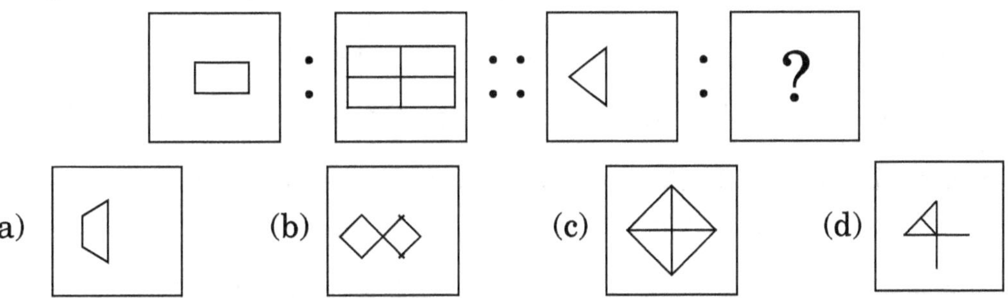

Ans. (c)

Explanation: The design in first figure is completed and divided into four equal parts to obtain the second figure.

LEVEL-1

Directions (Qs. 1-7): Choose the words that complete the second pair in the same way as the first pair.

1. Acting : Theatre : : Gambling : ?

   (a) Gym   (b) Bar   (c) Club   (d) Casino

2. Architect : Building : : Sculptor : ?

   (a) Chisel   (b) Stone   (c) Statue   (d) Museum

3. Doctor : Nurse : : ? : Follower

   (a) Employer   (b) Manager   (c) Leader   (d) Worker

4. Bread : Yeast : : Curd : ?

   (a) Fungi   (b) Virus   (c) Bacteria   (d) Milk

5. Clock : Time : : Thermometer ?

   (a) Temperature   (b) Energy

   (c) Heat   (d) Radiation

6. Flower : Bud : : Plant : ?

   (a) Twig   (b) Seed   (c) Flower   (d) Taste

7. Newspaper : Press : : Cloth ?

   (a) Tailor   (b) Fibre   (c) Textile   (d) Mill

8. Crime is related to police, in the same way flood is related to __________ ?

   (a) River   (b) Rain   (c) Dam   (d) Well

9. England is related to Atlantic Ocean, in the same way as Greenland is related to __________ ?

   (a) Atlantic Ocean   (b) Arctic Ocean

   (c) Pacific Ocean   (d) Antarctica Ocean

Directions (Qs. 10-11): Choose the pair of words that shows the relationship which is most similar to that of the given pair of words.

10. Water : Swim : : ? : ?

    (a) Knot : Tie   (b) Flood : Damage

    (c) Plant : Implement   (d) Ground : Play

11. Hot : Oven : : ? : ?

    (a) Ink : Pen   (b) Door : Bell

    (c) Cold : Refrigerator   (d) Ice : Cold

Directions (Qs. 12-30): Identify the relation between each of the given pair on either side of : : and find the missing figure/term.

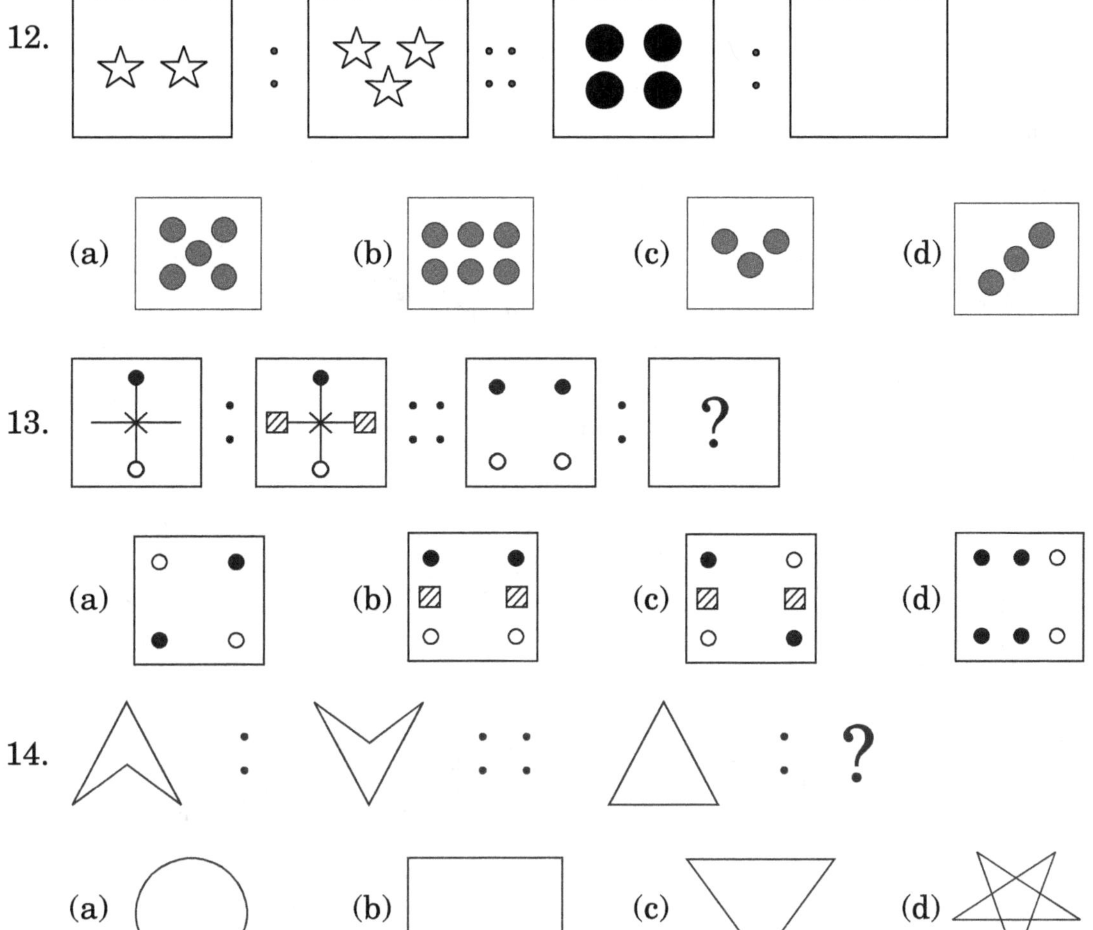

15.  : ?

(a) (b) (c) (d)

16.  : ?

(a) Root   (b) Vegetable   (c) Grain   (d) Salad

17. $10 + 4 + 5 : 19 :: 11 + 3 + 7 : \underline{\;\;?\;\;}$

(a) 12   (b) 20   (c) 21   (d) 25

18. 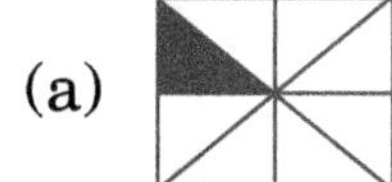 : ?

(a) (b) (c) (d)

19. 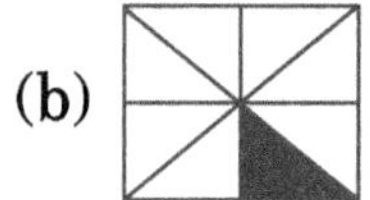 : ?

(a) (b) (c) (d)

20. $5\dfrac{1}{2} : \dfrac{11}{2} :: 3\dfrac{2}{5} : ?$

(a) $\dfrac{8}{4}$ (b) $\dfrac{17}{5}$ (c) $\dfrac{18}{5}$ (d) $\dfrac{16}{5}$

21. $\dfrac{1}{2} : \dfrac{2}{4} :: \dfrac{2}{3} : ?$

(a) $\dfrac{4}{8}$ (b) $\dfrac{4}{6}$ (c) $\dfrac{4}{7}$ (d) $\dfrac{3}{6}$

22. $\dfrac{6}{8} : \dfrac{3}{4} :: \dfrac{6}{24} : ?$

    (a) $\dfrac{3}{6}$ (b) $\dfrac{3}{8}$ (c) $\dfrac{3}{12}$ (d) $\dfrac{1}{12}$

23. $8 \times \dfrac{3}{4} : \dfrac{24}{4} :: 1 \times \dfrac{6}{7} : ?$

    (a) $\dfrac{1}{4}$ (b) $\dfrac{6}{7}$ (c) $\dfrac{9}{7}$ (d) None of these

24. 100 cm : 1 m : : 1000 m : ?

    (a) 2 kg   (b) 7 km   (c) 1 km   (d) None of these

25.  : Litre : :  : ?

    (a) Millilitres   (b) Miligram   (c) Kilogram   (d) Centimeter

26. 25 − 20 : 5 : : 75 − 65 : ?

    (a) 5   (b) 8   (c) 10   (d) None of these

27. Temperature : °C, °F : : Time : ?

    (a) Km, Cm   (b) A.M., P.M.   (c) L, Ml   (d) None of these

28. $2 \times 2 \times 2 : 8 ::$ ___?___ $:: 64$

    (a) $3 \times 3 \times 3$ (b) $4 \times 4 \times 4$ (c) $5 \times 5 \times 5$ (d) None of these

29. 50 : L : : 70 : ?

    (a) LIX   (b) LXX   (c) XL   (d) None of these

30. Exercise : Gym : : Eating : ?

    (a) Restaurant   (b) Drinking   (c) Fitness   (d) Dieting

31. The given pair of figures on either side of :: has a certain relationship. Identify the relationship and choose the missing figure. **(2022)**

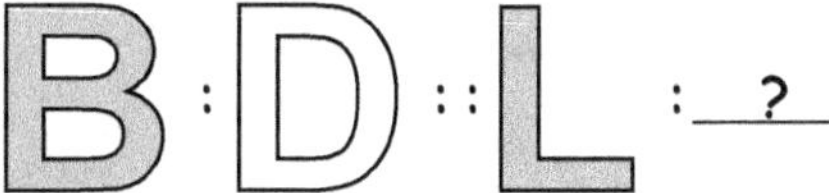

A. 　　B. 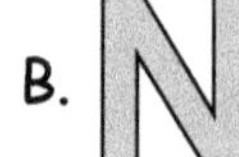　　C. 　　D. M

32. Select the related word from the given alternative that will replace (?).

   Fruit : Banana : : Mammal : ?   **(2022)**

   (a) Cow   (b) Snake   (c) Frog   (d) Sparrow

LEVEL-2

Directions (Qs. 1-4): Complete the second pair in the same way as the first pair.

1.  : 5 : :  : ?

   (a) 6   (b) 8   (c) 10   (d) 12

2. $12 + 7 : 19 :: 20 + 35 : ?$

   (a) 55   (b) 35   (c) 49   (d) 66

3. Antiseptic : Germs : : Antidote : ?

   (a) Allergy   (b) Poison   (c) Infection   (d) Wound

4. L : 50 :: C : ?

   (a) 60   (b) 85   (c) 95   (d) 100

5. Part is related to whole in the same way as Arc is related to ___?___

   (a) Rhombus   (b) Triangle   (c) Circle   (d) Square

6. Shoes are related to the cobbler. In the same way, Eye glasses are related to ______ ?

   (a) Optician   (b) Optometrist
   (c) Ophthalmologist   (d) Oculist

Directions (Qs. 7-8): Which figure will replace the question mark (?).

7. 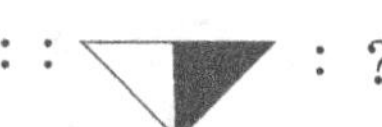 : ?

   (a)    (b) 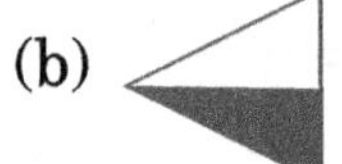   (c)    (d) None of these

8.  : 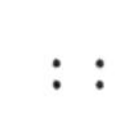 : : 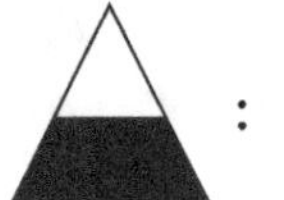 : ?

(a) ▮▮▮▮   (b) △   (c) ▽   (d) ✩

9. Tennis is related to court in the same way Boxing is related to _______ ?

    (a) Course   (b) Pool   (c) Arena   (d) Ring

10. Horse is related to the Hay in the same way a Cow is related to _______ ?

    (a) Leaves   (b) Fodder   (c) Milk   (d) Straw

Directions (Qs. 11-13): Complete the second pair in the same way as the first pair.

11. Darkness : Lamp

    (a) Study : Classroom   (b) Medicine : Illness

    (c) Thirst : Water   (d) Fatigue : Exercise

12. Iodine : Goitre

    (a) Mango : Anaemia   (b) Insulin : Diabetes

    (c) Hormones : Haemophilias   (d) Fat : Obesity

13. Blackboard : Chalk ::

    (a) Music : Song   (b) Ink : Pen

    (c) Nail : Wood   (d) Paper : Pencil

14. In the English alphabet, 'BDG' is to 'CFJ'. In the same way as 'EGJ' is to

    (a) FIN   (b) FJM   (c) FIL   (d) FIM

15. In the English alphabet, 'YTO' is to 'XSN'. In the same way as 'WRM' is to

    (a) TOJ   (b) VQL   (c) UPK   (d) RMH

16. Which word is related to the third word in the same way as the first two words are related?

    Potato : Carrot : : Radish : ?

    (a) Groundnut   (b) Spinach   (c) Sesame   (d) Tomato

17. 'College' is related to 'Student' in the same way as 'Hospital' is related to

    (a) Doctor   (b) Medicine   (c) Patient   (d) Nurse

18. Which figure will replace the question mark (?).

△ : ✡ : : ▭ : ?

(a) 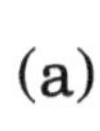   (b)    (c) 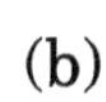   (d) 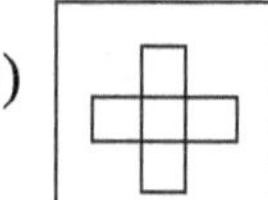

19. Which figure will replace the question mark (?).

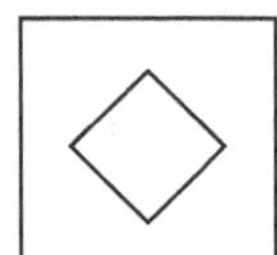 : 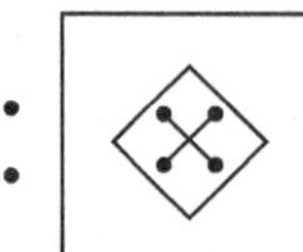 :: 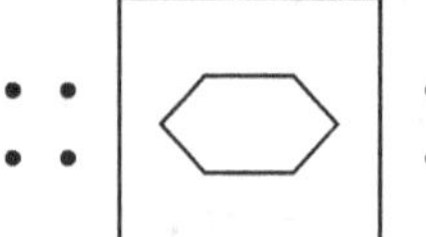 : ? 

(a)    (b) 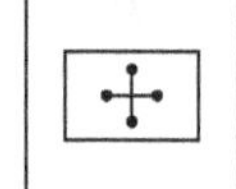   (c) 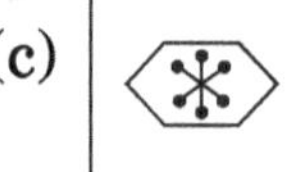   (d) 

20. Which figure will replace the question mark (?).

 : 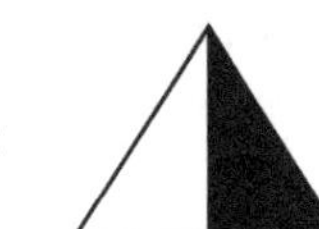 :: 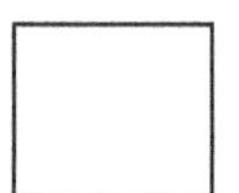 :

(a) 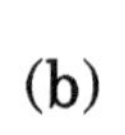   (b)    (c) 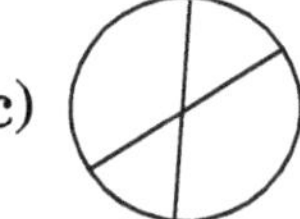   (d)

Directions (Qs. 21-28): Complete the second pair in the same way as the first pair.

21. $\dfrac{3}{5} : \dfrac{15}{25} :: \dfrac{2}{4} : ?$

   (a) $\dfrac{10}{20}$ (b) $\dfrac{8}{24}$ (c) $\dfrac{6}{24}$ (d) None of these

22. $\dfrac{8}{12} : \dfrac{2}{3} :: \dfrac{15}{25} : ?$

   (a) $\dfrac{3}{10}$ (b) $\dfrac{3}{5}$ (c) $\dfrac{4}{8}$ (d) $\dfrac{6}{8}$

23. $\dfrac{4}{16} : \dfrac{1}{4} :: \dfrac{5}{25} : ?$

   (a) $\dfrac{1}{4}$ (b) $\dfrac{1}{5}$ (c) $\dfrac{1}{6}$ (d) $\dfrac{1}{7}$

24. 1000 g : 1 Kg : : 1 gm : ?

(a) 0.1 Kg   (b) 0.001 Kg   (c) 0.2 Kg   (d) None of these

25. 125 ML : 0.125 L : : 68 ML : ?

(a) 1.250 L   (b) 0.68 L   (c) 0.068 L   (d) 68 L

26. 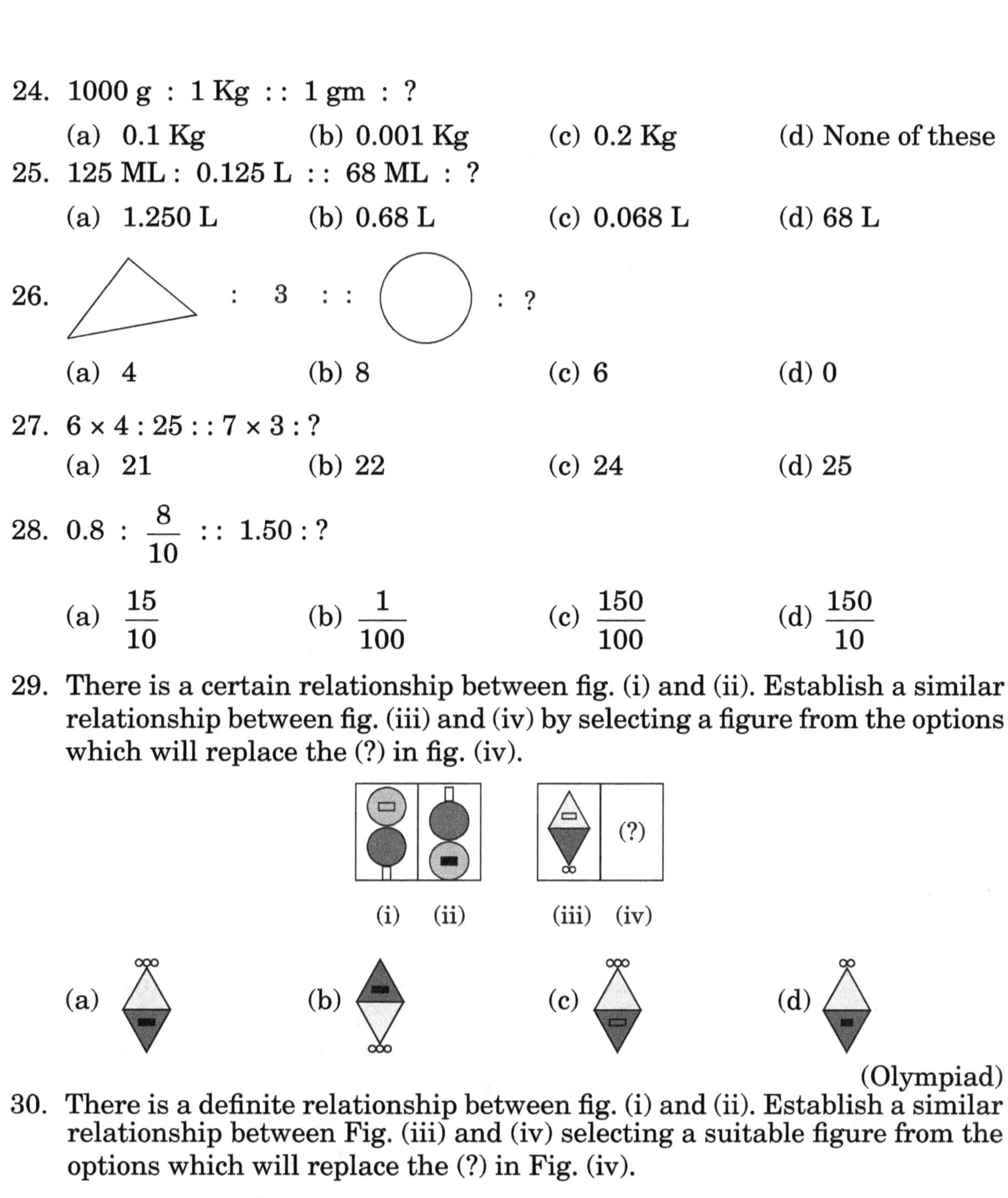 : 3 : : (circle) : ?

(a) 4   (b) 8   (c) 6   (d) 0

27. $6 \times 4 : 25 : : 7 \times 3 : ?$

(a) 21   (b) 22   (c) 24   (d) 25

28. $0.8 : \dfrac{8}{10} : : 1.50 : ?$

(a) $\dfrac{15}{10}$ (b) $\dfrac{1}{100}$ (c) $\dfrac{150}{100}$ (d) $\dfrac{150}{10}$

29. There is a certain relationship between fig. (i) and (ii). Establish a similar relationship between fig. (iii) and (iv) by selecting a figure from the options which will replace the (?) in fig. (iv).

(i)   (ii)   (iii)   (iv)

(a)   (b)   (c)   (d)

(Olympiad)

30. There is a definite relationship between fig. (i) and (ii). Establish a similar relationship between Fig. (iii) and (iv) selecting a suitable figure from the options which will replace the (?) in Fig. (iv).

(a)   (b)   (c)   (d)

(Olympiad)

31. There is a certain relationship between figures (i) and (ii). Establish the similar relationship between figures (ii) and (iv) by selecting a suitable figure from the options that would replace (?) in figure (iv). **(2020)**

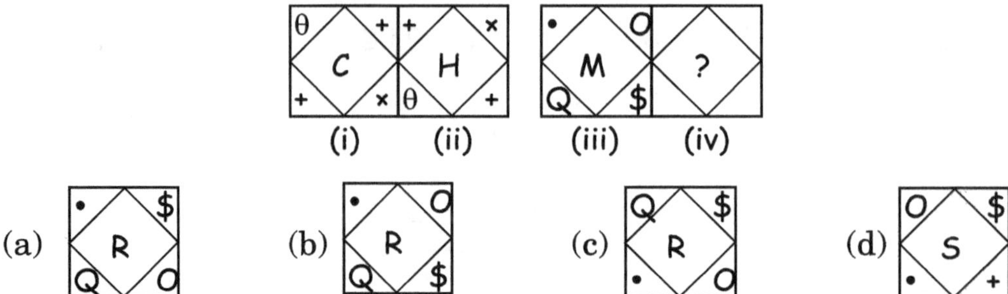

(i)   (ii)   (iii)   (iv)

(a)   (b)   (c)   (d)

32. There is a certain relationship between the figures on the either side of ::. Identify the relationship on left pair and find the missing figure. **(2021)**

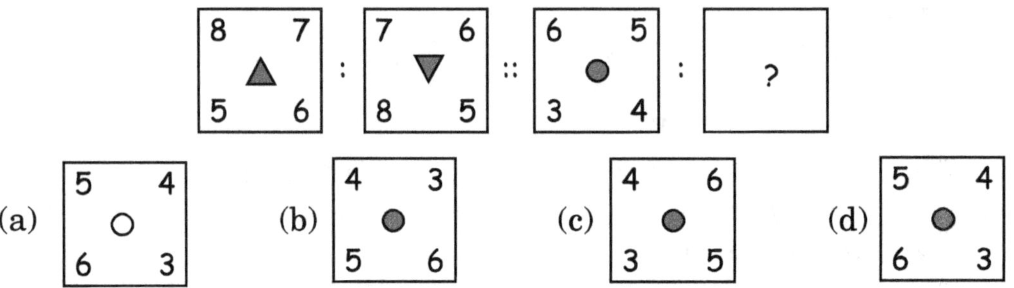

(a)   (b)   (c)   (d)

Answers and Explanation

Level-1

1. **(d)** Acting is performed in theatre. Similarly, Casino is a place where people gamble.

2. **(c)** As Architect makes Building, similarly, Sculptor makes statue.

3. **(c)** Nurse follows the instructions given by Doctor. In the same way, Followers follow the instructions of their Leaders.

4. **(c)** As Yeast is used to make Bread, in the same way, Bacteria is used to make curd.

5. **(a)** As clock measures time, Similarly, thermometer measures temperature.

6. **(b)** Flower grows from the Bud. In the same way, plant grows from the seed.

7. **(d)** As newspaper is prepared in a Press, similarly, Cloth is manufactured in the Mills.

8. **(c)** Police is meant to check the crime and Dam is constructed to prevent Flood.

9. **(b)** As England is situated in Atlantic Ocean, similarly,

Greenland is situated in Arctic Ocean.

10. (d) As Water is the medium to Swim, similarly, Ground is the place to Play.

11. (c) As Oven keeps the food hot, similarly, Refrigerator keeps the food cold.

12. (a) 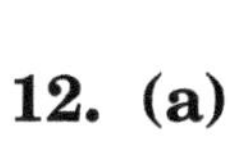

13. (b) 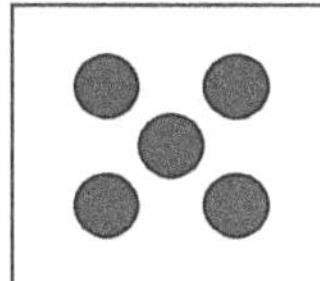

14. (c) 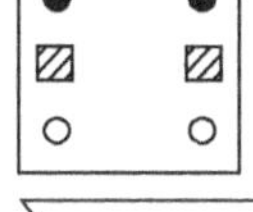

15. (d) 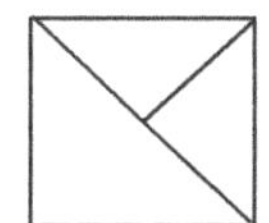

16. (b) As Pear is a fruit, similarly, spinach is a vegetable.

17. (c) As, $10 + 4 + 5 = 19$

similarly $11 + 3 + 7 = 21$.

18. (c) 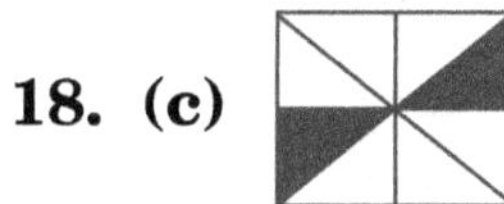

19. (c) 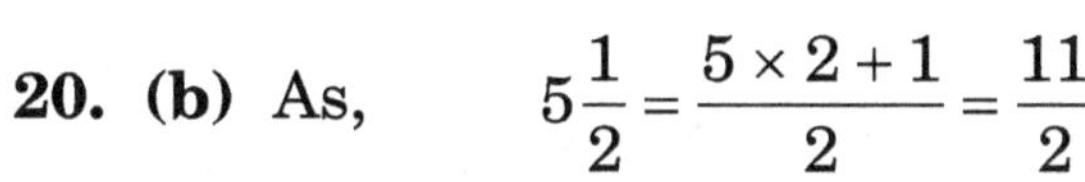

20. (b) As, $5\dfrac{1}{2} = \dfrac{5 \times 2 + 1}{2} = \dfrac{11}{2}$

Similarly,

$$3\dfrac{2}{5} = \dfrac{5 \times 3 + 2}{5} = \boxed{\dfrac{17}{5}}$$

21. (b) As,

$\dfrac{1}{2} \times \dfrac{2}{2} = \dfrac{2}{4}$ In the same way,

$$\dfrac{2}{3} \times \dfrac{2}{2} = \boxed{\dfrac{4}{6}}$$

22. (c) As,

$\dfrac{6 \, (\div 2)}{8 \, (\div 2)} = \dfrac{3}{4}$ In the same way,

$$\dfrac{6 \, (\div 2)}{24 \, (\div 2)} = \boxed{\dfrac{3}{12}}$$

23. (b) As, 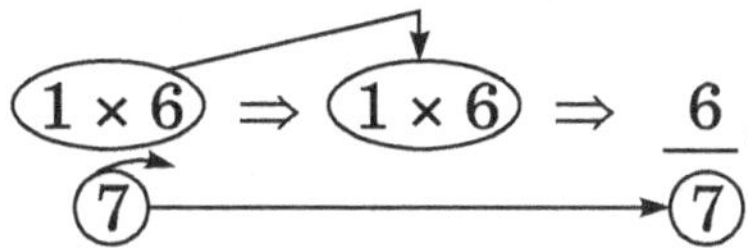

Similarly,

$\boxed{1 \times 6} \Rightarrow \boxed{1 \times 6} \Rightarrow \dfrac{6}{7}$.

with base $\dfrac{7}{7}$.

24. (c) As, 100 cm = 1 km

Similarly, 1000 m = 1 km

25. (c) As Water or any liquid counts or measures in litres/ millilitres, similarly, Fruits/ vegetables/grocery measure in kilogram/ gram.

26. (c) As, $25 - 20 = 5$

Similarly, $75 - 65 = 10$

27. (b) As Temperature measures in °C Celsius

°F Fahrenhiet, similarly, Time measures or counts in A.M. or P.M.

28. (b) As, $2 \times 2 \times 2 = 8$

Similarly, $4 \times 4 \times 4 = 64$.

29. (b) As, 50 $\Rightarrow$ Roman Number

$\Rightarrow$ L

Similarly, 70 $\Rightarrow$ Roman Number = LXX.

30. (a) As, we do exercise in gym. Similarly, we eat food in restaurant.

31. (a) 32. (a)

Level-2

1. (b) As, 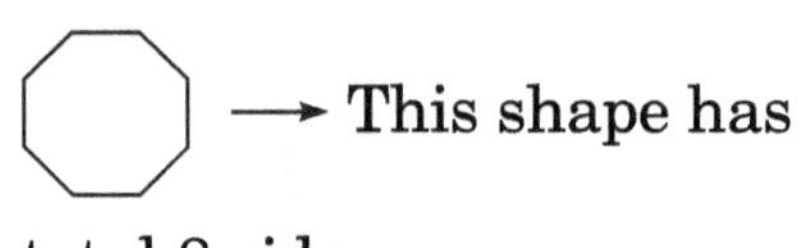 → This shape has total 5 sides

In the same way,

→ This shape has total 8 sides

2. (a) As, $12 + 7 = 19$

Similarly, $20 + 35 = \boxed{55}$

3. (b) First word counters the effect of second.

4. (d) As, L $\Rightarrow$ Roman Number = 50

Similarly, C = Roman Number = 100.

5. (c) In the given statement first is the part of the second.

6. (a) Second specialised in making the first.

7. (b) Shaded part in figure is changing clockwise.

8. (c)

9. (d) In the given statement second is the place where game/sport denoted by the first is held.

10. (b) Second is the food for the first.

11. (c) Lamp eliminates the darkness. Similarly, water eliminates the thirst.

12. (b) Lack of the first causes the second.

13. (d) As, we use chalk on a blackboard. In the same way, we use pencil to write on paper.

14. (d) As,

	B	D	G
	+1↓	+2↓	+3↓
	C	F	J

Similarly,

	E	G	J
	+1↓	+2↓	+3↓
	F	I	M

15. (b) As,

	Y	T	O
	−1↓	−1↓	−1↓
	X	S	N

Similarly,

	W	R	M
	−1↓	−1↓	−1↓
	V	Q	L

16. (a) Potato, Carrot, Radish and Groundnut are all grown under the ground.

17. (c) In the 'College', education is given to the 'Student', in the same way, treatment is given to the 'Patient' in the 'Hospital'.

18. (b) 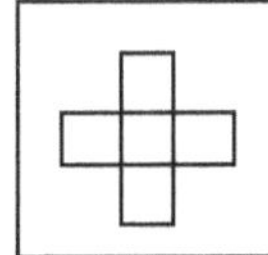

19. (c) 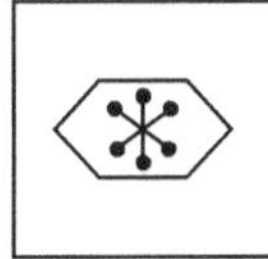

20. (b) 

21. (a) As, $\dfrac{3}{5} \times \dfrac{(5)}{(5)} = \dfrac{15}{25}$

Similarly, $\dfrac{2}{4} \times \dfrac{(5)}{(5)} = \dfrac{12}{24}$

22. (b) As, $\dfrac{8}{12} \div \dfrac{(4)}{(4)} = \dfrac{2}{3}$

Similarly, $\dfrac{15}{25} \div \dfrac{(5)}{(5)} = \dfrac{3}{5}$.

23. (b) As, $\dfrac{4}{16} \Rightarrow \dfrac{4 \times 1}{4 \times 4}$

Similarly, $\dfrac{5}{25} \Rightarrow \dfrac{5 \times 1}{5 \times 5}$

24. (b) As, $1\,g = \dfrac{1}{1000}$ Kg

In decimals, we write it as 1 gm = 0.001 Kg.

25. (c) $68\ \text{ML} = 68 \times \dfrac{1}{1000}\ \text{L}$

$= \dfrac{68}{1000}\ \text{L} \Rightarrow 0.068\ \text{L}.$

26. (d) A circle doesn't have any corner or sides.

27. (b) As, $6 \times 4 = 24 + 1 \Rightarrow 25$

Similarly,

$7 \times 3 = 21 + 1 \Rightarrow 22.$

28. (c) As, $0.8 \Rightarrow \dfrac{8}{10}$

Similarly, $1.50 = \dfrac{150}{100}$

29. (d) 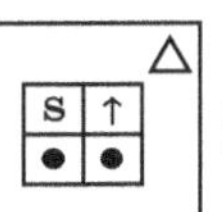 is correct answer.

30. (d) 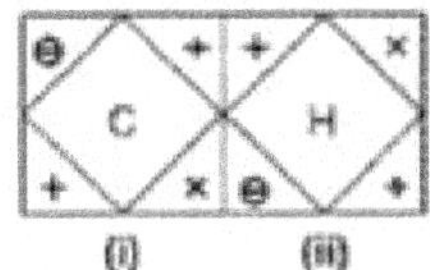 is correct answer.

31. (c)

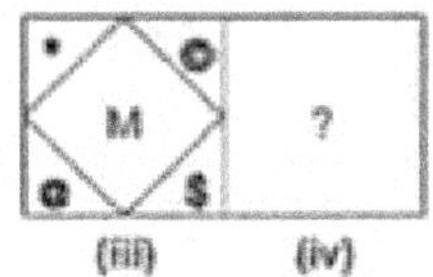

From the given fig. (i) and (ii), it can be observed that:

- $C + 5\ (D,E,F,G,H) \to H$

- Symbols interchange their position between top and bottom.

So, following the same pattern in image (iii), $M + 5(N, O, P, Q, R) \to R$ and interchanging the position of the symbols, we get the option C.

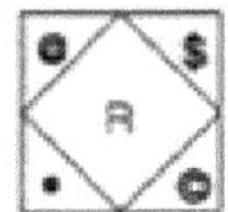

32. (d) In the given pattern, centre image flip vertically and the digits of the corners moves ahead anti-clockwise.

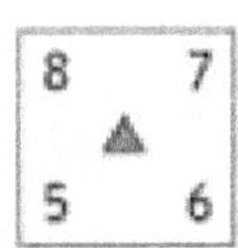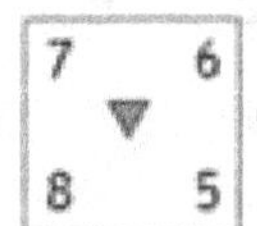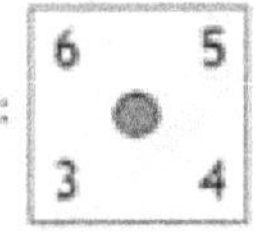

Patterns

INTRODUCTION

Patterns are

- repeated designs or recurring sequences.
- an ordered set of letters, words, numbers, shapes or other mathematical objects, arranged according to a particular rule.

Type I: To find the missing term or next term (number or letter)

- To find the missing term in the given pattern, identify the rule followed in rest of the given terms in pattern using mathematical operation: addition, subtraction, multiplication, division, skip counting and reverse counting.
- Identify the order of alphabetical series either from A to Z or Z to A.
- Skipping letters.

Type II: To find the missing part in the figure pattern.

- Complete the figure pattern by drawing its incomplete part in the pattern.

1. In the number pattern below, what are the values of A and B respectively?

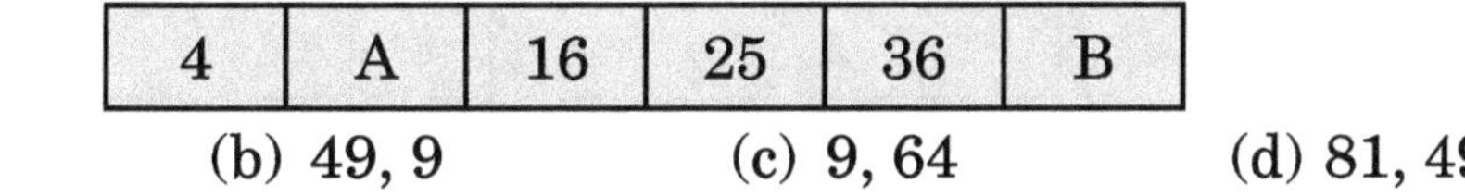

| 4 | A | 16 | 25 | 36 | B |

(a) 9, 49   (b) 49, 9   (c) 9, 64   (d) 81, 49

Ans. (a)

Explanation: Pattern followed in above series is

$$2 \times 2 = 4, \quad \boxed{3 \times 3 = 9}, \quad 4 \times 4 = 16, \quad 5 \times 5 = 25,$$
$$6 \times 6 = 36, \quad \boxed{7 \times 7 = 49}$$

2. Which is the missing square?

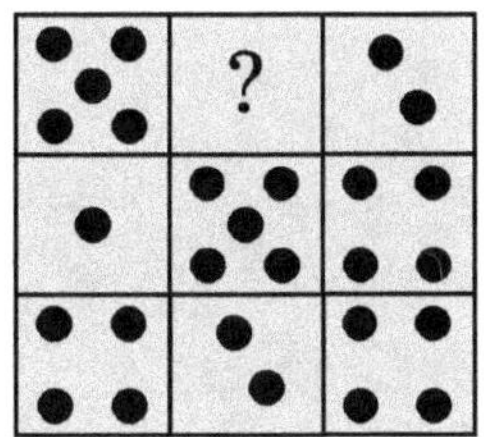

(a) (b) (c) (d)

Ans. (b)

Explanation: Sum of circles in each row or column is 10.

3. How many circles will be in pattern 7?

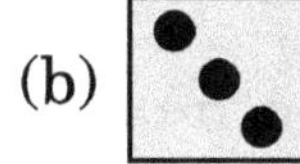 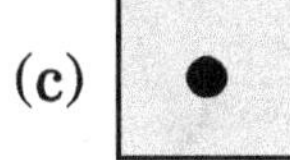 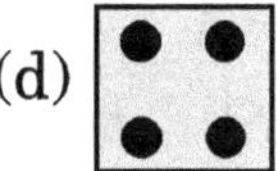

Pattern 1   Pattern 2   Pattern 3   Pattern 4

(a) 11   (b) 13   (c) 14   (d) 19

Ans. (b)

Pattern followed is

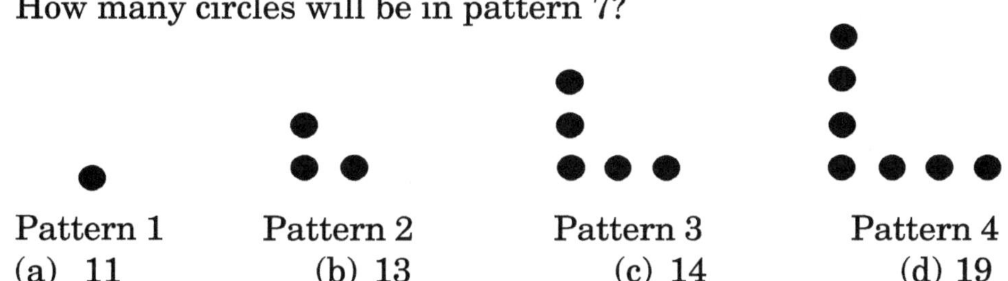

So, there will be 13 circles in Pattern 7.

4. Find the next letter in the pattern.

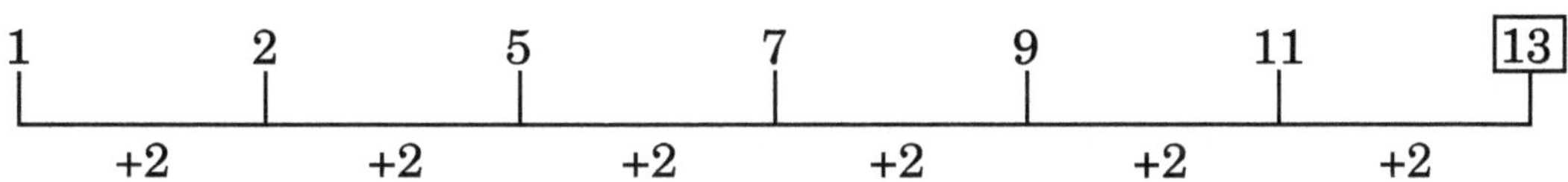

(a) K   (b) J   (c) H   (d) F

Ans. (a)

Explanation: The pattern is as follows.

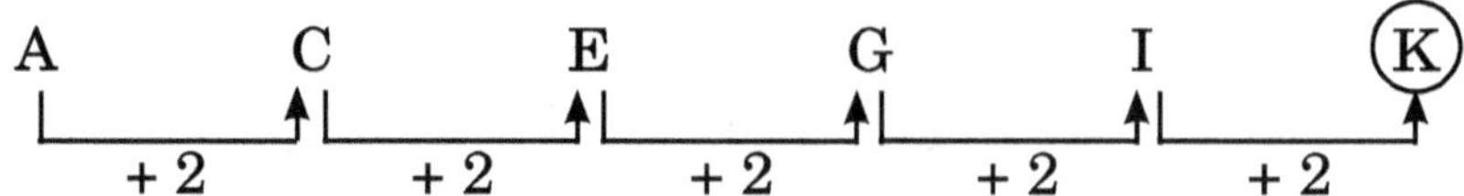

5. Look at the pattern.

Which set of letters best represents the pattern?
(a) ABC   (b) ABCC   (c) ABBC   (d) ABCD

Ans. (d)

Explanation:

The pattern is as follows:

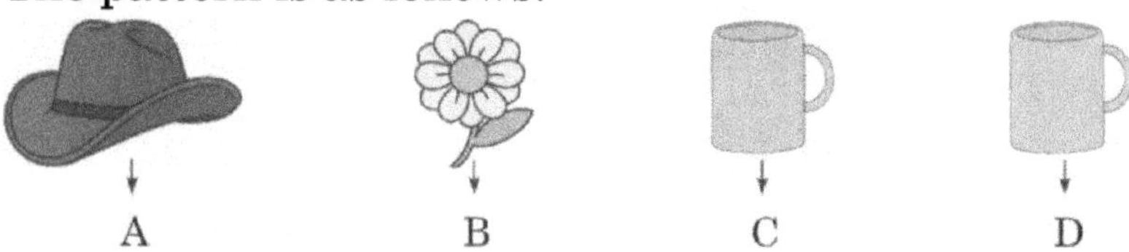

| A | B | C | D |

6. Which one of the following figures will continue the pattern?

(a)   (b)   (c)   (d)

Ans. (c)

Explanation: Figure is increased by one

LEVEL-1

1. Find the next figure in the given pattern?

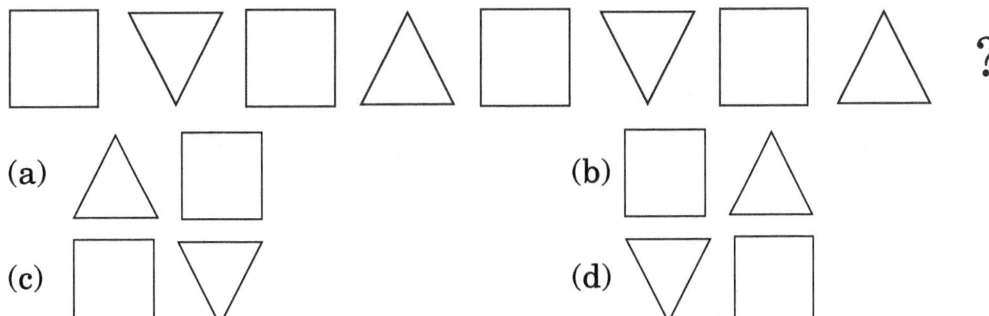

(a) (b)

(c) (d)

2. Piya draws 2 circles on the first page, 4 on the second page, 6 on the third page and 8 on the fourth page. If this pattern continues, then how many circles will she draw on the fifth page ?

(a) 10 (b) 14 (c) 12 (d) 20

3. Rachit and Tripti baked 3 cakes on Monday, 5 on Tuesday, 7 on Wednesday and 9 on Thursday. How many cakes will Rachit and Tripti baked on Saturday?

(a) 11 (b) 13 (c) 15 (d) 17

4. Write the rule followed by the pattern?

(a) BGBG (b) BBGBB (c) BGBBG (d) BBGBG

5. Identify the rule followed by the pattern?

(a) PQPR (b) QQPP (c) PPPQ (d) RRPQ

6. Mr. Kapoor reads 7 novels in March, 10 in April, 13 in May and 16 in June. How many novels will he be able to read in July?

   (a) 18   (b) 19   (c) 20   (d) 25

7. Find the missing number in the given pattern?

   ④, ⑧, ⑫, ⑯, __?__, ㉔, __?__, ㉜

   (a) 20, 28   (b) 26, 30   (c) 28, 30   (d) 25, 30

8. There are 80 books in shelf 1, 90 books in shelf 2, 100 books in shelf 3 and 110 books in shelf 4 of a library. How many books will be there in shelf 6?

   (a) 120   (b) 140   (c) 130   (d) 135

9. Meghna baked 9 pies in August, 15 pies in September, 21 pies in October and 27 pies in November. How many pies did Meghna baked in the month of December?

   (a) 40   (b) 36   (c) 33   (d) 30

10. Find the missing letter in the given series.

   | B | E | H | K | N | ? |

   (a) O   (b) P   (c) Q   (d) R

11. Find the number pattern of given series?

   | 1 | 2 | 3 | 1 | ? | 3 | ? |

   (a) 2, 1   (b) 1, 2   (c) 3, 2   (d) 3, 4

12. Write the rule followed by the pattern?

   (a) CCCBB   (b) AABBCC   (c) CCBBCC   (d) BBBCC

Direction (Qs. 13 and 14): Identify the rule followed by the pattern?

13.

   (a) PQQ   (b) QQP   (c) PPP   (d) QPQ

14. 

(a) MNPP   (b) MNOP   (c) OPNN   (d) MNNN

15. Find the missing number in the given pattern?

7   3   8   7   3   _____?_____.

(a) 10   (b) 5   (c) 8   (d) 15

16. Identify the figure that completes the pattern?

 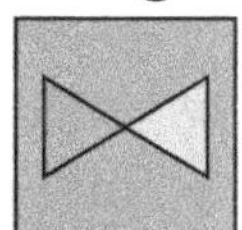 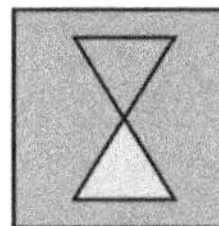  

(a) 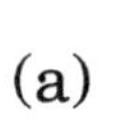 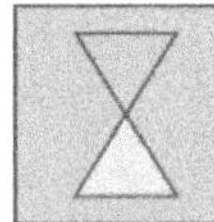   (b) 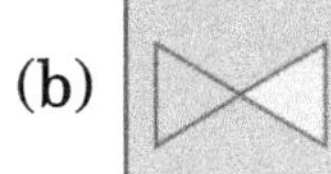   (c)    (d) 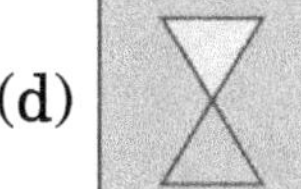

17. Identify the figure that completes the pattern?

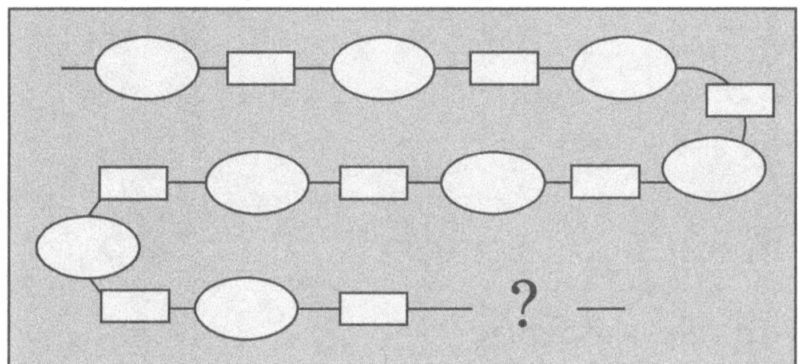

(a)   (b)   (c)   (d)

18. Identify the figure that completes the pattern?

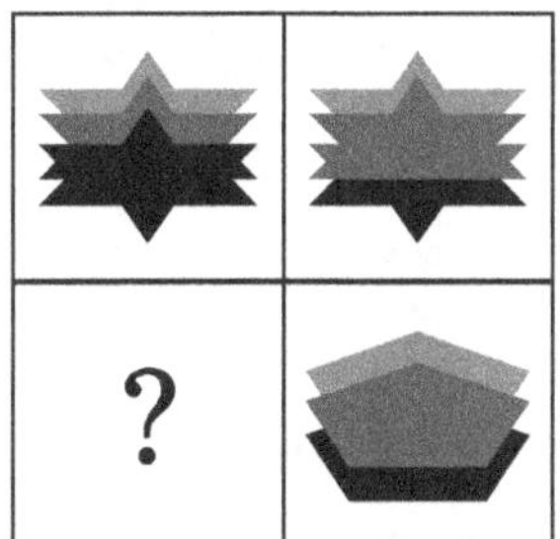

(a)    (b)    (c)    (d) 

19. Identify the figure that completes the pattern?

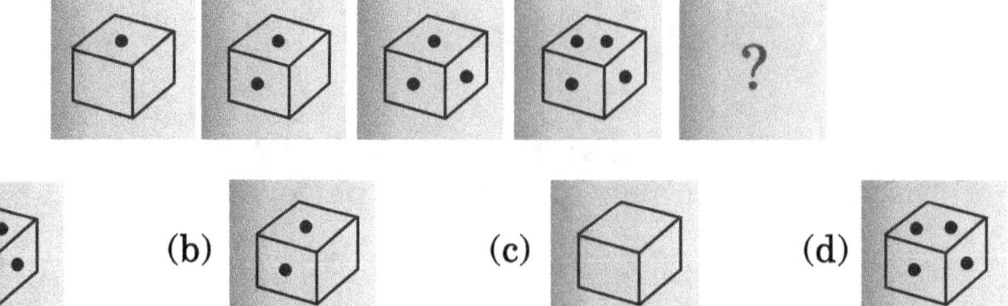

(a)   (b)   (c)   (d)

20. Identify the figure that completes the pattern?

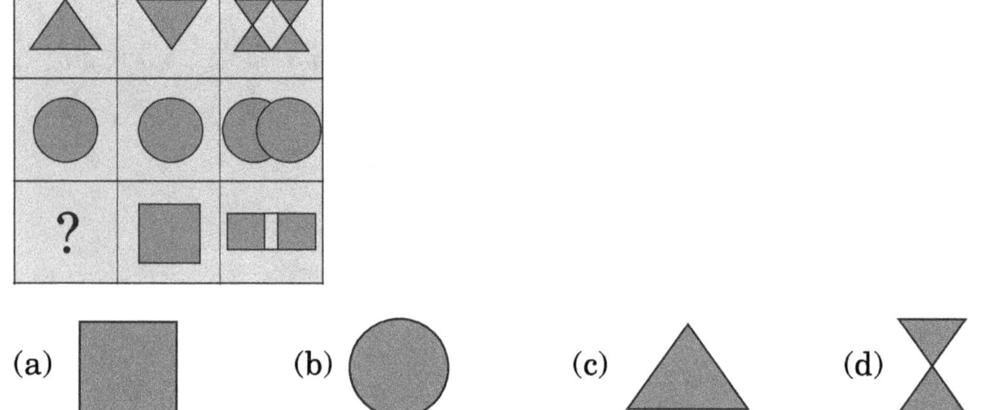

(a)   (b)   (c)   (d)

21. Complete the pattern with relevant figure?

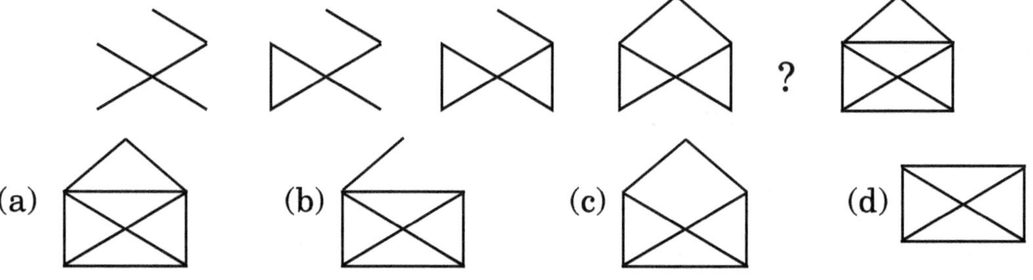

(a)   (b)   (c)   (d)

22. Complete the given pattern with relevant figure?

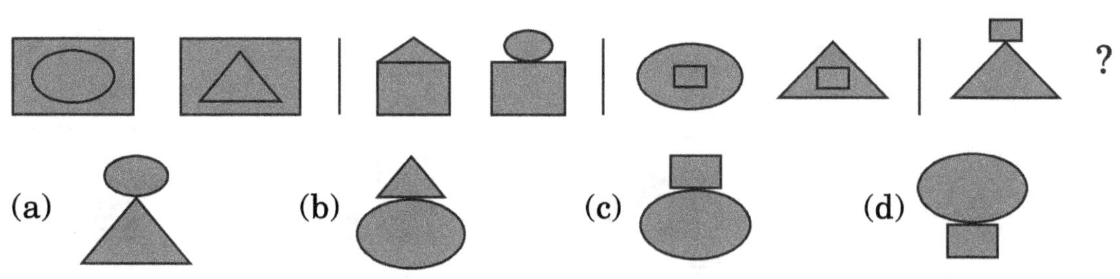

(a)   (b)   (c)   (d)

23. Which shape will complete the following pattern?

(a) 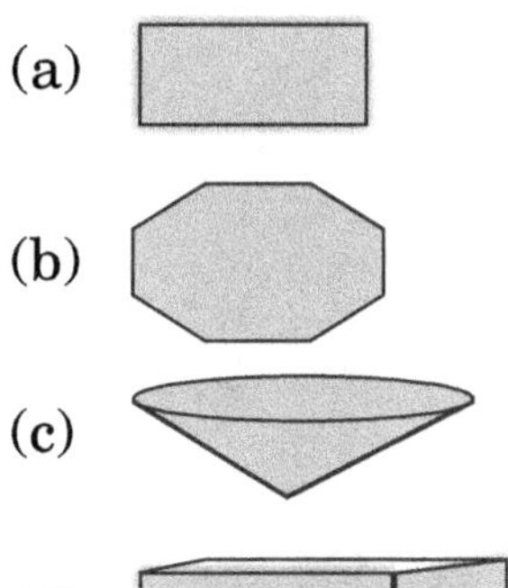

(b)

(c)

(d)

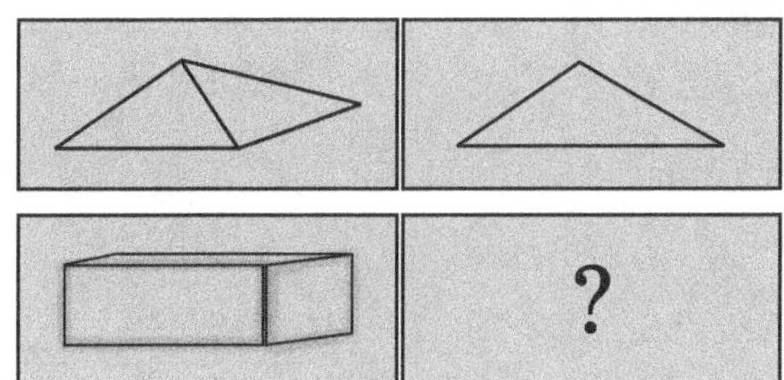

24. What is the missing in the given pattern?

(a) 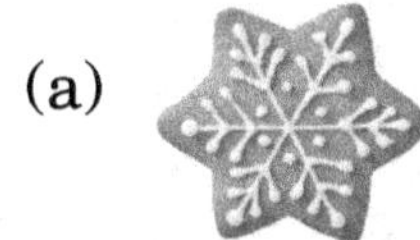   (b) 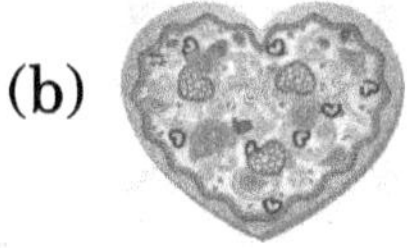   (c)    (d) 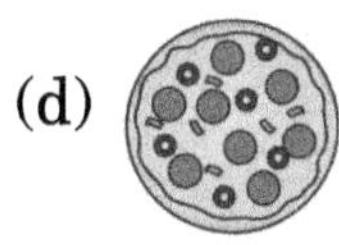

25. Complete the following pattern with relevant figure?

(a) 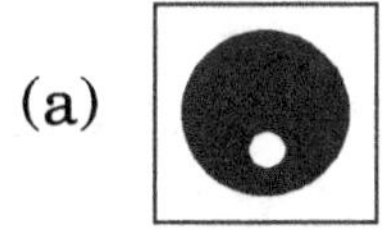   (b) 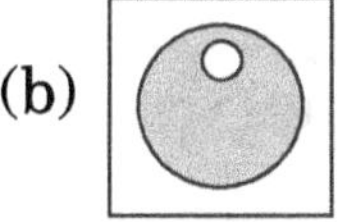

(c) 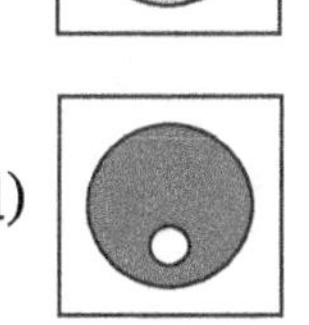   (d) 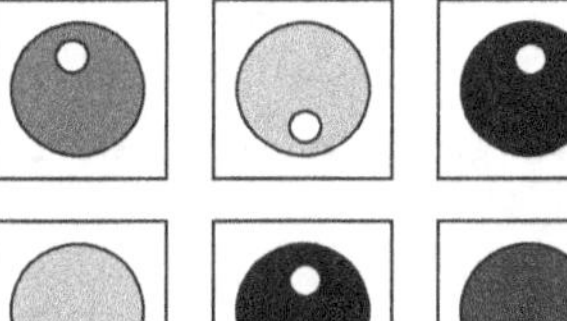

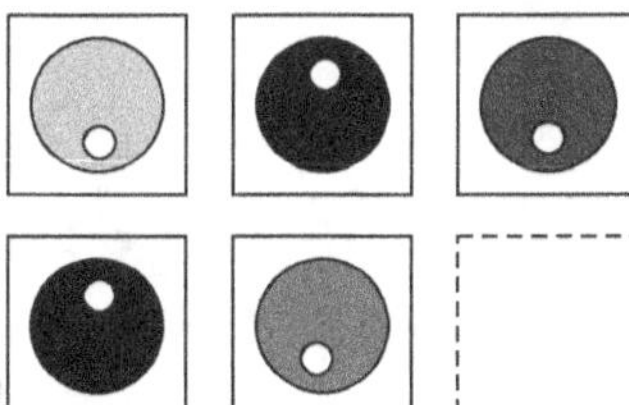

Direction (Qs. 26 to 30): Identify the missing numbers in the given patterns

26. 3, 6, 12, _______, ___________?

(a) 24, 48 (b) 24, 36 (c) 48, 36 (d) 48, 28

27. 4, 9, 16, 25, _______, _________ ?

(a) 88, 99 (b) 49, 58 (c) 36, 49 (d) 40, 49

28. 56, 52, 48, 44, 40, 36, 32, ___________?

(a) 48 (b) 55 (c) 66 (d) 28

29. 99, 88, 77, _________, ___________ ?

(a) 66, 55 (b) 60, 55 (c) 70, 66 (d) 66, 44

30. 1 : 45, 2 : 45, 3 : 45, _________, ___________ ?

(a) 12 : 45, 1 : 45 (b) 4 : 45, 5 : 45 (c) 5 : 45, 6 : 45 (d) 6 : 45, 7 : 45

31. Find the missing number in the number series given below. (2019)

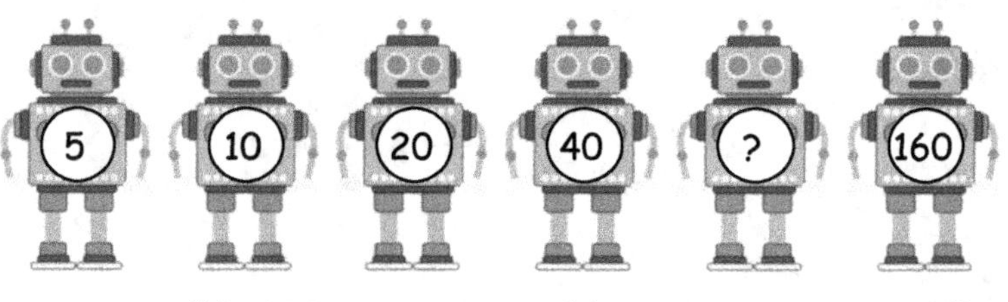

(a) 60 (b) 120 (c) 100 (d) 80

32. Which of the following figures will complete the given figure pattern? **(2021)**

(a)

(b)

(c)

(d)

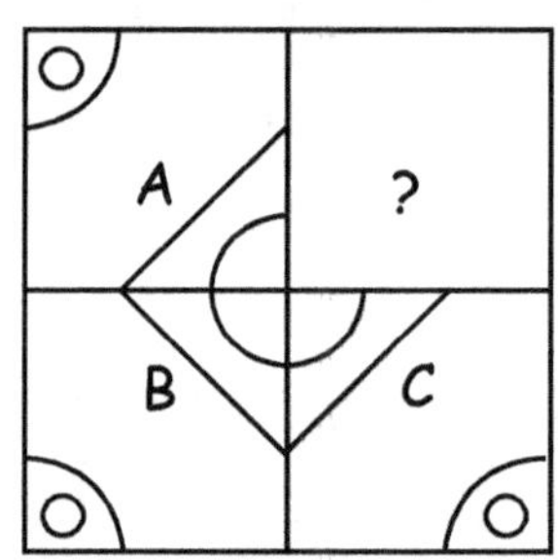

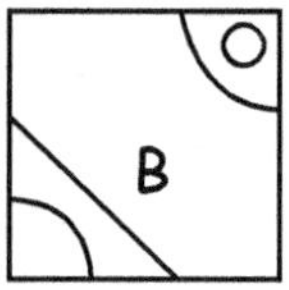

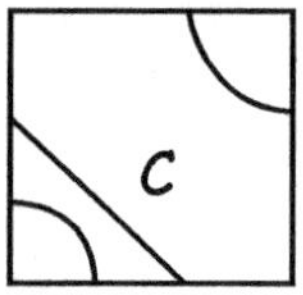

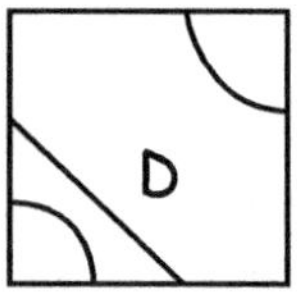

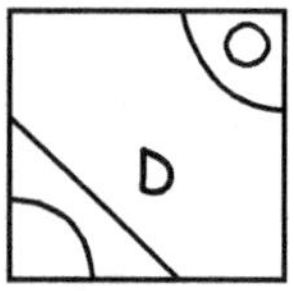

33. Study the given patterns carefully and tell the number of fish in Pattern 6. **(2022)**

Pattern 1

Pattern 2

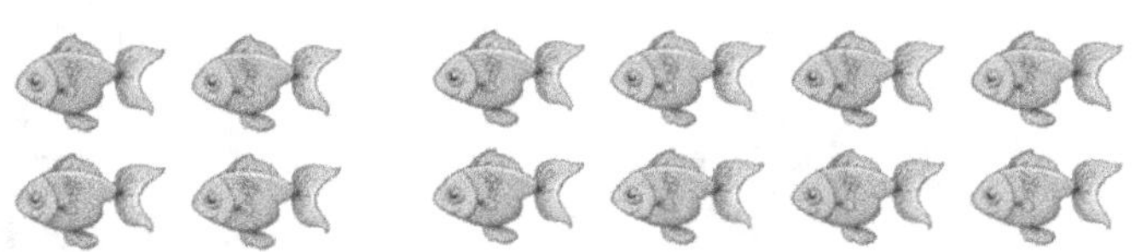

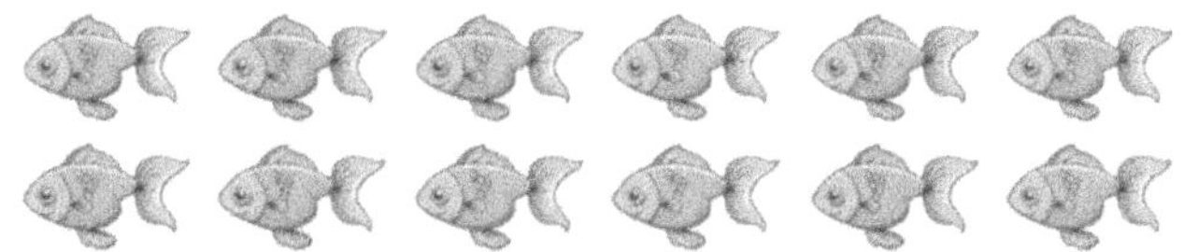

Pattern 3

   (a) 20   (b) 16   (c) 24   (d) 25

34. Find the next number in the following series: **(2022)**

7, 10, 9, 12, 11, 14, 13, ?

   (a) 15   (b) 16   (c) 12   (d) 17

35. Find the odd one out. **(2022)**

(a)   (b)   (c)   (d)

  Cow   Buffalo   Horse   Goat

LEVEL-2

1 Find the value of A and B in the number pattern given below?

   (a) 1,2   (b) 3,4   (c) 4,7   (d) 7,9

2 Which number will replace the question mark?

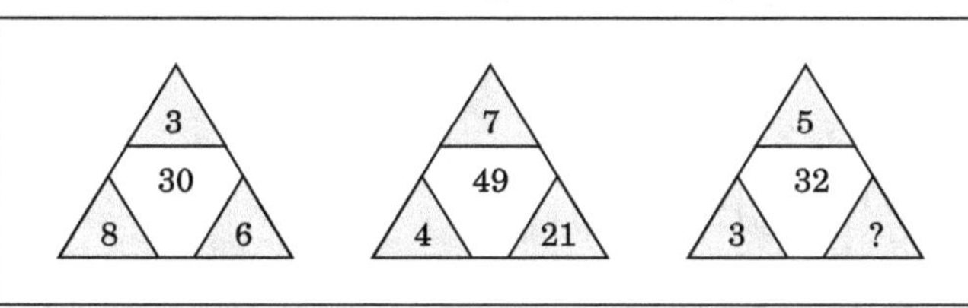

   (a) 15   (b) 16   (c) 17   (d) 18

3 Which of the following options will complete the fig. (X)?

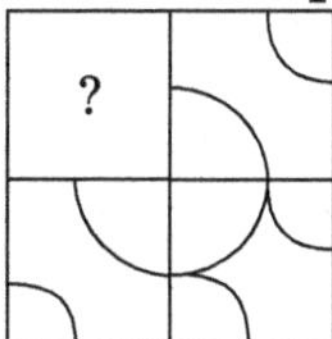

(a) 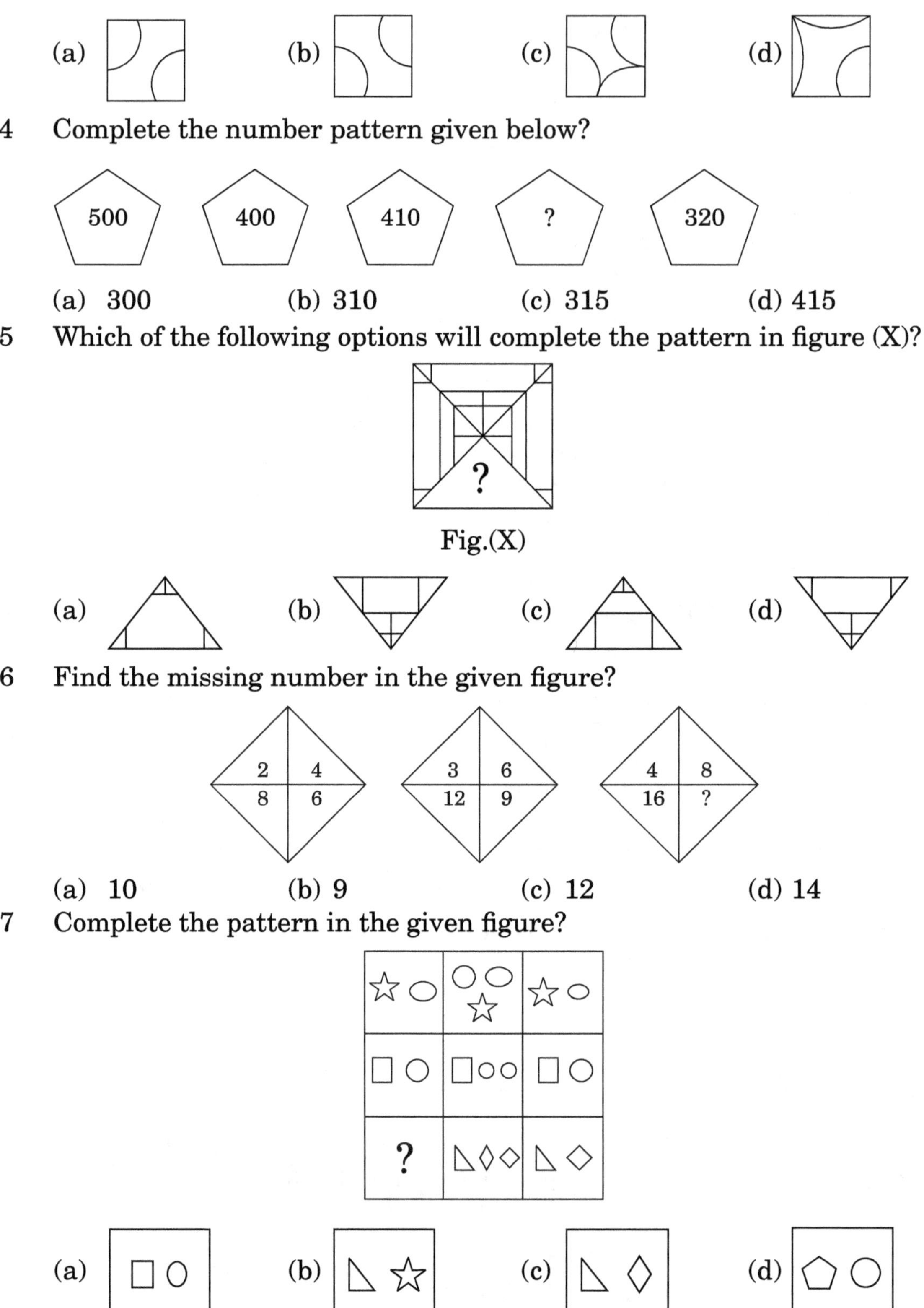

(b)

(c)

(d)

4 Complete the number pattern given below?

500   400   410   ?   320

(a) 300   (b) 310   (c) 315   (d) 415

5 Which of the following options will complete the pattern in figure (X)?

?

Fig.(X)

(a)   (b)   (c)   (d)

6 Find the missing number in the given figure?

| 2 | 4 |
| 8 | 6 |

| 3 | 6 |
| 12 | 9 |

| 4 | 8 |
| 16 | ? |

(a) 10   (b) 9   (c) 12   (d) 14

7 Complete the pattern in the given figure?

?

(a)   (b)   (c)   (d)

8   What comes next in the given figure pattern?

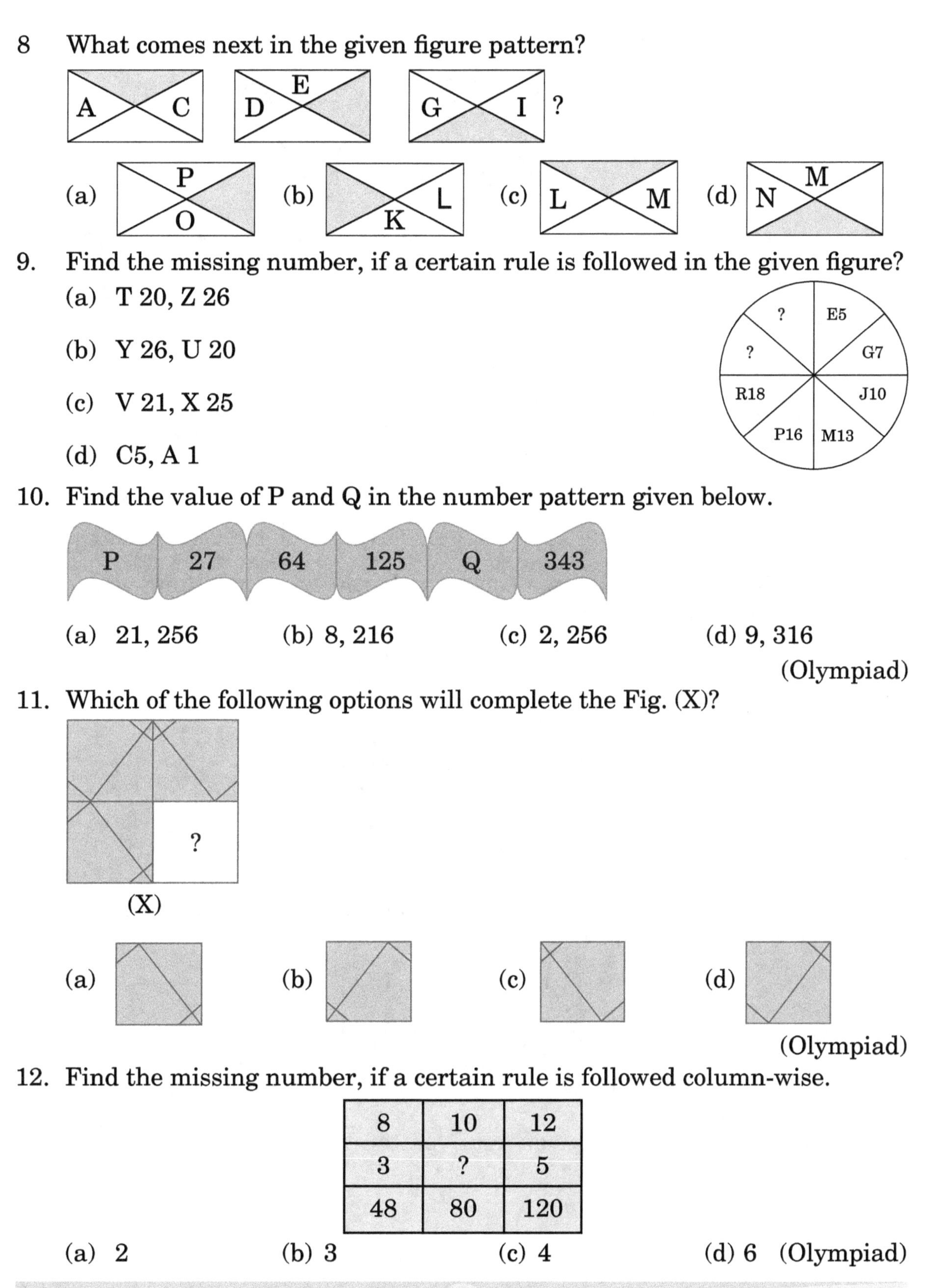

(a)   (b)   (c)   (d)

9. Find the missing number, if a certain rule is followed in the given figure?

(a) T 20, Z 26

(b) Y 26, U 20

(c) V 21, X 25

(d) C5, A 1

10. Find the value of P and Q in the number pattern given below.

| P | 27 | 64 | 125 | Q | 343 |

(a) 21, 256   (b) 8, 216   (c) 2, 256   (d) 9, 316

(Olympiad)

11. Which of the following options will complete the Fig. (X)?

(X)

(a)   (b)   (c)   (d)

(Olympiad)

12. Find the missing number, if a certain rule is followed column-wise.

8	10	12
3	?	5
48	80	120

(a) 2   (b) 3   (c) 4   (d) 6 (Olympiad)

13. Find the values of P and Q respectively in the given number pattern.

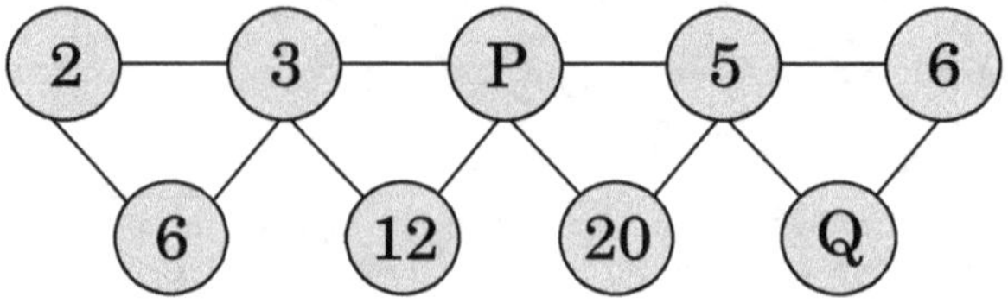

2 — 3 — P — 5 — 6

6   12   20   Q

(a) 5 and 28   (b) 4 and 30   (c) 3 and 30   (d) 2 and 18

(Olympiad)

14. Complete the number pattern given below.

11000   10000   10100   __?__   9200

(a) 9000   (b) 9100   (c) 10000   (d) 11100

(Olympiad)

15. If the given matrix follows a certain rule row-wise or column-wise, then find the missing number.

8	4	12
10	15	1
74	?	145

(a) 112   (b) 82   (c) 14   (d) 31

(Olympiad)

16. If the given matrix follows a certain rule row-wise or column-wise, then find the missing number.

12	8	16
13	15	52
100	92	?

(a) 272   (b) 181   (c) 77   (d) 50

(Olympiad)

17. What comes next in the given figure pattern?

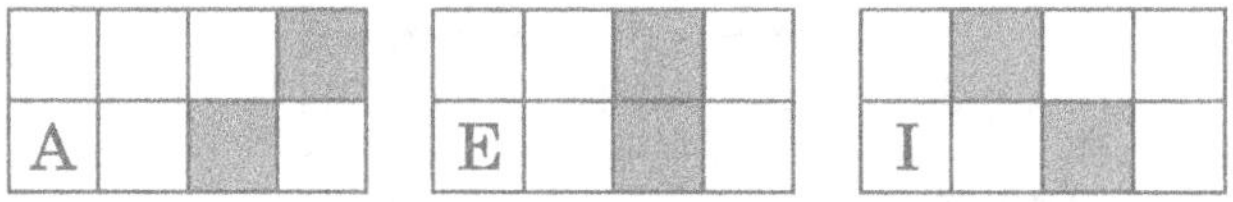

A   E   I

(a) 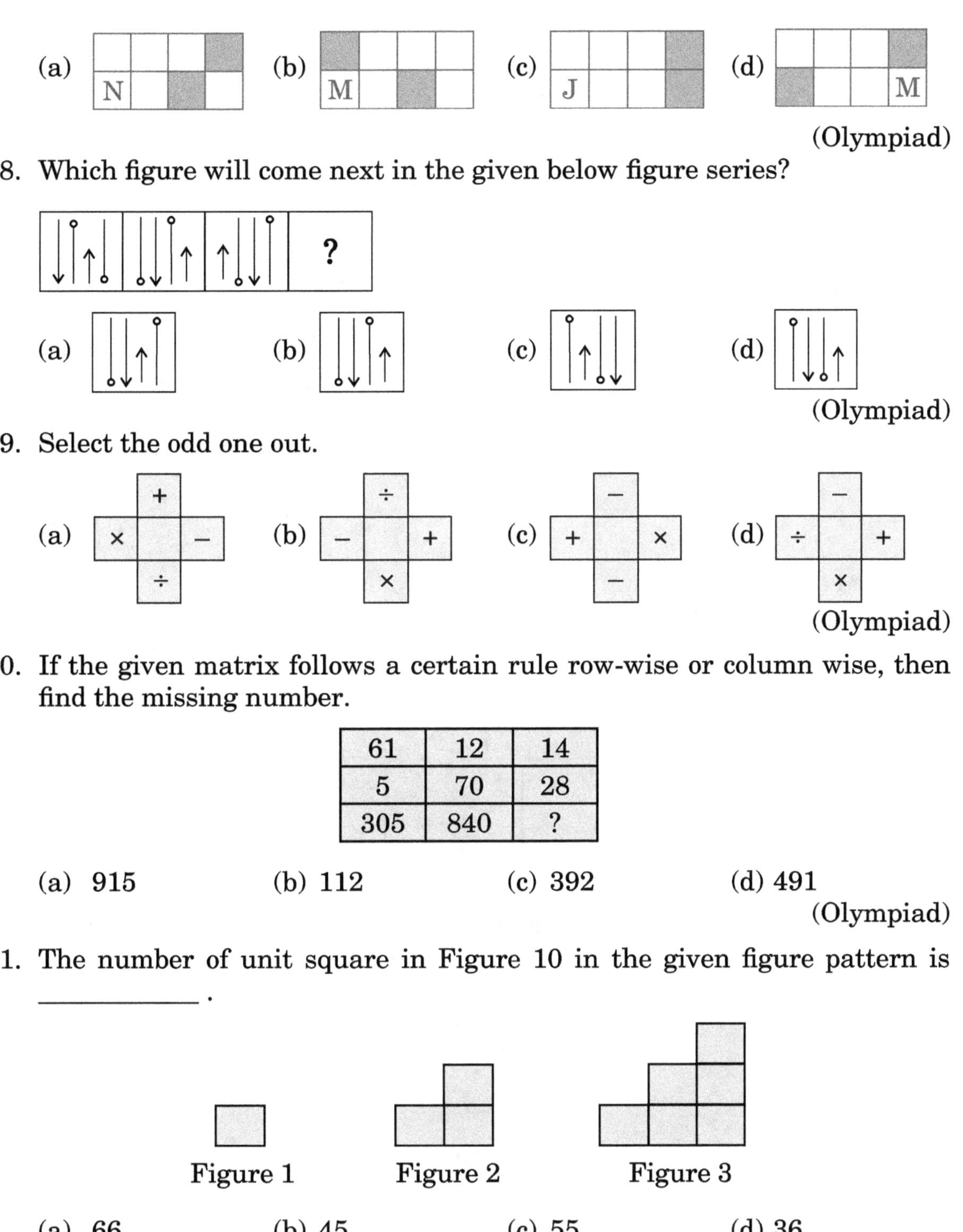 N   (b) M   (c) J   (d) M

(Olympiad)

18. Which figure will come next in the given below figure series?

(a)   (b)   (c)   (d)

(Olympiad)

19. Select the odd one out.

(a)   (b)   (c)   (d)

(Olympiad)

20. If the given matrix follows a certain rule row-wise or column wise, then find the missing number.

61	12	14
5	70	28
305	840	?

(a) 915   (b) 112   (c) 392   (d) 491

(Olympiad)

21. The number of unit square in Figure 10 in the given figure pattern is __________ .

Figure 1   Figure 2   Figure 3

(a) 66   (b) 45   (c) 55   (d) 36

(Olympiad)

22. A dog is chasing a cat as shown here.

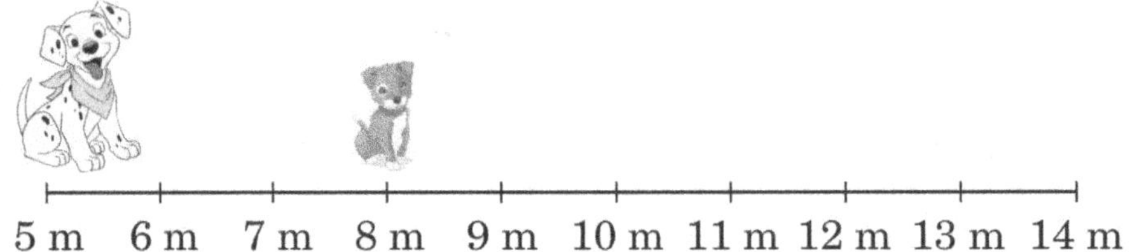

- The cat starts from 8 m and jumps 3 m every time.
- The dog starts from 5 m and jumps 5 m every time.

If they both start at the same time, in which jump will the dog overtake the cat?

(a) 1   (b) 2   (c) 3   (d) 4

(Olympiad)

23. Find the next figure in the given figure pattern.

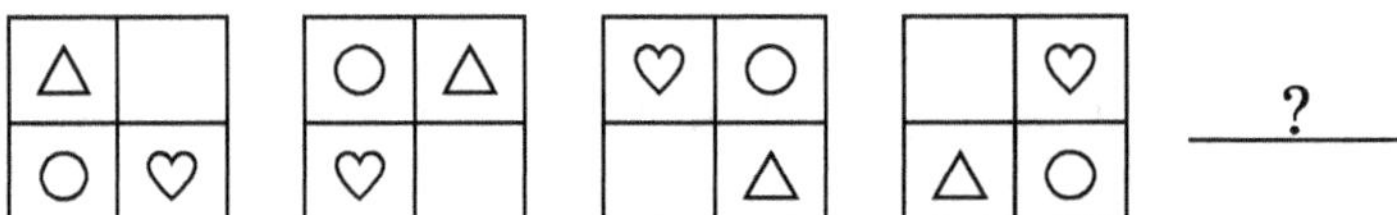

(a) 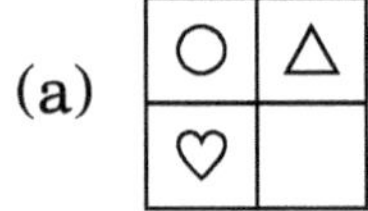   (b) 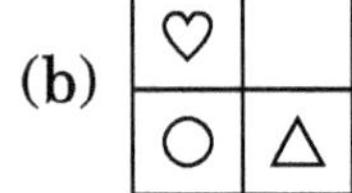   (c) 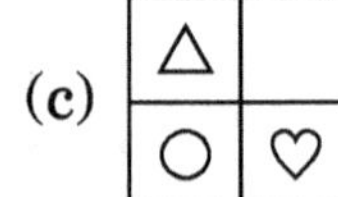   (d) 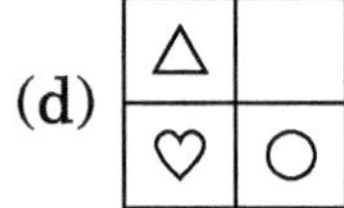

(Olympiad)

24. Which of the following options will complete the pattern in Figure (X)?

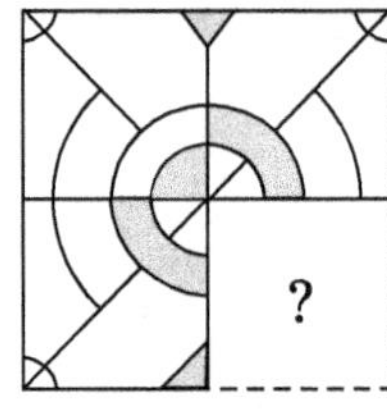

Figure (X)

(a)    (b)    (c)    (d) 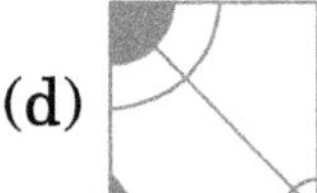

(Olympiad)

25. ___________ will replace the question mark in the given number pattern, if a certain rule is followed in the figures.

4	7
9	12

8	16
15	23

?	18
19	15

(a) 22

(b) 20

(c) 18

(d) 15

(Olympiad)

26. Which of the following figures will continue the given figure pattern?

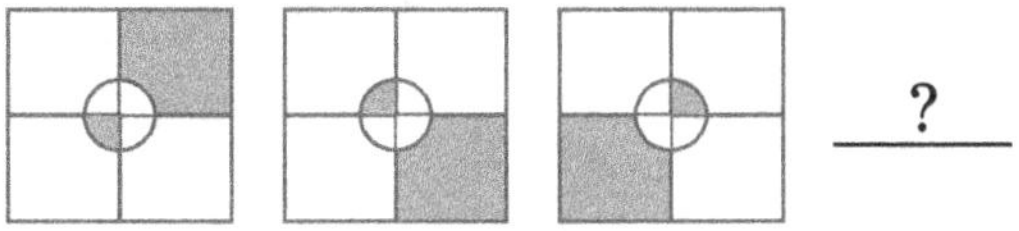

(a)

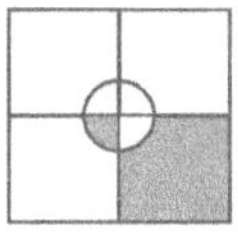

(b)

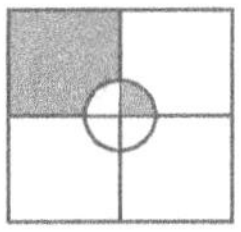

(c)

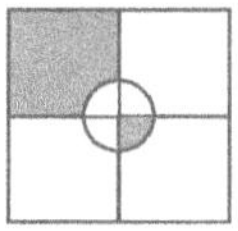

(d)

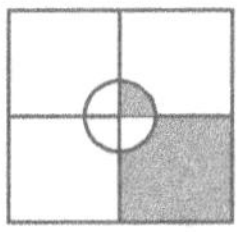

(Olympiad)

27. Find the missing number, if a certain rule is followed in the given figure.

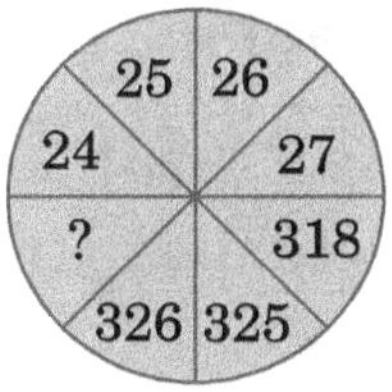

(a) 342

(b) 339

(c) 456

(d) 135

(Olympiad)

28. Select the figure from the options which when placed in blank space of Fig. (X) would complete the pattern.

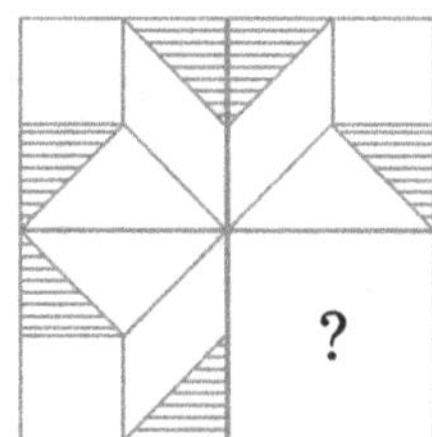

Fig. (X)

(a) 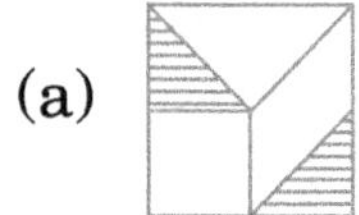   (b)    (c) 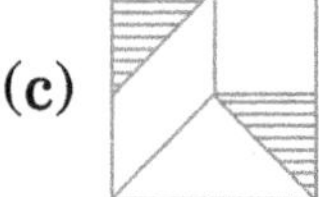   (d) 

(Olympiad)

29. Select a figure from the options which will complete the given figure pattern. **(2019)**

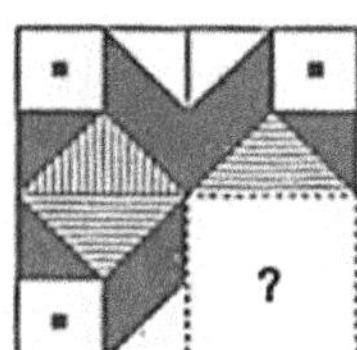

(a) 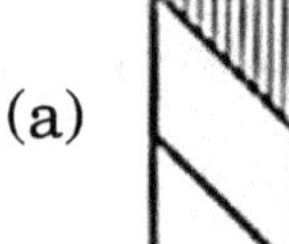   (b) 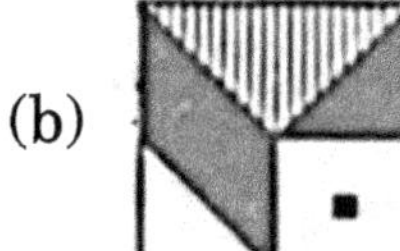   (c) 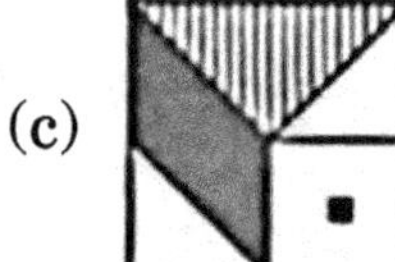   (d) 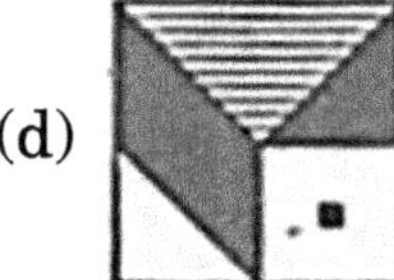

30. Select a figure from the options which when placed in the blank space of the given figure would complete the pattern. **(2021)**

(a) 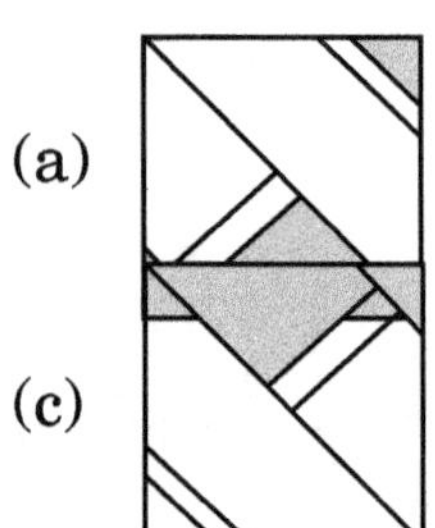

(b)

(c)

(d) 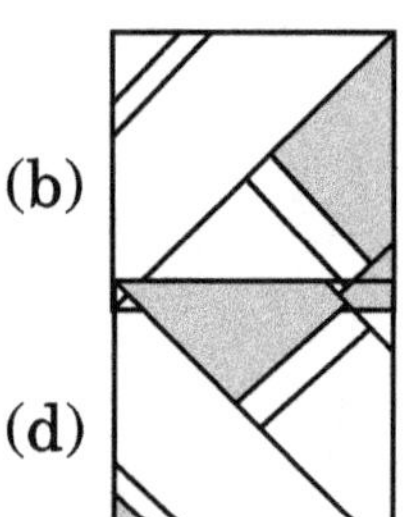

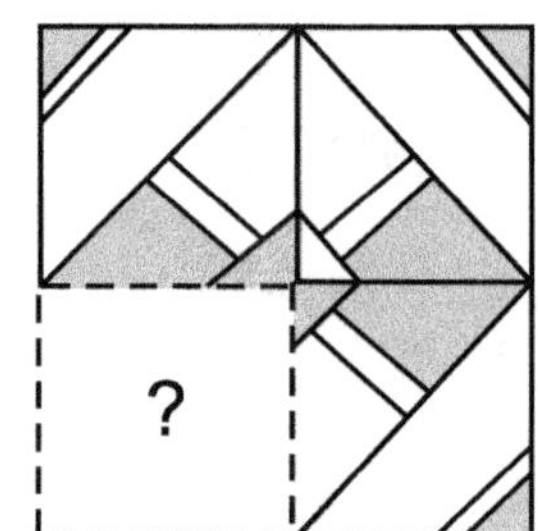

31. Find the number which replaces the question mark(?) in the following number series: **(2022)**

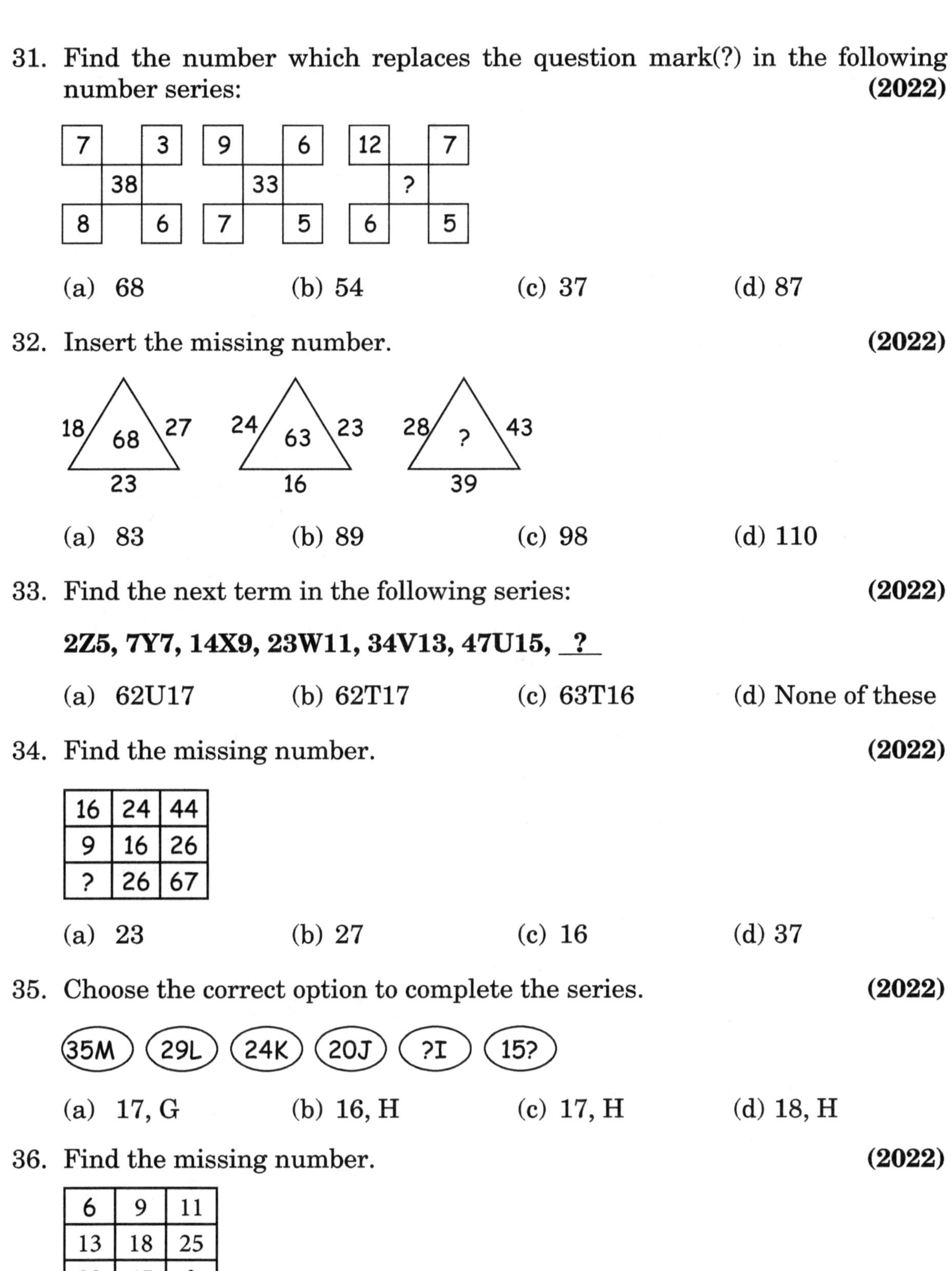

(a) 68   (b) 54   (c) 37   (d) 87

32. Insert the missing number. **(2022)**

(a) 83   (b) 89   (c) 98   (d) 110

33. Find the next term in the following series: **(2022)**

2Z5, 7Y7, 14X9, 23W11, 34V13, 47U15, _?_

(a) 62U17   (b) 62T17   (c) 63T16   (d) None of these

34. Find the missing number. **(2022)**

16	24	44
9	16	26
?	26	67

(a) 23   (b) 27   (c) 16   (d) 37

35. Choose the correct option to complete the series. **(2022)**

35M   29L   24K   20J   ?I   15?

(a) 17, G   (b) 16, H   (c) 17, H   (d) 18, H

36. Find the missing number. **(2022)**

6	9	11
13	18	25
29	45	?

(a) 81   (b) 77   (c) 64   (d) 52

Level-1

1. **(c)** 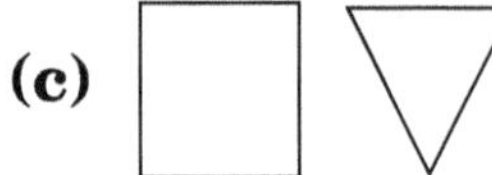

2. **(a)** The pattern is 2, 4, 6, 8 addition of 2 to each number.

So, Piya will draw 10 circles on fifth page.

3. **(b)** Rule of adding 2 to each number is followed. 3 cakes on Monday then 3 + 2 = 5 cakes on Tuesday then 5 + 2 = 7 cakes on Wednesday, then 7 + 2 = 9 cakes on Thursday, then 9 + 2 = 11 on Friday, at last they made 11 + 2 = 13 on Saturday.

4. **(d)** The pattern is as follows:

B	B	G	B	G
Boy	Boy	Girl	Boy	Girl

So, B B G B G is correct.

5. **(a)** The pattern is PQPR

6. **(b)** Rule of adding 3 to each number is followed.

Here, 7 in March

7 + 3 = 10 in April

10 + 3 = 13 in May

13 + 3 = 16 in June

16 + 3 = ⑲ in July

So, Mr. Kapoor will be able to read 19 novels in July.

7. **(a)** The pattern is as follows:

$$4 \quad 8 \quad 12 \quad 16 \quad \textcircled{20} \quad 24 \quad \textcircled{28} \quad 32$$
$$+4 \;\; +4 \;\;\; +4 \;\;\; +4 \;\;\; +4 \;\;\; +4 \;\;\; +4$$

8. **(c)** The pattern is as follows:

Shelf 1	80
Shelf 2	80 + 10 = 90
Shelf 3	90 + 10 = 100
Shelf 4	100 + 10 = 110
Shelf 5	110 + 10 = 120
Shelf 6	120 + 10 = 130

So, there will be 130 books in Shelf 6.

9. **(c)** Rule of adding 6 to each number is followed.

Aug.	Sep.	Oct.	Nov.	Dec.
9	15	21	27	㉝

$$+6 \qquad +6 \qquad +6 \qquad +6$$

10. **(c)** The pattern of the series is as follows:

$$B \xrightarrow{+3} E \xrightarrow{+3} H \xrightarrow{+3} K \xrightarrow{+3} N \xrightarrow{+3} \boxed{Q}$$

11. **(a)** The pattern is

$$1 \quad 2 \quad 3 \quad 1 \quad \boxed{2} \quad 3 \quad \boxed{1}$$

12. **(c)**

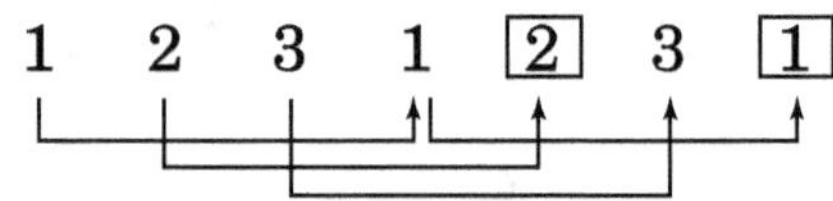

C	C	B	B
Cake	Cake	Balloon	Balloon

		C	C
		Cake	Cake

So, CCBBCC is correct.

13. (a) PQQ

14. (b) MNOP

15. (c) The digit repeats itself after two digits.

16. (d) 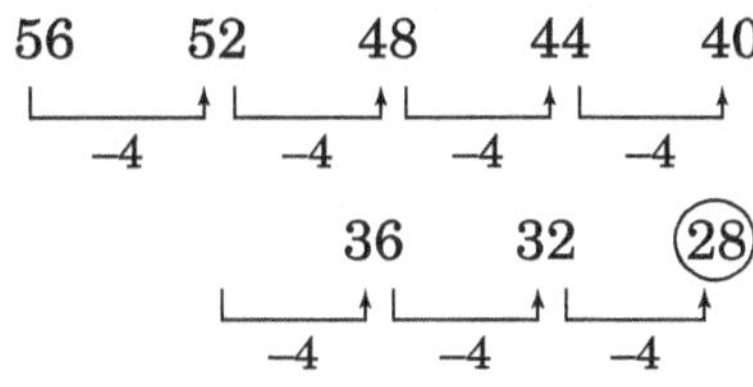

17. (d)

18. (d)

19. (a)

20. (a)

21. (c)

22. (c)

23. (a)

24. (c)

25. (b)

26. (a) The pattern is

$$3 \quad 6 \quad 12 \quad (24) \quad (48)$$
$$+3 \quad +6 \quad +12 \quad +24$$

27. (c) Rule followed in this pattern is square of each number

$$2^2 = 4, \quad 3^2 = 9, \quad 4^2 = 16,$$
$$5^2 = 25, \quad 6^2 = 36, \quad 7^2 = 49.$$

28. (d) Rule followed in this pattern is subtraction of 4 to each number.

$$56 \quad 52 \quad 48 \quad 44 \quad 40$$
$$-4 \quad -4 \quad -4 \quad -4$$
$$36 \quad 32 \quad (28)$$
$$-4 \quad -4 \quad -4$$

29. (a) Rule followed in this pattern is subtraction of 11 to each number.

$$99 \quad 88 \quad 77 \quad (66) \quad (55)$$
$$-11 \quad -11 \quad -11 \quad -11$$

30. (b) $1:45 \quad 2:45 \quad 3:45 \quad \boxed{4:45} \quad \boxed{5:45}$
$$+1 \quad +1 \quad +1 \quad +1$$

31. (d) $40 \times 2 = 80$

32. (d)

33. (c) Pattern 1 = (1 × 4) = 4 fishes; Pattern 2 = (2 × 4) = 8 fishes; Pattern 3 = (3 × 4) = 12 fishes; Pattern 4 = (4 × 4) = 16 fishes; Pattern 5 = (5 × 4) = 20 fishes; Pattern 6 = (6 × 4) = 24 fishes.

34. (b)   **35. (c)**

1. **(c)** The pattern is as follows:

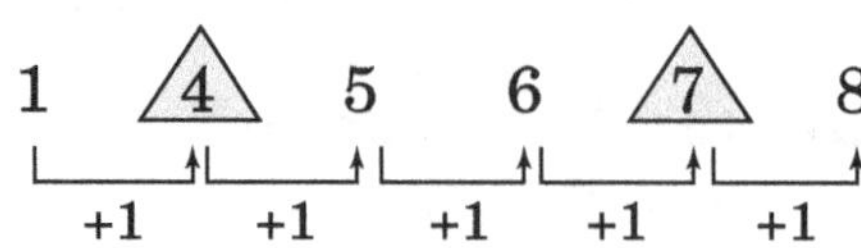

2. **(c)** The pattern is as follows:

As, in 1st Figure: $3 \times 8 = 24$, $24 + 6 = 30$

And in 2nd Figure: $4 \times 7 = 28$, $28 + 21 = 49$

Similarly, in 3rd Figure :

$3 \times 5 = 15$, $32 - 15 = \boxed{17}$.

3. **(c)**

4. **(b)** The pattern is as follows:

$$500 \quad 400 \quad 410 \quad \boxed{310} \quad 320$$
$$-100 \quad +10 \quad -100 \quad +10$$

5. **(d)**

6. **(c)** As, in 1st figure: $2 \times 1 = 2$
$2 \times 2 = 4$, $2 \times 3 = 6$, $2 \times 4 = 8$

And, in 2nd figure:

$3 \times 1 = 3$ $3 \times 2 = 6$, $3 \times 3 = 9$, $3 \times 4 = 12$

Similarly, in 3rd figure:

$4 \times 1 = 4$ $\quad 4 \times 2 = 8$,

$\boxed{4 \times 3 = 12}$, $\quad 4 \times 4 = 16$

7. **(c)**

8. **(b)** 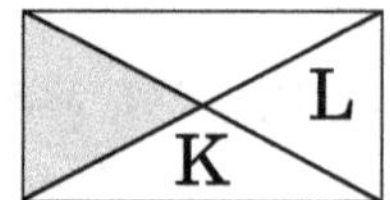

9. **(a)** Each block consists of letter and its corresponding positional value in English alphabetical order.

As, E $\rightarrow$ 5 (in English alphabet),

G $\rightarrow$ 7, J $\rightarrow$ 10, M $\rightarrow$ 13,

P $\rightarrow$ 16 and R $\rightarrow$ 18

So, the missing number and letter will be T 20, Z 26.

10. **(b)** The pattern is

$2^3 = 8$, $\quad 3^3 = 27$, $\quad 4^3 = 64$,
$5^3 = 125$, $\quad 6^3 = 216$, $\quad 7^3 = 343$.

11. **(b)** Option (b) will complete the fig (X).

12. **(c)** As, $\quad 48 \div 2 = 24$

$\quad\quad 24 = 8 \times 3$

and, $\quad 120 \div 2 = 60$

$\quad\quad 60 = 12 \times 5$

Similarly, $80 \div 2 = 40$

$\quad\quad 40 = 10 \times ?$

$\quad\quad ? = 4$.

13. **(b)** The pattern is as follows:

$$2 \quad 3 \quad \boxed{4} \quad 5 \quad 6$$
$$+1 \quad +1 \quad +1 \quad +1$$

and

$$6 \quad 12 \quad 20 \quad \boxed{30}$$
$$+6 \quad +8 \quad +10$$

14. (b) The pattern is as follows:

11000 10000 10100 $\boxed{9100}$ 9200

$-1000 \quad +100 \quad -1000 \quad +100$

15. (c) As $8^2 = 64 + 10 = 74$

and $12^2 = 144 + 1 = 145$

Similarly, $4^2 = 16 + 15 = \textcircled{31}$

So, option (c) is correct answer.

16. (a) As $13 + 12 = \quad 25 \times 4 = 100$

and $15 + 8 = \quad 23 \times 4 = 92$

Similarly, $16 + 52 = 68 \times 4 = \boxed{272}$

So, option (a) is correct answer.

17. (b) Option (b) is correct answer.

18. (c) Option (c) will come next.

19. (c) Option (c) is the odd one out.

20. (c) As, $61 \times 5 = 305$

and $12 \times 70 = 840$

Similarly, $14 \times 28 = 392$.

21. (c) The pattern is as follows:

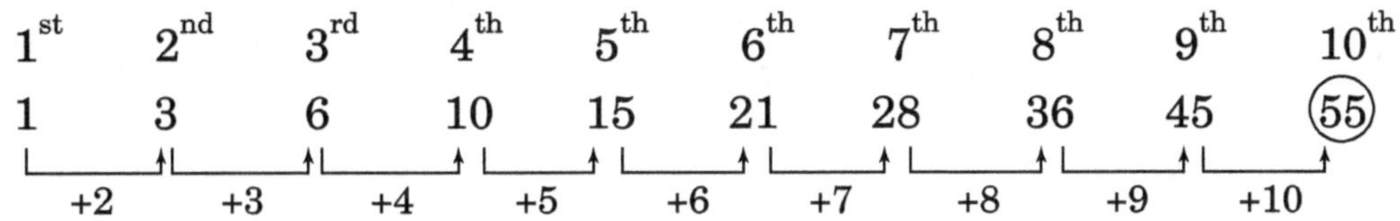

So, the number of unit square in figure 10 in the given pattern is 55.

22. (b) In 2nd jump the dog will overtake the cat.

23. (c) Option (c) will be the next figure.

24. (b) Option (b) will complete the pattern in figure (X).

25. (a) As $9 - 4 = 5$ and $12 - 7 = 5$

and $15 - 8 = 7$ and $23 - 16 = 7$

Similarly, $18 - 15 = 3$ and

$19 - ? = 3$

$? = 3 + 19$

$? = \boxed{22}$

So, option (a) is correct.

26. (c) Option (c) will continue the given figure pattern.

27. (b) Option (b) is correct.

28. (b) Option (b) would complete the pattern.

29. (b) Figure shown in option B will complete the given pattern.

30. (d) 

31. (c) **32. (d)**

33. (b) **34. (b)**

35. (c) **36. (d)**

Classification

OBJECTIVES

- These questions test the abilities of the students to observe the differences and similarities among objects or things.
- Students will learn assorting of the items of a given group on the basis of certain common quality.

INTRODUCTION

Classification means 'to assort the items of a given group on the basis of a certain common quality they possess and then spot the stranger or 'odd one out'. These questions are based on words, letters and numerals. In these types of problems, we consider the defining quality of particular things. In these questions, four elements or parts are given, out of which one doesn't belong to the group. You are required to find the 'odd one'.

Questions on Classification Types

These are the types of questions which we shall consider in classification:

Type I: Choosing the Odd Word

In these types of problems, some words are given which belong to real world. They have some common features except the odd one. You are required to find the 'odd one out'.

Directions (Examples 1-3):

In each of the following questions, four words have been given, out of which three are alike in some manner while the fourth one is different. Choose the odd one.

1. (a) Pear   (b) Apple   (c) Guava   (d) Orange

Ans. (d) **Explanation:** Out of given fruits orange is citrus fruit. So, it is different from others.

2. (a) Tomato   (b) Brinjal   (c) Cucumber   (d) Potato

Ans. (d)

Explanation: All the vegetables except potato grow above the ground level.

3. (a) Mustard   (b) Onion   (c) Olive   (d) Sesame

Ans. (b)

Explanation: All except onion are used for extracting oil.

Type II: Choosing the Odd Pair of Words

In this type of problems, different pairs are classified on the basis of some common features/properties like names, places, uses, situations, origin, etc.

Directions (Examples 4 to 5)

In each of the following questions, four pairs of words are given, out of which three pairs bear a certain common relationship. Choose the pair in which the words are differently related.

4. (a) Gold : Ornaments   (b) Cloth : Garments

   (c) Leather : Footwear   (d) Earthen pots : Clay

Ans. (d)

Explanation: Except pair (d), in all other pairs, the first is the raw material which is used to make the second.

5. (a) Petrol : Car   (b) Ink : Pen

   (c) Garbage : Dustbin   (d) Lead : Pencil

Ans. (c)

Explanation: Except pair (c), in all other pairs, first is required by the second for its functioning.

Type III: Choosing the Odd Letter/Letters Group

In these types of problems, some groups of letters are given. One out of them is different and this is to be chosen by the student as the answer.

Directions (Example 6): Choose the group of letters which is different from others.

6.   (a) H   (b) Q   (c) T   (d) Z

Ans. (b)

Explanation: All other letters except (b), occupy the even-numbered positions in the English alphabets.

Type IV: Choosing the Odd Numbers/Pair of Numbers

In these types of problems, certain numbers/pair of numbers are given, out of which except one, all have common characteristics and hence are alike. The 'different one' is to be chosen as the answer.

Directions (Example 7): Choose the one which is different from the rest three.

7.   (a) 57   (b) 87   (c) 131   (d) 133

Ans. (c)

Explanation: Except 131, all other numbers are non-prime (composite) numbers.

Type V: Choosing the odd picture/figure

In these types of problems, some groups of pictures/figures is given. One out of them is different and this is to be chosen by the candidate as the answer.

8.   Choose the one which is different from the others.

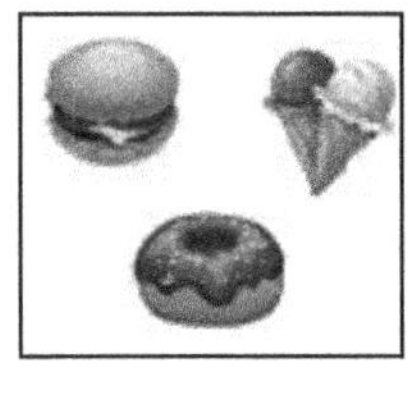

    (a)   (b)   (c)   (d)

Ans. (d) Except option (d), all others are eatable things.

LEVEL-1

Directions: (Qs 1 to 30) Find the odd one out (word/number pair/number/letter/figure) from the given options.

1. (a) 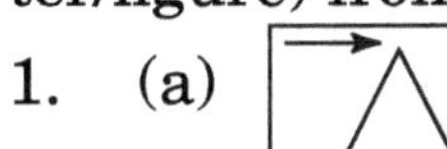 (b) 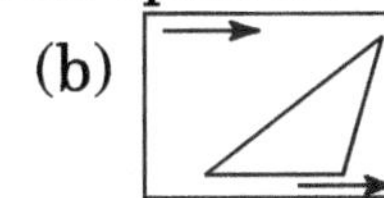 (c) 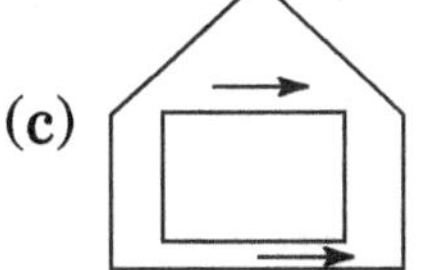 (d) 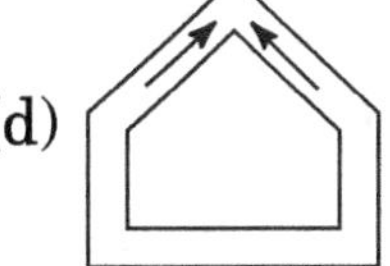

2. (a) Bottle : Wine   (b) Cup : Coffee
   (c) Pitcher : Water   (d) Tennis Racket : Ball

3. (a) Beautiful : Pretty   (b) Strong : Weak
   (c) Daring : Timid   (d) Youth : Adult

4. 1, 3, 5, 7, 11, 16, 17, 21
   (a) 3   (b) 5   (c) 16   (d) 7

5. 8, 27, 64, 100, 125
   (a) 8   (b) 27   (c) 125   (d) 100

6. 3, 6, 9, 18, 24, 27, 29, 30
   (a) 27   (b) 29   (c) 30   (d) 24

7. Wheat, Barley, Rice, Brinjal, Mustard
   (a) Barley   (b) Rice   (c) Brinjal   (d) Mustard

8. (a) (Man : Child)   (b) (Bee : Swarm)
   (c) (Cow : Herd)   (d) (Fish : Shoal)

9. (a) 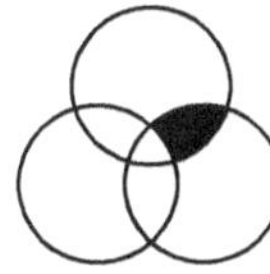 (b) 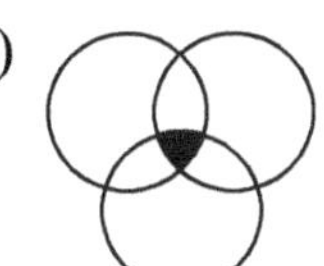 (c) 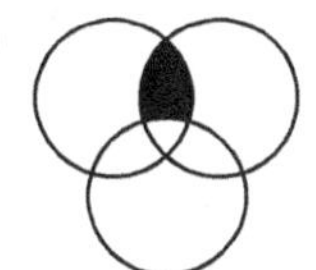 (d) 

10. (a) Circle   (b) Cone   (c) Cylinder   (d) Sphere

11. (a)  (b) 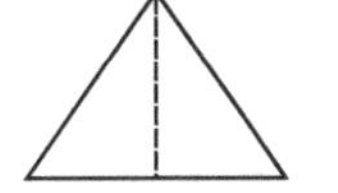 (c) 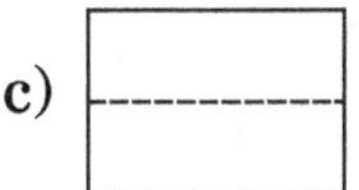 (d) 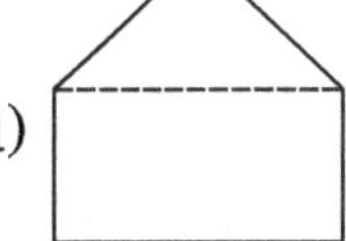

12. 2, 4, 6, 8, 10, 12, 17, 20
    (a) 8   (b) 17   (c) 10   (d) 6

13. (a) 55 – 44   (b) 121 ÷ 11   (c) 11 + 1   (d) 11 × 1

14. (a) 10 + 9   (b) 19 – 0   (c) 95 ÷ 5   (d) 19 × 0

15. (a) 3, 6   (b) 6, 9   (c) 9, 12   (d) 2, 11

16. (a) 2, 4   (b) 8, 12   (c) 16, 18   (d) 5, 7

17. 51,   144,   64,   121,   81

    (a) 51   (b) 64   (c) 121   (d) 81

18. (a) 55 – 44   (b) 12 – 1   (c) 14 – 3   (d) 20 – 8

19. (a) 12 – 24   (b) 14 – 35   (c) 8 – 16   (d) 13 – 26

20. (a) 5 + 5   (b) 7 + 3   (c) 6 + 4   (d) 8 + 4

21. (a) 768   (b) 668   (c) 448   (d) 384

22. (a) 1082   (b) 2012   (c) 2802   (d) 8012

23. (a) Apple   (b) Litchi   (c) Pear   (d) Orange

24. (a) Ostrich   (b) Kiwi   (c) Eagle   (d) Penguin

25. (a) 514 > 298   (b) 333 > 222   (c) 223 = 223   (d) 445 > 356

26. (a)    (b)    (c)    (d) 

27. (a) 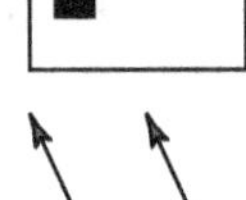   (b) 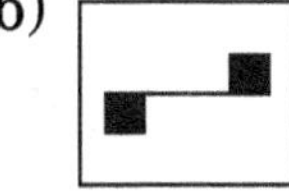   (c) 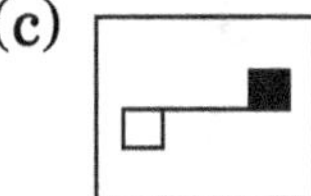   (d) 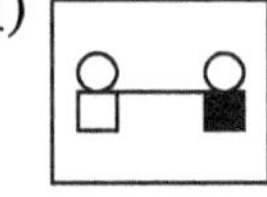

28. (a) 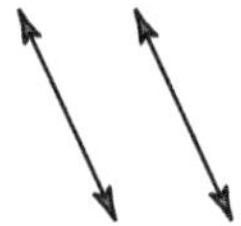   (b) 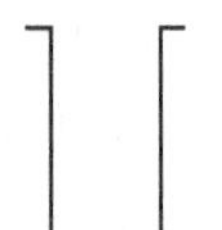   (c)    (d) 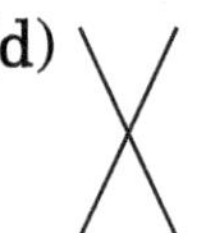

29. (a) 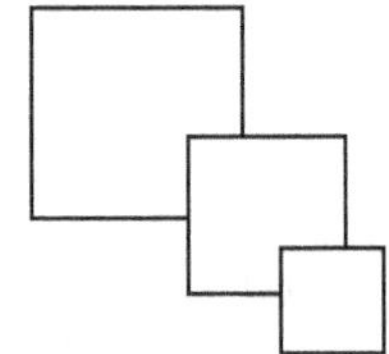   (b)    (c) 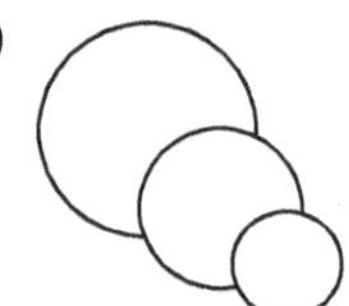   (d) 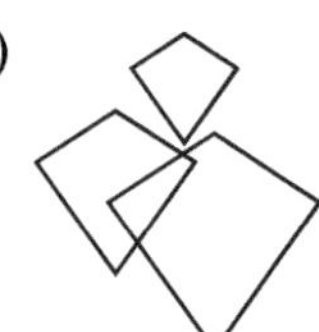

30. Choose the odd one.

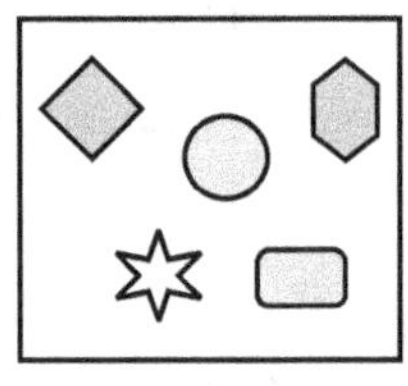

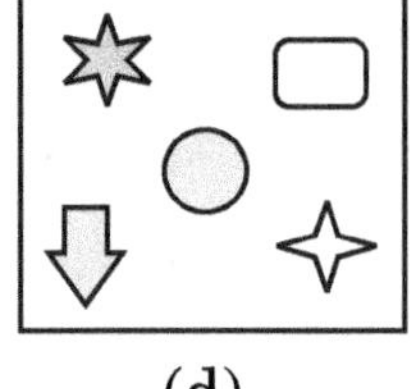

    (a)   (b)   (c)   (d)

Direction (Qs. 1-6): Choose the odd one out.

1. (a) 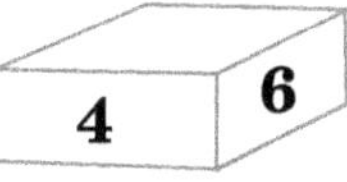   (b)   (c) 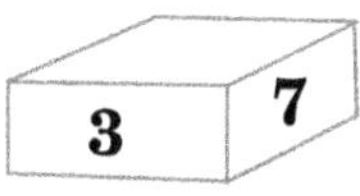   (d) 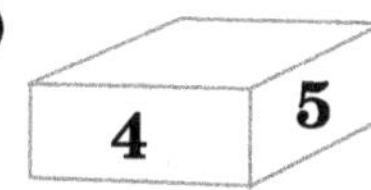

2. (a) ADE   (b) ILM   (c) VYZ   (d) JLM

3. (a) Tyre   (b) Ring   (c) Plate   (d) Bangle

4. (a) (2, 8)   (b) (3, 27)   (c) (4, 32)   (d) (5, 125)

5. 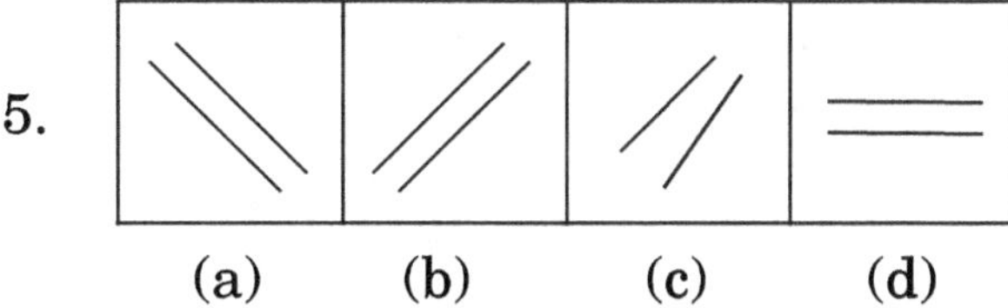

    (a)   (b)   (c)   (d)

6. (a) White : Dirty   (b) Easy : Difficult

   (c) Brave : Coward   (d) End : Beginning

7. Which number in this square is the odd one.

2	10	6	18
8	144	24	36
16	4	48	72
20	60	84	125

   (a) 144   (b) 84   (c) 48   (d) 125

Direction (Qs. 8-29): Choose the odd one out.

8. (a) 41   (b) 43   (c) 81   (d) 47

9.    

    (a)   (b)   (c)   (d)

10. (a) Painter : Gallery   (b) Worker : Factory

   (c) Farmar : Field   (d) Mason : Wall

11. (a) 13   (b) 17   (c) 63   (d) 23

12. (a) 28   (b) 64   (c) 125   (d) 216

13. (a) Wool   (b) Silk   (c) Wax   (d) Honey

14. (a) 49   (b) 56   (c) 21   (d) 36

15. (a) 244   (b) 324   (c) 352   (d) 514

16. (a) 385   (b) 572   (c) 425   (d) 671

17. (a) 331   (b) 482   (c) 551   (d) 383

18. (a) 2384   (b) 3756   (c) 4298   (d) 3629

19. (a) 2, 3, 5, 8   (b) 4, 5, 7, 10   (c) 7, 8, 9, 11   (d) 10, 11, 13, 16

20. (a) 844   (b) 633   (c) 954   (d) 762

21. (a) 34 – 43   (b) 55 – 62   (c) 62 – 71   (d) 83 – 92

22. (a) 7 – 3   (b) 3 + 5   (c) 4 + 4   (d) 6 + 2

23. (a) 1 – 0   (b) 3 – 8   (c) 7 – 50   (d) 6 – 35

24. (a) OPQ   (b) ABD   (c) EFH   (d) JKM

25. (a) 343 : 7   (b) 512 : 8   (c) 243 : 9   (d) 216 : 6

26. (a) 18 – 45   (b) 23 – 14   (c) 29 – 82   (d) 36 – 27

27. (a) Peninsula   (b) Island   (c) Bay   (d) Cape

28. (a) Fog   (b) Cloud   (c) Rain   (d) Mist

29. (a) MOR   (b) XZB   (c) PRU   (d) HJM

30. Select the odd one out.

(a)   (b)   (c)   (d)

(Olympiad)

Level-1

1. (d) 

2. (d) Except (d) all others are complementary to each other.

3. (a) Except (a) all others are antonyms.

4. (c) Each number in the series is an odd number. The number '16' is the only even number.

5. (d) The pattern is
$$2^3 = 8$$
$$3^3 = 27$$
$$4^3 = 64$$
$$5^3 = 125$$
But 100 is not perfect cube.

6. (b) Each number except 29, is a multiple of 3.

7. (c) Except Brinjal all the other things are crops. But brinjal is a vegetable.

8. (a) In all other pairs, second word is the collection group of the first.

9. (b) Except (b) in other shaded area covers only two circles.

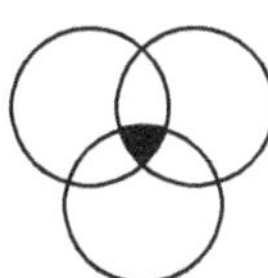

10. (a) All are solid shapes except circle. Circle is a flat shape.

11. (d)

12. (b) Number 17 is the odd number.

13. (c) As $55 - 44 = 11$
$$121 \div 11 = 11$$
$$11 \times 1 = 11$$
But, $\boxed{11 + 1 = 12}$

14. (d) As $10 + 9 = 19$
$$19 - 0 = 19$$
$$95 \div 5 = 19$$
But, $\boxed{19 \times 0 = 0.}$

15. (d) Except (d) all the other numbers are divisible by 3.

16. (d) Except option (d) all the others are divisible by 2.

17. (a) Except option (a) all others are perfect square.

18. (d) Subtract the numbers
$$55 - 44 = 11$$
$$12 - 1 = 11$$
$$14 - 3 = 11$$
So, $\boxed{20 - 8 = 12}$ Odd one out.

19. (b) Except (b) in all others first number is multiplied by 2 to get the second number.
$$12 \times 2 = 24$$
$$\boxed{14 \times 2 = 28}$$
$$8 \times 2 = 16$$
$$13 \times 2 = 26.$$

20. (d) Add the numbers

$$5 + 5 = 10$$
$$7 + 3 = 10$$
$$6 + 4 = 10$$

$\boxed{8 + 4 = 12}$ Odd one out

21. (d) Except option (d), in all other options 8 is at ones place but in option (d) 8 is at tens place.

22. (c) Except (c) in all other options '0' is at hundreds place.

23. (d) Only Orange is citrus fruit. So, it is different from others.

24. (c) All except Eagle are flightless birds.

25. (c) Except (c) in all other options first number is greater than second number.

26. (d) Option (d) is different.

27. (d) 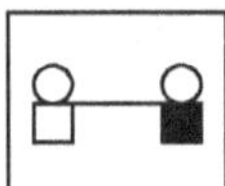

28. (d) Only in option (d) lines are intersecting each other.

29. (d) Except (d) all other figures are connected in the sequence from bigger to small.

30. (d) Except option (d) all others have similar figures.

Level-2

1. (d) All the numbers have the total of 10 as a result except option (d).

$6 + 4 = 10$, $8 + 2 = 10$, $7 + 3 = 10$

$5 + 4 = 9$, therefore option (d) is the odd one.

2. (d) As,

$$A \xrightarrow{+3} D \xrightarrow{+1} E,$$
$$I \xrightarrow{+3} L \xrightarrow{+1} M,$$
$$\text{and, } V \xrightarrow{+3} Y \xrightarrow{+1} Z$$
$$\text{But, } J \xrightarrow{+2} L \xrightarrow{+1} M$$

3. (c) Except Plate, all other things have hollow body.

4. (c) As, $2^3 = 8$, $3^3 = 27$, $5^3 = 125$

But, $\boxed{4^3 = 64}$ not $\bigcirc\!\!\!\!32$

Therefore (4, 32) is the odd one.

5. (c) Except option (c), in all other figures, the two line segments are parallel to each other.

6. (a) Except (a) in all other pairs, the two words are antonyms of each other.

7. (d) Except (d) all other numbers are divisible by 2.

8. (c) Each of the numbers is a Prime number except 81.

9. (d) Except option (d), in all others, the eyes are in the same direction.

10. (d) In all the other pairs, second is the working place of the first.

11. (c) Each number except 63 is a prime number. Therefore (c) is the odd one.

12. (a) Each number except 28, is a perfect cube.

13. (c) Wool, silk and honey we get from animals but not wax. So, wax is the odd one.

14. (d) Each of the number except 36 is divisible by 7.

15. (b) Except (b) all others have the sum of 10.

$$244 = 2 + 4 + 4 = 10$$
$$\boxed{324 = 3 + 2 + 4 = 9}$$
$$352 = 3 + 5 + 2 = 10$$
$$514 = 5 + 1 + 4 = 10$$

16. (c) In all the numbers, the middle digit is the sum of the other two numbers except (c) i.e. 425.

17. (d) Except (d), in each number, the product of first and third digits is the middle one.

18. (d) Except (d) in all other numbers, the last digit is two times the first one.

19. (c) Except (c), in all groups, second number is one more than first number, third number is two more than second number and fourth number is three more than third number.

20. (d) In all other numbers, the last digit is equal to the difference between the first digit and the second digit.

21. (b) In all other pairs, second number is 9 more than the first except (b).

22. (a) In all other pairs, the sum of two numbers is 8 except (a) = 7 − 3.

$$\boxed{7 + 3 = 10}$$
$$3 + 5 = 8$$
$$4 + 4 = 8$$
$$6 + 2 = 8.$$

23. (c) In all other pairs, the second number is one less than the square of the first number except (c).

24. (a) As,

A B D,   E F H,   J K M
+1 +2   +1 +2   +1 +2

But,   O P Q.
+1 +1

25. (c) Except (c) in all other pairs, the first number is the cube of the second number.

26. (c) In all other pairs, the difference between the two numbers is the multiple of 9 except (c).

27. (c) A peninsula, island, and cape are all landforms. A bay is a body of water.

28. (b) Except clouds others are different forms of precipitation.

29. (b) As,

M O R,   P R U,   H J M
+2 +3   +2 +3   +2 +3

X Z B
But,   +2 +2

30. (d) Option (d) is odd one out.

Alphabet Test

OBJECTIVES

- Students will learn how to arrange a single series of alphabets.
- They will learn to decode the logic involved in the alphabetical sequence.

INTRODUCTION

Alphabet test is a group of English letters. It is a test to solve the problems based on letters of English alphabet.

Some basic facts related to Alphabet Test are given below:

I. The Alphabet Series:

The English Alphabet contains 26 letters as shown below:

A	B	C	D	E	F
G	H	I	J	K	L
M	N	O	P	Q	R
S	T	U	V	W	X
		Y	Z		

II. Letters positions in forward alphabetical order:

A	B	C	D	E	F	G	H
1	2	3	4	5	6	7	8
I	J	K	L	M	N	O	P
9	10	11	12	13	14	15	16
Q	R	S	T	U	V	W	X
17	18	19	20	21	22	23	24
Y	Z						
25	26						

III. Letters positions in backward or reverse alphabetical order:

Z	Y	X	W	V	U	T	S
1	2	3	4	5	6	7	8
R	Q	P	O	N	M	L	K
9	10	11	12	13	14	15	16
J	I	H	G	F	E	D	C
17	18	19	20	21	22	23	24
B	A						
25	26						

- Remember the word E J O T Y

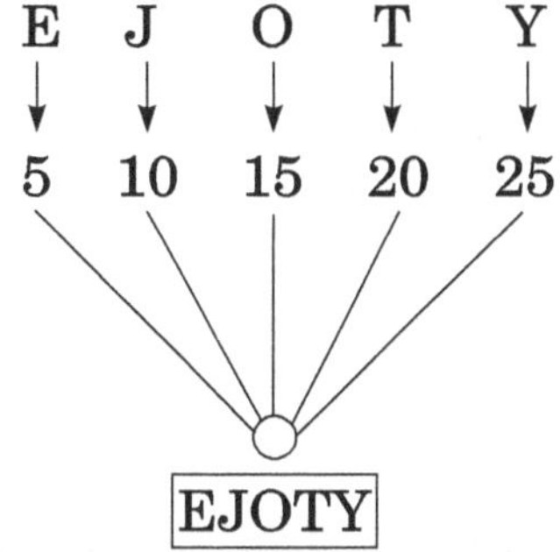

IV. A, E, I, O, U are vowels and remaining letters are consonants of English alphabet respectively:

V. A-M (1-13) letters are the first half of English alphabet.

VI. N-Z (14-26) letters are the second half of English alphabet.

Type 1: Alphabetical Order of Words

Arranging words in alphabetical order implies 'to arrange them in the order as they appear in a dictionary'. First consider the first letter of each word. Arrange the words in the order in which these letters appear in the English alphabet.

Examples

1. Arrange the following words as per order in the dictionary.

   A. Nose　　　**B. Mouth**　　　**C. Eyes**　　　**D. Hair**

   (a) D, C, A, B　　　(b) C, D, B, A　　　(c) A, B, D, C　　　(d) D, C, B, A

Ans. (b)

Explanation: The given words begin with letters N, M, E, H respectively. Their order in English alphabet is E, H, M, N. Thus, the correct alphabetical order of these words is as follows:

Eyes → Hair → Mouth → Nose i.e. C, D, B, A.

So, option (b) is correct.

2. Arrange the following words as given in dictionary.

   1. Across　　　**2. Admit**　　　**3. Advise**　　　**4. Alone**

   (a) 1, 2, 3, 4　　　(b) 1, 2, 4, 3　　　(c) 1, 3, 2, 4　　　(d) 4, 3, 2, 1

Ans. (a)

Explanation: Here, first letter of all words is 'A'. For the second letter, two of the words have 'd'. We now move on to the third letter in each of these two words and then arranging the words accordingly, we get

Across → Admit → Advise → Alone.

So, 1, 2, 3, 4 is the correct order of the words.

Hence, option (a) is correct.

Note: In some cases, two or more words begin with the same letter. Such words should be arranged in the order of second or third letters in the alphabet.

3. Which of the following words will come fourth in the English dictionary?

   (a) False　　　(b) Follow　　　(c) Faithfully　　　(d) Fool

Ans. (d)

Explanation: The given words can be arranged in the alphabetical order as:

$$1 \qquad 2 \qquad 3 \qquad 4$$

Faithfully → False → Follow → Fool

Now, Clearly, 'Fool' comes fourth. So, the correct answer is (d).

Type 2: Letter-Gap Problems

In letter-gap problems, one has to find out as many letters in the same sequence between them in the given word as in the English alphabet.

4. How many letters are there in the word '**MOUTH**' which have as many letters between them in the word as in the English alphabet?

   (a) One (b) Two (c) Three (d) None

Ans. (a)

Explanation: According to the question:

M   O   U   T   H

So, such number of letters is TU.

Hence, option (a) is correct answer.

Type 3: Rule Detection

In rule detection, four options are given as the group of letters and out of these four groups of letters, students are asked to choose the correct alternative which follows a certain rule in a particular manner.

5. Find out which of letter groups contains more than two vowels?

   (a) B D E J O L (B) J K A P I X (c) P R A Q E O (d) Z I L E R S

Ans. (c)

Explanation: P R A Q E O has more than two vowels – A, E and O

Type 4: Alphabetical Quibble

In this type of questions, generally a letter-series is given of English alphabets from A to Z or a randomised sequence of letters. The students are required to find out how many times a letter satisfying the certain condition.

6. The given question is based on the following alphabet series:

   A B C D E F G H I J K L M N O P Q R S T U V W X Y Z

In the English alphabet, which letter will be the seventh from the right end?

   (a) S (b) T (c) Q (d) P

Ans. (b)

Explanation: Counting from the right end of the given alphabet series, i.e. from Z, the seventh letter will be T.

A B C D E F G H I J K L M N O P Q R S T U V W X Y Z

7th From the right end

So, option (b) is correct.

Type 5: Word Formation By Unscrambling Letters

In this type of questions, a set of English letters is given in a jumbled order. The student is required to arrange these letters to form a meaningful word.

7. Select the combination of numbers so that the letters arranged accordingly will form a meaningful word.

T	R	I	F	U
1	2	3	4	5

   (a) 4, 2, 5, 3, 1   (b) 3, 1, 2, 4, 5   (c) 4, 3, 2, 1, 5   (d) 5, 3, 2, 1, 4

Ans. (a)

Explanation: From the given letters, when arranged in the order 4, 2, 5, 3, 1 form the word 'FRUIT'. Hence, option (a) is correct.

Type 6: Word Formation Using Letters of a Given Word

In this type of questions, students have to form words using letters of a given word.

8. In the following question, choose one word which can be formed from the letters of the given word.

A R R A N G E

   (a) REAL   (b) CARE   (c) RANGE   (d) FARE

Ans. (c)

Explanation: Only 'RANGE' can be formed from the given word 'ARRANGE'.

   (a) REAL cannot be formed as there is no 'L' in the given word.

   (b) CARE cannot be formed as there is no 'C' in the given word.

   (d) FARE cannot be formed as there is no 'F' in the given word.

So, option (c) is correct.

LEVEL-1

Direction (Qs. 1-2): In each of the following questions, arrange the given words in the sequence in which they occur in the dictionary and then choose the correct sequence.

1. 1. Eagle   2. Earth   3. Eager   4. Early   5. Each

    (a) 1, 5, 2, 4, 3   (b) 2, 1, 4, 3, 5   (c) 2, 3, 5, 4, 1   (d) 5, 3, 1, 4, 2

2. 1. Select   2. Seldom   3. Send   4.Selfish   5. Seller

    (a) 1, 2, 4, 5, 3   (b) 2, 1, 5, 4, 3   (c) 2, 1, 4, 5, 3   (d) 2, 5, 4, 1, 3

3. Arrange the given words in Alphabetical order and choose the one that comes first?

    (a) Warp   (b) Waste   (c) War   (d) Wrinkle

4. How many pairs of letter are there in the word 'BUCKET' which have as many letters between them in the word as in the alphabet?

    (a) One   (b) Two   (c) Three   (d) Four

5. Which group of letters should not contain more than two vowels?

    (a) B D E J O L Y   (b) J K A P I X U

    (c) P R A Q E O S   (d) Z I L E R A M

6. In the following alphabets, which letter is eight to the right of the fourteenth letter form the right end?

    Z A B C D E F G H I J K L M N O P Q R
    S T U V W X Y

    (a) H   (b) R   (c) S   (d) T

7. A B C D E F G H I J K L M N O P Q R S
    T U V W X Y Z

    Which letter is exactly midway between G and Q in the given alphabet?

    (a) K   (b) L   (c) M   (d) N

Direction (Qs. 8-9): Unscramble the words below to form a meaningful word. Choose the correct option.

8. RANGE

    (a) Geanr   (b) Anger   (c) Narge   (d) Ganre

9. WINGS

    (a) Sing   (b) Swim   (c) Win   (d) Swing

Direction (Qs. 10-12): Choose the option which gives the correct order of the letters as indicated by the numbers to form words.

10.

    H N R C A B
    1 2 3 4 5 6

    (a) 2, 5, 3, 4, 1, 6   (b) 3, 5, 6, 4, 1, 2

    (c) 4, 1, 5, 6, 2, 3   (d) 6, 3, 5, 2, 4, 1

11.

    D I F E R N
    1 2 3 4 5 6

    (a) 1, 4, 3, 6, 2, 5   (b) 6, 4, 3, 5, 2, 1   (c) 3, 5, 2, 4, 6, 1   (d) 5, 4, 3, 2, 6, 1

12.

    R U S G A
    1 2 3 4 5

    (a) 1, 5, 4, 2, 3   (b) 3, 2, 4, 5, 1   (c) 4, 5, 3, 2, 1   (d) 5, 3, 4, 1, 2

13. How many D's are there in the following series which are immediately followed by W and immediately preceded by K?

    K D W C K D W N K G D W W D H K V D W
    K D W

    (a) One   (b) Two   (c) Three   (d) Four

14. In the given series of letters, how many T's are preceded and followed by T?

    P T P T T P P T P T P P P Q Q P T P T T
    P P P T

    (a) 0   (b) 2   (c) 3   (d) 4

15. In the following list of letters, how many B's are followed by Q's but not preceded by D's ?

D B Q B D Q B D B D Q D B Q D S D Q P
B Q D S S S Q D B Q B Q D B Q D D D B Q

(a) 0   (b) 2   (c) 3   (d) 4

16. Arrange the words in a logical and meaningful order.

    1. Food   2. Cutting   3. Market   4. Vegetables   5. Cooking

(a) 1, 2, 5, 3, 4   (b) 4, 3, 1, 2, 5   (c) 1, 5, 2, 4, 3   (d) 3, 4, 2, 5, 1

17. How many pairs of letters are there in the word 'PARROT' which have as many letters between them in the word as in the alphabet?

(a) One   (b) Two   (c) Three   (d) None

Direction (Qs. 18-22): In each of the following questions, insert the letter that complete the first word and begins the second word.

18. M A N (?) A R D

(a) L   (b) T   (c) K   (d) Y

19. B A R R O (?) E I G H T

(a) D   (b) W   (c) I   (d) K

20. S T A (?) E A D

(a) B   (b) V   (c) R   (d) G

21. P L A (?) A T C H

(a) Y   (b) C   (c) N   (d) W

22. S P I N A (?) A T E

(a) M   (b) L   (c) U   (d) S

23. In the given letter series, which letter is 16th from the left end?

M N O P Q R S T U V W X Y Z A B C D E F G H I J K L

(a) Z   (b) A   (c) B   (d) D

24. Arrange the given words in alphabetical order.

   1. House   2. Elephant   3. Tiger   4. Lion

   (a) 1, 2, 3, 4   (b) 2, 1, 4, 3   (c) 3, 4, 1, 2   (d) 4, 3, 2, 1

25. How many pairs of letters are there in the word 'COMPUTER' which have as many letters between them in the word as in the alphabet?

   (a) Three   (b) Two   (c) One   (d) None

Direction (Qs. 26-28): In each of the following questions, find the two words, one from each group that together make a new meaningful word. The word from the first group always comes first.

26.

1	2	3
Crow	Wall	Cloth

A	B	C
ton	lane	paper

   (a) 1 B   (b) 3 A   (c) 2 B   (d) 2 C

27.

1	2	3
Sleek	Pain	Seek

P	Q	R
search	green	killer

   (a) 3 Q   (b) 1 P   (c) 2 R   (d) 1 Q

28.

P	Q	R
Dem	Play	Under

1	2	3
caue	ful	cut

   (a) P 3   (b) Q 2   (c) R 1   (d) P 2

29. If a meaningful word can be formed with 1st, 5th and 8th letters of the alphabetical order of the letters of the word 'SHORTAGE', then Ist letter of the word is your answer. If more than one such word can be formed, then 'X' is your answer, and if no such word can be formed then 'N' is your answer.

   (a) E   (b) S   (c) X   (d) N

30. In the given letter series, which letter is sixth to the right of the seventeenth from the right end?

   Y U V M N O P E F G H A B C D I J K L Q R S T W X Z

   (a) S   (b) M   (c) H   (d) I

31. Which one of the following words cannot be made from the letters of the given word? **(2022)**

UNIVERSITY

(a) Virtue   (b) Invite   (c) Turn   (d) Routine

32. Find the missing term in the series given below. **(2022)**

CE · DF · GI · HJ · KM · ?

(a) NP   (b) MP   (c) LM   (d) LN

LEVEL-2

Direction (Qs. 1-2): Answer the following questions based on the letter-sequence given below:

1. Which letter is 8th to the right of 12th letter from the right?

A B C D E F G H I J K L M N O P Q R S
T U V W X Y Z

(a) D   (b) W   (c) G   (d) T

2. Which letter is 6th to the left of 12th letter from the right?

A B C D E F G H I J K L M N O P Q R S
T U V W X Y Z

(a) R   (b) J   (c) I   (d) S

3. Find the two letters in the word EXTRA which have as many letters between them in the word as in the alphabet. If these two letters are arranged in alphabetical order which letter will come second?

(a) E   (b) X   (c) T   (d) R

4. A B C D E F G H I J K L M N O P Q R S T U V W X Y Z F.
In the English alphabet which letter will be to the immediate left of M?

(a) N   (b) L   (c) O   (d) K

5. Which letter is midway between 22nd letter from the left and 21st letter from the right?

A B C D E F G H I J K L M N O P Q R S T U V W X Y Z

(a) L   (b) M   (c) O   (d) None of these

6. A B C D E F G H I J K L M N O P Q R S T U V W X Y Z.
If the second half of the given alphabet is written in reverse order, which letter will be seventh to the right of the twelfth letter from the left end?

(a) R   (b) S   (c) U   (d) V

7. How many letters are there in the word 'HONEY' which have as many letters between them in the word as in the alphabet?

(a) 1   (b) 2   (c) 3   (d) 4

8. In the word 'CHEAT', how many pairs of letters are there which have as many letters between them in the word as in the alphabet?

(a) One   (b) Two   (c) Three   (d) Four

9. Arrange the given words in the alphabetical order and choose the one that comes first?

(a) Science   (b) Scripture   (c) Scramble   (d) Script

10. Arrange the following words in the meaningful order?

1. Year   2. Week   3. Month   4. Day

(a) 4, 3, 1, 2   (b) 4, 2, 3, 1   (c) 1, 3, 2, 4   (d) 1, 2, 4, 3

11. Arrange the following words as given in dictionary and find the word which will appear at second place.

(a) Accept   (b) Able   (c) Apple   (d) Angle

Direction (Qs. 12-13): Find two words, one from each group, which when joined together to make new words.

1	2	3		P	Q	R
Nail	Tooth	Skin		Paste	Part	Pat

12.

(a) 2P   (b) 3R   (c) 2Q   (d) 1P

13.

1	2	3
arm	face	head

X	Y	Z
waste	enjoy	ache

   (a) 2Z   (b) 2Y   (c) 3Z   (d) 1X

Direction (Qs. 14-15): In each of the following questions, insert the letters that complete the first word and begin the second word.

14. TOR ___ AIR

   (a) AH   (b) HE   (c) CH   (d) HC

15. RISE ☐ HOUT

   (a) N   (b) S   (c) T   (d) U

16. How many such pairs of letters are there in word 'TURBAN', each of which has as many letters between them as in the English alphabet?

   (a) Three   (b) Two   (c) One   (d) None

17. In the following letter series, how many M's are followed by

N M W V M N V W N M W V N W N M

   (a) 0   (b) 2   (c) 3   (d) 4

18. How many such pairs of letters are there in word 'LEMON', each of which has as many letters between them as in the alphabet?

   (a) Three   (b) Two   (c) Four   (d) One

19. The following question is based on the following alphabet series.

L M N O P Q R S T A B C D E F G H I J K U V W X Y Z

Which letter is exactly midway between T and U?

   (a) E   (b) F   (c) G   (d) H

20. How many meaningful English words can be formed from the letters IENF using each letter only once in each word?

   (a) One   (b) Two   (c) Three   (d) None of these

21. If a meaningful word be formed using the four letters ARCE each only once, then the fourth letter of that word is your answer. If more than one such word can be formed, your answer would be 'Z' and if no such word can be formed, your answer is 'X'.

   (a) X   (b) Z   (c) E   (d) A

22. Arrange the following words in a logical sequence and find the word which will appear at third place?

1. Tens   2. Hundred   3. Ones   4. Thousand   5. Lakh

(a) Ones   (b) Hundred   (c) Lakh   (d) Tens

23. Find the combination of numbers from the options so that letters arranged accordingly form a meaningful word.

$$\begin{array}{cccccc} W & L & I & A & D & I \\ 1 & 2 & 3 & 4 & 5 & 6 \end{array}$$

(a) 1, 4, 2, 3, 5, 6 (b) 1, 2, 3, 4, 5, 6 (c) 5, 6, 1, 4, 2, 3 (d) 3, 2, 4, 1, 6, 5

Direction (Qs. 24-25): In each of the following questions, choose one word which can be formed from the letters of the given word.

24. ENVIRONMENT

(a) MOST   (b) RENT   (c) RIDE   (d) MUTE

25. RHINOCEROS

(a) RENAL   (b) SURE   (c) HIND   (d) HORSE

26. From the word 'BEHIND', how many independent words can be made without changing the order of the letters and using each letter only once?

(a) 1   (b) 2   (c) 3   (d) 4

Direction (Qs. 27-28): In each of the following questions, a word has been given followed by four other words, one of which cannot be formed by using the letters of the given word. Find that word.

27. CARPENTER

(a) PEN   (b) CARE   (c) PAINTER   (d) RATE

28. TRANSFORM

(a) TRAIN   (b) FORT   (c) ROAM   (d) RANSOM

29. Find which one word can be made from the letters of the given word?

CORRESPONDING

(a) DISCERN   (b) RESPONSE   (c) REPENT   (d) CORRECT

(Olympiad)

30. Some letters are given which are numbered 1, 2, 3, 4, 5 and 6 followed by four options containing combinations of these numbers. Find the combination of numbers so that letters arranged accordingly form a meaningful word?

A U I G R T

1 2 3 4 5 6

(a) 4, 3, 5, 6, 1, 2   (b) 4, 3, 2, 1, 5, 6

(c) 4, 2, 3, 1, 6, 5   (d) 4, 2, 3, 6, 1, 5

(Olympiad)

31. Some letters are given which are numbered 1, 2, 3, 4 and 5. Find the combination of numbers so that letters are arranged accordingly to form a meaningful English word. **(2021)**

O T N H R

1 2 3 4 5

(a) 3, 1, 2, 5, 4   (b) 3, 1, 5, 2, 4

(c) 3, 2, 4, 1, 5   (d) 1, 3, 5, 2, 4

32. Some letters are given which are numbered as 1, 2, 3, 4, 5 and 6. Find the combination of numbers so that the letters are arranged accordingly to form a meaningful English word. **(2022)**

N E C G H A

1 2 3 4 5 6

(a) 3, 5, 6, 1, 4, 2 (b) 5, 6, 4, 2, 1, 3 (c) 3, 5, 1, 6, 2, 4 (d) 4, 6, 3, 2, 1, 5

33. Find the odd one out. **(2022)**

(a) A P M   (b) B Q N   (c) E R P   (d) D S P

34. Choose the option that will replace (?) in the given pattern. **(2022)**

(a) PZ   (b) LZ   (c) QZ   (d) RY

35. What will come in place of the question mark(?)? **(2022)**

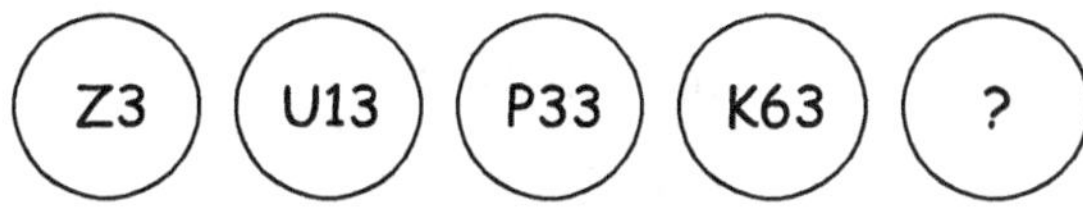

(a) G83   (b) H96   (c) F103   (d) F107

Level-1

1. (d) The order is as follows:
Each → Eager → Eagle → Early → Earth i.e. 5, 3, 1, 4, 2.

2. (c) The order is as follows:
Seldom → Select → Selfish → Seller → Send i.e. 2, 1, 4, 5, 3.

3. (c) The alphabetical order is:

War → Wasp → Waste → Wrinkle
  1   2   3   4

It is clearly shown that 'War' comes first.

4. (a)
B U C K E T

So, such number of letter is CE.

5. (a) B D E J O L Y
      1 2

6. (d) The fourteenth letter from the right is L. The eight letter to the right of L is T.

7. (b) There are nine letters between G and Q– H, I, J, K, L, M, N, O, P. Clearly the middle letter is L.

8. (b) Anger

9. (d) Swing

10. (d) Clearly, the given letters, when arranged in the order 6, 3, 5, 2, 4, 1 form the word 'BRANCH'. Hence, the answer is (d).

11. (c) Clearly, the given letters, when arranged in the order 3, 5, 2, 4, 6, 1 form the word 'FRIEND'. Hence, the answer is (c).

12. (b) Clearly, the given letters, when arranged in the order 3, 2, 4, 5, 1 form the word 'SUGAR'. Hence, the answer is (b).

13. (c) Here,

| K D W | C | K D W | N K G D |

W W D H K V D W | K D W |

So, in the above series, KDW occur 3 times. Hence, option (c) is correct.

14. (a) Since there are no T's in consecutive order.

15. (b) Sequence we are looking:

| Not D | B | Q |

D B Q B D Q B D B D Q D B Q
D S D Q | P B Q | D S S S D B
| Q B Q | D B Q D D D B Q

This sequence occurs two times. Hence, the answer is (b).

16. (d) The logical order is as follows:

Market → Vegetables → Cutting → Cooking → Food i.e., 3, 4, 2, 5, 1.

17. (b) According to the question:

P A R R O T

So, such number of letters are PR and RT.

18. (d) M A N (Y) A R D ie, M A N (Y) and (Y) A R D

19. (b) BARRO (W) EIGHT

So, BARRO (W)

and (W) EIGHT

20. (c) STA(R)EAD

So, STA(R)

and (R)EAD

21. (a) PLA(Y)ATCH

So, PLA(Y)

and (Y)ATCH

22. (b) SPINA(L)ATE

So, SPINA(L)

and (L)ATE

23. (c) The letter is 16th from the left end is B.

24. (b) The order is as follows:

Elephant → Horse → Lion → Tiger i.e. 2, 1, 4, 3.

25. (b) According to the question,

C O M P U T E R

So, such number of letters are TU and RT.

26. (d) Here,

$\dfrac{\overset{2}{\text{Wall}} + \overset{C}{\text{paper}}}{}$ = Wallpaper = 2C

27. (c) Here,

$\overset{2}{\text{Pain}} + \overset{R}{\text{killer}}$ = Painkiller = 2R

28. (b) Here,

$\overset{Q}{\text{Play}} + \overset{2}{\text{ful}}$ = Playful = Q 2

29. (b) Given word: S H O R T A G E

1 2 3 4 5 6 7 8

Meaningful word with letters, S, T, E will be 'SET' and the first letter of the word is 'S'. So, option (b) is correct.

30. (d) The letter is sixth to the right of the seventeenth from the right end is 'I'.

31. (d) **32. (d)**

Level-2

1. (b) The letter is 8th to the right of 12th letter from the right is 'W".

2. (c) The letter is 6th to the left of 12th letter from the right is 'I'.

3. (a) E X T R A

Arranged in alphabetical order, AE. It is clear that E will come second.
When E and A are arranged in alphabetical order them i.e. AE, E will be second.

4. (b) Clearly, L is the letter to the immediate left of M.

5. (d) 22nd letter from the left is V. 21st letter from the right is F. Now, the letter midway between F and V is N.

6. (c) The new alphabet series is

A B C D E F G H I J K
L M Z Y X W V U T S R
Q P O N

The twelfth letter from the left is L. The seventh letter to the right of L is U.

7. (b) As, H O N E Y

So, such number of letters are EH and NO.

8. (a) As, C H E A T

So, such number of letters is CE.

9. (a) As,

Science → Scramble →
(1)   (2)

Script $\rightarrow$ Scripture
$\quad\quad$ (3) $\quad\quad\quad$ (4)
and the word comes first is 'Science.'

10. (b) The meaningful order is
$$4 \quad 2 \quad 3 \quad 1$$
Day $\rightarrow$ Week $\rightarrow$ Month $\rightarrow$ Year
i.e. 4, 2, 3, 1.

11. (a) The order is:
Able $\rightarrow$ Accept $\rightarrow$ Angle $\rightarrow$ Apple
and the word appear at second place will 'Accept'.

12. (a) Here,
$$\overset{2}{\text{Tooth}} + \overset{P}{\text{Paste}} = \text{Toothpaste}$$
$$= \quad 2P$$

13. (c) Here,
$$\overset{3}{\text{Head}} + \overset{Z}{\text{ache}} = \text{Headache}$$
$$= \quad 3Z$$

14. (c) TOR [CH] AIR i.e., TOR [CH] and [CH] AIR.

15. (b) RISE [S] HOUT i.e., RISE [S] and [S] HOUT.

16. (a) As, T U R B A N
So, such number of letters are AB, RT and TU.

17. (c) The series is as follows:
[N M] W V M N V W [N M] W V N W [N M]
So, there are three N's which are followed by M.

18. (b) As, L E M O N
So, such pairs of letters are NO and LO.

19. (b) The letter is exactly midway between T and U is 'F'.

20. (a) Given letters, I E N F
Meaningful word, F I N E.

21. (b) Meaningful words — C A R E, R A C E

22. (b) The logical sequence is:
$$3 \quad\quad 1 \quad\quad 2$$
Ones $\rightarrow$ Tens $\rightarrow$ Hundred $\rightarrow$
$$4 \quad\quad\quad 5$$
Thousand $\rightarrow$ Lakh
and the word which will appear at third place is 'Hundred'.

23. (c) Given letters –
$$W \ L \ I \ A \ D \ I$$
$$1 \ 2 \ 3 \ 4 \ 5 \ 6$$
Meaningful word –
$$D \ I \ W \ A \ L \ I$$
$$5 \ 6 \ 1 \ 4 \ 2 \ 3$$

24. (b) Only RENT can be formed from the letters of the given word ENVIRONMENT.

25. (d) Only HORSE can be formed form the letters of the given word RHINOCEROS.

26. (b) The words are BE and HIND.

27. (c) The word 'CARPENTER', does not contain the letter I. So, the word 'PAINTER' can not be formed.

28. (a) The word 'TRANSFORM' does not contain the letter I. So the word 'TRAIN' can not be formed.

29. (a) Only 'DISCERN' can be formed from the letters of the given word CORRESPONDING.

30. (d) Given letters A U I G R T
$$1 \ 2 \ 3 \ 4 \ 5 \ 6$$
Meaningful word
$$G \ U \ I \ T \ A \ R$$
$$4 \ 2 \ 3 \ 6 \ 1 \ 5$$

31. (b) 3, 1, 5, 2, 4; NORTH

32. (a) 3, 5, 6, 1, 4, 2; CHANGE

33. (c) **34. (c)** **35. (c)**

Order and Ranking

- Students will be able to identify the position of an objects/a person from left end or right end.
- They will be able to identify interchanging positions of two persons.

INTRODUCTION

In this chapter generally the ranks of a person from both sides left or right or from top and from bottom are mentioned and total numbers of persons are asked.

TYPES OF QUESTIONS

1. Total number of persons and positions of one person (either from left or right) are given.
2. Position of more than one person is given.
3. Ascending/Descending order – according to age, height, weight, marks etc.

FORMULAS FOR ORDER AND RANKING

Finding rank either from left or from right

Total – (given rank – 1) = required rank

Finding total numbers

Case 1

When ranks of one person are given from both sides of the row.

Ranks of common person from both sides (R1 + R2) – 1

Case 2

When ranks of two persons and numbers of the persons who are sitting between these two persons are given.

(R1 + R2) + number of middle persons

Finding the numbers of persons who are sitting between any two persons

Total – (Rank from left + Rank from the right)

Finding Rank of Middle Person

Step 1: Convert both ranks from the same side.

Step 2: Find the average of both ranks.

Example 1:

Here is a table

Name	Rank from top	Rank from bottom
Rahul	5	1
Kavita	4	2
Chetan	3	3
Aryan	$\boxed{2}$	$\boxed{4}$
Raj	1	5

Let us discuss about 'Raj'

Raj's rank from top = 1 and from bottom = 5

Total number of persons in the row = 5

- Means total rank = (rank from top + rank from bottom) – 1

$$= (1 + 5) – 1 = 5$$

- Rank from top = total rank – (rank from bottom – 1)

$$= 5 – (5 – 1) = 1$$

- Rank from bottom = total rank – (rank from top – 1)

$$= 5 – (1 – 1) = 5$$

Example 2:

Abhishek is fifteenth from the right end in a row of 40 boys. What is his position from the left end?

(a) 24th (b) 25th (c) 26th (d) 27th

Ans. (c)

Explanation: Clearly, number of boys towards the right of Abhishek = 14.

So, Abhishek's rank from left end = 40 − 14 = 26th

Example 3:

Raj is sixth from left and Rohan is eighth from right.

If there are seven students between them then how many students are there in a row?

(a) 14   (b) 15   (c) 21   (d) 22

Ans. (c)

Explanation:

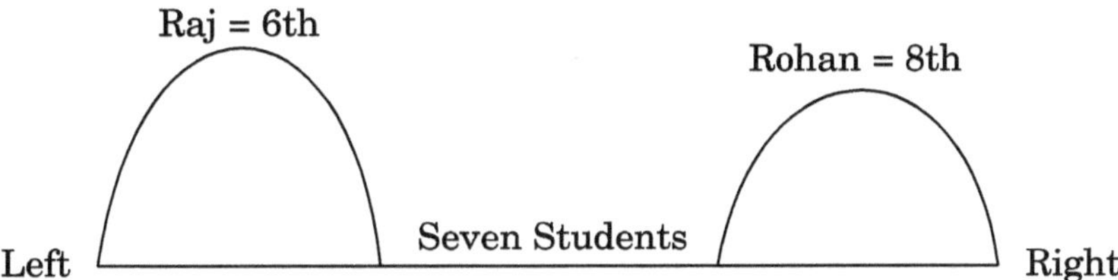

Total number of students in a row = 6 + 8 + 7 = 21

Example 4:

Jyoti is seventh from left end and is fourth to the left of Manya who is seventh from right end. Then how many students are there in a row?

(a) 17   (b) 18   (c) 16   (d) 14

Ans. (a)

Explanation:

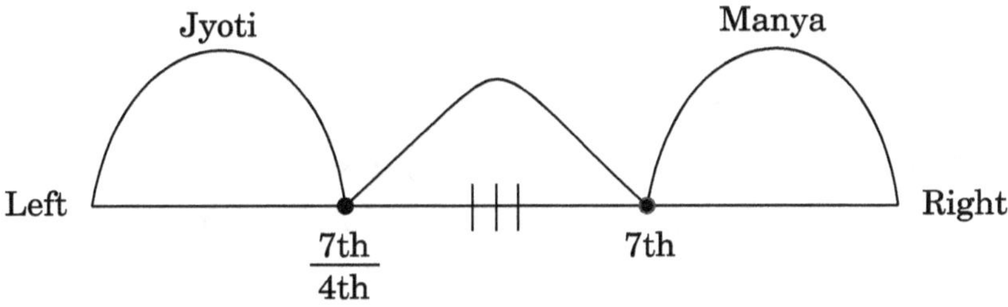

Total students in a row = 7 + 3 + 7 = 17

Example 5:

Jai is 15th from left and Vijay is 14th from right. When they interchange their positions respectively then Vijay becomes 21st from right end. What will be Jai's position from left after interchanging?

(a) 25　　　　　(b) 22　　　　　(c) 27　　　　　(d) 28

Ans. (b)

Explanation:

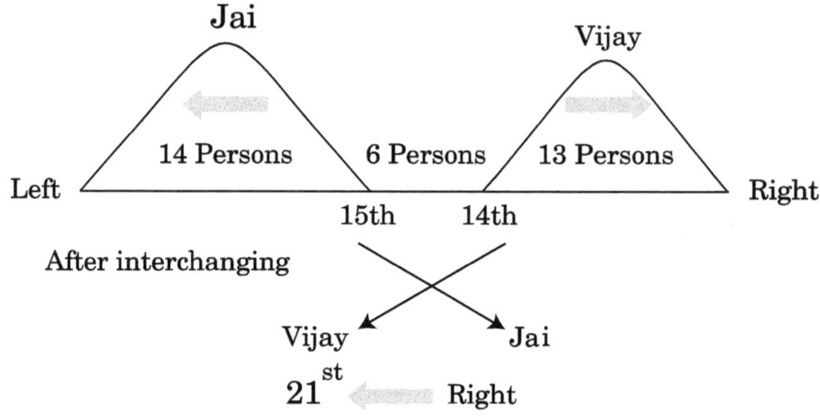

Jai's position from the left after interchanging = 15 + 6 + 1 = 22.

Example 6:

Among five persons, Raja secured more marks than only Kapil. Ashok and Jagdish secured less marks than only Nikhil. Who among them secured third least marks?

(a) Nikhil　　　　　　　　　(b) Raja

(c) Jagdish　　　　　　　　　(d) Cannot be determined

Ans. (d)

Explanation:

Nikhil > Ashok / Jagdish > Raja > Kapil

Third least marks = Either Ashok or Jagdish

Hence, it cannot be determined who secured third least marks.

LEVEL-1

1. In a garden there is a row of trees, one tree is fifth from the either ends of this row. How many trees are there in the row?
   (a) 5   (b) 8
   (c) 10   (d) 9

2. Asha ranks sixth from the top and fourteenth from the bottom in class. How many students are there in the class?
   (a) 20   (b) 18
   (c) 19   (d) 25

3. Megha is seventh from the top and twenty eighth from the bottom in class. How many students are there in the class?
   (a) 35   (b) 34
   (c) 30   (d) 38

4. Among five children P, Q, R, S and T each having a different height, P is taller than only S and R is shorter than only T. Who among them is the third in order of height?
   (a) T   (b) Q
   (c) R   (d) S

5. Ramesh is 9th from downwards in a class of 31 students. What will be his position from upwards?
   (a) 21st (b) 22nd
   (c) 23rd (d) 24th

6. Some girls are sitting in a line. Meeta is on 10th place from left and Simran is on 11th place from right. There are 4 girls between them. How many girls are there in the line?

7. Mahendra is 12th from downwards in a class of 35 students. What will be his position from upwards?
   (a) 23   (b) 24
   (c) 25   (d) 26

8. Srishti is ranked 8th from the top and 20th from the bottom among those who passed the examination. Six did not participate in the examination and five failed in it. How many girls were there in the class?
   (a) 30   (b) 35
   (c) 37   (d) 38

9. Maya is 7 rank ahead of Ritu in a class of 39 students. If Ritu's rank is seventeenth from the last, what is Maya's rank from the start?
   (a) 12th (b) 15th
   (c) 10th (d) 18th

10. Prerika is fourth from the right end in the row of 10 girls. What is her position from the left?
    (a) 4th (b) 5th
    (c) 6th (d) 7th

11. Preeti is 16th from the top and 29th from the bottom in class. How many students are there in the class?
    (a) 40   (b) 42
    (c) 44   (d) 48

12. Mehak is 12th in the class of 28 students. What is her rank from the last?
   (a) 14th (b) 16th
   (c) 18th (d) 17th

13. In a single line of girls, one girl is at 20th position from both the sides. How many girls are there in the class?
   (a) 40   (b) 39
   (c) 38   (d) 37

14. Ruchika ranked 9th from the top and 28th from the bottom in a class. How many students are there in the class?
   (a) 33
   (b) 35
   (c) 36
   (d) 37

15. If Anika finds that she is 10th from the right in a line of girls and fourth from the left. How many girls should be added to the line such that there are 28 girls in the line?
   (a) 11   (b) 12
   (c) 13   (d) 15

16. The seventh flower from the left end is ____________ ?

Left   P   Q   R   S   T   U   V   W   Right

   (a) V   (b) W   (c) U   (d) T

17. The ____________ is 4th from the right end.

Left   Kite   Sun   Shape   Bell   Flower   Right

   (a) Shape   (b) Flower   (c) Sun   (d) Kite

18. If we remove shape X and shape Y from the series given below, then ____________ will come on the middle rank?

M   X   R   Q   P   S   Y   T   U

   (a) P   (b) Q   (c) R   (d) T

19. If Payal is behind Ratna, Meena is last in the queue and Prabha is not behind Ratna, then who will be the first person in the queue?
   (a) Payal   (b) Prabha   (c) Ratna   (d) Meena

20. Shanaya's position is 11th from upwards in a class of 30 students. What will be her position from downwards?

(a) 17th (b) 18th

(c) 19th (d) 20th

21. In a queue, Raina is 12th from the front and Pratiksha is 19th from the end. While Dally is in between Raina and Pratiksha. There be 38 persons in the queue, how many persons are in between Raina and Pratiksha.

(a) 5 persons   (b) 6 persons

(c) 4 persons   (d) 7 persons

22. How many 5s are there in the following number sequence which are immediately preceded by 7 and immediately followed by 6 ?

Terms : 7 5 5 9 4 5 7 6 4 5 9 8 7 5 6 7 6 4 3 2 5 6 7 8

(a) 1   (b) 2

(c) 3   (d) 4

23. The positions of how many digits in the number 3 5 1 4 6 2 9 8 7 will remain unchanged after the digits are rearranged in ascending order within the number ?

(a) None   (b) One

(c) Two   (d) Three

Direction (Qs. 24-26): Answer the following questions based on the arrangement given below:-

A D 4 R % G 1 # O I + F E 2 M S 5 $
Q @ L O C & 8 S X

24. How many such numbers are there which are immediately preceded by letter and immediately followed by symbol ?

(a) More than three (b) One

(c) Two   (d) Three

(e) None of these

25. Which element is third to the left of the eight from the right end?

(a) 5   (b) S

(c) M   (d) F

(e) None of these

26. If all the numbers are dropped from the above the sequence, then which element is eight to the right of seventh from the left end?

(a) C   (b) @

(c) $ (d) Q

Direction (Qs. 27-29): Study the following arrangement and answer the questions given:

81   47   56   38   79   67

27. If the positions of first and second digits are changed in each number, which is the lowest number?

(a) 47   (b) 81

(c) 56   (d) 38

28. If in each number 1 is added to first digit, then which is the largest number?

(a) 38   (b) 81

(c) 56   (d) 47

29. If all numbers are arranged in ascending order, then what is the difference between the numbers which is second from the left and third from the right?

(a) 36   (b) 9

(c) 12   (d) 20

30. Study the following arrangement to answer the given question.

456   789   145   392   1
40   653   806

Which of the following is the sum of the first and third digit of the third largest number?

(a) 14   (b) 9

(c) 11   (d) 10

31. In a class, Akash ranks seventh from the top and seventeenth from the bottom. How many students are there in the class?   **(2022)**

(a) 23   (b) 22

(c) 20   (d) 24

32. In a class, Rakesh ranks 9th from the top and 28th from the bottom. How many students are there in the class?   **(2022)**

(a) 25   (b) 19

(c) 36   (d) 38

LEVEL-2

1. Some girls are sitting in a row. M is sitting 12th from the left and N is 8th from the right. If there are four girls between M and N, how many girls are there in row?

(a) 20   (b) 22

(c) 24   (d) 26

2. Shantanu ranks 7th in class of 20 students. What will be his rank from the last?

(a) 10th (b) 12th

(c) 13th (d) 14th

3. Aakriti and Akansha are ranked fourth and fifth respectively from the top in a class of 25 students. What will be their respective ranks from the bottom in the class?

(a) 22nd and 21st

(b) 23rd and 21st

(c) 22nd and 24th

(d) 25th and 22nd

4. In a line, Shreya is 8th from the left and Bhavna is 17th from the right. If they interchange their positions, Shreya becomes 14th from the left. How many girls are there in the row?

(a) 25   (b) 27

(c) 28   (d) 30

5. Jack remembers that his brother Paresh's birthday falls after 20th May but before 28th May, while Tripti remembers that Paresh's birthday falls before 22nd May but after 12th May. On what date Paresh's birthday falls?

(a) 26th May   (b) 18th May

(c) 20th May   (d) 21st May

6. Nisha leaves her house at 20 minutes to seven in the morning, reaches Pooja's house in 25 minutes, they finish their breakfast in another 15 minutes and leave for their office. What time do they leave Pooja's house to reach their office?

(a) 7 : 20 a.m.   (b) 7 : 25 a.m.

(c) 7 : 40 a.m.   (d) 7 : 55 a.m.

7. In a row of pine trees, one tree is 4th from either end of the row. How many trees are there in the row?

(a) 4   (b) 6

(c) 7   (d) 9

8. In class of 35 students, among those students who passed, Aishwarya secured 11th position from upwards and 15th from downwards. How many students failed?

(a) 4   (b) 5

(c) 7   (d) 10

9. Vidit remembers that his father's birthday was certainly after eight but before thirteenth of December. His sister Mitali remembers that their father's birthday was definitely after ninth but before fourteenth of December. On which date of December was their father's birthday?

(a) 10th

(b) 11th

(c) 12th

(d) Data inadequate

10. In a row of 10 girls, when Poonam was shifted by two places towards the left, she became sixth from the left end. What was her earlier position from the right end of the row?

(a) First   (b) Second

(c) Third   (d) Fourth

11. Some boys are sitting on a bench.

- Raj and Vijay are sitting at one of the ends.
- There are three persons between Vijay and Ankur.
- Aryan is sitting midway between Vijay and Ankur.
- Ankur is sitting just next to Raj

How many people are sitting on the bench?

(a) 4   (b) 5

(c) 6   (d) 7

12. The peach cake is not smaller than the lemon cake. The lemon cake is bigger than the chocolate cake. Which cake is the smallest?

(a) The peach cake

(b) The lemon cake

(c) The chocolate cake

(d) None of these

13. Harsh is older than Raj and Raj is older than Anshul. Which of the following statements must be true?

(a) Harsh is older than Anshul.

(b) Harsh is younger than Anshul.

(c) Harsh is the same age as Anshul.

(d) Anshul is the oldest.

14. Nitin is younger than Jatin and older than Amit. Anshul is as old as Jatin.

Which of the following statements is wrong?

(a) Jatin is older than Amit.

(b) Anshul is older than Amit.

(c) Nitin is younger than Anshul.

(d) Amit is not the youngest.

15. Miss Kapoor is taking a Maths test. The marks (out of 50) scored by each student are given below.

Priya	Jatin	Poonam	Dev	Manav	Tanu	Komal	Amit	Raj	Latika
30	15	25	45	42	47	12	20	49	10

Who scored the highest and who scored the lowest marks respectively?

(a) Raj, Jatin   (b) Tanu, Latika

(c) Dev, Jatin   (d) Raj, Latika

16. Four runners Simran, Rohit, Latika and Anuj took part in a 100m race.

Simran : I was faster than Rohit.

Rohit   : I was the second.

Latika : I was neither at the first nor at the last place.

Who stood last in the race?

(a) Simran   (b) Rohit

(c) Anuj   (d) Latika

17. The child A is less intelligent than the child B. The child C is less intelligent than the child D. The child B is less intelligent than the child C. Which child is the most intelligent?

(a) B   (b) A

(c) D   (d) C

18. Ashish is heavier than Govind. Mohit is lighter than Jack. Pawan is heavier than Jack but lighter than Govind.

Who among them is the heaviest?

(a) Govind   (b) Jack

(c) Pawan   (d) Ashish

Direction (Qs. 19-20): Read the following information and answer the following questions. Five boys participated in a competition.

Rohit   : I was ranked lower than Sanjay.

Vikas : I was ranked higher than Dinesh.

Kamal : I was between Rohit and Vikas.

19. Who was ranked highest?

(a) Sanjay   (b) Vikas

(c) Dinesh   (d) Kamal

20. Who was ranked lowest?

(a) Sanjay   (b) Kamal

(c) Dinesh   (d) Vikas

21. Hitesh is richer than Jaya where as Mohan is richer than Pritam. Amit is richer than Hitesh?

Which conclusion can be definitely drawn from the above statement?

(a) Jaya is poorer than Pritam.

(b) Mohan is richer than Amit.

(c) Jaya is poorer than Hitesh.

(d) Pritam is richer than Amit.

22. There are five friends Latika, Garima, Megha, Priya and Beena. Latika is taller than Priya. Garima and Beena are of the same height. Megha is shorter than Beena. Priya is taller than Garima. Who is the tallest?

(a) Latika   (b) Beena

(c) Garima   (d) Priya

(Olympiad)

23. Mohit, Rohit, Tanuj, Varun and Amit are comparing the flavours of milkshake they like

- Mohit, Tanuj and Amit are the only ones who like vanilla milkshake.
- Rohit is the only one who dislikes strawberry milkshake.
- Varun's favourite is chocolate milkshake.
- Everyone except Tanuj likes banana milkshake.
- The only child who does not like chocolate milkshake is Mohit.

Who likes the least flavours of milkshake?

(a) Amit   (b) Varun

(c) Mohit   (d) Rohit

(Olympiad)

24. The Vanilla cake is larger than the Coconut cake. The Chocolate cake is larger than the Vanilla cake but smaller than the Mango cake. Which of the following is the correct order of cakes from the largest to the smallest?

(a) Vanilla > Coconut > Chocolate > Mango

(b) Mango > Chocolate > Coconut > Vanilla

(c) Mango > Vanilla > Chocolate > Coconut

(d) Mango > Chocolate > Vanilla > Coconut

(Olympiad)

25. Neha is standing in a row of children. If she is 13th from the right end and 19th from the left end, then how many children are standing in the row?

(a) 31   (b) 29   (c) 28   (d) 27

(Olympiad)

26. Select the correct order from the heaviest to the lightest.

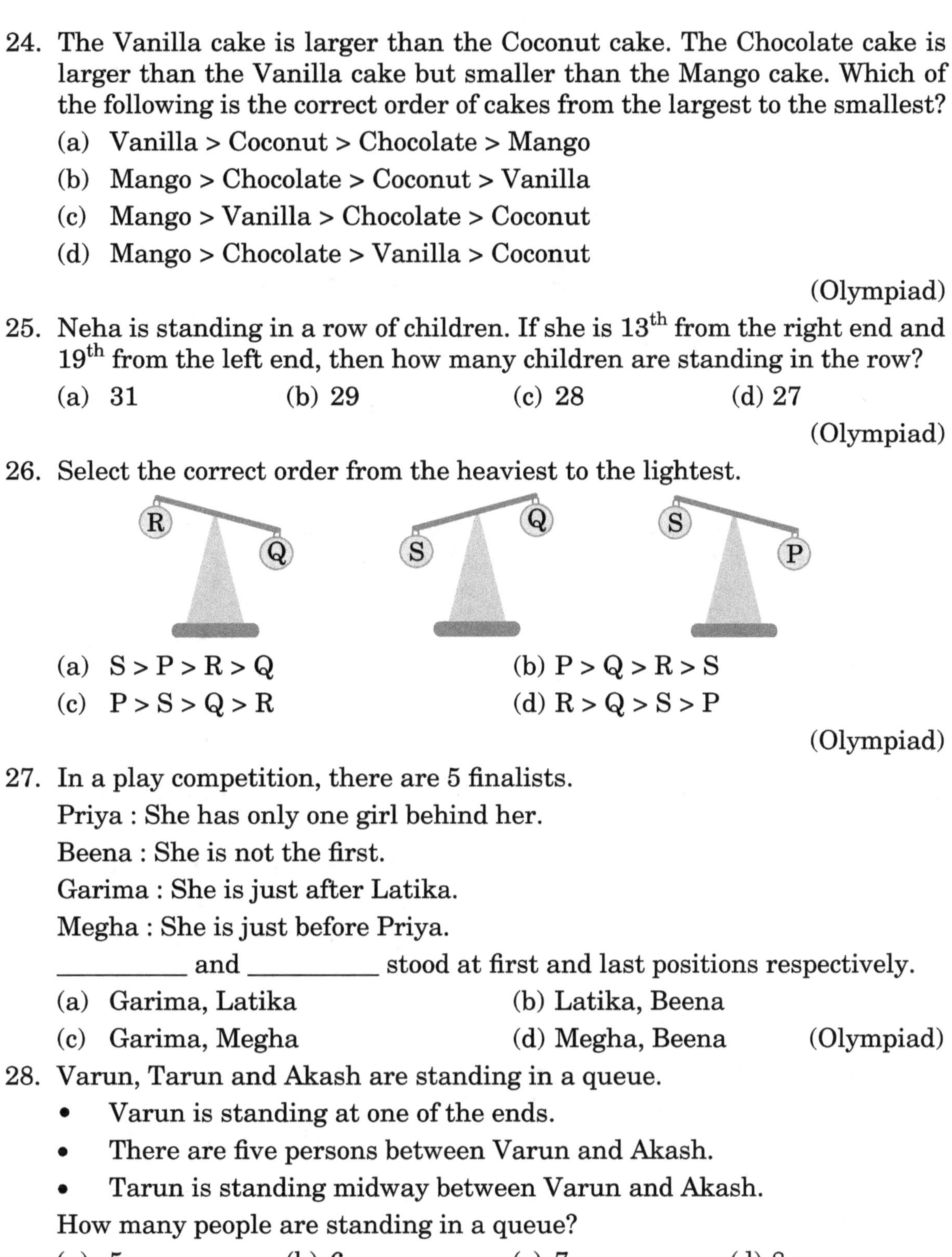

(a) S > P > R > Q

(c) P > S > Q > R

(b) P > Q > R > S

(d) R > Q > S > P

(Olympiad)

27. In a play competition, there are 5 finalists.

Priya : She has only one girl behind her.

Beena : She is not the first.

Garima : She is just after Latika.

Megha : She is just before Priya.

__________ and __________ stood at first and last positions respectively.

(a) Garima, Latika

(c) Garima, Megha

(b) Latika, Beena

(d) Megha, Beena   (Olympiad)

28. Varun, Tarun and Akash are standing in a queue.

• Varun is standing at one of the ends.

• There are five persons between Varun and Akash.

• Tarun is standing midway between Varun and Akash.

How many people are standing in a queue?

(a) 5   (b) 6   (c) 7   (d) 8

(Olympiad)

29. If Nisha is 2nd from the left end and Preeti is 3rd from the right end, and 4 girls are standing between them, then number of girls in the row is ___________.

   (a) 10   (b) 11   (c) 8   (d) 9

30. Study the given arrangement carefully.

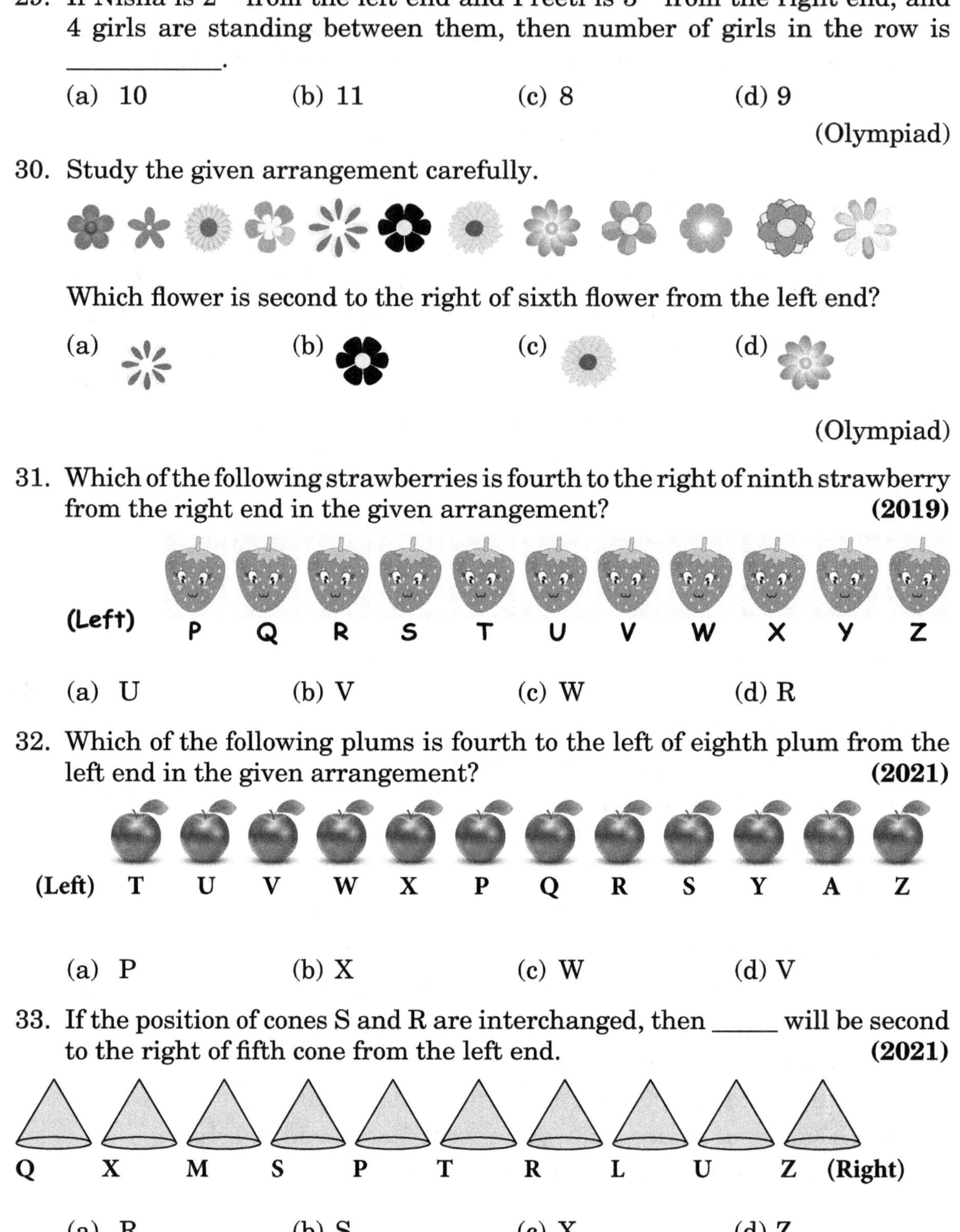

   Which flower is second to the right of sixth flower from the left end?

   (a)   (b)   (c)   (d)

31. Which of the following strawberries is fourth to the right of ninth strawberry from the right end in the given arrangement?   **(2019)**

   (Left)   P   Q   R   S   T   U   V   W   X   Y   Z

   (a) U   (b) V   (c) W   (d) R

32. Which of the following plums is fourth to the left of eighth plum from the left end in the given arrangement?   **(2021)**

   (Left)   T   U   V   W   X   P   Q   R   S   Y   A   Z

   (a) P   (b) X   (c) W   (d) V

33. If the position of cones S and R are interchanged, then ______ will be second to the right of fifth cone from the left end.   **(2021)**

   Q   X   M   S   P   T   R   L   U   Z   **(Right)**

   (a) R   (b) S   (c) X   (d) Z

Level-1

1. **(d)** Tree 1, Tree 2, Tree 3, Tree 4 — (Tree 5) — Tree 6, Tree 7, Tree 8, Tree 9

    Total trees = 4 + 1 + 4 = 9.

2. **(c)** Total students in the class = (rank from top + rank from bottom) − 1 = (6 + 14) − 1 = 19.

3. **(b)** Total students = (rank from top + rank from bottom) − 1

    $$= (7 + 28) - 1$$
    $$= 34.$$

4. **(b)** P > only S and R < only T.

    Descending order of is

    $$\text{T} > \text{R} > (\text{Q}) > \text{P} > \text{S}$$
    $$1 \quad\ 2 \quad\ 3 \quad\ 4 \quad\ 5$$

    Hence, Q is third in order of height.

5. **(c)** Ramesh's position from upwards = (Total students − Ramesh's position from down) + 1

    $$= (31 - 9) + 1 = 23^{\text{rd}}$$

6. **(a)** Meeta's place from left + Simran's place from right) + (Girls between them)

    $$= (10 + 11) + (4) = 25 \text{ girls.}$$

7. **(b)** Mahendra's position from upwards = (Total students − Mahendra's position from down)

    $$= (35 - 12) + 1 = 24.$$

8. **(d)** Number. of girls who passed = (7 + 19 + 1) = 27

    Total Number of girls in class = 27 + 6 + 5 = 38

9. **(c)** Ritu is seventeenth from the last and Maya is 7 ranks ahead of Maya.

    So, Maya is 10th from the start.

10. **(d)** Number of girls towards the left of Prerika = (10 − 4) = 6

    Prerika's position from the left end = 6 + 1 = 7

11. **(c)** Total Students = (Preeti's rank from top + Preeti's rank from bottom) − 1

    $$= (16 + 29) - 1$$
    $$= 44 \text{ students}$$

12. **(d)** Mehak's rank from last = Total rank − (Rank from top − 1)

    $$= 28 - (12 - 1)$$
    $$= 28 - 11 = 17$$

13. **(b)** Number of girls in the class = (20 + 20) − 1 = 39 girls.

14. **(c)** Total students = (rank from top + rank from bottom) − 1

    $$= (9 + 28) - 1 = 36$$

15. **(d)** Number of girls in the line = (10 + 4) − 1 = 13

    Number of girls to be added = 28 − 13 = 15 girls.

16. (a) V is the seventh flower from the left end.

17. (c) Sun is 4th from the right end.

18. (a) Series after removing shape X and shape Y

Middle

= $\longleftarrow$ M R Q (P) S T U $\longrightarrow$

19. (b) Sequence in queue:

I. Prabha
II. Ratna
III. Payal
IV. Meena

Hence, Prabha is the first person in the queue.

20. (d) Shanaya's position from downwards

= (Total students – Shanaya's position from forward) + 1

= (30 – 11) + 1

= 19 + 1

= 20th.

21. (d) Number of persons between Raina and Pratiksha

= 38 – (12 + 19) = 38 – (31)

= 7 persons

22. (a) Sequence we are looking 756

Number Sequence 7 5 5 9 4 5 7 6 4 5 9 8 756 7 6 4 3 2 5 6 7 8

Preceded by 7 and followed by 6 So, there is only one such 5

23. (c) Given Order   3 5 1 4 6 2 9 8 7

Ascending Order   1 2 3 4 5 6 7 8 9

Hence, 4 and 8 digit remain unchanged after the rearrangement.

24. (c) Sequence looking for:

Letter	Number	Symbol

A D 4 R % G1# O I + F E 2 M S5$ Q @ L O C & 8 S X

Hence, there are only two such sequences.

25. (a) A D 4 R % G 1 # O I + F E 2 M S(5)$ Q @ L O C & 8 S X

$\longleftarrow$

11th from right

Third to the left of the eight from the right end = 8 + 3 = 11 from right = 5

26. (d) Sequence after dropping numbers:

A D R % G # O I + F E M S $ (Q) @ L C & S X

$\longrightarrow$

15th from left

Element Q eight to the right of seventh from the left end = 8 + 7 = 15 from left.

27. (b) Rearrangement:

18   74   65   83   97   76

Number 81 is the lowest.

28. (b) Rearrangement:

91   57   66   48   89   77

Number 81 is the largest.

29. (d) Ascending Order :

38   47   56   67   79   81

2nd from left   third from right

$\therefore$ Difference = $67 - 47 = 20$.

30. (b) Descending Order:

806   789   653   456   392

145   146

$653 = 6 + 3 = 9$

Hence, the sum of the first and third digit of the third largest number is 9.

31. (a) $7 + 17 - 1 = 23$.

32. (c)

Level-2

1. (c) Number of girls in the row = Number of girls up till M + Number of girls between M and N + Number of girls including N.

= 12 + 4 + 8 = 24 girls

2. (d) Number of students behind Shantanu rank = $(20 - 7) = 13$

So, Shantanu's rank from the last is 14th.

3. (a) Number of students behind Aakriti in rank = $(25 - 4) = 21$

Aakriti is 22nd from the bottom.

Number of students behind Akansha in rank = $(25 - 5) = 20$

So, Akansha is 21st from the bottom.

4. (d) Shreya and Bhawna interchange their positions. So, Shreya's new position is the same as Bhawna's earlier position. This position is 14th from the left and 17th from the right is Bhawna's new position.

Number of girls in the row = $(13 + 1 + 16) = 30$

5. (d) According to Jack, Paresh's birthday falls on, ㉑ˢᵗ 22nd, 23rd, 24th, 25th, 26th and 27th of May.

According to Tripti, Paresh's birthday falls = 13th, 14th, 15th, 16th, 17th, 18th, 19th, 20th and ㉑ˢᵗ May.

The common day is 21st.

Paresh's birthday falls on 21st.

6. (a) Nisha leaves her house 6 : 40 a.m.

Reaches Pooja's house = 6.40 + 25 minutes = 7.05 a.m.

Finish their breakfast = 7.05 + 15 minutes = 7.20 a.m.

7. (c)

			Middle			
1	2	3	④	5	6	7
Tree	Tree	Tree		Tree	Tree	Tree

Number of trees in the row = $(3 + 1 + 3) = 7$ trees

8. (d) (Total students) – (Aishwarya's position from upwards + Aishwarya's position from downwards) – 1

$$= 35 - (11 + 15) - 1$$
$$= 35 - (26) - 1 = 10$$

9. (d) According to Vidit his father's birthday falls on 9th, 10th, 11th and 12th December.

According to Mitali, Father's birthday falls on 10th, 11th, 12th and 13th December.

The days common are 10th, 11th and 12th December.

So, data is inadequate.

10. (c) Row Arrangement

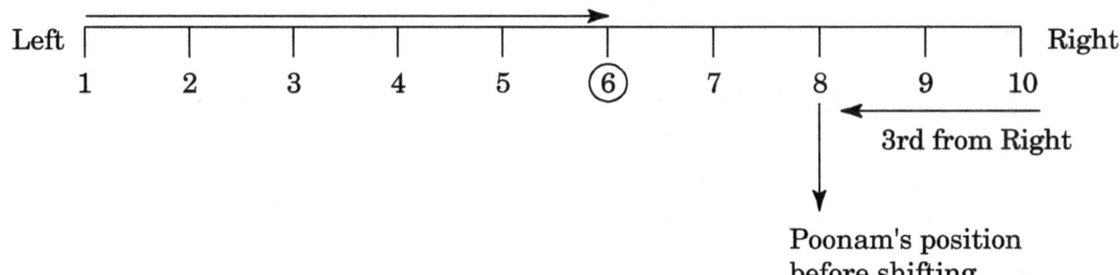

11. (c) Raj   Ankur   Aryan   Vijay

Total persons = 4 + 2 = 6.

12. (c) Peach cake > Lemon cake > Chocolate cake

So, the chocolate cake is smallest.

13. (a) Harsh > Raj > Anshul

Hence, Harsh is older than Anshul.

14. (d) The Sequence is :

Anshul = Jatin > Nitin > Amit.

Clearly, Amit is the youngest.

Hence, option (d) is the incorrect statement.

15. (d) Raj scored the highest marks = 49

Latika scored the lowest marks = 10

16. (c) Simran > Rohit > Latika > Anuj.
      (1)   (2)   (3)   (4)

Hence, Anuj stood last in the race.

17. (c) The order of children is :

D > C > B > A

Hence, the child D is the most intelligent.

18. (d) The Sequence is :

Mohit < Jack < Pawan < Govind < Ashish

Hence, Ashish is the heaviest.

The Sequence is :

Dinesh < Vikas < Kamal < Rohit < Sanjay

19. (a) Sanjay ranked highest.

20. (c) Dinesh ranked lowest.

21. (c) In terms of richness we have:

Jaya < Hitesh < Amit and Pritam < Mohan

Hence, Jaya is poorer than Hitesh.

22. (a) Order is :

Latika > Priya > Garima = Beena > Megha

Hence, Latika is the tallest.

23. (d)

	Vanilla	Strawberry	Chocolate	Banana
Mohit	√	√	×	√
Rohit	×	×	√	√
Varun	×	√	√	√
Tanuj	√	√	√	×
Amit	√	√	√	√

So, it is clearly shown from the above arrangement that Rohit likes the least flavours of milkshake.

24. (d) Option (d) is correct according to the given information.

25. (a) Total children in a row = (Neha's position from the right end + Neha's position from the left end) − 1
= (13 − 19) − 1
= 31.

26. (c) Option (c) is the correct order.

27. (b) Finalists Ranking:

Latika > Garima > Megha >
↓ ↓ ↓
Rank 1 Rank 2 Rank 3

Priya > Beena
↓ ↓
Rank 4 Rank 5

So, Latika and Beena stood at first and last position respectively.

28. (c)

Varun   Tarun   Akash

Five persons between Varun and Akash

Total persons = 1 + 5 + 1 = 7.

29. (d)

Raj = 2nd Preeti = 3rd

Left   4 girls   Right

Total number of girls in a row = 2 + 4 + 3 = 9.

30. (d) Second to the right of sixth flower from the left end = 8th from left end.

31. (b) Ninth strawberry from the right end is R and its fourth to the right is V.

32. (b) Eighth plum from the left is R. Its fourth to the left is W.

33. (b) If position of S and R is interchanged.

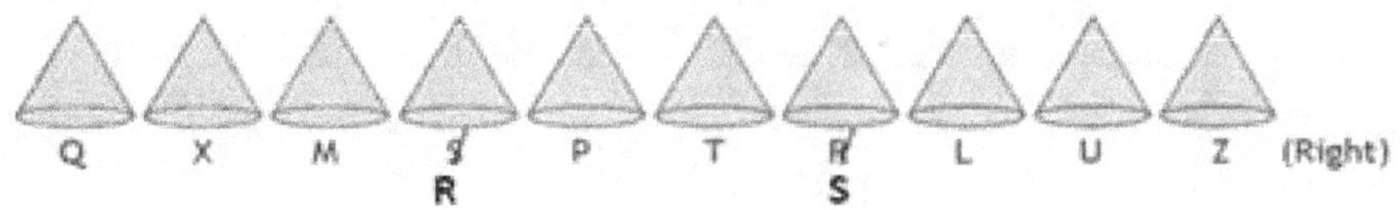

The fifth cone from the left is P and its second to the right is S.

Direction and Distance

OBJECTIVES

- Students will develop the ability to trace and follow the logical path correctly and sense of direction correctly as well.

INTRODUCTION

Direction is a measurement of position of one thing with respect to another thing.

Displacement is the measurement of distance between initial and the final point. Direction and distance test mainly deals with two types of directions i.e. main directions and cardinal directions.

MAIN DIRECTIONS

There are four type of directions, viz, East, West, North and South as shown below. The word 'NEWS' stands for the information of all four directions.

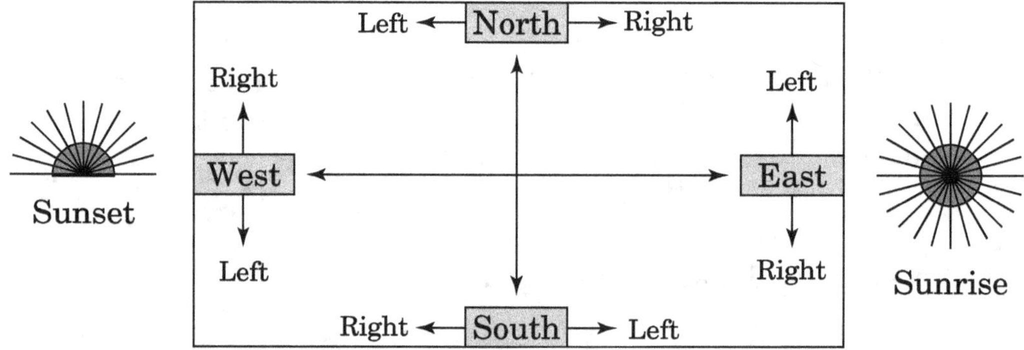

A direction between two main directions is called cardinal direction. Clearly, there are four cardinal directions.

(i)   N-E (North-East)

(ii) N-W (North-West)

(iii) S-E (South-East) and

(iv) S-W (South-West)

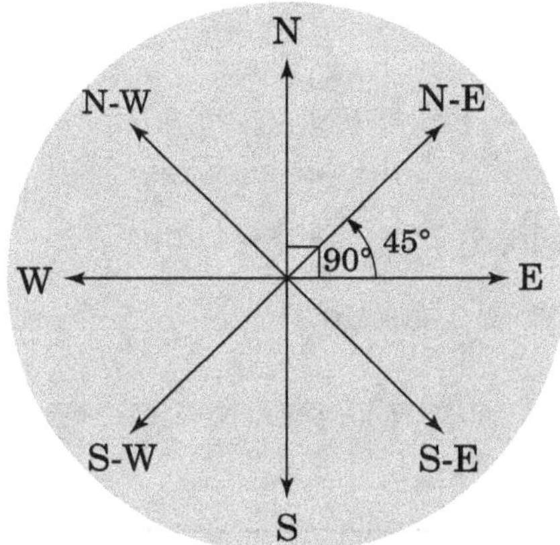

Note: Angle formed between two main directions is 90° and angle formed between a cardinal direction and main direction is 45° as shown in the above diagram.

ROTATION OF ANGLES

To solve angle movement questions, it is necessary to know about the rotations of angles which are given below.

(i)   For right direction movement (Clockwise)

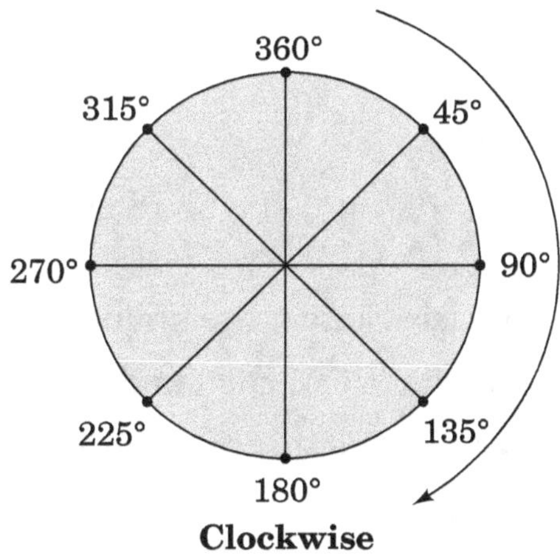

(ii) For left direction movement (Anti-clockwise)

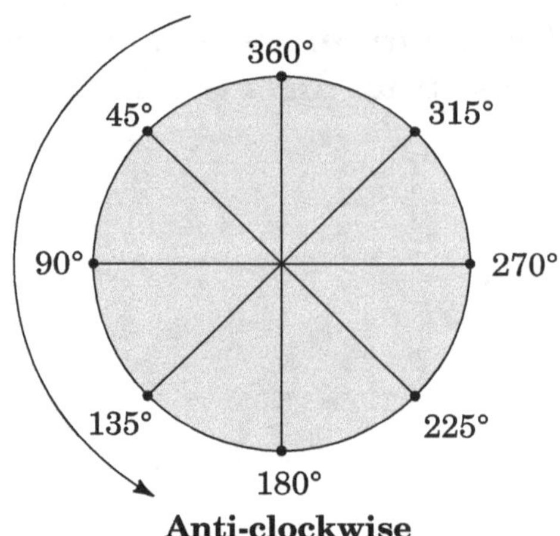

Left turn Anti-clockwise direction

Right turn Clockwise direction

The change in direction when a person or vehicle takes a right or a left turn

Direction before taking the turn	Direction in which the person or vehicle will be moving after taking turn	
	Right	**Left**
North	East	West
South	West	East
East	South	North
West	North	South

SHADOW CASE

In Morning/Sunrise time

(a) If a person facing towards Sun, the shadow will be towards his back or in west.

(b) If a person facing towards South, the shadow will be towards his right.

(c) If a person facing towards West, the shadow will be towards his front.

(d) If a person facing towards North, the shadow will be towards his left.

In Evening/Sunset time

(a) If a person facing towards Sun, the shadow will be towards his back or in East.

(b) If a person facing towards North, the shadow will be towards his right.

(c) If a person facing towards East, the shadow will be towards his front.

(d) If a person facing towards South, the shadow will be towards his left.

Note: At 12:00 noon there is no shadow because the rays of the Sun are vertically downward.

Type 1: Final Direction Based

In these types of questions, we have to ascertain the final direction with respect to the initial point or the directional relations between two points/things.

Examples

1. A man is facing towards West and turns through 45° clockwise, again 180° clockwise. In which direction is he facing now?

   (a) West

   (b) North-West

   (c) North

   (d) South-East

Ans. (d)

Explanation:

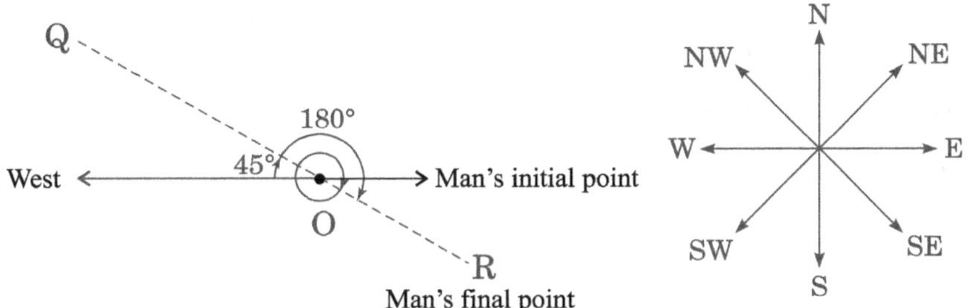

Finally on moving 180° clockwise, he faces in the direction which is South-East.

Type 2: Distance (Displacement) Based

In this type of questions, we deal with the final distance between starting and final point or between two points/persons/things. There are various formats/patterns of displacement.

2. Mayank walks 20 m North. Then, he turns right and walks 30 m. Now, he turns right and walks 20 m. How far is he from his original position?

(a) 15 m

(b) 30 m

(c) 25 m

(d) 45 m

Ans. (b)

Explanation:

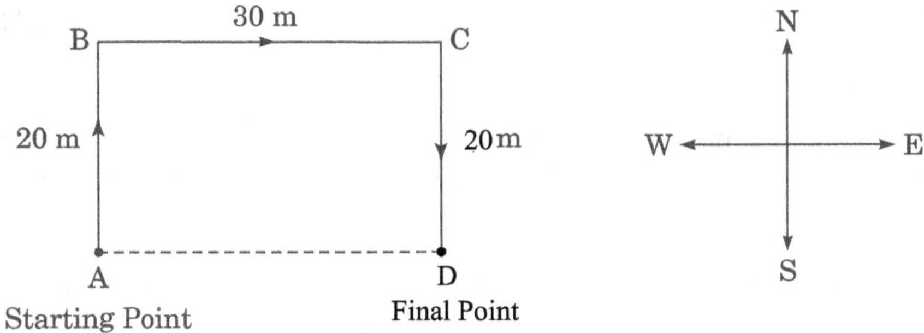

Here, required distance (AD) = AD = BC = 30 m

AD = 30 m.

Type 3: *Distance (Displacement) and Direction Based*

In this type of questions, we deal with the final distance between starting and final point of any person/object/thing. There are various formats/patterns of distance and direction.

3. A tourist drives 10 Km towards East and turns to the right hand and drives 3 Km. Then, he drives towards West (turning to his right) 10 Km. He, then turns to his left and drives 2 Km. How far is he from his starting point and in which direction would he be?

(a) 10 Km, East   (b) 5 Km, North   (c) 8 Km, West   (d) 5 Km, South

Ans. (d)

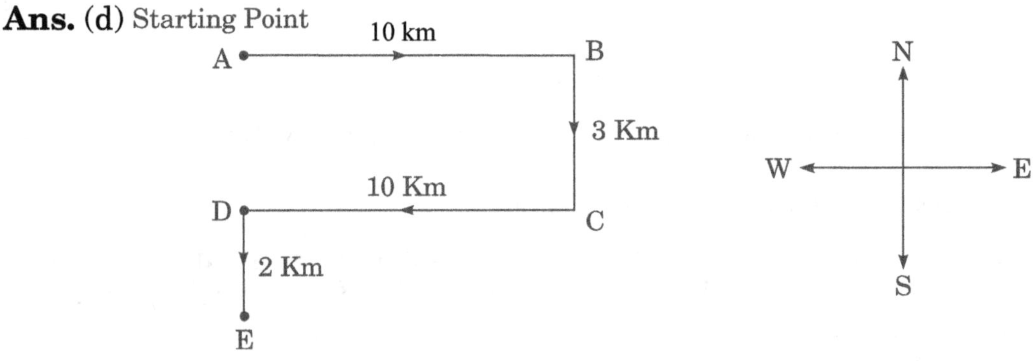

Here, $\quad$ AD = BC = 3 Km

$\therefore \quad$ Required distance AE = AD + DE = 3 + 2 = 5 Km

$\quad$ His final point is E which is in South direction from starting point A.

4. Sunny is facing the temple. If he turns to his left, he will face the Mall. He turns _________ to his left.

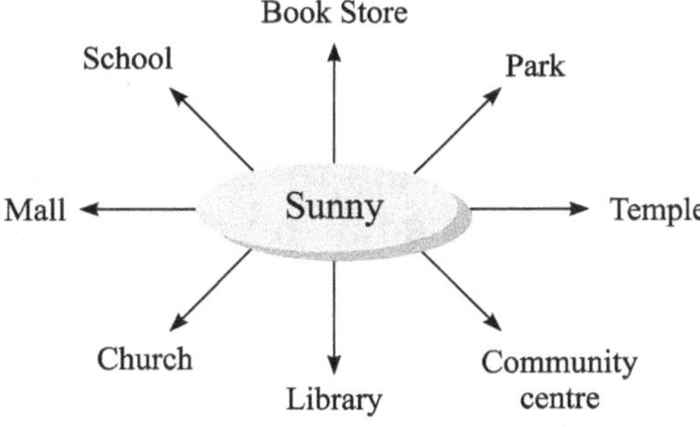

(a) $\dfrac{1}{4}$ turn $\qquad$ (b) $\dfrac{1}{3}$ turn $\qquad$ (c) $\dfrac{1}{2}$ turn $\qquad$ (d) $\dfrac{3}{4}$ turn

Ans. (c)

Explanation:

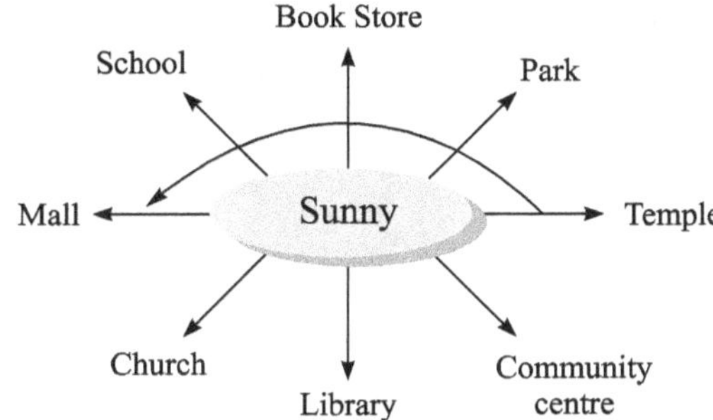

So, Sunny turns $\dfrac{1}{2}$ turn to his left.

5. Which point is east of B?

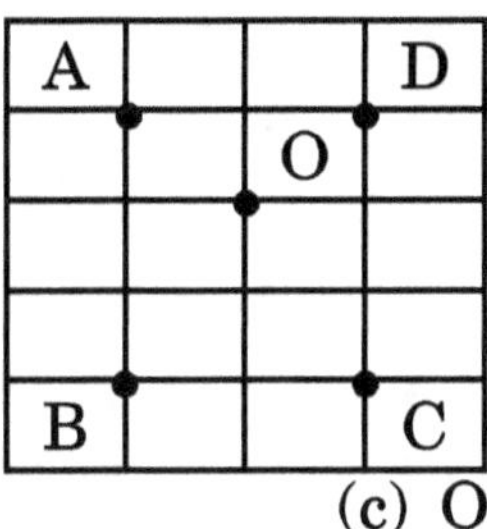

(a) A $\qquad$ (b) D $\qquad$ (c) O $\qquad$ (d) C

Ans. (d)

Explanation:

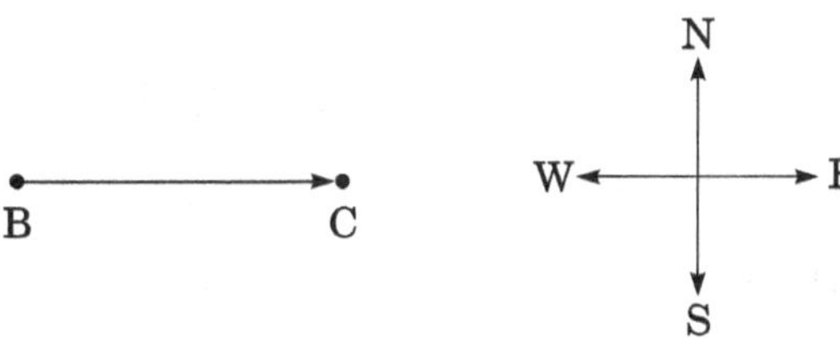

So, point C is east of B.

LEVEL-1

1. In a timepiece at 6 P.M., hour hand points to south. In which direction the minute hand will point at 9.15 P.M.?

   (a) East   (b) West   (c) South   (d) North

2. One morning Rani started to walk towards the sun. After covering some distance she turned to right then again to the right. Now in which direction is she facing?

   (a) East   (b) West   (c) South   (d) North

3. A man goes 4 km towards east, then he takes left turn and goes 3 km. What is the distance between 2 points.

   (a) 4 Km   (b) 3 Km   (c) 7 Km   (d) 6 Km

4. Anil wants to go to school. He starts from his house which is in the East and comes to crossing. In which direction is the school?

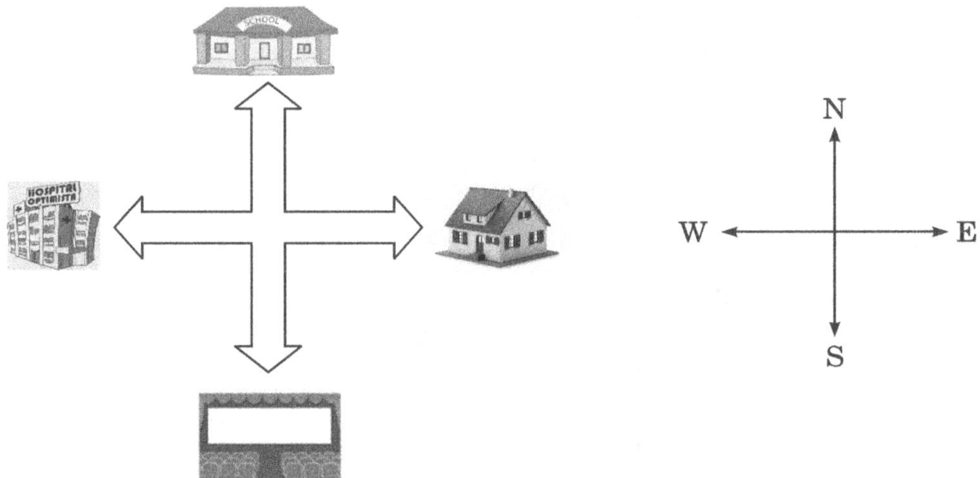

   (a) East   (b) North   (c) South   (d) West

Direction (Qs. 5 and 6): Observe the given diagram carefully and answer the following questions.

5. If South-East becomes North, then what will South-West become?

   (a) West   (b) North   (c) East   (d) North-West

6. Considering the above question, what will West become?

   (a) North-East   (b) South-East   (c) North-East   (d) South-East

Direction (Qs. 7 and 8): Observe the diagram carefully and answer the following questions.

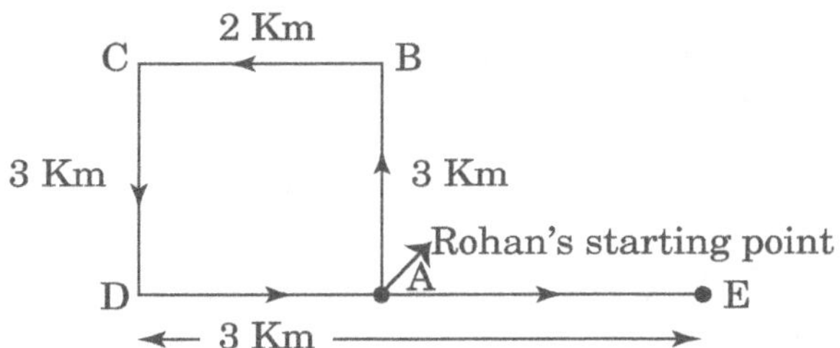

7. Rohan walks a distance of 3 Km towards North and he turns left. In which direction is he now?

    (a) East   (b) West   (c) North   (d) South

8. Rohan's starts walking at point A and finishes at point E. What is total distance between his starting point and finishing point?

    (a) 10 Km   (b) 9 Km   (c) 11 Km   (d) 12 Km

9. Observe the following diagram and answer the following question:

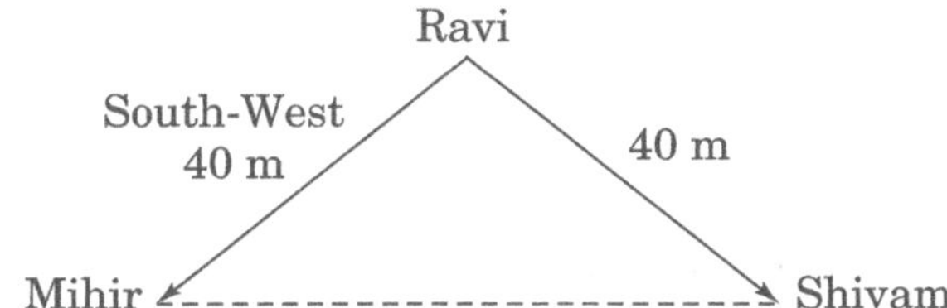

    Mihir is 40 m South-West of Ravi. Shivam is 40 m South-East of Ravi, then Shivam is in which direction of Mihir.

    (a) East   (b) West   (c) North-East   (d) South

Direction (Qs. 10-13): Read the given information carefully and answer the following questions.

Four friends A, B, C and D live in the same locality. The locality of their houses has been given below:

A's House

B's House

C's House

D's House

10. The house of B is in the ______________ of A's house

    (a) East   (b) West   (c) South   (d) North

11. The house of B is in the ______________ of C's house

    (a) East   (b) West   (c) North   (d) South

12. The house of C is in the ______________ of D's house

    (a) East   (b) West   (c) North   (d) South

13. D's house is in which direction of A's house?

    (a) South-East   (b) North-East

    (c) East   (d) Data is inadequate

14. To walk from his home to school Tom has to cycle towards South. In which direction does he cycle on his way back home?

    (a) East   (b) West   (c) South   (d) North

15.

The diagram shows a crossroads.

Jim approaches the crossroads in his car from the South, and then turns right. In which direction is he then headed?

    (a) East   (b) North   (c) South   (d) West

16. Pihu is facing the bookshop. If she turns to her right, she will face the church. She turns _________ to her right.

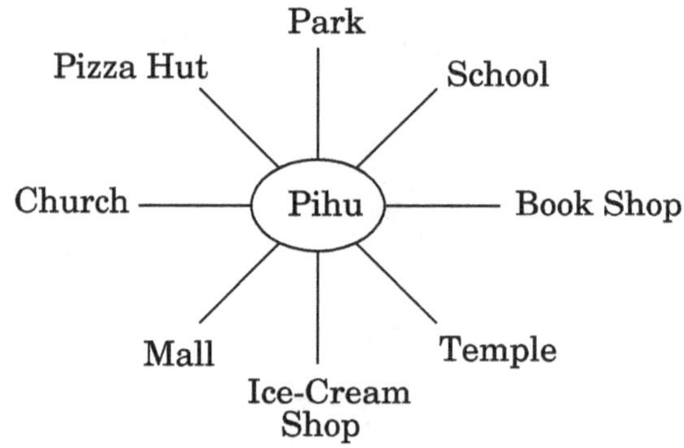

    (a) $\frac{3}{4}$ turn   (b) $\frac{1}{3}$ turn   (c) $\frac{1}{2}$ turn   (d) $\frac{1}{4}$ turn

Direction (Qs. 17 and 18): Read the following information and answer the following questions.

- Shivani, Anju, Aryan and Dev are playing cards.
- Shivani and Anju are partners.
- Aryan faces towards North.
- Shivani faces towards West.

17. Who faces towards East?
    (a) Shivani   (b) Anju   (c) Dev   (d) Aryan

18. Who faces towards South?
    (a) Shivani   (b) Anju   (c) Dev   (d) Aryan

Direction (Qs. 19 and 20): Consider the following information and answer the following questions.

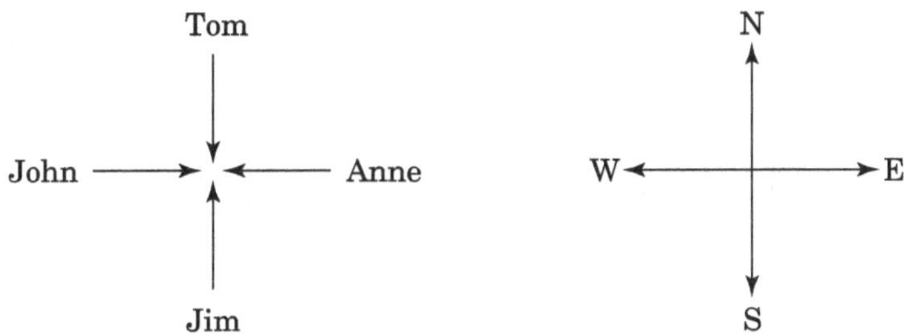

Tom, Jim, John and Anne are playing a game of Carrom. Tom, Jim and John, Anne are partners.

19. If Anne exchanges her position with Tom, who will be the partner of John?
    (a) Anne   (b) John   (c) Tom   (d) Jim

20. If Tom exchanges his position with John who will be the partner of Jim?
    (a) John   (b) Tom   (c) Anne   (d) None

21. Given map is showing the distances between Akram's house, his school and shopping mall. Which of the following statements is correct?

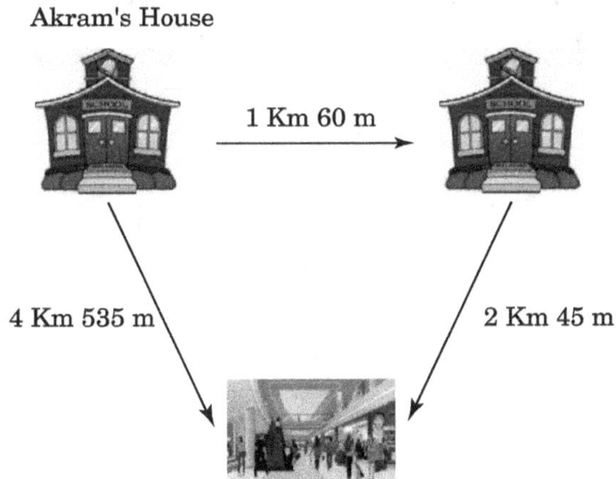

(a) The distance between the shopping mall and Akram's house is shorter than the distance between his school and the shopping mall.

(b) The distance between Akram's house and his school is greater than the distance between his school and the shopping mall.

(c) The distance between Akram's house and his school is 1600 m.

(d) The distance between the shopping mall and Akram's house is 4535m.

22. Rohit takes 1/2 turn clockwise and faces North-East in the end. Which direction was Rohit facing at first? Observe the diagram given below and answer the questions.

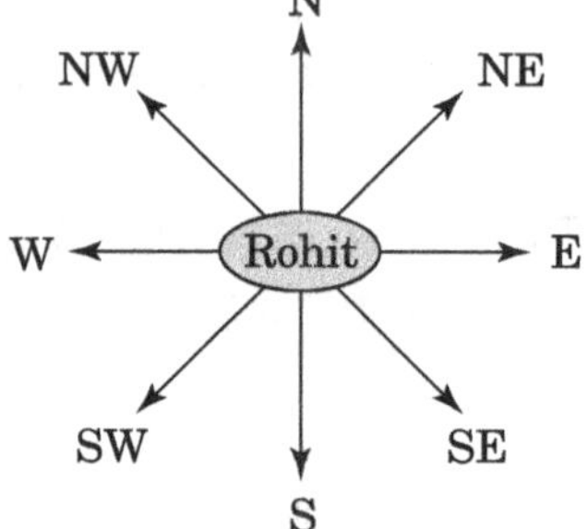

(a) South-west

(b) South-east

(c) North-west

(d) North-west

23. I am facing the market. If I make 1/2 turn to the right, I will be facing the
____________.

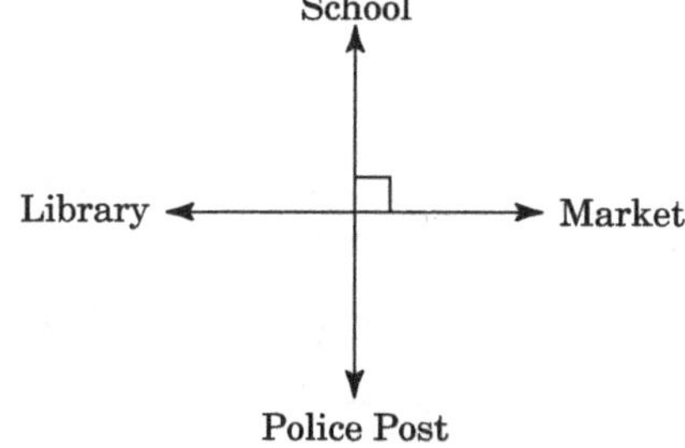

(a) School

(b) Library

(c) Market

(d) Police Post

24. Rahul faces North. He made a $\frac{3}{4}$ clockwise turn first followed by $1\frac{1}{2}$ anti-clockwise turn. In what direction is he facing now ?

(a) East   (b) West   (c) North   (d) South

Direction (Qs. 25 and 26): Study the given diagram carefully and answer the following questions.

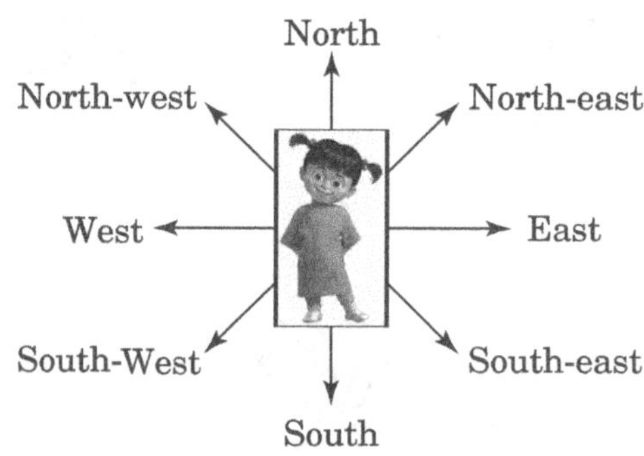

25. If the girl is facing West and makes $1\frac{1}{2}$ turn in a clockwise-direction, in which direction will she be facing?

(a) South-east   (b) East   (c) North   (d) South

26. If the girl is facing South-West and makes 3/4 turns in a anticlockwise direction, in which direction will she be facing?

(a) South-east   (b) North-east   (c) North-west   (d) South-west

Direction (Qs. 27 and 28): Study the information carefully to answer the questions.

27. 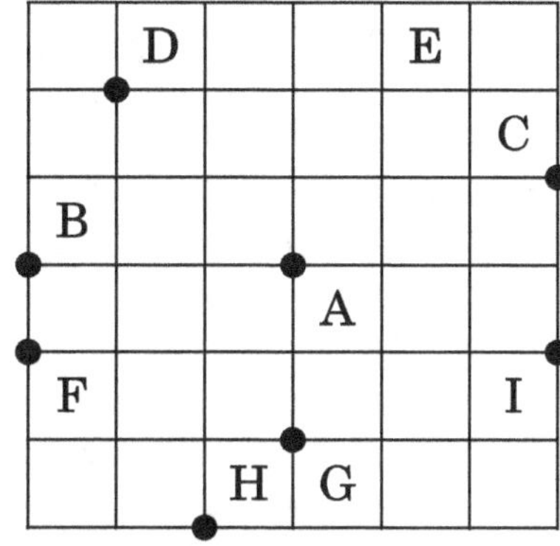

Which point is North-West of A?

(a) D   (b) E   (c) E   (d) I

28. Which point is South-East of A?

(a) I   (b) F   (c) D   (d) C

29. Megha is facing West. If she makes $2\frac{1}{2}$ turns clockwise, which direction will she face in the end?

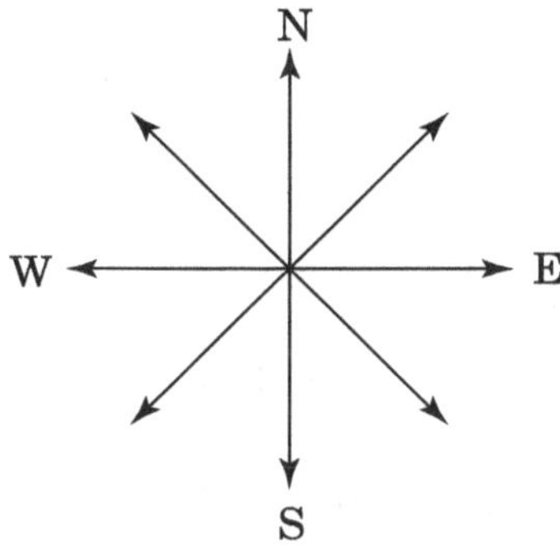

(a) East   (b) West   (c) North   (d) South

30. Reema is facing North and makes 3/4 turn in a clockwise direction, what will she be facing finally?

(a) East   (b) West   (c) South   (d) North

31. Rahul is facing west. He walks 35 km and takes a right turn. He again walks 35 km and takes a right turn and walks 35 km. Then how much and in which direction he has to walk to reach his starting point? **(2022)**

(a) 35 km South   (b) 35 km North   (c) 35 km East   (d) 35 km West

LEVEL-2

Direction (Qs. 1-4): Some boys are sitting in three rows and all facing North. Observe the given diagram and answer the following questions.

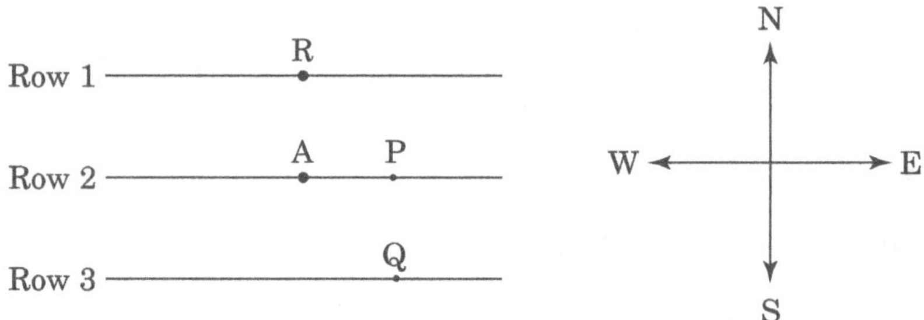

1. In which direction of R is A?

(a) East   (b) West   (c) South   (d) North

2. In which direction of Q is P?

(a) East   (b) West   (c) South   (d) North

3. Who is sitting east of A?

(a) R   (b) P   (c) Q   (d) None

4. In which diretion of R is Q?

(a) South   (b) East   (c) South-East   (d) South-West

Direction (Qs. 5-7): Study the information and answer the following questions.

5. Rajan starts towards south from point A. After walking 5 m, he turned to his left. After walking 3 m, he turned to his right. Now in which direction he is facing?

(a) South   (b) North   (c) East   (d) West

6. What is the total distance Rajan walked from point A to point C?

   (a) 10 m   (b) 8 m   (c) 13 m   (d) 12 m

7. After reaching point D Rajan turns right, to which direction he is facing?

   (a) East   (b) West

   (c) South   (d) North

Direction (Qs. 8-11): Each of the following questions is based on the following information.

Six flats on a floor in two rows facing North and South are alloted to P, Q, R, S, T and U.

Flats Alloted

```
P ———————— R ———————— U   ↓ Facing South

S ———————— T ———————— Q   ↑ Facing North

                N
                ↑
        W ←—————+—————→ E
                ↓
                S
```

8. If the flats R and T are interchanged then whose flat will be next to U?

   (a) R   (b) T   (c) P   (d) S

9. Which of the following combinations gets South facing flats?

   (a) QTS   (b) RTS

   (c) URP   (d) SUT

10. Whose flat is between Q and S?

    (a) T   (b) R

    (c) U   (d) P

11. Which of the following statements is definitely true?

    (a) Q gets a South facing flat.

    (b) Flat R is between S and Q.

    (c) STQ get North facing flats.

    (d) U gets a North facing flat and is next to P.

Direction (Qs. 12-15): Read the following information carefully and answer the questions.

There are 5 shops A, B, C, D and E.

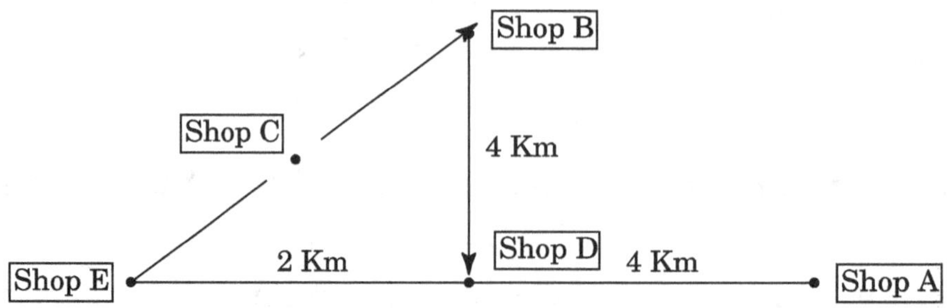

12. What is the distance between Shop D and Shop A?

    (a) 6 m   (b) 4 m   (c) 3 m   (d) 2 m

13. In which direction is A with respect to B?

    (a) Southeast   (b) Southwest   (c) Northeast   (d) Northwest

14. What is the distance between shop E and shop A?

    (a) 6 m   (b) 4 m

    (c) 3 m   (d) 2 m

15. D is _____________ to East of _____________.

    (a) 2 m, shop E   (b) 4 m, shop E

    (c) 2 m, shop A   (d) 4 m, shop A

Direction (Qs. 16-18): Read the given information carefully and answer the following questions.

A, B, C, D, E, F, G and H are sitting around a circular table facing the centre in the English alphabetical order for a discussion at equal distance. Their positions are clockwise. Observe diagram given below:

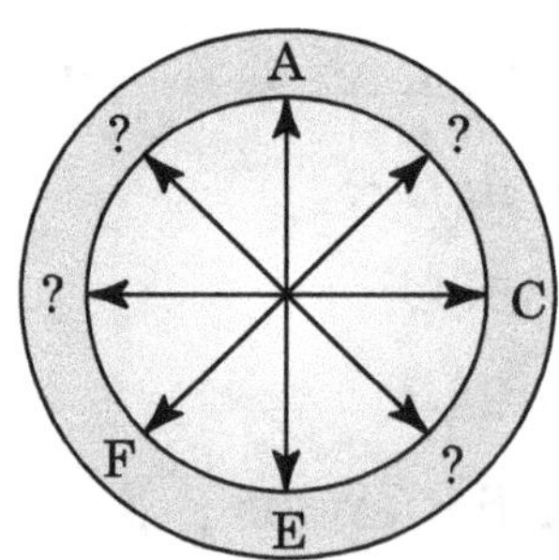

16. If A sits in the North, then what will be the position of D? (Refer diagram given above).

(a) South   (b) East   (c) Southeast   (d) Northeast

17. Who is sitting facing East?

(a) C   (b) G   (c) A   (d) E

18. Who is sitting North-East direction?

(a) F   (b) H   (c) B   (d) D

19. Initial direction and movements of a rat are given through arrows showing the face of rat. Choose the correct diagram of movement of rat.

Note: Sign ■——▶ shows the initial point of a rat in which arrow shows the face of rat.

Movement:

Start ■——▶ right ——▶ left ——▶ left ——▶ right ——▶ right ——▶ South
                                                     Final direction.

(a) 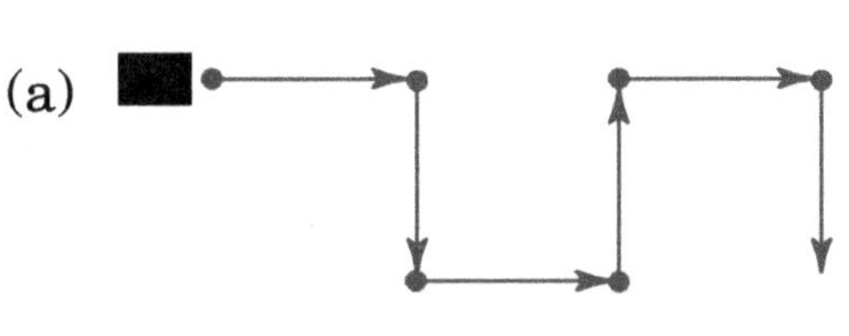

(b) 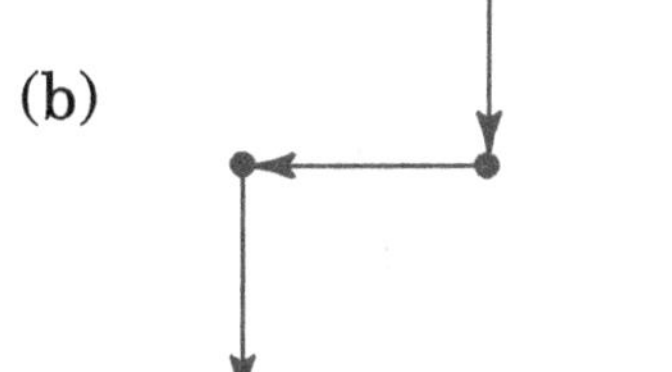

(c) 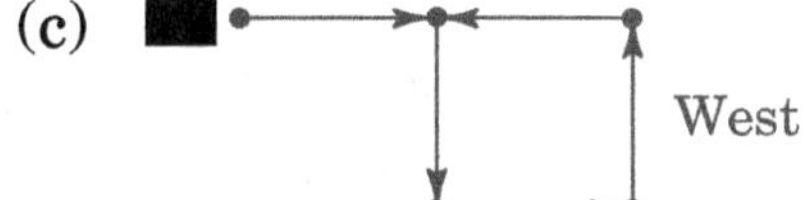

(d) 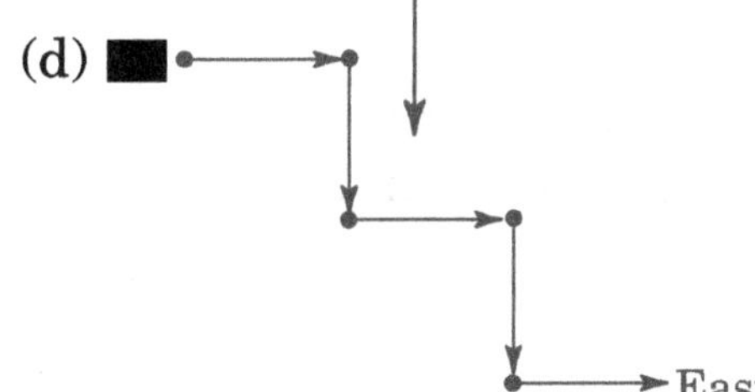

Direction (Qs. 20): Initial direction and movements of a person are given in the following questions in which arrow (■——▶) shows the face of person. Find the final direction.

20. Movements

South ■——▶ left ——▶ right ——▶ right ——▶ left ——▶ left ——▶
                                                    Final direction.

(a) East   (b) West   (c) South   (d) North

21. Raja starts from point A and walks 1 Km towards South, turns left and walks 1 Km. Then he turns left again and walks 1 Km. Now he is facing which direction.

(a) East   (b) West   (c) North   (d) South

22. The door of Aditya's house faces the East. From the back side of his house he walks straight 50 metres, then turns to the right. Now, he is in which direction?

(a) East   (b) West   (c) South   (d) North

Direction (Qs. 23-24): Observe the given diagram and answer the following questions.

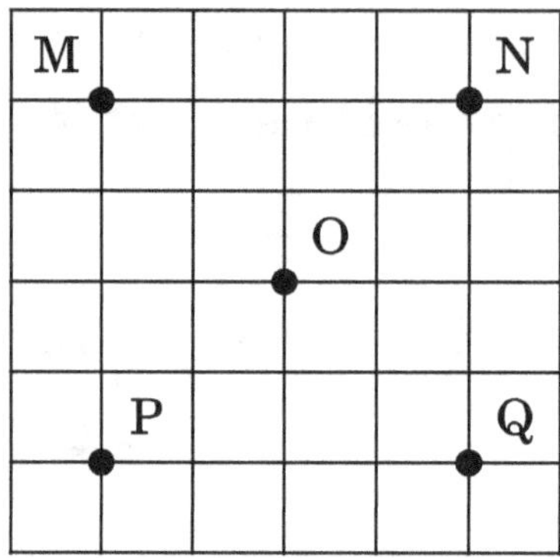

23. Which point is South-West of O?

(a) M   (b) N   (c) P   (d) Q

24. Which point is North-East of O?

(a) M   (b) N   (c) P   (d) Q

25. If Varun is facing west and he takes $(3/4)^{th}$ turn anticlockwise, 1/2 turn clockwise and finally $(2/8)^{th}$ turn antilockwise, where will he be facing?

(a) House   (b) Park   (c) Playground   (d) Mall

(Olympiad)

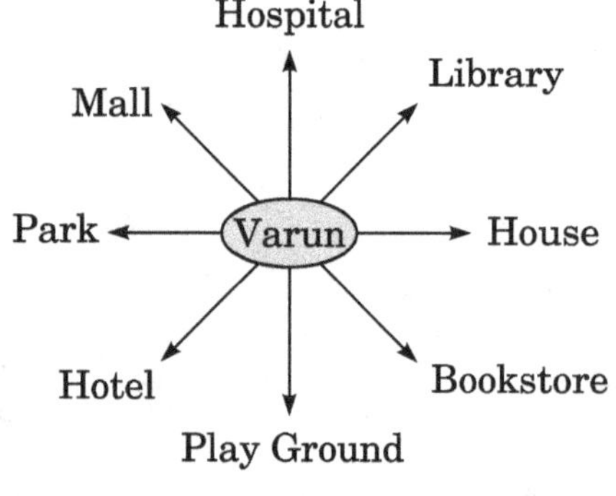

26. Arnav is facing towards north. He makes $\dfrac{3}{4}$ turns to his right and $\dfrac{1}{2}$ turns in clockwise direction. Now if he wants to reach the book store, then what turn will he make?

(a) $\dfrac{1}{4}$ turns anticlockwise

(b) $\dfrac{5}{8}$ turns clockwise

(c) $\dfrac{3}{4}$ turns towards right

(d) $\dfrac{7}{8}$ turns towards left

(Olympiad)

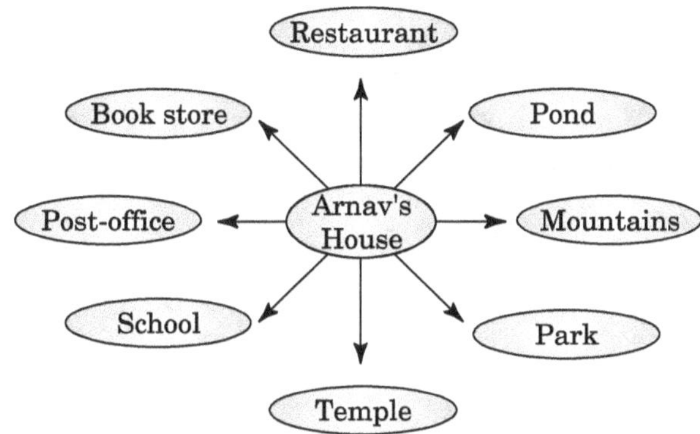

27. If P and Q as well as R and S interchange their positions, then what is the position of T with respect to P?

(a) East   (b) West

(c) North   (d) South

(Olympiad)

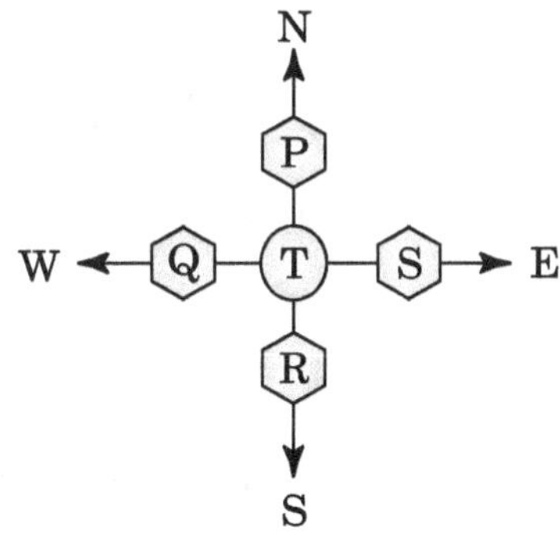

28. How many letters appear the same when rotated by $\frac{1}{2}$ turn?

A B C D E F G H I J L K M
N O P Q R S T U V W X Y Z

(a) 7   (b) 6   (c) 5   (d) 4

(Olympiad)

29. Mohit was facing the library. He made a 3/4 turn anticlockwise. Where would he be facing?

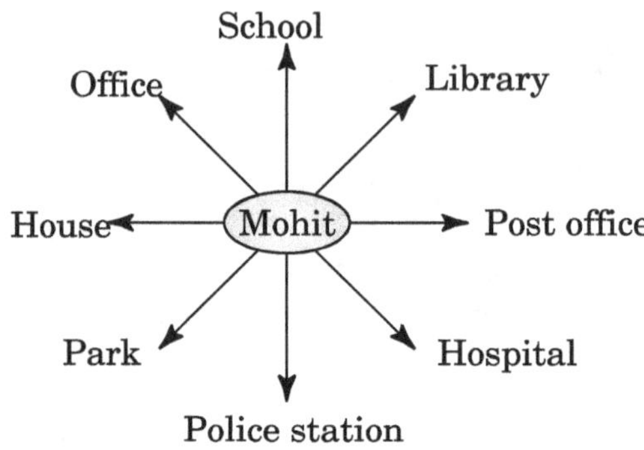

(a) Park   (b) Home   (c) Hospital   (d) Office

(Olympiad)

30. Latika is facing towards her home. How many turns she must move in the clockwise direction to face the school?

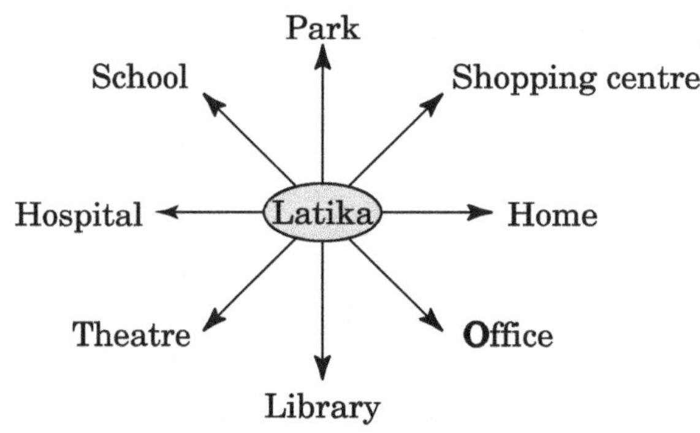

(a) 5/4   (b) 3/8   (c) 5/8   (d) 3/4

(Olympiad)

31. Garima starts walking towards the East and after walking some distance she takes a left turn. Again after walking some distance, she turns to

the left and finally stops after walking some more distance. Which of the following shows the correct path travelled by Garima? **(2018)**

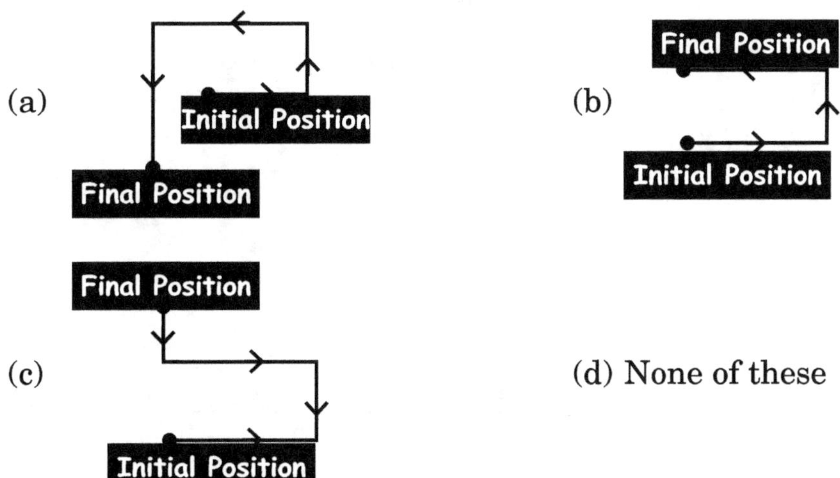

(a)

(b)

(c)

(d) None of these

32. Pooja moves from one point to another point as marked. She starts from point L and moves towards North to reach a point. She then turns and moves in East direction to reach another point. Finally, she turns and moves in South direction and reaches end point. On which point is she right now? **(2022)**

(a) R

(b) Z

(c) P

(d) C

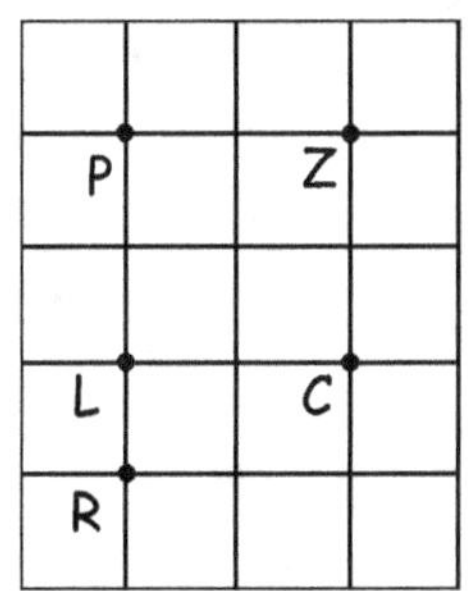

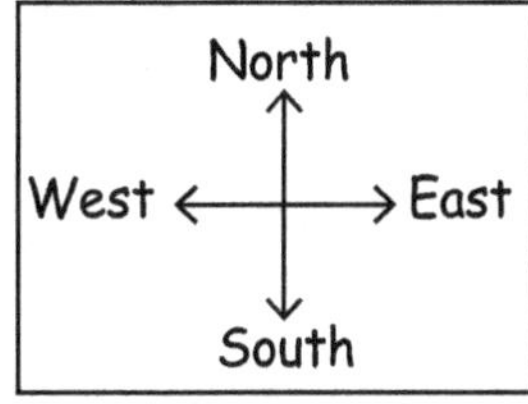

33. Kiran starts for her school from her house, heading towards East. She walks 8 km and takes a right turn. Again she walks 4 km and takes a right turn. Again she walks 4 km to reach her school. How much distance she has covered and in which direction her school is from her house? **(2022)**

(a) 4 km North-East

(b) 12 km North-West

(c) 16 km South-West

(d) 16 km South-East

34. How many letters of the given word will appear the same if it is rotated by $\frac{1}{2}$ turn? **(2022)**

H A Z E L N U T

(a) 3

(b) 4

(c) 2

(d) 1

Level-1

1. (a)

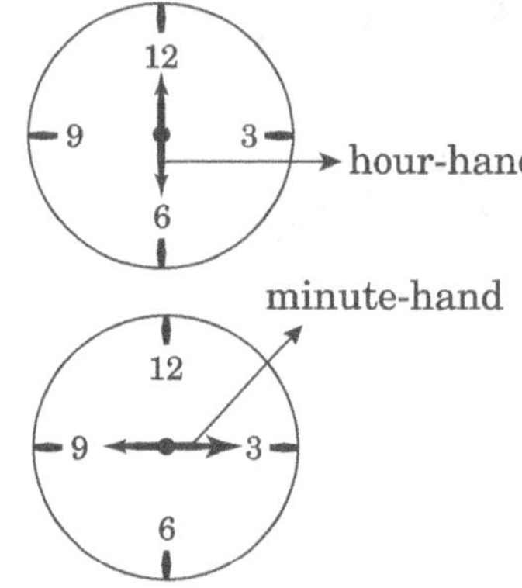

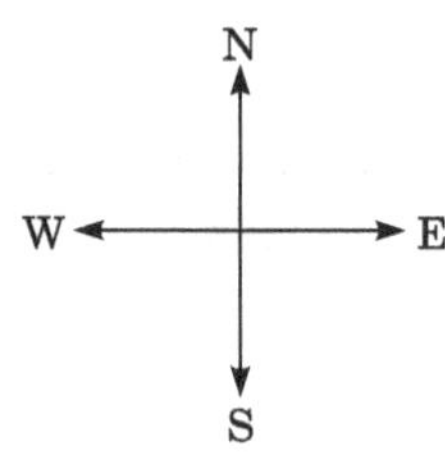

At 9.15 P.M., the minute hand will point towards east.

2. (b) Starting Point

It is clearly shown from the above diagram that now Rani is facing west direction.

3. (c)

4 km towards east + 3 km = 7 km. Hence, the distance between two points is 7 km.

4. (b) School is in the north direction.

Solutions 5 and 6

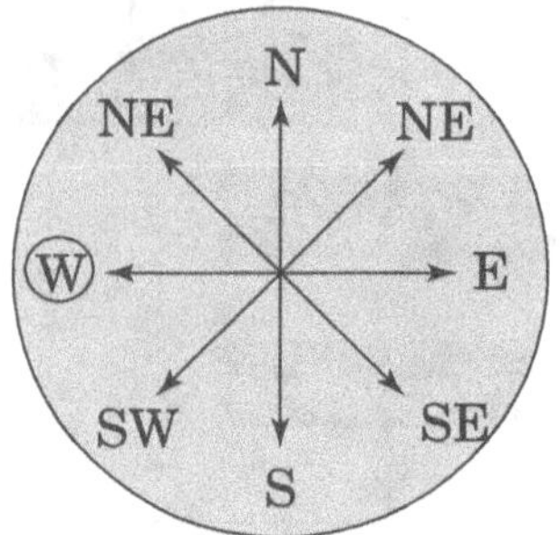

5. (c) So, south-west becomes East.

6. (b) So, West will become South-East.

7. (b) Now, Rohan is in West direction, shown in diagram B to C.

8. (c) Here, AB + BC + CD + DE = 3 + 2 + 3 + 3 = 11 Km

9. (a) Shivam is in the East of Mihir.

10. (a)

A's House $\xrightarrow{\text{East}}$ B's House

So, the house of B is in the east of A's House.

11. (c)

A's House   B's House

North

C's House

So, the house of B is in the north of C's house.

12. (b)

C's House $\xleftarrow{\text{West}}$ D's House

So, the house of C is in the west of D's house.

13. (a)

A's House   B's House

South-East

C's House   D's House

So, D's house is in South-east direction of A's house.

14. (d) Tom cycles in the opposite direction to South, which is North.

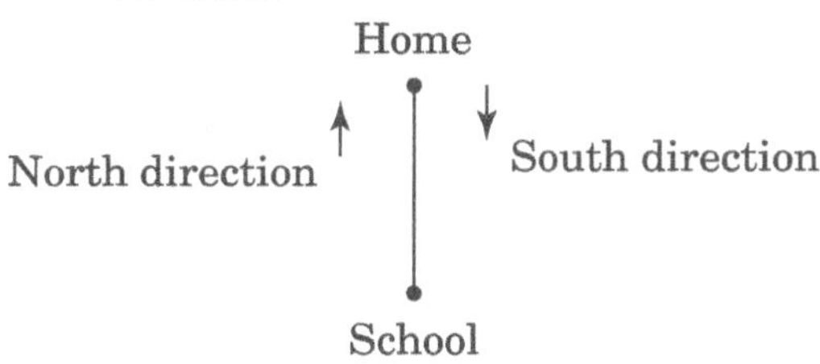

15. (a)

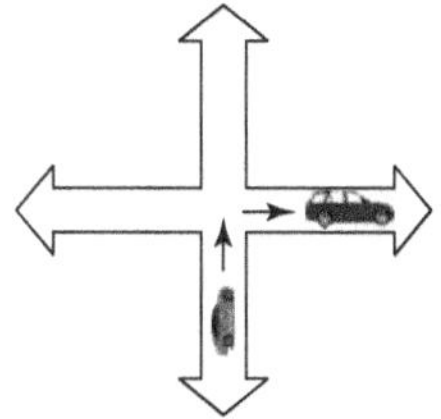

He is headed in East direction.

16. (c)

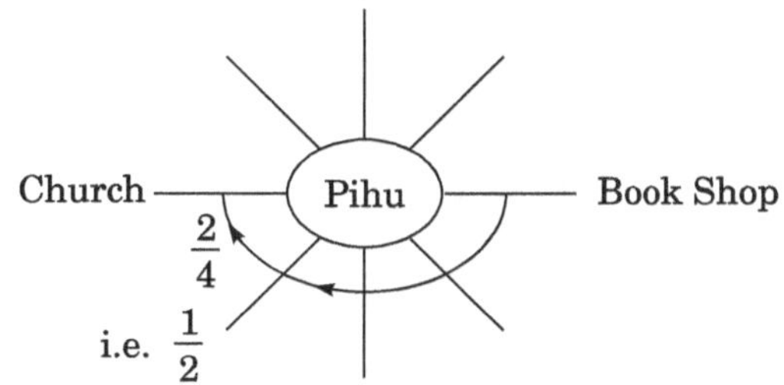

So, she turns $\frac{1}{2}$ to her right.

Solutions 17 and 18

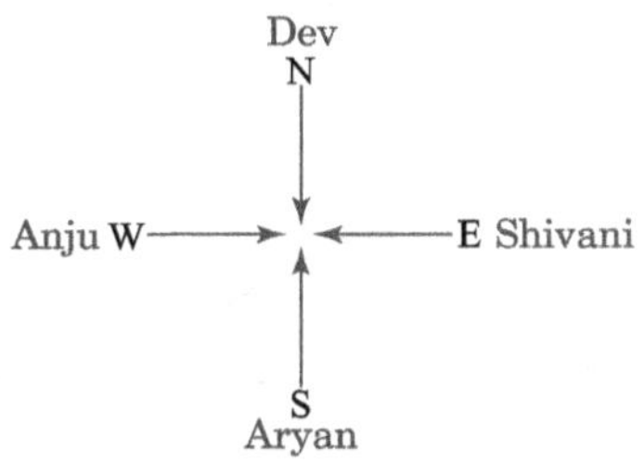

17. (b) As per the given infomation Shivani and Anju are partners, if Shivani faces West then Anju will face East.

18. (c) It is clearly shown from the diagram that Dev faces towards South.

19. (c)

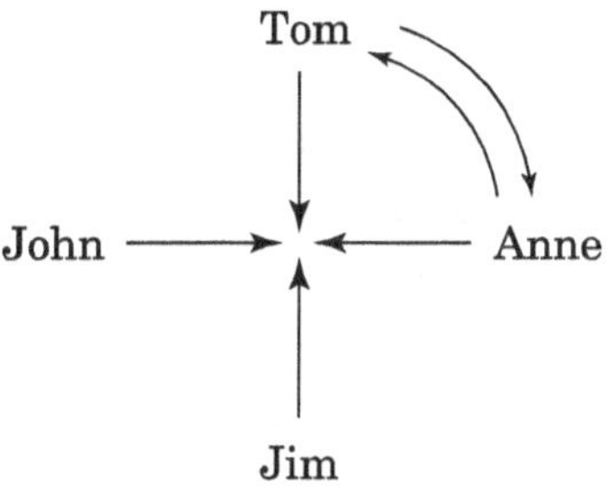

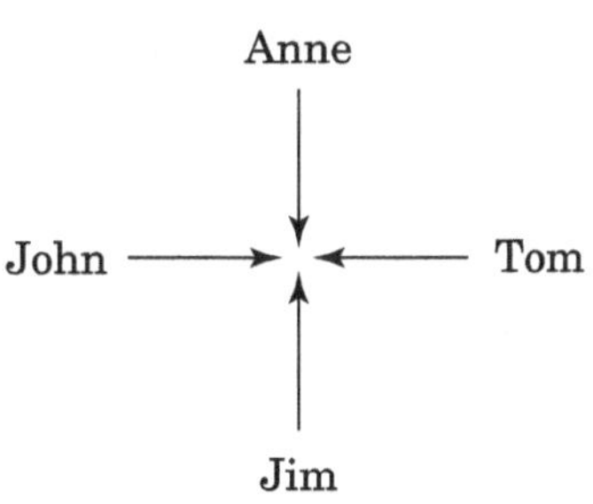

So, Tom will be the partner of John.

20. (a)

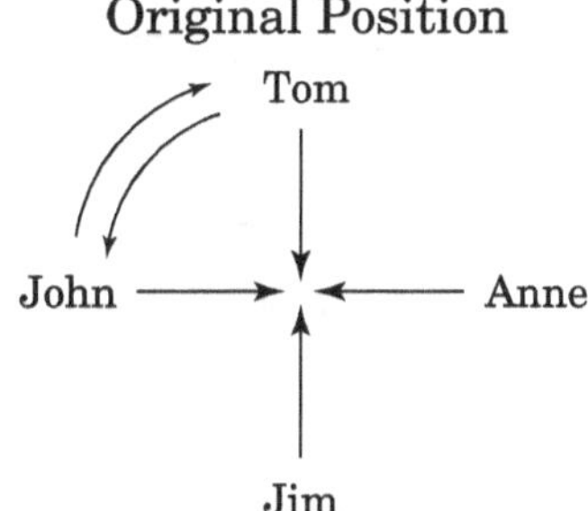

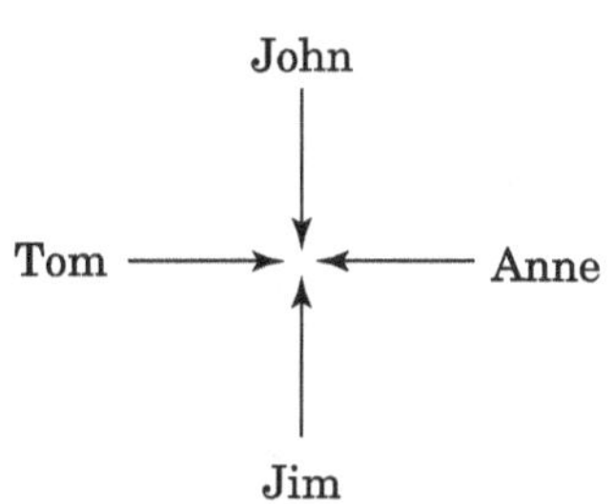

So, John will be the partner of Jim.

21. (d) Option (d) is the correct statement.

22. (a)

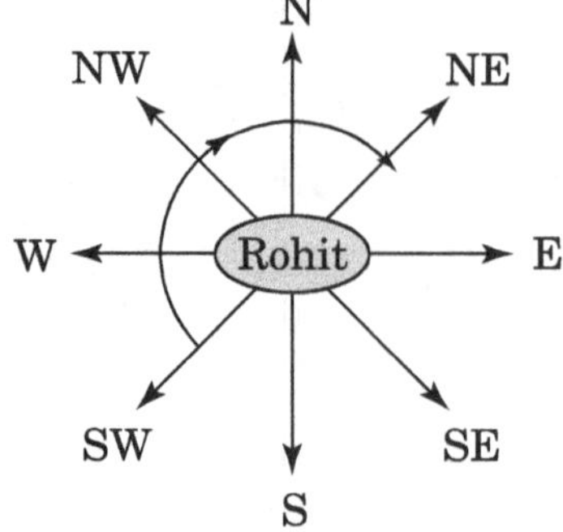

So, Rohit was facing South-West direction at first.

23. (b)

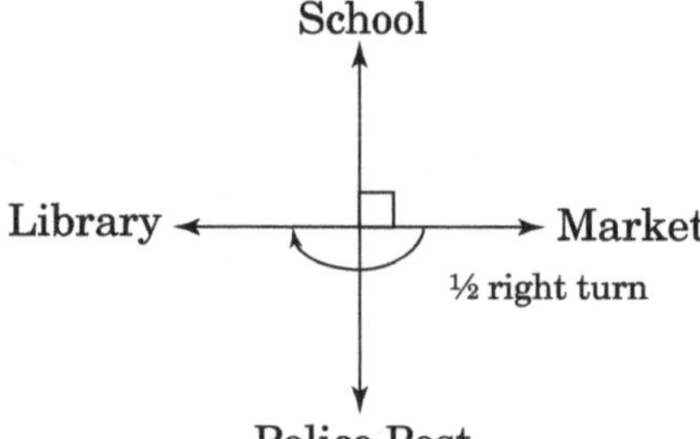

So, I will be facing the Library.

24. (b) He is facing east now.

25. (b)

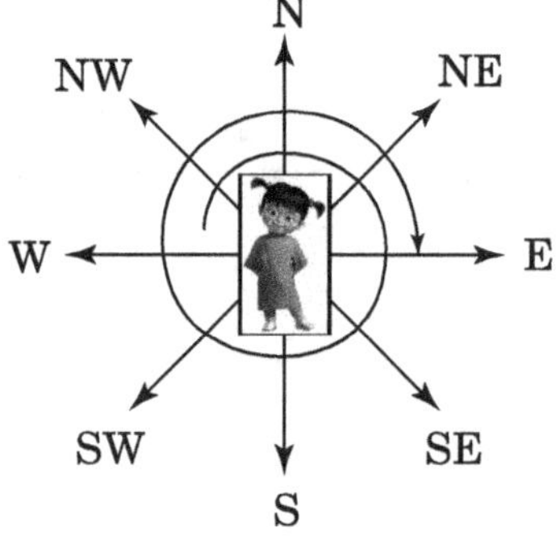

So, she will be facing east direction.

26. (c)

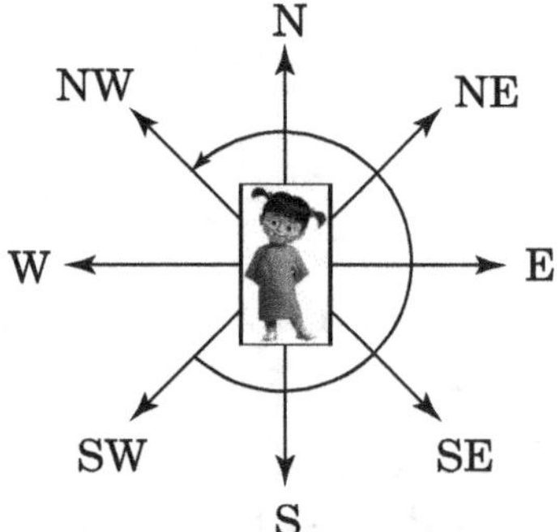

So, she will be facing North-West direction.

27. (a)

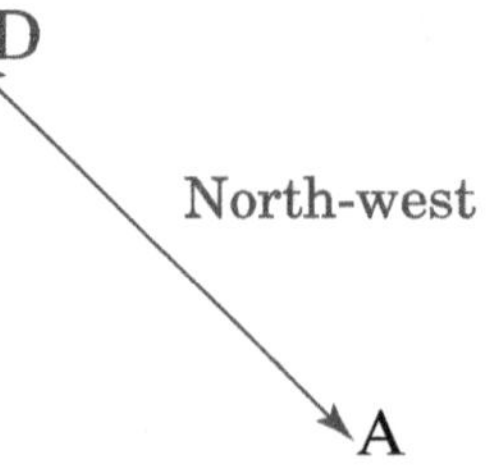

Point D is North-West of A.

28. (a)

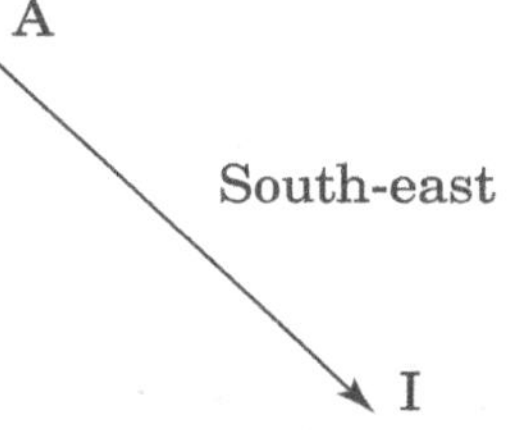

Point I is South-East of A

29. (a)

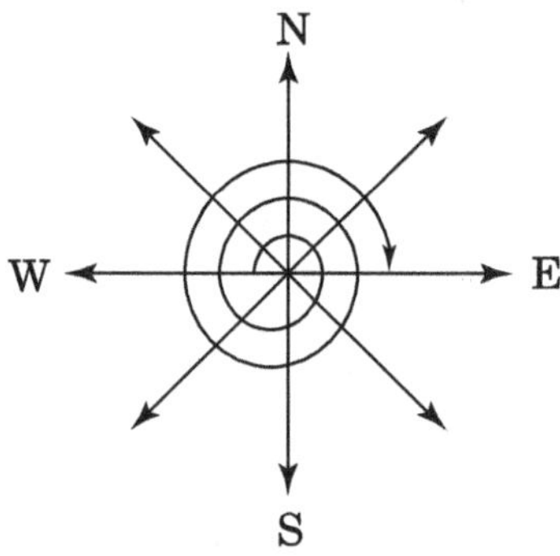

She will face east direction in the end.

30. (b)

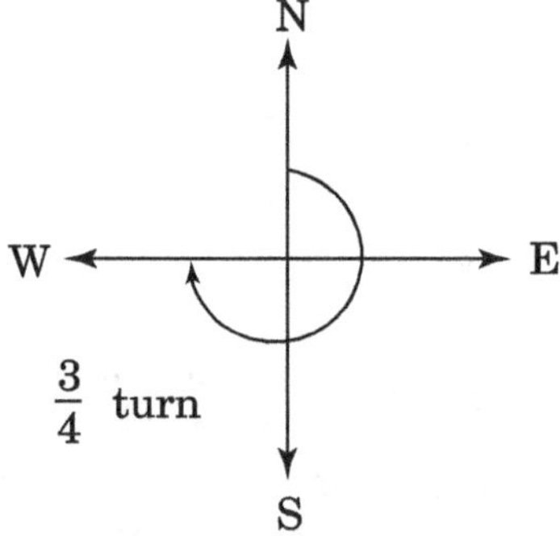

She will be facing west.

31. (b) 35 km in souath.

1. (c)

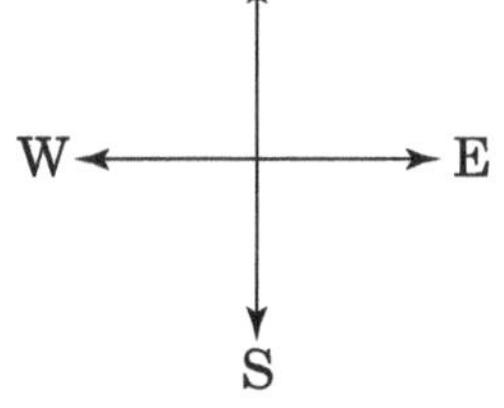

A is in South of R.

2. (d)

P is in North of Q.

3. (b)

P is sitting east A.

4. (c)

Q is in South-East of R.

5. (a)

Now, Rajan is facing South direction.

6. (b) Total distance = 5 m + 3 m

= 8 m

7. (b)

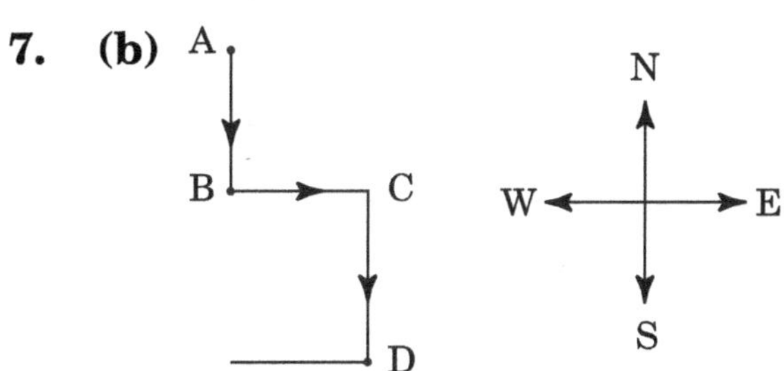

Rajan is facing West direction.

8. (b) Interchanging flats R and T.

Flat T will be next to U.

9. (c)

URP flat combination gets South facing flats.

10. (a)

Flat T is between Q and S.

11. (c)

12. (b)

13. (a)

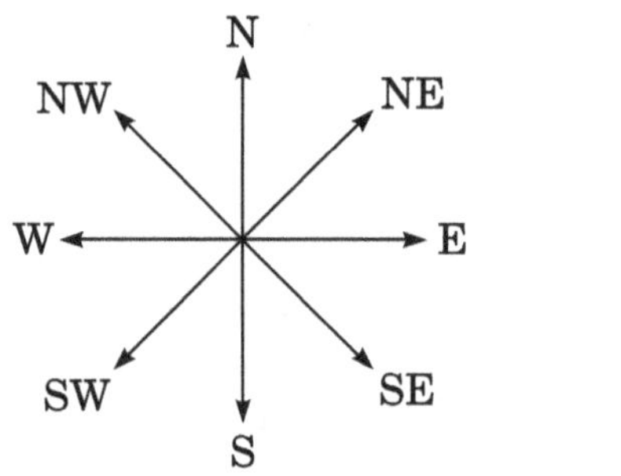

14. (a)

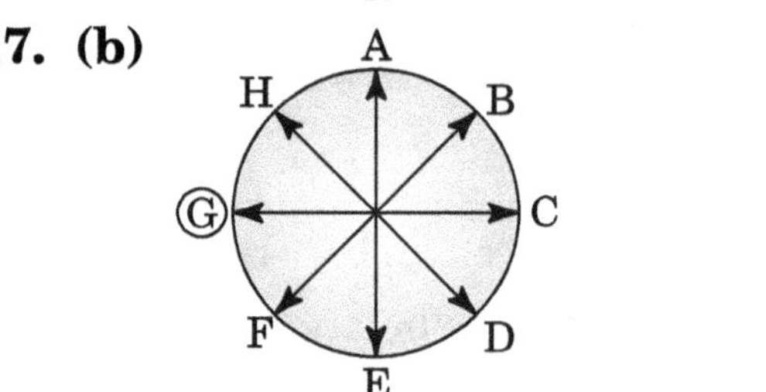

The distance between shop E and shop A is 6 m.

15. (a)

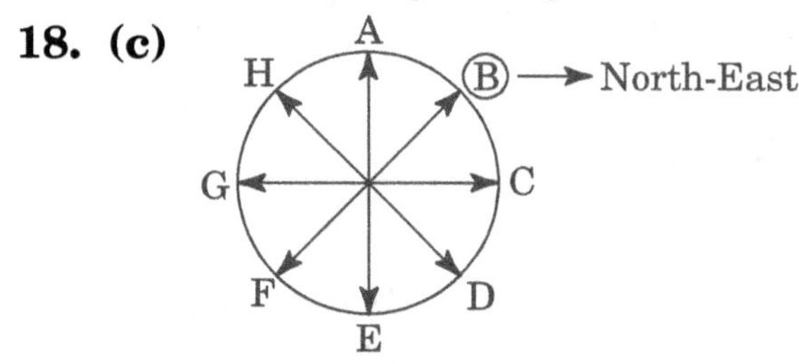

16. (c)

G is sitting facing East.

18. (c)

B is sitting North-east direction.

19. (a) Option (a) represents the correct sequence of movement of rat.

20. (a)

He is facing East direction.

21. (c)

It is clear from the diagram that Raja is facing towards North.

22. (d)

Now, Aditya is facing North direction.

23. (c)

24. (b)

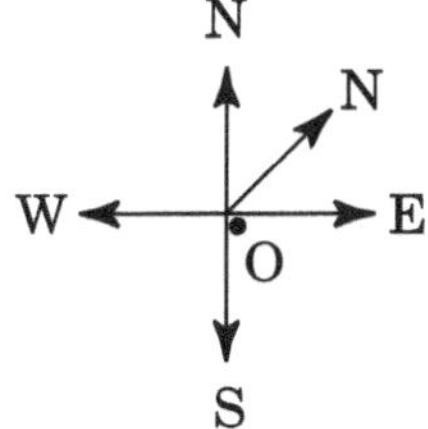

25. (a)

So, he will be facing house.

26. (b)

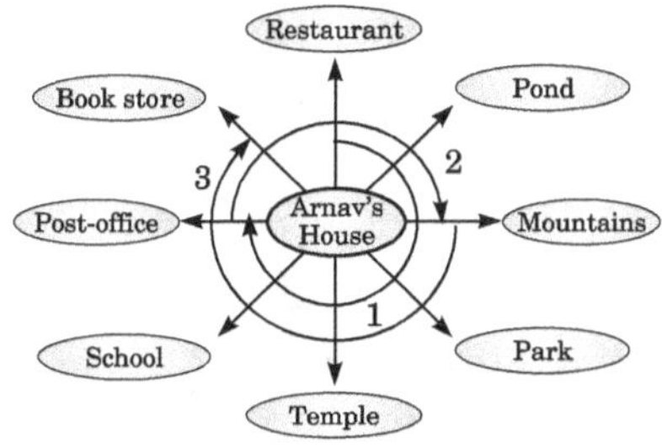

So, if he wants to reach the book store, then he will make $\frac{5}{8}$ turns clockwise.

27. (a) After Interchanging their positions

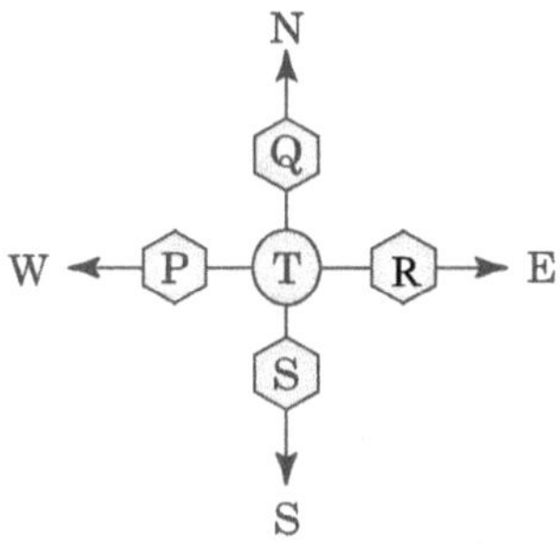

From the above diagram, it is clear that T is in east with respect to P.

28. (a) There are seven letters i.e., H, I, N, O, S, X and Z appear the same when rotated by $\frac{1}{2}$ turn.

29. (c)

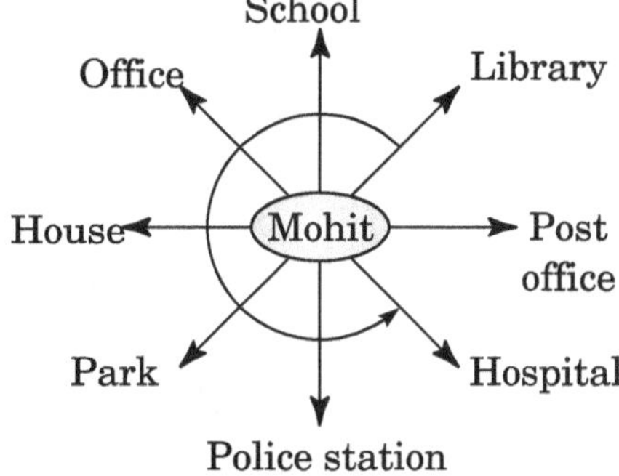

So, he would be facing hospital.

30. (c) She needs $\frac{5}{8}$ turns in the clockwise direction to face the school.

31. (b)

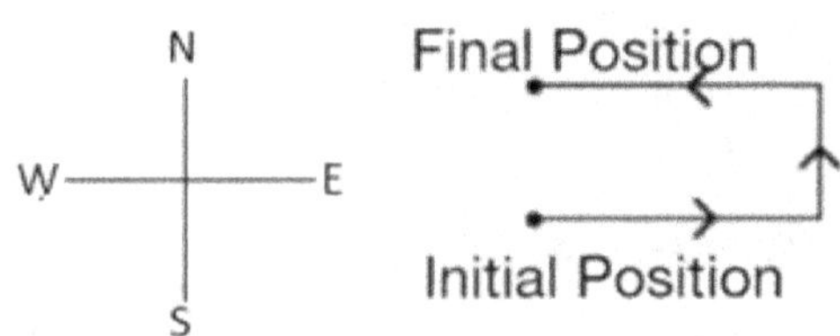

32. (d) Point C. When Pooja moves from point L towards North, she reaches at point P. Then she moves in East direction to reach point Q. Then finally, she moves towards South at point C.

33. (d)

34. (a)

Coding Decoding

OBJECTIVES

- Students will develop the ability to understand the logic that codes a particular message to read the message.

INTRODUCTION

A code means arrangement of letters. Therefore, coding is a method of transforming any instruction from the given form to the required form.

CODING

A particular code pattern is used to express a word in English language to express it as a different word. The coded word itself does not make any sense unless we know the code, i.e. unless we know the pattern or code that has been followed.

DECODING

Decoding helps in tracing out the actual meaning of a coded letter/word/ sentence.

TYPES OF CODING

1. Letter Coding
2. Number Coding
3. Substitution Coding
4. Sentence Coding
5. Symbols Coding

1. Letter Coding

In these questions, code values are given to a word in terms of letters. A particular letter stands for another letter in letter coding.

1. In a certain code language, TEACHER is written as VGCEJGT, then how will CHILDREN be written in that code language?

   (a) ENAGITEV
   (b) PGTFNKJE
   (c) EJKNFTGP
   (d) MGAETVIE

Ans. (c)

Explanation:

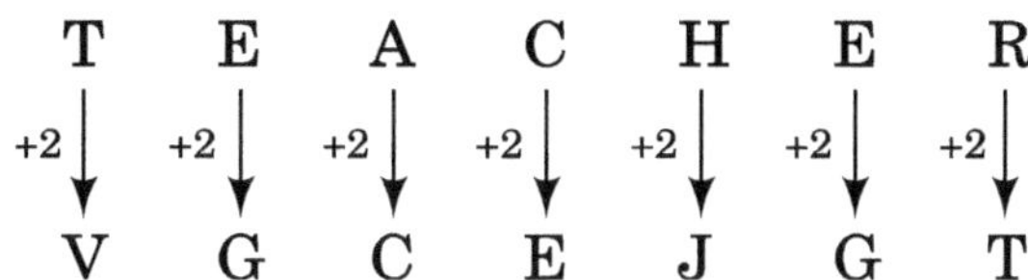

Similarly,

Hence, answer is (c).

2. Number Coding

In these questions, either numerical code values are assigned to a word or alphabetical code values are assigned to numbers.

2. If in a certain code ROPE is coded as 6821, CHAIR is coded as 73456 what will be code for CRAPE?

   (a) 73456
   (b) 76421
   (c) 77246
   (d) 77123

Ans. (b)

Explanation:

The alphabets are coded as follows:

R	O	P	E	C	H	A	I
6	8	2	1	7	3	4	5

So, CRAPE is coded as 76421, so the answer is (b).

3. Substitution Coding

In this type of questions, a particular word is assigned to a certain substituted name and a question is asked to be answered in that substituted name.

3. If sky is star, star is cloud, cloud is earth, earth is tree and tree is book, then where do the birds fly?

   (a) Star
   (b) Sky
   (c) Cloud
   (d) Earth

Ans. (a)

Explanation:

In reality birds fly in the sky but in this question, as given sky is called star. So, star is the answer.

4. Sentence Coding

In this type of questions, a group of words will be coded.

4.   If 'drink fruit juice' is written as 'tee see pee', 'juice is sweet' is written as 'see kee lee' and 'he is intelligent' is written as 'lee ree mee'. What will be the code for 'sweet' in that code language?

    (a) see   (b) kee   (c) pee   (d) lee

Ans. (b)

Explanation:

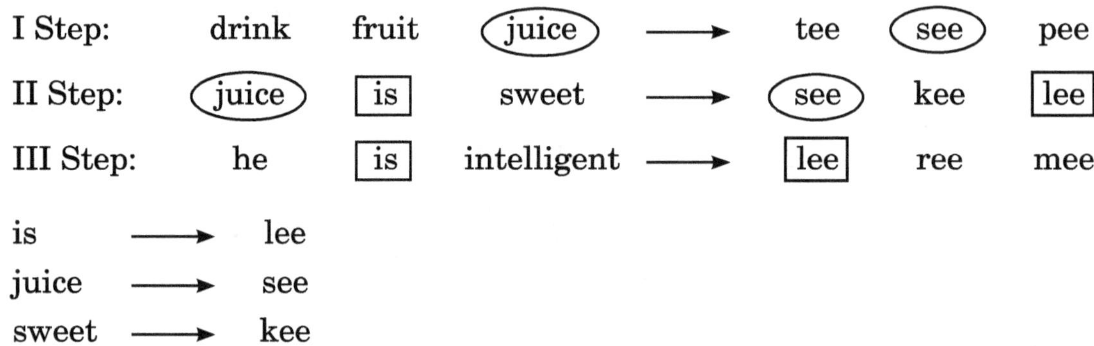

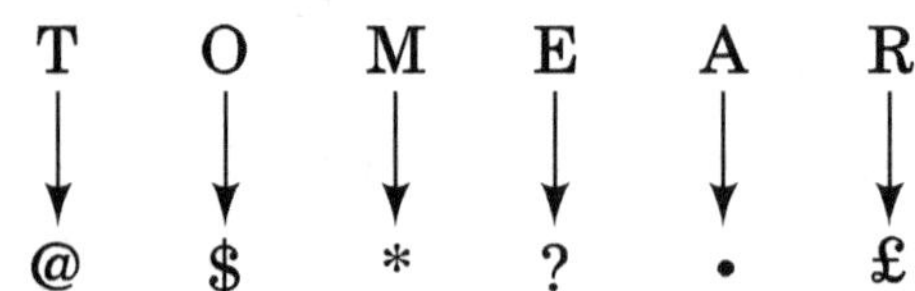

In first and second step we get the code of 'juice' which is 'see'. In the same manner, from second and third step we get the code of 'is' which is 'lee'. In the second step, the remaining word is "sweet" and the remaining code is "kee".

Hence, answer is (b).

5. Symbols Coding

In this type of questions, either alphabetical code values are assigned to symbols or symbols are assigned to alphabets.

5.   In a certain code 'TOME' is written as '@ $ * ?' and ARE is written as '• £ ?'. How can 'REMOTE' be written in that code.

    (a) £ ? • $ @ ?   (b) @ ? * $ @ ?

    (c) £ ? □ $ @ ?   (d) None of these

Ans. (c)

Explanation:

From the data we have

$$\begin{array}{cccccc} T & O & M & E & A & R \\ \downarrow & \downarrow & \downarrow & \downarrow & \downarrow & \downarrow \\ @ & \$ & * & ? & • & £ \end{array}$$

Hence, REMOTE is coded as £ ? * $ @ ?

So, (c) is the answer.

1. If the code of PRESENT is TNESERP and code of PAPER is REPAP, then what will be the code of MONDAY?
   - (a) YADOMN
   - (b) YADNOM
   - (c) YADMNO
   - (d) YADMON

2. If the code of FARTHER is REHTRAF, then what is the code of FREEDOM?
   - (a) MODEERF
   - (b) MODREEF
   - (c) DOMREEF
   - (d) MODREEF.

3. If water is called stone, stone is called tree, tree is called ship, ship is called boat and boat is called car, then where do the birds live?
   - (a) Boat
   - (b) Water
   - (c) Ship
   - (d) Stone

4. If RISHIKA is coded as 2345367, how will SHIKHA coded?
   - (a) 473762
   - (b) 466374
   - (c) 4777363
   - (d) 453657

5. If POND is written as ONMC, how LAKE is written in that code?
   - (a) KZJD
   - (b) KBJD
   - (c) MZJD
   - (d) MBJD

6. In a certain code, RIPPLE is written as 613382 and LIFE is written as 8192. How is PILLER written in that code?
   - (a) 318286
   - (b) 318826
   - (c) 338826
   - (d) 618826

7. If in a certain code REMOVE is coded as EVOMER. Then how will INFORM be coded?
   - (a) MROFNI
   - (b) MORFNI
   - (c) MRONFI
   - (d) MRONIF

8. If in a certain code 24685 is written as 35796, how will 35776 be written in the same code?
   - (a) 44826
   - (b) 46887
   - (c) 45998
   - (d) 54328

9. If △ means ◯, ◯ means □, □ means ▭ and ▭ means ◉ then which has exactly four lines of symmetry?
   - (a) △
   - (b) ◯
   - (c) □
   - (d) ▭

10. If table is called furniture, furniture is called desk, desk is called almirah, almirah is called bench and bench is called bed, then where the clothes are kept?
    - (a) Furniture
    - (b) Table
    - (c) Desk
    - (d) Bench

11. If the code of 46895 is 24673, then what will be the code of 3865?
    (a) 1554   (b) 1643   (c) 1779   (d) 1843

12. If VI means XI, XI means C, C means XII, then which comes immediately after X in counting?
    (a) VI   (b) C   (c) XI   (d) XII

13. If in a certain code BROKEN is written as NEKORB. What will be the code of DIVISION?
    (a) NISINOD   (b) NOISIVID
    (c) NOISVIID   (d) NOIISVID

14. If ☐ means △, △ means ☐, ☐ means ◯, then which is formed using triangle?
    (a) ◯   (b) ☐   (c) ☐   (d) △

15. If Flower is called Letter, Letter is called Purple, Purple is called Red, Red is called Pink and Pink is called Blue, then what is offered to God?
    (a) Ring   (b) Flower
    (c) Letter   (d) Pink

16. If Road is called Water, Water is called Cloud, Cloud is called Sky, Sky is called Sea. Where do aeroplanes fly?
    (a) Road   (b) Cloud   (c) Sea   (d) Sky

Direction (Qs. 17-19): The number in each question below is to be codified in the following code.

Digit	7	2	1	5	3	9	8	6	4
Letter	W	L	M	S	I	N	D	J	B

17. What is the code for 18 46?
    (a) MDJB   (b) MDJB   (c) MDJB   (d) MDBJ

18. What is the code for 9341?
    (a) NIBS   (b) NBIM   (c) NIBM   (d) WBIM

19. What is the code for 64928?
    (a) JBNLD   (b) JBLND   (c) BJNLD   (d) DBNLS

20. If △ = C, ◯ = R, ☐ = E and ☐ = A, then what is the code for the given figures?

    △ ☐ ◯ ☐

    (a) CREA   (b) CARE   (c) REAC   (d) RAEC

21. First key is coded as CD. if its number is '34'. How will second key coded in the same way, if its number is '56'?

First key   Second key

(a) EE   (b) FF   (c) EF   (d) FE

22. If PEAR is coded as EPRA, then how will WEAK be coded in the same language?

(a) WEKA   (b) EWAK   (c) EAWK   (d) EWKA

23. If 2 means 3, 3 means 4, 4 means 6, which number is an odd number?

(a) 2   (b) 3   (c) 4   (d) 6

24. If C means D, D means E and E means F, which alphabet is a vowel?

(a) D   (b) E   (c) F   (d) C

25. Select the correct letter code for the shape or pattern given at the end of the line?

AB   XZ   LB   XB

(a) XB   (b) LZ   (c) AZ   (d) LB

26. 123456 is the code for FATHER, 4526 is the code for?

(a) HAER   (b) HARE   (c) HEAR   (d) HATE

27. If 567 is code for CAR and 234 is the code for TOY, 5672 is the code for?

(a) PART   (b) CART   (c) TART   (d) FART

28. Book is coded as @ ^ ^ #, Lock is coded as % ^ * #, How is BLOCK coded?

(a) @ % ^ ^ #   (b) @ ^ * # #   (c) @ % ^ * #   (d) @ ^ % * #

29. In a certain code language, 'GIVE' is written as 'GVIE' and 'TAKE' is written as 'TKAE'. How will 'DISK' be written is that same code?

(a) SIDK   (b) SKDI   (c) DSIK   (d) DSKI

30. If 3 means 5, 5 means 7 and 7 means 13, then which is prime factor of 25?

(a) 3   (b) 5   (c) 7   (d) 13

31. If 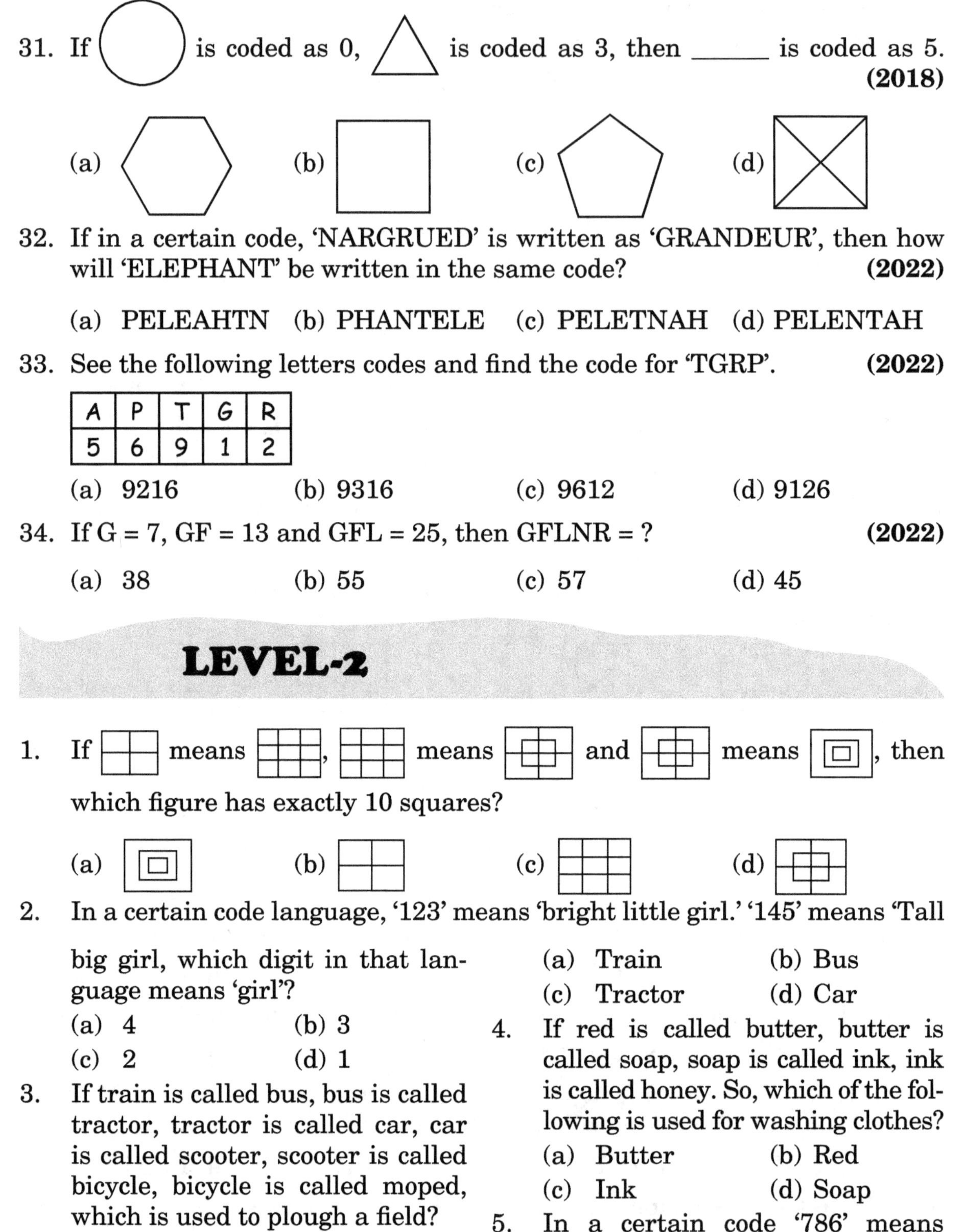 is coded as 0, △ is coded as 3, then ______ is coded as 5. **(2018)**

(a) hexagon   (b) square   (c) pentagon   (d) square with cross

32. If in a certain code, 'NARGRUED' is written as 'GRANDEUR', then how will 'ELEPHANT' be written in the same code? **(2022)**

(a) PELEAHTN   (b) PHANTELE   (c) PELETNAH   (d) PELENTAH

33. See the following letters codes and find the code for 'TGRP'. **(2022)**

A	P	T	G	R
5	6	9	1	2

(a) 9216   (b) 9316   (c) 9612   (d) 9126

34. If G = 7, GF = 13 and GFL = 25, then GFLNR = ? **(2022)**

(a) 38   (b) 55   (c) 57   (d) 45

LEVEL-2

1. If ⊞ means ⊞⊞, ⊞⊞ means ⊞ and ⊞ means ▢, then which figure has exactly 10 squares?

(a) ▢   (b) ⊞   (c) ⊞⊞   (d) ⊞

2. In a certain code language, '123' means 'bright little girl.' '145' means 'Tall big girl, which digit in that language means 'girl'?

(a) 4   (b) 3
(c) 2   (d) 1

3. If train is called bus, bus is called tractor, tractor is called car, car is called scooter, scooter is called bicycle, bicycle is called moped, which is used to plough a field?

(a) Train   (b) Bus
(c) Tractor   (d) Car

4. If red is called butter, butter is called soap, soap is called ink, ink is called honey. So, which of the following is used for washing clothes?

(a) Butter   (b) Red
(c) Ink   (d) Soap

5. In a certain code '786' means "Study very hard", 958 means

"Hard work pays" which of following is the code for 'Hard'?
(a) 7   (b) 8
(c) 9   (d) 6

6. If Pink is called Red, Red is called Purple, Purple is called Blue, Blue is called Orange and Orange is called Yellow. Then what is the colour of clear sky?
(a) Blue   (b) Yellow
(c) Purple   (d) Orange

7. If GIVE is coded as 5137 and BAT is coded as 924. How is GATE coded?
(a) 4475   (b) 5379
(c) 7924   (d) 5247

8. In a certain code STAR is written as 5$*2 and TORE is written a $32@. How is OATS written in that code?
(a) 3*5$ (b) 3*$5
(c) 3$*5   (d) 35*$

9. If PALE is coded as 2153, EARTH is coded as 51490. How is PEARL coded?
(a) 24153   (b) 23145
(c) 29530   (d) 25430

10. In a certain language, if 'BOYS' is written as 'SOYB', how is 'GIRL' is coded in that language?
(a) LRIG   (b) LIRG
(c) LRIG   (d) LGIR

11. In a certain code, 47 means 'which class' and '543' means 'Caste and Class'. What is the code for 'Class'?
(a) 3   (b) 4
(c) 8   (d) Either 5 or 8

12. If III means IV, IV means V, V means VI and VI means VII, then which comes immediately before V in counting?
(a) III   (b) IV
(c) V   (d) VI

13. If REASON is coded as 5 and MUSIC as 4, what is the code number for STUDENT?
(a) 4   (b) 5
(c) 6   (d) 8

14. If light is called morning, morning is called night, night is called afternoon, afternoon is called noon, then when do we sleep?
(a) Night   (b) Noon
(c) Morning   (d) Afternoon

15. In certain code WIPE is written as '2%7#' and MORE is written as '94*#' then how ROPE will be coded?
(a) *74#   (b) *47#
(c) 7*4#   (d) 47#*

16. In certain code MATE is written as '3%6#' and METAL as 3#6%1 then, how TELL will be written in that code?
(a) 36%#
(b) 6%#1
(c) 6#11
(d) None of these

17. In a certain code ATE is written as 146 and CHAIR is written as 08173 then how TEACHER can be written in that code?
(a) 4501953
(b) 4610863
(c) 4310934
(d) None of these

18. If ◯ means △, △ means ▭, ▭ means ⬤ then which has three corners?

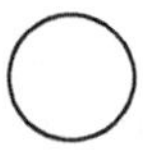

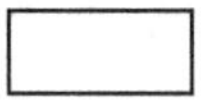

(a) 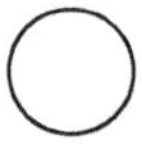 ◯   (b)  △
(c) 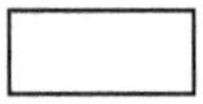 ▭   (d) 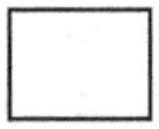 ▭

19. If White is called Blue, Blue is called Red, Red is called Yellow, Yellow is called Green, Green is called Black, Black is called Violet. What would be the colour of human blood?
    (a) Green   (b) Yellow
    (c) Red   (d) Violet

20. If SHARP is coded as 98034 and PUSH as 4598, then RUSH is coded as?
    (a) 3598   (b) 3568
    (c) 3885   (d) 8335

21. If Cook is called Butler, Butler is called Manager, Manager is called Teacher, Teacher is called Clerk and Clerk is called Principal, who will teach in a class?
    (a) Cook   (b) Butler
    (c) Manager   (d) Clerk

22. If rose is called popy, popy is called lily, lily is called lotus and lotus is called glandiola, which is the king of flowers?
    (a) Rose
    (b) Lotus
    (c) Popy
    (d) Glandiola

23. If ELCSUM is the code for MUSCLE, which word has the code LATIPAC?
    (a) CONFESS
    (b) CONDUCE
    (c) CAPITAL
    (d) CAPRICE

24. If book is called watch, watch is called bag, bag is called dictionary and dictionary is called window, which is used to carry the books?
    (a) Dictionary   (b) Bag
    (c) Book   (d) Watch

25. If paper is called wood, wood is called straw, straw is called grass, grass is called rubber and rubber is called cloth, what is the furniture made up of?
    (a) Paper   (b) Wood
    (c) Straw   (d) Grass

26. If 10 means 20, 20 means 30, 30 means 40 and 40 means 50, then which is multiple of 6?
    (a) 10   (b) 20
    (c) 30   (d) 40

27. In the figures given below the word and its code is written on the leaves of first figure. Following the same rule, find the code for the word in the leaf of second figure.

First- Fig.   Second- Fig.

    (a) OPPPY
    (b) OPPYP
    (c) OPPPY
    (d) YPPPO

28. If 'Basketball' is called 'Ludo', 'Ludo' is called 'Football', 'Football' is called 'Cricket', 'Cricket' is called 'Carrom' and 'Carrom' is called 'Volleyball', then which game is played with a bat?

(a) Basketball   (b) Ludo

(c) Cricket   (d) Carrom

(Olympiad)

29. If in a certain code '97452' is written as 'PRIME', '503' is written as 'MUG' and '6813' is written as 'TANG', then how will '304687' be written in the same code?

(a) GUTIAR   (b) GUIATR
(c) GUITAR   (d) GUITRA

(Olympiad)

30. In a certain code language, if BOARD is written as \$3%#6 and ROPE is written as #35@, then PEAR will be written as __________?

(a) 5%6#   (b) 5^%#
(c) #6%5   (d) 5@%#

(Olympiad)

31. The codes for some letters are given below   **(2019)**

Letters	N	S	U	R	A	V	E	O
Codes	–	©	+	@	!	×	\$	#

Find the code for REASON.

(a) @\$!©#–   (b) @\$!#×#   (c) @\$©!#–   (d) @!\$©#×

32. In a certain code language, some letters are coded as follows.   **(2022)**

Letters	T	C	S	K	R	E	I	B
Codes	©	!	7	#	6	%	1	\$

Find the code of KITES

(a) #@167   (b) #1@%7   (c) 6#@!\$ (d) %1©7#

33. If '+' means '×', '–' means '÷', '×' means '–' and '÷' means '+', then what will be the value of $36 ÷ 64 – 8 × 4 + 4$.   **(2022)**

(a) 32   (b) 15   (c) 28   (d) None of these

Level-1

1. (b) Letter of word are written in reverse order to get the decoded word. Hence, the code for Monday is YADNOM.

2. (a) Letters of word are written in reverse order to get the decoded word. Code for FREEDOM is MODEERF

3. (c) Birds live on trees. But here the code for tree is ship. Therefore, the answer is (c).

4. (d) As,

$$
\begin{array}{ccccccc}
R & I & S & H & I & K & A \\
\downarrow & \downarrow & \downarrow & \downarrow & \downarrow & \downarrow & \downarrow \\
2 & 3 & 4 & 5 & 3 & 6 & 7
\end{array}
$$

Similarly,

$$
\begin{array}{cccccc}
S & H & I & K & H & A \\
\downarrow & \downarrow & \downarrow & \downarrow & \downarrow & \downarrow \\
4 & 5 & 3 & 6 & 5 & 7
\end{array}
$$

5. (a) As,

$$
\begin{array}{cccc}
P & O & N & D \\
-1\downarrow & -1\downarrow & -1\downarrow & -1\downarrow
\end{array}
$$

Coded as : O   N   M   C

Similarly,

$$
\begin{array}{cccc}
L & A & K & E \\
-1\downarrow & -1\downarrow & -1\downarrow & -1\downarrow
\end{array}
$$

Coded as : K   Z   J   D

6. (b) Alphabets are coded as shown:

R	I	P	L	E	F
6	1	3	8	2	9

Thus, the code for PILLER is 318826.

7. (a) Letters of word are written in reverse order to get the decoded word. Hence, the code for INFORM is MROFNI.

8. (b) As,

$$
\begin{array}{ccccc}
2 & 4 & 6 & 8 & 5 \\
+1\downarrow & +1\downarrow & +1\downarrow & +1\downarrow & +1\downarrow
\end{array}
$$

Coded as : 3   5   7   9   6

Similarly,

$$
\begin{array}{ccccc}
3 & 5 & 7 & 7 & 6 \\
+1\downarrow & +1\downarrow & +1\downarrow & +1\downarrow & +1\downarrow
\end{array}
$$

Coded as : 4   6   8   8   7

9. (b) 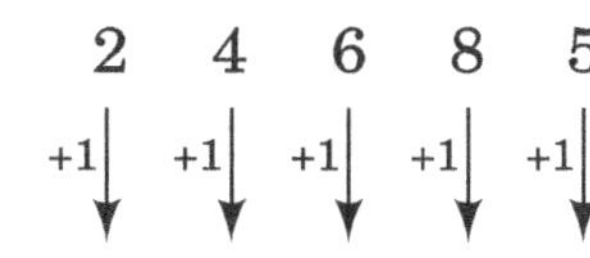 has exactly four lines of symmetry and ◯ means ▢.

10. (d) Clothes are kept in Almirah but here, Almirah is called Bench. So, option (d) is the correct answer.

11. (b) As,

    4   6   8   9   5
    $\downarrow_{-2}$ $\downarrow_{-2}$ $\downarrow_{-2}$ $\downarrow_{-2}$ $\downarrow_{-2}$

Coded as : 2   4   6   7   3

Similarly,

    3   8   6   5
    $\downarrow_{-2}$ $\downarrow_{-2}$ $\downarrow_{-2}$ $\downarrow_{-2}$

Coded as : 1   6   4   3

12. (a) In roman numerals, XI comes imediately after X and VI means XI.

13. (b) Letters of words are written in reverse form to get the decoded word. Hence, the code of DIVISION is NOISIVID.

14. (b) 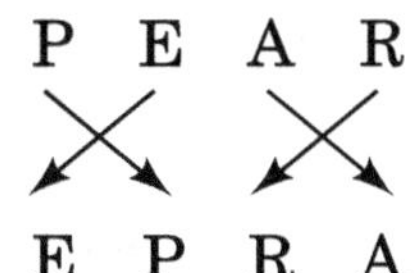 is formed by triangle and △ means ▯.

15. (c) Flower is offered to God, but here Flower is letter. So, (c) is the correct answer.

16. (c) Aeroplanes fly in the sky but according to statement sky is called sea.

17. (d) As given, 1 is coded as M, 8 as D, 4 as B, 6 as J, So, 1846 is coded as MDBJ.

18. (c) As given, 9 as N, 3 as I, 4 as B and 1 as M. So, 9341 is coded as NIBM.

19. (a) As given, 6 is coded as J, 4 as B, 9 as N, 2 as L and 8 as D. So, 64928 is coded as JBNLD.

20. (b) Codes are:

△ ⇒ C
▭ ⇒ A
◯ ⇒ R
▢ ⇒ E

The given figures are the code for the word CARE.

Hence, option (b) is correct.

21. (c) Since '34' means CD according to the position of letters in the English alphabet. In the same way, '56' means 'EF'.

22. (d) As,

P E A R
E P R A

Similarly,

W E A K
E W K A

Hence, option (d) is correct.

23. (a) 3 is an odd number and 2 means 3.

24. (a) E is a vowel and D means E.

25. (b) The shapes are coded as

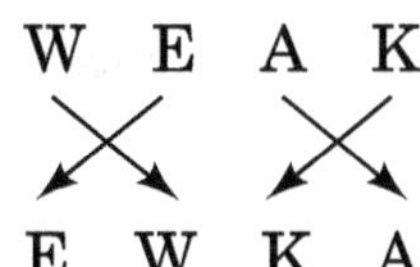 → A, ▦ → X

and ▭ → L

And, the arrows are coded as

⟶ B and ⟵ Z

So, the code for 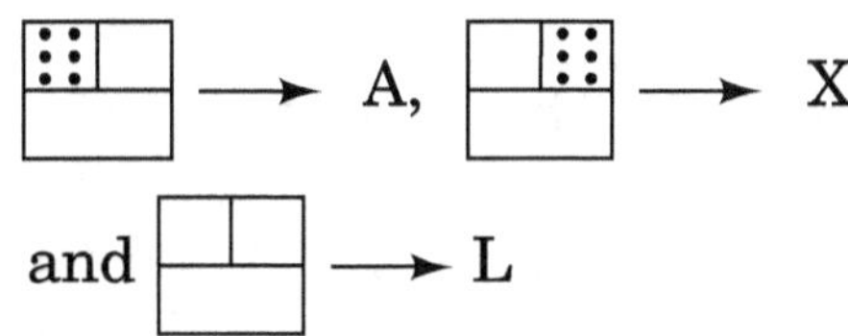 LZ.

26. (c)

1	2	3	4	5	6
F	A	T	H	E	R

So, 4526 is the code for HEAR.

27. (b)

5	6	7
C	A	R

2	3	4
T	O	Y

5	6	7	2
C	A	R	T

Hence, the correct answer is option (b).

28. (c) As,

B O O K   L O C K

and

Coded as : @ ^ ^ #   % ^ * #

So,

B   L   O   C   K

@   %   ^   *   #

29. (c) As, G ⟶ G and T ⟶ T

I ⤬ V   A ⤬ K
V   I   K   A
E ⟶ E   E ⟶ E

Similarly,

D ⟶ D
I ⤬ S
S   I
K ⟶ K

Hence, option (c) is correct.

30. (a) Prime factor of 25 is 5 and 3 means 5.

31. (c) Digit is related to number of sides. Circle has no side. Triangle has 3 sides. Pentagon has 5 sides.

32. (d) 33. (d) 34. (c)

Level-2

1. (c) 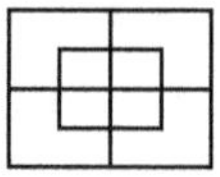 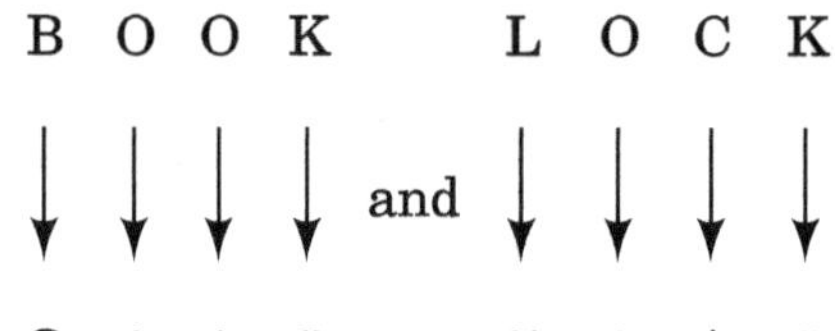 has exactly 10 squares and [grid] means [grid].

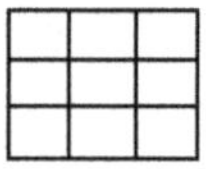

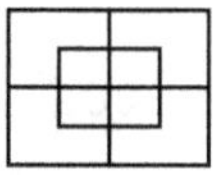

2. (d) The first and second statements has the common code digit is 1 and the common word girl. So, 1 is coded as girl.

3. (d) A 'tractor' is used to plough a field. But a 'tractor is called 'car'.

So, a 'car' will be used to plough the field.

4. (c) Soap is used for washing clothes but according to the statement soap is called ink.

5. (b) In the first and second statement the common code is 8 and the common word is hard. Therefore, 8 means hard.

6. (d) The colour of clear sky is blue but according to statement orange is called blue.

7. (d) As,

Code as :

G	I	V	E	B	A	T
5	1	3	7	9	2	4

Similarly, Code as :

G	A	T	E
5	2	4	7

8. (b) Following table depicts the code of used letters in the two given words:

Letters	S	T	A	R	O	E
Code	5	$	*	2	3	@

Therefore, OATS = 3*$5.

9. (b)

P	A	L	E	R	T	H
2	1	5	3	4	9	0

So, PEARL is coded as

P	E	A	R	L
2	3	1	4	5

10. (b) As,

Coded as :

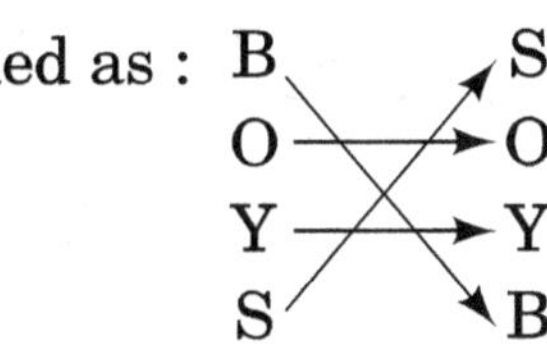

`Similarly,

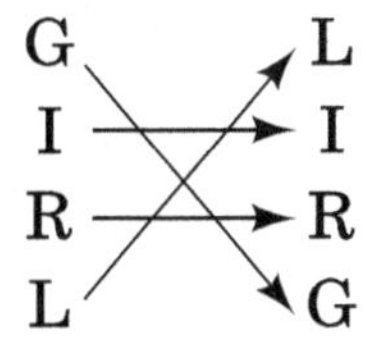

Hence, option (b) is the correct answer.

11. (b) In statement first and second the common code digit is 4 and the common word is class. Therefore, 4 is the code for class.

12. (a) In roman numerals, IV comes before V but here III means IV. So, III comes before V.

13. (c) Code for the given word = (Number of letters in the word) −1

So, code for STUDENT = 7 − 1 = 6

14. (d) We sleep in night but according to statement night is called afternoon.

15. (b)

W	I	P	E	M	O	R
2	%	7	#	9	4	*

Therefore, ROPE will coded as

R	O	P	E
*	4	7	#

16. (c)

M	A	T	E	L
3	%	6	#	1

Therefore, TELL will be coded as

T	E	L	L
6	#	1	1

17. (b)

A	T	E	C	H	I	R
1	4	6	0	8	7	3

Therefore, TEACHER will be coded as

T	E	A	C	H	E	R
4	6	1	0	8	6	3

18. (a) 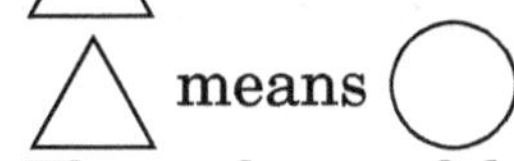 has three corners and means

19. (b) The colour of human blood is red. But according to the statement red is called yellow. Therefore, the colour of human blood is yellow.

20. (a)

S	H	A	R	P	U
9	8	0	3	4	5

Therefore, RUSH will be coded as

R	U	S	H
3	5	9	8

21. (d) Clearly, a 'Teacher' teaches in a class and as given 'Teacher' is called 'Clerk'. So, a 'Clerk' will teach in the class.

Hence, the answer is (d).

22. (d) The king of flowers is the 'lotus'. But 'lotus' is called 'glandiola'.

So, 'glandiola' is the king of flowers.

23. (c) In the code, the letters of the word are put in the reverse order of positions.

24. (a) Clearly, a 'bag' is used to carry the books but a 'bag' is called 'dictionary'.

So, a 'dictionary' will be used to carry the books.

25. (c) The furniture is made up of 'wood' and as given 'wood' is called 'straw'.

So, the sky is made up of 'straw'.

26. (b) Multiple of 6 is 30 and here 20 means 30.

27. (b) As,
H A P P Y

A H P Y P

Similarly,
P O P P Y

O P P Y P

So, the code for the word POPPY is OPPYP.

28. (d) 'Cricket' is played with a bat. But 'Cricket' is called 'Carrom'. So, Carrom is played with a bat.

29. (c)

Numbers:	9	7	4	5
Codes:	P	R	I	M
	2	0	3	6
	E	U	G	T
	8	1		
	A	N		

Numbers:	3	0	4	6	8	7
Codes:	G	U	I	T	A	R

So, option (c) is correct.

30. (d) As,

B	O	A	R	D	P	E
↓	↓	↓	↓	↓	↓	↓
$	3	%	#	6	5	@

Similarly,

P	E	A	R
↓	↓	↓	↓
5	@	%	#

31. (a) REASON : @$!©#-

32. (b) K → #, I → 1, T → @, E → %, S → 7

So, KITES = #1@%7

33. (c)

Arithmetic Reasoning

OBJECTIVES

- This test measures student's ability to perform basic arithmetic operations and to solve problems that involve fundamental arithmetic concepts.

INTRODUCTION

Arithmetic reasoning focuses on word problems and delivers mathematical questions and equations in a format that must be synthesized.

Examples

1. After buying 2 erasers at Rs. 10 each, Akram has Rs. 3 left. How much amount did he have at first?

    (a) 20   (b) 22   (c) 23   (d) 26

Ans. (c)

Explanation:

Cost of one eraser = Rs. 10

Cost of two erasers = 10 × 2 = 20

$$= \text{Rs. } 20$$

After buying 2 erasers Akram has left = Rs. 3

Total amount first he had = 20 + 3 = 23

2. Sania has 12 chocolates. Suraj has one fourth as many chocolates as Sania. Ridhima has 8 more chocolates than Suraj. How many total chocolates are there?

    (a) 12   (b) 14   (c) 26   (d) 28

Ans. (c)

Explanation:

Total number of chocolates Sania has = 12

Suraj has = 12 × 1/4 = 3

Ridhima has = 3 + 8 = 11

Total chocolates = 12 + 3 + 11 = 26

3. One pan can fry 2 pieces of meat at one time. Every piece of meat takes two minutes to be cooked (one minute for each side). Using only one pan, what is the least possible time to cook 1000 pieces of meat?

   (a) 1000 minutes (b) 1500 minutes (c) 2000 minutes (d) 2500 minutes

Ans. (a)

Explanation:

One pan can fry at one time = 2 pieces of meat

Every piece of meat takes time = 2 minutes

Possible time to cook 1000 pieces = 1000 × 2 = 2000 minute

but 2 pieces can be fried at one time = 2000/2 = 1000 minutes

4. Manav wrote the number sentences below,

   $20 = \boxed{} \times 4$

   $\boxed{} \times \$ = 15$

The value of $\boxed{}$ is the same in both the sentences. Both of Manav's number sentences are true. What is the value of \$?

   (a) 1 (b) 2 (c) 3 (d) 5

Ans. (c)

Explanation:

Value of $\boxed{5}$ is = 5

Value of \$ is = 3

$20 = \boxed{5} \times 4$

$\boxed{5} \times 3 = 15$

5. Mr. Kapoor brought 5 oranges to a picnic. All the oranges were cut into halves. Each person ate one half of an orange and there were no oranges left over. How many people ate oranges?

   (a) 5 (b) 7 (c) 8 (d) 10

Ans. (d)

Explanation:

Total oranges = 5

Pieces of oranges after cut into halves = 5 × 2 = 10

Hence, 10 people ate oranges.

1. A tailor had a number of shirt pieces to cut from a roll of fabric. He cut each roll of equal length into 10 pieces. He cut at the rate of 45 cuts in a minute. How many rolls would be cut in 24 minutes?

   (a) 30 rolls   (b) 58 rolls

   (c) 120 rolls   (d) 150 rolls

2. At the zoo Geeta saw 21 lions and tigers. There were five more lions than tigers. How many were tigers

   (a) 15   (b) 16

   (c) 17   (d) 19

3. Raju has 84 cows in his farm. He has 6 times as many cows as he has horses. The number sentence below can be used to find the number of horses, h, he has

   $$84 \div h = 6$$

   How many horses, h, does Raju have?

   (a) 14 horses   (b) 12 horses

   (c) 66 horses   (d) 78 horses

4. Tom scored 4 more points in the basket ball game than Mary. Lindy scored 22 points, which was twice as many as Tom. How many points did Mary score?

   (a) 7   (b) 8

   (c) 11   (d) 14

5. Priya cuts a cake into two halves and cuts one half into smaller piece of equal size. Each of the small pieces is twenty grams in weight. If she has seven pieces of cake in all with her. What is the weight of cake in all?

   (a) 220 gm   (b) 250 gm

   (c) 240 gm   (d) 225 gm

6. The table shows the number of cans of different coloured paint in Mr. Donald's garage. Each can is the same size.

   Mr Donald's Paint Cans

Colour	Number
Pink	4
Yellow	3

   Mr. Donald chooses one paint can without looking. What is the probability the first can chosen will be a can of pink paint?

   (a) $\dfrac{3}{4}$ (b) $\dfrac{3}{4}$

   (c) $\dfrac{4}{7}$ (d) $\dfrac{4}{3}$

7. A shepherd had 27 sheep. All but 10 died. How many was he left with?

   (a) 27   (b) 10

   (c) 17   (d) 8

8. A bird shooter was asked how many birds he had in the bag. He replied that there were all sparrows but 6, all pigeons but 6 and all ducks but 6. How many birds he had in the bag in all?

   (a) 36   (b) 18

   (c) 27   (d) 9

9. At the end of birthday party, ten children present all shake hands with each other once. How many handshakes will there be altogether?

(a) 20   (b) 45

(c) 55   (d) 90

10. If you write 1 to 100 counting, then how many times do you write 3?

(a) 21   (b) 20

(c) 18   (d) 11

11. A group of 1200 persons consisting of captains and soldiers is travelling in a train. For every 16 soldiers there is one captain. The number of captains in the group is?

(a) 70   (b) 85

(c) 80   (d) 75

12. Use the picture below to answer the question

John will use one marker to colour half of the circles. What is the colour of the marker John will use?

(a) blue   (b) green

(c) yellow   (d) red

13. Wilson is buying curd for a party.

- He needs to buy 50 kg of curd.
- Curd is sold only in 8 and 12 kg packages.

Which choice shows the least amount of curd Wilson can buy to have enough for a party?

(a) Five 12 kg packages

(b) Three 12 kg packages and two 8 kg packages

(c) Two 12 kg packages and three 8 kg packages

(d) Six 8 kg packages

14. Patrick has a set of green, white and black marbles.

- The green marbles make up exactly $\frac{1}{2}$ of the set.
- The set has 2 black marbles.
- The number of white marbles is twice the number of black marbles.

How many marbles are in Patrick's set?

(a) 6   (b) 4

(c) 8   (d) 12

15. Simran has 6 carrots. Sara has 3 more carrots than Simran. Denny has 3 times as many carrots as Sara. How many carrots does Denny have?

(a) 6   (b) 9

(c) 18   (d) 27

16. A is 4 years older to B and 4 years younger to C, while B and D are twins. How many years older is C to D?

(a) 5 years   (b) 6 years

(c) 8 years   (d) 4 years

17. On Friday Mary was a referee at 3 soccer games. She arrived at the soccer field 20 minutes before the first game. Each game lasted for $1\frac{1}{2}$ hours. There were 5 minutes

brake between each game. Mary left 15 minutes after the last game. How long, in minutes, was Mary at the soccer field?

(a) 300 minutes

(b) 305 minutes

(c) 315 minutes

(d) 320 minutes

18. A pouch contains 6 blue marbles, 3 red marbles, 1 green marble, and 2 pink marbles.

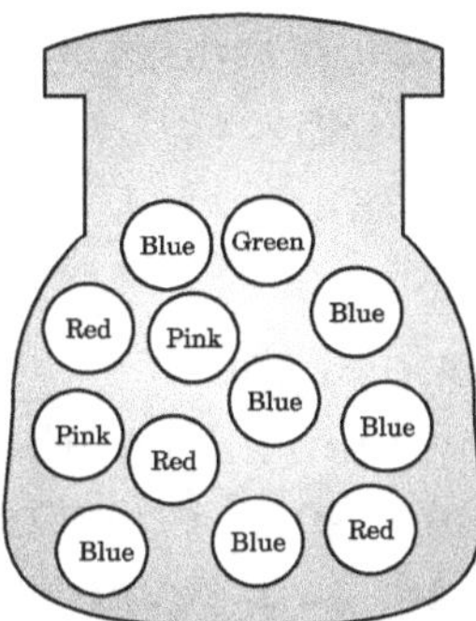

What is the probability that Tom will select, without looking, a blue marble on the first try?

(a) $\dfrac{6}{12}$

(b) $\dfrac{3}{12}$

(c) $\dfrac{1}{12}$

(d) $\dfrac{2}{12}$

19. In Aporva's class there are twice as many girls as boys. There are 9 boys in the class. What is the total number of boys and girls is the class?

(a) 9

(b) 18

(c) 24

(d) 27

20. Ankur wanted to use his calculator to add 1479 and 246. He entered 1379 + 246 by mistake. Which of these could he do to correct the mistake?

(a) Add 100

(b) Add 1

(c) Subtract 1

(d) Subtract 100

21. A number machine takes a number and operates on it. When the Input Number is 6 the output number is 11, as shown below,

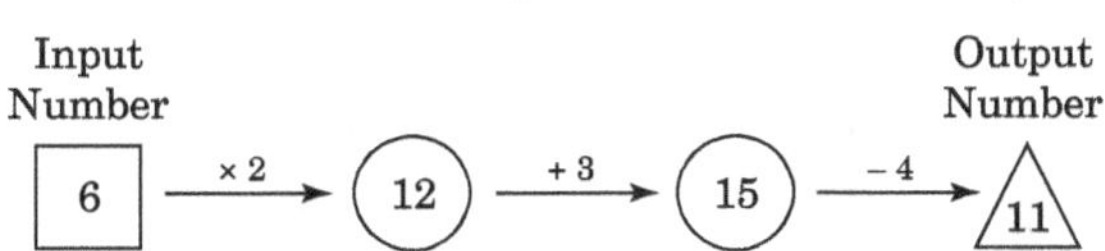

When the Input Number is 8, which of these is the Output Number?

(a) 14

(b) 13

(c) 15

(d) 19

22. ☐ represents the number of books that Riya reads each week. Which of these represents the total number of books that Riya reads in 5 weeks?

(a) 5 + ☐

(b) 5 × ☐

(c) ☐ + 5

(d) (☐ + ☐) × 6

23. How many minutes are there in 1/12 of a day?

(a) 15

(b) 30

(c) 60

(d) 120

24. Tell the numbers that will replace ▲, ◼ and ★ in the given square so that the sum of numbers from every side is 105.

(a) 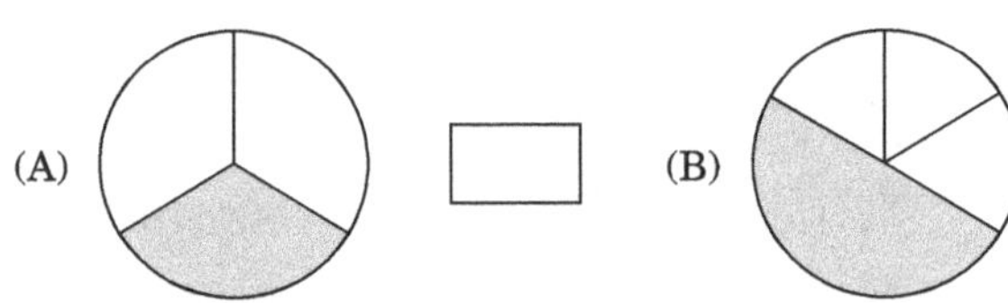 34, ▲ = 37, ★ 31

(b) ■ 31, ▲ = 34, ★ 37

(c) ■ 37, ▲ = 31, ★ 34

(d) ■ 30, ▲ = 31, ★ = 34

25. Compare the shaded regions. Which symbol belong to the square?

(A) ⬤ ▭ (B) ⬤

(a) <
(b) >
(c) =
(d) None of these

26. Raj bought 12 plums and ate $\frac{1}{3}$ of them Shivam bought 12 plums and ate $\frac{1}{4}$ of them. Which statement is true?

(a) Raj ate 4 plums and Shivam ate 3 plums.
(b) Raj ate 3 plums and Shivam ate 4 plums.
(c) Raj and Shivam ate the same number of plums.
(d) Raj had 9 plums remaining.

27. When Pinocchio lies, his nose gets 5 cm longer. When he tells the truth, his nose gets 3 cm shorter. When his nose was 10 cm long, he told three lies and made two true statements. How long was Pinocchio's nose afterwards?
(a) 18 cm (b) 19 cm
(c) 21 cm (d) 22 cm

28. The product of all numbers in the dial of a telephone is __________?
(a) 1,58,480
(b) 1,00,000
(c) zero
(d) None of these

29. Shivam had 23 candies. He put the same number in each of two bags and had seven candies left over. How many did he put in each bag?
(a) 6 (b) 7
(c) 8 (d) 9

30. Find out the two signs to be interchanged for making following equation correct
$$5 + 3 \times 8 - 12/4 = 3$$
(a) + and − (b) − and /
(c) + and × (d) + and /

31. Supriya remembers the first eight digits of her phone number but she forgot the last ninth digit of it. She only remembers that the last digit is amongst 1, 2, 3, 5, 6 and 8. How many possible combinations of numbers can be formed? **(2018)**
(a) 6 (b) 7
(c) 9 (d) 10

32. Find the missing number. **(2020)**

(a) 270   (b) 207   (c) 215   (d) 300

LEVEL-2

1. The total of the ages of Amar, Anaya and Ashish is 80 years. What was the total of their ages three years ago?
   - (a) 72 years
   - (b) 74 years
   - (c) 71 years
   - (d) 77 years

2. 30 members of a club decided to play a badminton singles tournament. Every time a member loses a game he is out of the tournament. There are no ties. What is the minimum number of matches that must be played to determine the winner?
   - (a) 61
   - (b) 15
   - (c) 29
   - (d) None of these

3. In a garden, there are 10 rows and 12 columns of mango trees. The distance between the two trees is 2 metres and a distance of one metre is left from all sides of the boundary of the garden. The length of the gardan is
   - (a) 24 m
   - (b) 20 m
   - (c) 22 m
   - (d) 26 m

4. I have a few sweets to be distributed. If I keep 2, 3 or 4 in a pack, I am left with one sweet. If I keep 5 in a pack. I am left with none. What is the minimum number of sweets I have to pack and distribute?
   - (a) 54
   - (b) 65
   - (c) 37
   - (d) 25

5. A motorist knows four different routes from Bristol to Birmingham. From Birmingham to Sheffield he knows three different routes and from Sheffield to Carlisle he knows two different routes. How many routes does he know from Bristol to Carlise?
   - (a) 8
   - (b) 12
   - (c) 24
   - (d) 46

6. Nina joined a short term course in art and craft on 20th April. The course classes got over on 9th June. What is the total duration of the class?
   - (a) 30 days
   - (b) 45 days
   - (c) 51 days
   - (d) 100 days

7. Rishika's exam started on 2nd March and the last exam was on 3rd April. What is the total duration of her exams?
   - (a) 30 days
   - (b) 33 days
   - (c) 44 days
   - (d) 60 days

8. A farmer built a fence around his plot. He used 27 fence poles on each side of the square plot. How many poles did he need altogether?

   (a) 108

   (b) 100

   (c) 104

   (d) None of these

9. In a class, 20% of the students own only two cars each, 40% of the remaining own three cars each and the remaining members own only one car each. Which of the following statements is definitely true from the given statements?

   (a) Only 20% of the total members own three cars each.

   (b) 48% of the total members own only one car each.

   (c) 60% of the total members own at least two cars each.

   (d) 80% of the total members own at least one car.

10. When Rahul born, his father was 32 years older than his brother and his mother was 25 years older than his sister. If Rahul's brother is 6 years older than him and his mother is 3 years younger than his father, how old was Rahul's sister when he was born?

    (a) 10 years   (b) 7 years

    (c) 14 years   (d) 20 years

11. The top shelf held 27 books. The bottom shelf held 43 books. 11 books from the top shelf were checked out. 6 books from the bottom shelf were missing. How many total books are left on both shelves?

    (a) 51   (b) 52

    (c) 53   (d) 54

12. A monkey climbs 30 feet at the beginning of each hour and rests for a while when he slips back 20 feet before he again starts climbing in the beginning of the next hour. If he begins his ascent at 8.00 a.m., at what time will he first touch flag at 120 feet from the ground?

    (a) 4 p.m.

    (b) 5 p.m.

    (c) 6 p.m.

    (d) None of these

13. For every soft drink bottle that Tom collected, Maria collected 4. Tom collected a total of 8 soft drink bottles. How many bottles did Maria collect?

    (a) 4   (b) 16

    (c) 24   (d) 32

14. Raja and Ritu collect baseball cards. Each has the same number of cards. If John gives Raja and Ritu 6 more baseball cards each, who will have the greater number of baseball cards, Raja or Ritu?

    (a) Raja

    (b) Ritu

    (c) Raja and Ritu will have the same number of baseball cards.

    (d) None of the above

15. Ajay place these animals cards into a bag.

What is the probability that he will draw a card with an elephant?

(a) $\dfrac{2}{9}$ (b) $\dfrac{4}{9}$ (c) $\dfrac{2}{9}$ (d) $\dfrac{1}{9}$

16. Mrs. Kapoor ordered 3 different colours of markers.
   - She ordered 20 of each colour markers.
   - She also ordered some pencils.
   - She ordered 2 times as many pencils as markers.

   How many pencils did Mrs. Kapoor order?

   (a) 20   (b) 60
   (c) 100   (d) 120

17. Manav's mother prepares sandwiches with two slices of bread each. A package of bread has 24 slices. How many sandwiches can she prepare from two and half packages of bread?

   (a) 12   (b) 24
   (c) 30   (d) 34

18. If Anne ate two slices more than half of a 12 $\triangle$-slice pizza, than how many slices did Anne eat?

   (a) 6   (b) 7
   (c) 8   (d) 5

19. Rahul is 10 years younger than Vijay. Vijay is 5 years older than Raj. Raj is twice as old as John. John is 5 years old. What is the combined age of these four people?

   (a) 35 years   (b) 50 years
   (c) 55 years   (d) 25 years

20. Akshat cut each cake into 8 slices, and ended up with 64 slices altogether. How many cakes did he cut up?

   (a) 8   (b) 7
   (c) 9   (d) 10

21. The number of red frogs exceeded the number of blue frogs by 50. The number of green frogs was 20 less than the number of blue frogs. If there were 100 blue frogs, what was the sum of the reds, the blues, and the greens?

(a) 250   (b) 80   (c) 330   (d) 230

22. Shalini's mother baked five pies for her birthday party. Each person who came to the party ate one piece, and all the pieces were the same size. The pies that were left over are shown below. How many people came to the party?

(a) 28   (b) 29   (c) 27   (d) 30

23. On his farm Mr. Donald had 3 ducks, 15 chickens, 4 mice and 2 dogs. How many legs were on his animals?

(a) 60   (b) 24   (c) 30   (d) 55

24. Jenny bought a ball that bounces exactly half the height from which it is dropped. He drops it from the top of a building that is 40 meters tall. How high will the ball bounce after its fourth bounce?

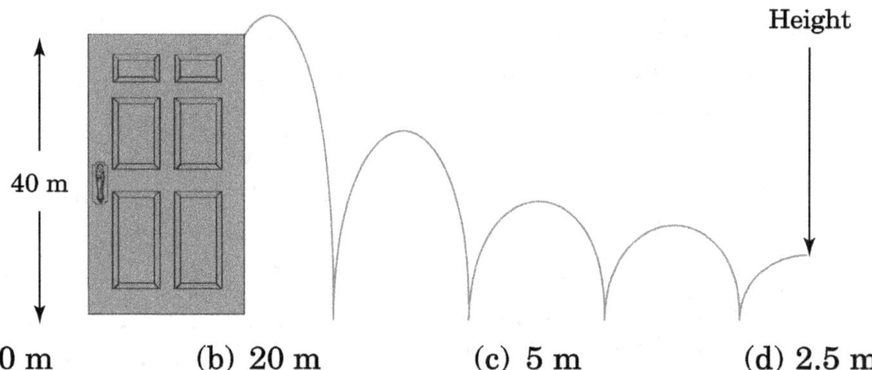

(a) 10 m   (b) 20 m   (c) 5 m   (d) 2.5 m

25. In a fourth-grade class, two out of four students bring their lunch to school. There are 30 students in this class. How many students in the class bring their lunch to school?

(a) 30   (b) 15   (c) 10   (d) 5

26. Harshita makes necklaces out of beads. Her choices of shapes and colours of beads are shown below.

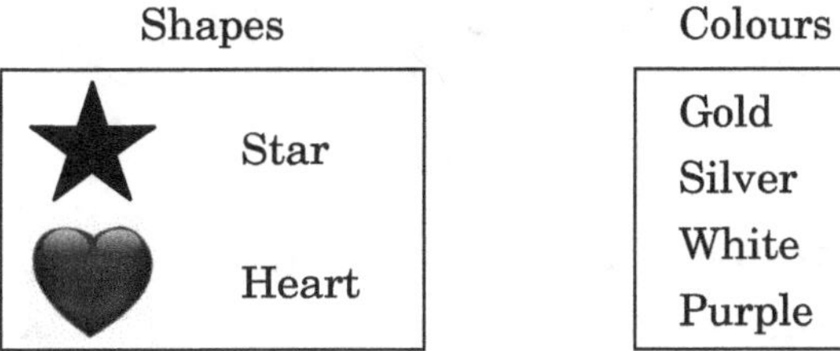

Which tree diagram shows all the possible combinations of 1 shape and 1 colour?

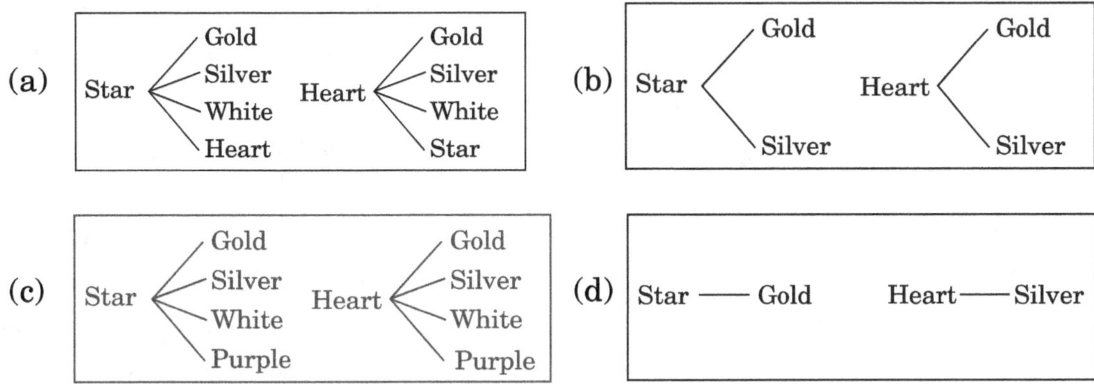

27. Tom and Jerry have boxes of chalk.

- Tom has 6 boxes with 9 pieces each box.

- Jerry has 9 boxes with 6 pieces in each box.

Who has more pieces of chalk?

(a) Tom

(b) Jerry

(c) Both have same

(d) Data Inadequate

28. Suzen had 81 chickens. He sold an equal number of chickens to each of 3 customers and had 54 chickens left. How many chickens did suzen sell to each customer?

(a) 8   (b) 9   (c) 10   (d) 11

29. Swati needs 2 eggs for every cake she bakes. Which pair describes cakes and eggs correctly?

(a) 2 cakes, 6 eggs

(b) 2 cakes, 3 eggs

(c) 3 cakes, 5 eggs

(d) 3 cakes, 6 eggs

30. Pulkit put the following blocks in a bag. Without looking Pulkit has the greatest probability of picking which number?

(a) 1

(b) 2

(c) 3

(d) 4

Level-1

1. (c) Number of cuts made to cut a roll into 10 pieces = 9

∴ Required number of rolls

= 45 × 24/9

= 120.

2. (b) Total number of lions = 21

Total number of tigers

= 21–5 = 16

3. (a) 84 ÷ h = 6

h = 84 ÷ 6 = 14

Raju has 14 horses.

4. (a) Lindy scored = 22 points

Tom scored = 22/2 = 11 points

Mary scored = 11 – 4 = 7 points

5. (c)

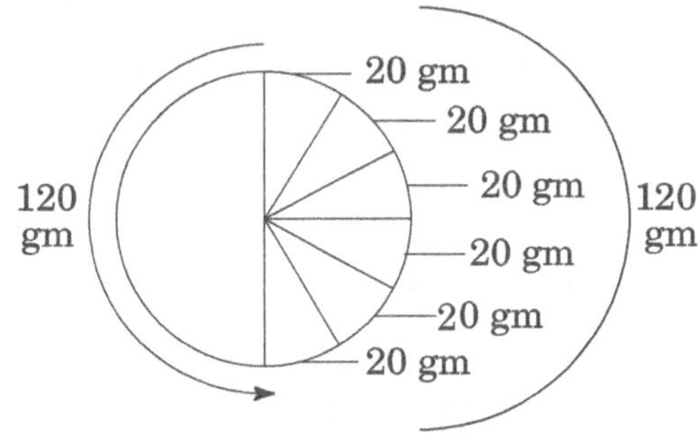

The weight of cake is 240 gm.

6. (c) Total number of cans = 7

Probability of pink can = $\dfrac{4}{7}$

7. (b) "All but 10 died" means all except 10 died i.e. 10 sheep remained alive.

8. (d) Number of sparrows + Number of ducks = 6 and number of sparrows + Number of pigeon = 6.

This is possible when there are 3 sparrows, 3 pigeons and 3 ducks i.e. 9 birds in all.

9. (b) Clearly the total number of handshakes

= (9 + 8 + 7 + 6 + 5 + 4 + 3 + 2 + 1) = 45.

10. (b) Clearly from 1 to 100, there are ten numbers with 3 as the unit's digit – 3, 13, 23 33, 43, 53, 63,73, 83, 93 and ten number with 3 as tens digit – 30, 31, 32, 33, 34, 35, 36, 37, 38, 39.

So, required number = 10 + 10 = 20.

11. (d) Clearly, out of every 16 persons, there is one captain.

So, number of captains

$= \dfrac{1200}{16} = 75.$

12. (d) Total number of circles = 12

Number of red circles = 6

Number of blue circles = 2

Number of green circles = 3

Numbr of yellow circles = 1

Red circles is the half of total. So, John will use red marker.

13. (b) Three 12 kg packages = 12 × 3 = 36 kg

Two 8 kg packages = 8 × 2 = 16 kg

Total curd = 36 + 16 = 52 kg

14. (d) Number of black marbles = $\boxed{2}$

Number of white marbles = 2 × 2 = 4

Total number of black and white marbles = 4 + 2 = 6

Total marbles (n) = n = $\dfrac{1}{2}$ × n + 6

$$n = 6 \times 2 = 12$$

Number of green marbles = 12 × $\dfrac{1}{2}$ = 6.

15. (d) Number of carrots Simran has = 6

Number of carrots Sara has = 6 + 3 = 9

Number of carrot Denny has = 9 × 3 = 27.

16. (c) C > A > B = D

   (4 years) (4 years) Twins

C is = 4 + 4 = 8 years older to D.

17. (c)

- Mary arrived at soccer field = 20 minutes before the first game.

- Each game duration = $1\dfrac{1}{2}$ hours = 90 minutes

  Three games duration = 90 × 3 = 270 minutes

- Minutes brake between each game = 5 minutes

  Total minutes among games = 5 × 2 = 10 min.

- Mary left soccer field after 15 minutes of last game.

  Total minutes = 20 + 270 + 10 + 15 = 315 minutes

18. (a) Total marbles = 12

Blue marbles = 6

Probability of selecting blue marbles = $\dfrac{6}{12}$.

19. (d) Number of boys in the class = 9

Number of girls in the class = 9 × 2 = 18

Total number of boys and girls = 18 + 9 = 27.

20. (a) Actual calculation

= 1479 + 246 = 1725

Calculation done by mistake = 1379 + 246 = 1625

∴ Difference = 1725 − 1625 = 100.

21. (c)

Input Number   Output Number

$\boxed{8} \xrightarrow{\times 2} (16) \xrightarrow{+3} (19) \xrightarrow{-4} \triangle{15}$

The Output Number will be 15.

22. (b) 5 × $\square$

23. (d) One day has 24 hours

$$1/12 \text{ of a day} = 24 \times \frac{1}{12} = 2 \text{ hours}$$

1 hour = 60 minutes

2 hours = 2 × 60 = 120 minutes

24. (a) ■ 34, ▲ = 37, ★ 31

32	39	34	= 105
37	35	37	= 105
36	31	38	= 105
= 105	105	105	

25. (a) Shaded region in figure (A)

$$= \frac{1}{3}$$

Shaded region in figure (B)

$$= \frac{3}{6} = \frac{1}{2}$$

$$\frac{1}{3} < \frac{1}{2}.$$

26. (a) Raj ate $= 12 \times \frac{1}{3} = 4$ plums

Shivam ate $= 12 \times \frac{1}{4} = 3$ plums

So, Raj ate 4 plums and Shivam ate 3 plums.

Hence, statement (a) is correct.

27. (b) Pinnocchio's nose length = 10 cm

Pinnocchio's nose length after three lies = 10 + (5 x 3) = 10 + 15 = 25 cm

Pinnocchio's nose length after two true statements

$$= 25 - (2 \times 3)$$

25 − 6 = 19 cm.

28. (c) Since one of the number on the dial of a telephone is 0, so the product of all the numbers on it is 0.

29. (d) Total candies = 23

Candies leftover = 7

Candies in each bag

= 23 − 7 = 16

= 16/2 = 8

30. (b) On interchanging − and /, we get the equation as

$$5 + 3 \times 8 / 12 - 4 = 3$$

$$5 + 3 \times (2/3) - 4 = 3$$

or   3 = 3, which is true.

31. (a) As 6 options are available for the last digit.

32. (a)

335 - 65 = 270.

1. (c) Required sum = $(80 - 3 \times 3)$ years

$$= (80 - 9) \text{ years}$$
$$= 71 \text{ years.}$$

2. (c) Clearly, every member except one (i.e. the winner) must lose one game to decide the winner.

So, minimum number of matches to be played = $30 - 1$ = 29.

3. (a) Each row contains 12 plants.

There are 11 gaps between the two corner trees (11×2) metres and 1 metre on each side is left.

$\therefore$ Length = $(22 + 2)$ m = 24 m.

4. (d) The required number will be such that it leaves a reminder of 1 when divided by 2, 3 or 4 and no reminder when divided by 5. Such a number is 25 among options.

5. (c) Total number of routes from Bristale to Carlisle = $(4 \times 3 \times 2)$ = 24.

6. (c) Number of days left in April
$$= 30 - 19$$
$$= 11 \text{ days}$$
(Since April has 30 days)

Number of days in May = 31 days
(Since May has 31 days)

Number of days in June = 9 days

Total duration of class
$$= 11 + 31 + 9 = 51 \text{ days.}$$

7. (b) Number of days left in March
$$= 31 - 1 = 30 \text{ days}$$

Number of days in April = 3 days

Total duration of her exams
$$= 30 + 3$$
$$= 33 \text{ days.}$$

8. (c) Since each pole at the corner of the plot is common to its two sides, so we have

Total number of poles needed
$$= 27 \times 4 - 4$$
$$= 108 - 4$$
$$= 104$$

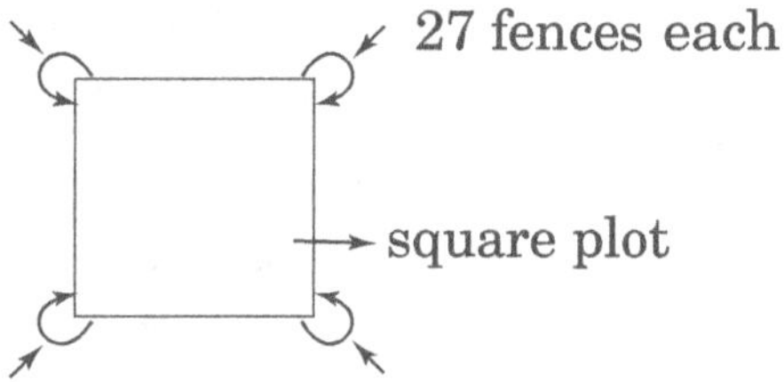

9. (b) Let total number of members be 100.

Then, Number of members owning only 2 cars = 20

Number of members owning 3 cars = 40% of 80
$$= 32$$

Number of members owning only 1 car = $100 - (20 + 32)$
$$= 48$$

Thus, 48% of the total members own one car each.

10. **(a)** When Rahul was born, his brother's age = 6 yrs

His father's age = (6 + 32) yrs = 38 yrs.

His mother's age = (38 – 3) yrs = 35 yrs

His sister's age = (32 – 25) yrs = 10 yrs.

11. **(c)** Number of books on top shelf = 27

Number of books on bottom shelf = 43

Total missing books = 11 + 6 = 17

Number of books left on = 27 + 43 –17 = 53

12. **(c)** Net ascend of monkey in 1 hr = (30 – 20) = 10 feet

So, the monkey ascends 90 feet in 9 hrs i.e. till 5 p.m. Clearly, in the next 1 hour i.e. till 6 p.m. the monkey ascend remaining 30 feet to touch the flag.

13. **(d)** Total soft drink bottles collected by Tom = 8

Total soft drink bottles collected by Maria = 8 × 4 = 32.

14. **(c)** As both has the same number of card John also gives both 6 more baseball cards. So, Raja and Ritu will have the same number of baseball cards.

15. **(b)** Total number of cards = 9

Cards with elephant = 4

Probability of a card with an elephant = $\dfrac{4}{9}$.

16. **(d)** Total order of markers = 3 × 20 = 60

Total order of pencils = 60 × 2 = 120.

17. **(c)** A package of bread has = 24 slices

Sandwiches made by one packages of bread = 12

Sandwiches made by two packages of bread = 12 × 2 = 24

Sandwiches made by half packages of bread = 6

Total sandwiches = 24 + 6 = 30.

18. **(c)** Total slices = 12

Half of 12 slices = 6

Anne ate = 6 + 2 = 8 slices.

19. **(a)** John's age = 5 years

Raj's age = 5 × 2 = 10 years

Vijay's age = 10 + 5 = 15 years

Rahul's age = 15 – 10 = 5 years

Total combined age = 5 + 10 + 15 + 5 = 35 years.

20. **(a)**

Total slices = 64

Cakes he cut up = 64 ÷ 8 = 8.

21. **(c)** Number of blue frogs = 100

Number of red frogs = 100 + 50 = 150

Number of green frogs = 100 − 20 = 80

Total frogs = 100 + 150 + 80 = 330.

22. **(d)** Total pies = 5

Each pie has equal pieces = 8

Total pieces = 8 × 5 = 40

Pieces eaten = 30

Hence, total persons = 30.

23. **(a)**

Animals	Number of Animals	Total legs
Ducks	3	3 × 2 = 6
Chickens	15	15 × 2 = 30
Mice	4	4 × 4 = 16
Dogs	2	2 × 4 = 8
	Total	= 60

24. **(d)** After the first bounce the ball bounced = 40/2 = 20 metres

After the second bounce = 20/2 = 10 metres

After the third bounce = 10/2 = 5 metres

After the fourth bounce = 5/2 = 2.5 metres.

25. **(b)** One half of 30 is 15.

26. **(c)** Option (c) is correct answer.

27. **(c)** Tom has = 6 × 9 = 54 pieces

Jerry has = 9 × 6 = 54 pieces

So, both have same.

28. **(b)** Total chickens = 81

Chickens left = 54

Chickens sold = 81 − 54 = 27

Chickens sold to each customer = 27 / 3

= 9 Chickens.

29. **(d)** Swati needs to make a cake = 2 eggs

To bake 3 cakes she will need = 3 × 2

= 6 eggs

So, 3 cakes, 6 eggs.

30. **(b)** Number 2 has the greatest probability of picking as, there are three blocks of number 2.

Calendar/Day/Date

OBJECTIVES

- Students will be able to distinguish between events occurring in time using terms.
- They will get the qualitative feel of long and short duration.

INTRODUCTION

TIME

Time is measured with the help of a clock or a watch. A clock has two hands.

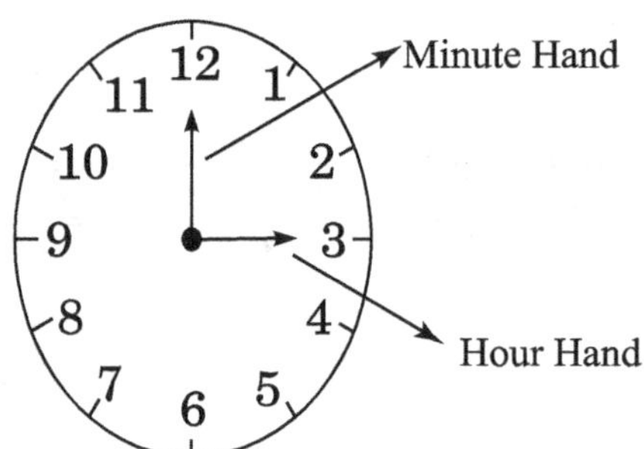

- The shorter hand is called the Hour Hand.
- The longer hand is called the Minute Hand.
- The face of the clock is divided into 12 equal divisions.
- The hour hand takes 12 hours to complete 1 round. It moves round the clock twice a day.
- The minute hand takes 1 hour to complete one round. In 1 round, minute hand moves through 60 small divisions, each of which is equal to 1 minute.

- On the clock, there are 5 minutes between the two consecutive numbers.

- The minute hand moves 24 times round the clock in one day.

DAYS

The duration of 24 hours (from one mid-night to the next mid-night) is called 1 day.

$$1 \text{ day} = 24 \text{ hours}$$

Days of a Week

- There are 7 days in a week.

- The names of the seven days of the week in order are:

Monday	Tuesday	Wednesday	Thursday	Friday	Saturday	Sunday
First	Second	Third	Fourth	Fifth	Sixth	Seventh
1st	2nd	3rd	4th	5th	6th	7th

Yesterday, Today, Tomorrow

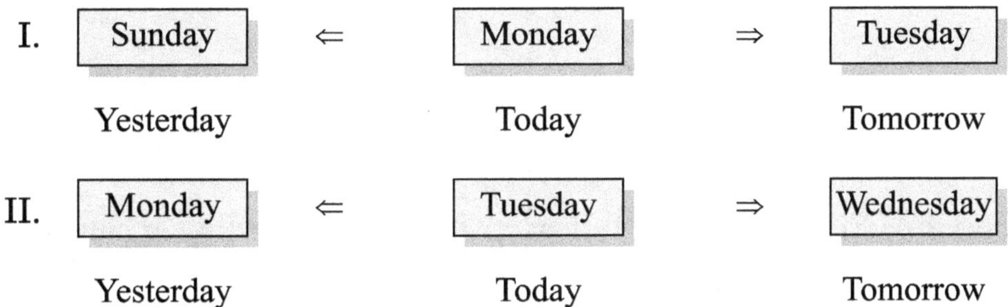

MONTHS

Some months have 30 days and some have 31 days except February which has 28 days. But in a leap year, the month February has 29 days.

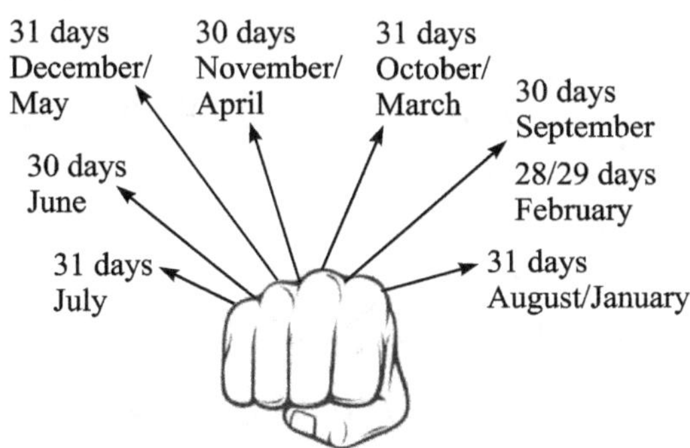

If yesterday was Monday, what day will be the fifth day from today?

    (a) Friday   (b) Saturday   (c) Sunday   (d) Monday

Ans. (b)

Explanation: If yesterday was Monday. So, today is Tuesday. Then, Fifth day from Tuesday will be Saturday.

Example 2:

Raju correctly remembers that Priya's birthday was after Tuesday but before Friday. Shivam correctly remembers that Priya's birthday was after Wednesday but before Sunday, on which day of the week does Priya's birthday definitely fall?

    (a) Monday   (b) Thursday   (c) Saturday   (d) Friday

Ans. (b)

Explanation:

According to Raju, Priya's birthday falls = Wednesday or | Thursday. |

According to Shivam Priya's birthday falls = | Thursday. |, Friday or Saturday.

So, Priya's birthday falls on Thursday.

Example 3:

Babli has a dental appointment on April 15. April 1 is Thursday. On which day of the week is her appointment?

    (a) Monday   (b) Tuesday   (c) Wednesday   (d) Thursday

Ans. (d)

Explanation: April 1 is Thursday.

$$1 + 7 = 8^{th} \text{ will be Thursday.}$$

$$8 + 7 = 15^{th} \text{ will be Thursday.}$$

Example 4:

The clock shows the time a magic show started. The magic show ended $1\frac{1}{2}$ hours later. When did the magic show end?

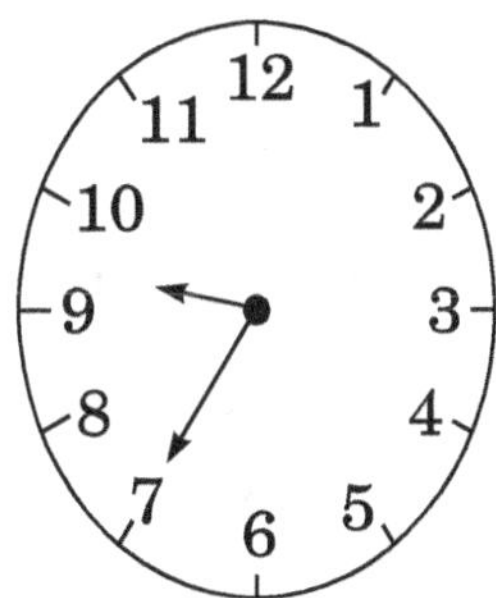

   (a) 11 : 05 p.m.   (b) 10 : 30 p.m.   (c) 11 : 15 p.m.   (d) 10 : 00 p.m.

Ans. (a)

Explanation: The clock shows = 9 : 35 p.m.

After $1\frac{1}{2}$ hours = 9 : 35 + 1 : 30 = 11 : 05 p.m.

Example 5:

180 seconds earlier than 14:25 is _________ ?

   (a) 2 : 22 p.m.   (b) 2 : 45 p.m.   (c) 2 : 22 a.m.   (d) 2 : 45 a.m.

Ans. (a)

Explanation:

$$1 \text{ minute} = 60 \text{ seconds}$$
$$180 \text{ seconds} = 180/60 = 3 \text{ minute}$$

3 minutes earlier than 14 : 25 is 2 : 22 p.m.

LEVEL-1

1. Reeta spent 25 minutes on her homework last night. She started at 5 : 50 p.m. What time did she finish her work?

   (a) 6 : 15 p.m. (b) 5 : 10 p. m.
   (c) 5 : 15 p.m. (d) 6 : 10 p.m.

Direction (Qs. 2-5): Read the calendar and answer the following questions.

January 2016						
Sun	Mon	Tue	Wed	Thu	Fri	Sat
					1 New year	2
3	4	5	6	7	8	9
10	11	12	13	14	15	16
17	18 Martin Luther king's Birthday	19	20	21	22	23
24	25	26	27	28	29	30
31						

2. When is Martin Luther King's Birthday falling?
   (a) 4   (b) 18
   (c) 25   (d) 1

3. How many Sundays are there in this month?
   (a) 2   (b) 3
   (c) 4   (d) 5

4. How many working days are there in this month?
   (a) 26   (b) 28
   (c) 25   (d) 31

5. 19th Jan 2016 is falling on which day?
   (a) Monday   (b) Tuesday
   (c) Friday   (d) Wednesday

6. It takes 12 minutes to bathe a dog at Dr. Rishi's Dog home. How long would it take to bathe 10 dogs?
   (a) 60 minutes
   (b) 100 minutes
   (c) 120 minutes
   (d) None of these

7. How many weeks are there in 1 year?
   (a) 55   (b) 53
   (c) 51   (d) 52

8. The month with neither 31 nor 30 days is?
   (a) April   (b) November
   (c) February   (d) March

9. Number of weekend days in a week are ________ ?

   (a) 4   (b) 2
   (c) 1   (d) 5

10. Shruti wanted to travel around the world. She worked it out that the trip would take her five years. How many months would that be?

   (a) 15 months   (b) 65 months
   (c) 60 months   (d) 52 months

11. Maya will arrive at the Taj Palace on 10th July and will stay three nights. What date will Maya check out the hotel?

   (a) 12th July   (b) 13th July
   (c) 15th July   (d) 11th July

12. If today is Tuesday, 24th February, then previous Tuesday fell on ________.

   (a) 19th (b) 18th
   (c) 17th (d) 16th

13. Rohan was born on September 8th, Jaspreet was born on November 8th of the same year. How many months older is Rohan?

   (a) 3 months   (b) 5 months
   (c) 4 months   (d) 2 months

14. If today is Friday and Anita's birthday is on 3rd day after today, then on which day she will celebrate her birthday?

   (a) Sunday   (b) Tuesday
   (c) Monday   (d) Friday

15. If today is Monday, then what day will be 8th day?

   (a) Thursday   (b) Monday
   (c) Friday   (d) Saturday

Direction (Qs. 16-20): Read the statement and use the correct options. Use the words which best estimate the time of activity.

16. Watching a baseball match?

   (a) Minutes   (b) Hours
   (c) Days   (d) Weeks

17. Painting a house?

   (a) Hours   (b) Weeks
   (c) Years   (d) Months

18. Pratima visits a museum. How long does she spends in the museum?

   (a) Hours   (b) Weeks
   (c) Month   (d) Year

19. Practising for a play?

   (a) Hours
   (b) Days
   (c) Year
   (d) None of these

20. Cooking Food.

   (a) Seconds   (b) Hours
   (c) Days   (d) Months

21. Meghna was born on April 8, 1985. How old will she be on her birthday in 2016?

   (a) 29   (b) 30
   (c) 31   (d) 35

22. Which month comes before May and after March?

   (a) January
   (b) June
   (c) April
   (d) None of these

Directions (Qs. 23 -30): Read the Calendar and answer the following questions.

January 2014						
Sun	Mon	Tue	Wed	Thu	Fri	Sat
			1	2	3	4
5	6	7	8	9	10	11
12	13	14	15	16	17	18
19	20	21	22	23	24	25
26	27	28	29	30	31	

23. What is the day after two days of Wednesday 1 Jan 2014?

   (a) Monday   (b) Saturday

   (c) Sunday   (d) Friday

24. What will be the day of 21st of January 2014?

   (a) Monday   (b) Sunday

   (c) Tuesday   (d) Saturday

25. How many days are there in January?

   (a) 27   (b) 30

   (c) 31   (d) 29

26. What is the day before 27th January?

   (a) Saturday   (b) Monday

   (c) Sunday   (d) Friday

27. How many full weeks are there in January?

   (a) 5   (b) 3

   (c) 2   (d) 4

28. What day is the 1st day of the month?

   (a) Tuesday

   (b) Wednesday

   (c) Friday

   (d) Saturday

29. Riya goes on holiday on the 4th January for 10 days. What date does she return?

   (a) 15th Jan

   (b) 14th Jan

   (c) 12th Jan

   (d) None of these

30. What will be the last day of the month?

   (a) Wednesday

   (b) Tuesday

   (c) Saturday

   (d) Friday

31. Gaurav's birthday falls just after 4th Tuesday of September 20XX. The day on which Gaurav celebrates his birthday is _________ ?

September 20XX						
Sun	Mon	Tue	Wed	Thu	Fri	Sat
		1	2	3	4	5
6	7	8	9	10	11	12
13	14	15	16	17	18	19
20	21	22	23	24	25	26
27	28	29	30			

(a) 23rd September

(b) 30th September

(c) 1st October

(d) 29th September

(Olympiad)

32. How many possible combinations of 1 watch and 1 mobile phone can be formed using the given information?

Watches	Mobile phones
Titan	Nokia
Maxima	Motorola
Fastrack	Samsung
Sonata	Tata
	Reliance
	HTC
	Blackberry

(a) 18

(b) 14

(c) 11

(d) 28

(Olympiad)

33. Garima goes to office everyday in July 20XX. If each Sunday and all multiples of 5 are holidays, then how many days she will go to office?

July 20XX						
Sun	Mon	Tue	Wed	Thu	Fri	Sat
		1	2	3	4	5
6	7	8	9	10	11	12
13	14	15	16	17	18	19
20	21	22	23	24	25	26
27	28	29	30	31		

(a) 21

(b) 23

(c) 22

(d) 24

(Olympiad)

34. If the given clock is 45 minutes slow, then the correct time after half an hour will be _________ ?

(a) 6 O'clock

(b) 6 : 30

(c) 7 O'clock

(d) 5 : 30

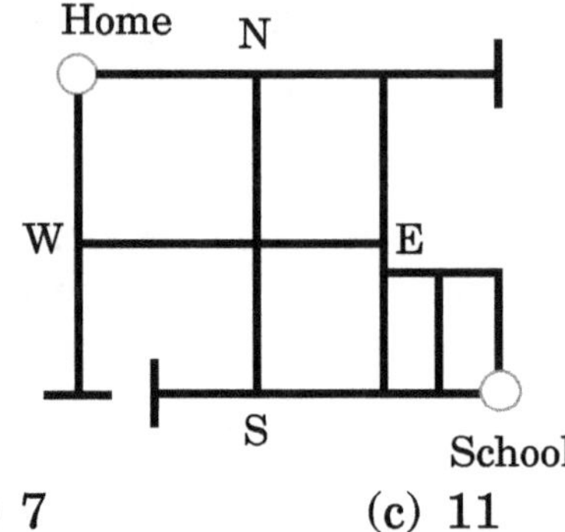

(Olympiad)

35. In how many ways can Garima travel from Home to School, if moving North and West are not permitted?

(a) 0   (b) 7   (c) 11   (d) None of these

(Olympiad)

36. Maahi's swimming classes starts from 15th October and lasts till 30th October. If every Sunday is a holiday, then for how many days will she go for swimming classes? **(2020)**

(a) 12

(b) 14

(c) 15

(d) 17

OCTOBER 20XX						
Sun	Mon	Tue	Wed	Thu	Fri	Sat
				1	2	3
4	5	6	7	8	9	10
11	12	13	14	15	16	17
18	19	20	21	22	23	24
25	26	27	28	29	30	31

37. Mukul's birthday falls on the day just before the 4th Tuesday of June 2019. The date on which Mukul celebrates his birthday is ______________.

(2022)

June 2019						
SUN	MON	TUE	WED	THU	FRI	SAT
						1
2	3	4	5	6	7	8

(a) 18th June (b) 26th June (c) 24th June (d) 25th June

Answers and Explanations

Level-1

1. (a) $5:50 + 25$ minutes $= 6:15$.
2. (b) Martin Luther's birthday is falling on 18th of Jan.
3. (d) There are 5 Sundays in this month.
4. (a) $31 - 5 = 26$ working days.
5. (b) 19th Jan 2016 is falling on Tuesday.
6. (c) Time taken for 1 dog
   $= 12$ Minutes
   Time taken for 10 dogs $= 12 \times 10 = 120$ minutes
7. (d) There are 52 weeks in a year.
8. (c) The month with neither 31 nor 30 day is February.
9. (b) Number of weekend days in week are 2.
10. (c) $12 \times 5 = 60$ months
11. (b) Maya will stay 3 nights in the hotel

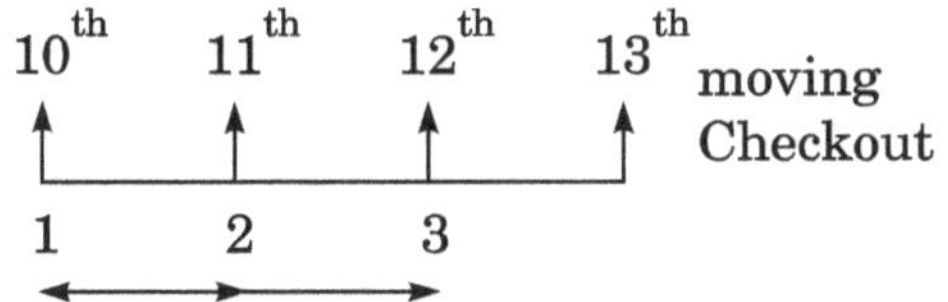

12. (c) Previous Tuesday falls on 7 days before 24th February, i.e., 17th February.
13. (d) 2 months.
14. (c)

Today	Next day	Second day	Third day
Friday	Saturday	Sunday	Monday

So, she will celebrate her birthday on Monday.

15. (b) If today is Monday, then the 8th day will be Monday.

16. (b) Hours
17. (d) Months
18. (a) Hours
19. (b) Days.
20. (b) Hours.
21. (c) Meghna on April 8, 1985
    Her age is $= 2016$

    $= 31$ years
22. (c) April
23. (b) Saturday
24. (c) Tuesday
25. (c) 31
26. (c) Sunday
27. (b) 3 weeks
28. (b) Wednesday
29. (b) 14th Jan
30. (d) Friday
31. (a) The day on which Gaurav celebrates his birthday is 23rd September.
32. (d) There are 28 possible combinations of 1 watch and 1 mobile phone can be formed.
33. (c) She will go to office 22 days.
34. (a) The correct time after half an hour will be 6 O'clock.
35. (c) 11 ways can Garima travel from Home to school, if moving north and west is not permitted.
36. (b) No. of days from 15th October to 30th October $= 16$ days

   No. of Sundays $= 2$

   Days left for swimming classes $= 16 - 2 = 14$.
37. (c)

Problem-Solving

OBJECTIVES

- Students will develop the ability to understand what the goal of the problem is and what rules could be applied that represent the key to solving the problem.
- They will develop abstract thinking and creative approach.

INTRODUCTION

The process of working through details of a problem to reach a solution. Problem solving may include mathematical or systematic operations and can be a gauge of an individual's critical thinking skills.

Four Stages of Problem Solving

Stage 1 :   Understand and explore the problem;

Stage 2 :   Find a strategy;

Stage 3 :   Use the strategy to solve the problem;

Stage 4 :   Look back and reflect on the solution.

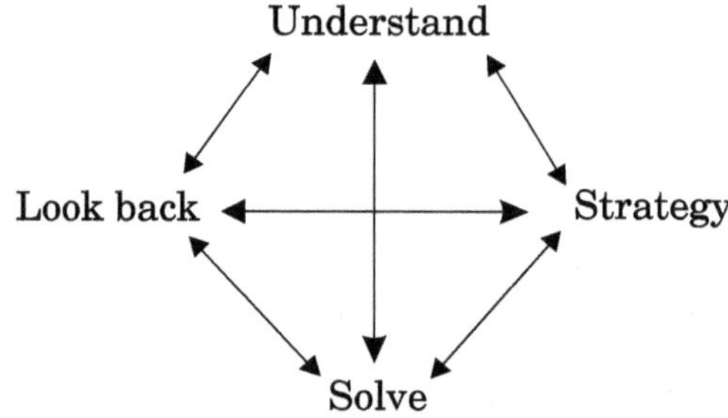

Example 1:

Jay is 85 cm tall. His father is twice as tall as Jay. How tall is Jay's mother if she is 15 cm shorter than his father?

    (a) 1 m 55 cm   (b) 1 m 66 cm   (c) 1 m 72 cm   (d) 1 m 90 cm

Ans. (a)

Explanation:

$$\begin{aligned}
\text{Jay's height} &= 85 \text{ cm} \\
\text{His father's height} &= 85 \times 2 = 170 \text{ cm} \\
\text{His mother's height} &= 170 - 15 = 155 \text{ cm} \\
&= 1 \text{ m } 55 \text{ cm.}
\end{aligned}$$

Example 2:

There are 18 pupils in a group. There are 10 boys and the rest are girls. 7 pupils are wearing glasses. If 3 girls are wearing glasses, how many boys are not wearing glasses?

    (a) 3   (b) 6   (c) 8   (d) 9

Ans. (b)

Explanation:

$$\begin{aligned}
\text{Total pupils} &= 18 \\
\text{Number of boys} &= 10 \\
\text{Number of girls} &= 18 - 10 = 8 \\
\text{Number of pupils wearing glasses} &= 7 \\
\text{Number of girls wearing glasses} &= 3 \\
\text{Number of boys wearing glasses} &= 7 - 3 = 4 \\
\text{Number of boys not wearing glasses} &= 10 - 4 = 6.
\end{aligned}$$

Example 3:

If $\bigcirc > \triangle$, $\triangle > \heartsuit$ and $\heartsuit > \diamondsuit$, then which of the following is definitely wrong?

    (a) $\bigcirc > \diamondsuit$ (b) $\bigcirc > \triangle$

    (c) $\triangle > \diamondsuit$ (d) $\diamondsuit > \bigcirc$

Ans. (d)

Explanation:

$$\bigcirc > \triangle > \heartsuit > \diamondsuit$$

Options (a), (b) and (c) are correct but option (d) is definitely wrong as $\bigcirc > \diamondsuit$.

Example 4:

Tom is $6\frac{3}{4}$ years old. John is $6\frac{1}{2}$ years old. Jim is 6.25 years old. Mark is 6.5 years old. Which two children are at the same age?

    (a) Tom and Mark   (b) John and Jim

    (c) Tom and Jim   (d) John and Mark

Ans. (d)

Explanation:

$$1 \text{ year} = 12 \text{ months}$$
$$\frac{3}{4} \text{ year} = 9 \text{ months}$$
$$\text{Hence, Tom's age} = 6 \text{ years } 9 \text{ months}$$
$$\frac{1}{2} \text{ year} = 6 \text{ months.}$$
$$\text{Hence, John's age} = 6 \text{ years } 6 \text{ months}$$
$$\text{Jim's age} = 6 \text{ years } 3 \text{ months}$$
$$\text{Mark's age} = 6 \text{ years } 6 \text{ months.}$$

Therefore, John and Mark are at the same age.

Direction (Examples. 5–8): Read the information given below carefully and answer the following questions. A, B, C, D, E, F and G are sitting in a row facing north.

- A is sitting at the right end and G is sitting at the left end.
- F is the immediate right of E.
- E is 4th to the right of G.
- C is the neighbour of B and D.
- D is third to the left of A.

Example 5:

Who is/are to the left of C?

    (a) Only B   (b) G, B and D   (c) G and B   (d) D, E, F and A

Ans. (c)

Explanation:

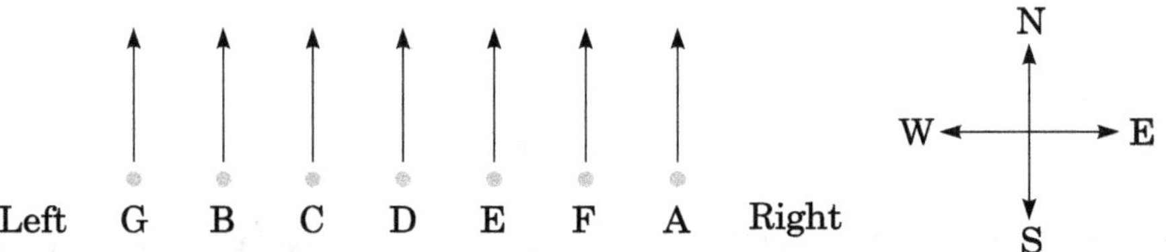

G and B are to the left of C.

Example 6:

Which of the following statements is not true?

    (a) A is at one of the ends.   (b) E is to the immediate right of D.

    (c) G is at one of the ends.   (d) F is sitting between E and A.

Ans. (b)

Explanation:

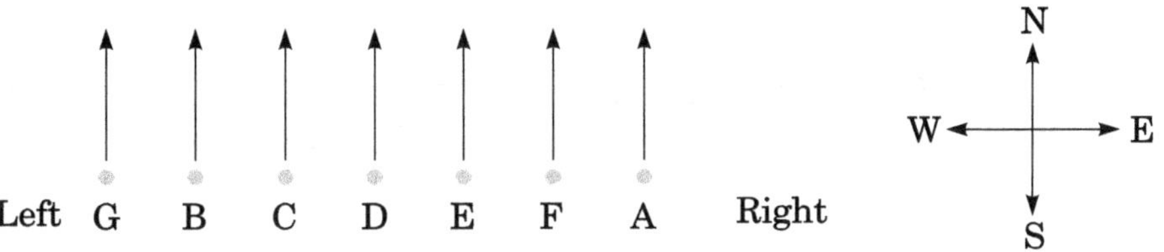

E is to the immediate right of D.

Example 7:

Who are the neighbours of B?

    (a) C and D   (b) G and F   (c) C and G   (d) C and E

Ans. (c)

Explanation:

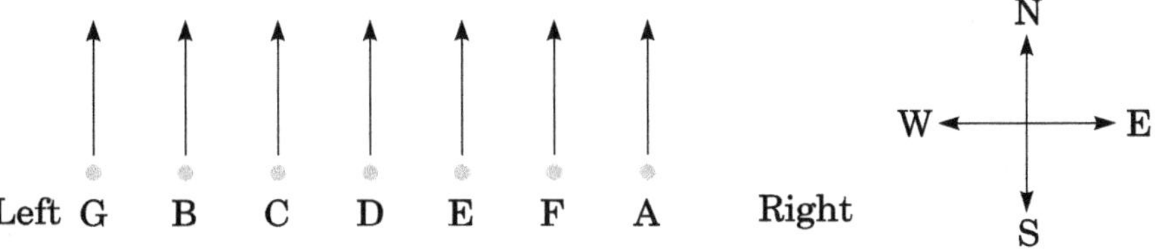

C and G are the neighbours of B.

Example 8:

What is the position of D?

    (a) Between B and C   (b) Extreme left

    (c) Centre   (d) Extreme right

Ans. (c)

Explanation:

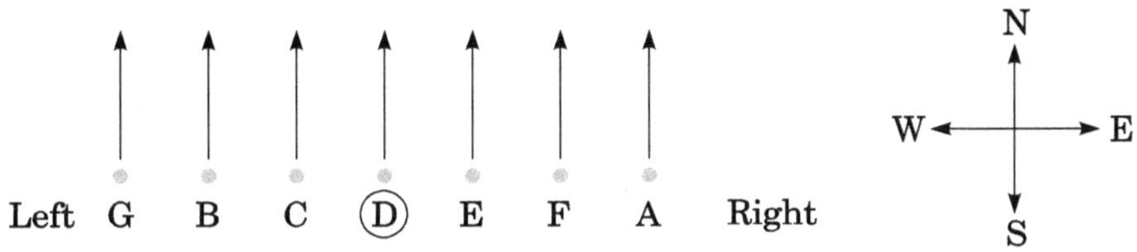

D is in Centre.

LEVEL-1

1. Tanni broke half as many balloons as Ritika. Altogether they broke 18 balloons. Ritika broke 12 balloons. How many balloons did Tanni break?

    (a) 9   (b) 8   (c) 10   (d) 6

Direction (Qs. 2–3): Study the given information carefully and answer the questions.

- There are four friends A, B, C and D.
- Each one is proficient in one of the games, Namely: Badminton, Volleyball, Cricket and Hockey.
- D Plays hockey.
- C does not play either Badminton or Cricket.
- A does not play cricket.

2. Who plays cricket?

    (a) A   (b) B   (c) C   (d) D

3. Which game is played by C?

    (a) Hockey   (b) Badminton   (c) Cricket   (d) Volleyball

4. A blacksmith has three iron articles A, B and C, each having a different weight ?

- A weighs twice as much as C.
- B weighs half as much as C.

    Which of the following represents the descending order of weighs of the articles?

    (a) A, B, C   (b) B, A, C   (c) A, C, B   (d) C, A, B

5. If A * B means A and B are of the same age; A – B means B is younger than A; then Vijay * Saurabh – Reena means?

    (a) Reena is the youngest   (b) Reena is the oldest

    (c) Saurabh is younger than Reena   (d) None of these

Direction (Qs. 6–7): Four boys took part in a race. Raj finished before Mohit but behind Gaurav. Ashish finished behind Mohit.

6. Who won the race?

    (a) Raj   (b) Mohit   (c) Gaurav   (d) Ashish

7. Who was on the second position?

    (a) Raj   (b) Gaurav   (c) Mohit   (d) Ashish

8. Paresh started with 32 baseball cards. He sold 8 cards. Then he bought 12 more. How many cards does he have now?

    (a) 36   (b) 40   (c) 24   (d) 30

9. Rani's desk is in the third row from the front and the second row from the back of classroom. The desks in the classroom are lined up in straight rows. Her desk is also the third from the left and first from the right. How many desks are there?

    (a) 9 desks   (b) 12 desks   (c) 15 desks   (d) 16 desks

10. Cocky the Hen lays eggs this week.

    - There are more than 4 eggs.

    - There are fewer than 7 eggs.

    - There are not 5 eggs.

    How many eggs does Cocky lay?

    (a) 5   (b) 6   (c) 7   (d) 4

11. 2 Pineapples produce 3 glasses of juice. How many Pineapples are needed to produce 6 glasses of juices?

    (a) 3 Pineapples   (b) 4 Pineapples

    (c) 5 Pineapples   (d) 6 Pineapples

Direction (Qs. 12 and 13): A, B, C, D and E are five boys sitting in a line facing to south as shown in the figure.

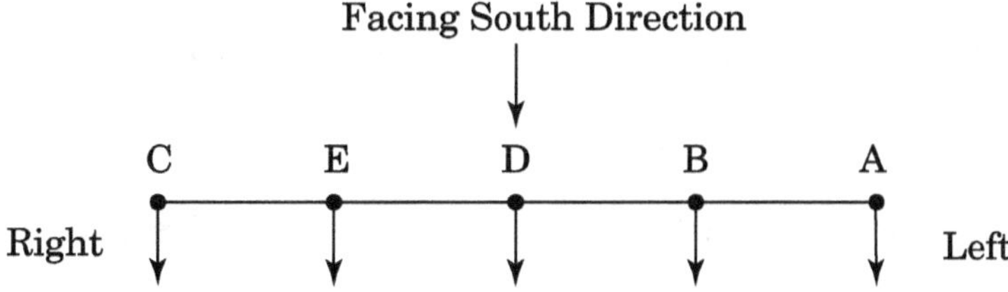

Now, answer the following questions.

12. If B shifts to place of E, E shifts to the place of A and A shifts in the place of B, then who will be second to the right?

(a) B   (b) E   (c) A   (d) D

13. If C and D interchange their positions then, who will be second to the right of A?

(a) C   (b) D   (c) E   (d) B

14. Four families A, B, C and D are living in houses in a row. B has A and D as neighbours. D has B and C as neighbours. Who lives next to A?

(a) A   (b) B   (c) C   (d) D

15. There are 35 boats. If each boat can hold 49 people. How many people in total do all the boats hold?

(a) 1500   (b) 1800   (c) 2000   (d) 1715

Direction (Qs. 16-18): Read the given information carefully and answer the following questions.

Five children are standing in line waiting for the ice-cream shop to open.

- Shivam is in the exact middle of the line.
- Raj is directly behind Shubam.
- Abhay is not first or last.
- Kavya is on the first.

16. Who is standing at last?

(a) Abhay   (b) Raj   (c) Shivam   (d) Kavya

17. Who is standing between Shivam and Raj?

(a) Kavya   (b) Abhay   (c) Shubam   (d) None of these

18. What is the correct order of line?

(a) Kavya ← Shubam ← Shivam ← Raj ← Abhay

(b) Kavya ← Abhay ← Shivam ← Shubam ← Raj

(c) Kavya ← Raj ← Shivam ← Abhay ← Shubam

(d) Kavya ← Raj ← Shivam ← Shubam ← Abhay

19. Neha, Radhika, Riya and Tara are playing in the park. On one of the see-saws, Neha is sitting on the left and Riya on the right. The see-saw tilts towards the right. On another see-saw, it tilts towards Radhika when Tara and Radhika sit on opposite sides. The four of them then decide to play on one see-saw. If Riya and Radhika sit together on one side and Neha and Tara both sit on the other side, to which side will the see-saw tilt?

(a) Neha, Radhika

(b) Riya, Radhika

(c) Neha, Tara

(d) None of these

Direction (Qs. 20 and 21): Read the given information and answer the following questions.

Four friends, Raj, Amit, Manav and Raghav like to play four different sports namely Cricket, Tennis, Football and Hockey, but not in the same order.

- Raj likes neither Tennis nor Hockey.
- Amit likes to play Cricket.
- Manav does not like to play Tennis.

20. Which sport is played by Raj?

(a) Cricket   (b) Hockey   (c) Tennis   (d) Football

21. Who plays Tennis as his favourite sport?

(a) Amit   (b) Raj   (c) Manav   (d) Raghav

Direction (Qs. 22-24): Read the given information carefully and answer the following questions.

"My name is Mukul. I live between Mayank and Anshul."

"My name is Mayank. I don't live in house number 3."

22. Who lives in house number 1?

    (a) Mukul   (b) Anshul   (c) Mayank   (d) None

23. In which house number does Mukul live?

    (a) 1   (b) 2   (c) 3   (d) None

24. Who lives in house number 3?

    (a) Mukul   (b) Mayank   (c) Anshul   (d) None

25. There are three separate large black boxes, and inside each large box there are two separate small red boxes, inside each of these small boxes, there is one smaller blue box. How many boxes are there altogether?

    (a) 9   (b) 12   (c) 15   (d) 18

Direction (Qs. 26 and 27): Read the given information carefully and answer the following questions.

- Five Girls receive gifts.
- These gifts are: a scooter, a shirt, a nintendo, a computer and a radio.
- Mayra loves clothing.
- Antra loves the outdoors.
- Sanya hates electronic games.
- Neha dislikes music and computers.
- Sapna loves to type.

26. Who receives radio as a gift?

    (a) Mayra   (b) Antra   (c) Sanya   (d) Anna

27. Sapna receives which gift?

    (a) Shirt   (b) Scooter   (c) Radio   (d) Computer

28. Four people are standing in a queue outside the ATM for cash withdrawal. The two persons standing at the extreme ends are Raj and Abhay. Anita is in front of Abhay. Reena is standing behind Raj.

    Counting from the front, at which place is Anita?

    (a) First   (b) Second   (c) Third   (d) Fourth

29. Nancy's mom baked cookies. Nancy wants to share the cookies equally with five friends. What information is needed to determine how many cookies each person could get?

    (a) The size of the cookies

    (b) The kind of cookies

(c) The time it took to bake the cookies

(d) The number of cookies baked

30. Diya asked the students in her class if they have any pets. Her results are shown below.

- 5 students have cats.
- 9 students have fish.
- 6 students have parrots.
- 13 students have dogs.
- No student has a frog.

Based on the above information, which statement is most likely to be true?

(a) Frogs are the least popular pets.

(b) Fish are better pets than dogs.

(c) Cats are better pets than fish.

(d) Frogs are the most popular pets.

31. There is a certain relationship between the pair of figures on the either side of ::. Identify the relationship of the given pair and find the missing figure. **(2022)**

△ : 12 :: △(▽) : ?

(a) 7   (b) 15   (c) 9   (d) 12

LEVEL-2

1. Six friends Ansh, Raj, Dev, Vinay, Raghav and Amit met up to go bowling together and then split into 2 teams, three in each. If Ansh, Dev and Amit were in one team, who did they play against?

(a) Ansh, Raj and Vinay   (b) Dev, Vinay and Raghav

(c) Dev, Raghav and Ansh   (d) Raj, Vinay and Raghav

Direction (Qs. 2-4): Read the given information carefully and answer the following questions.

Five boys are sitting on a bench facing north. Avi is to the left of Aarav and right of Nikunj. Vipul is sitting on the right end. Atul is between Aarav and Vipul.

2. Who is in sitting in the middle?

(a) Avi   (b) Aarav   (c) Nikunj   (d) Vipul

3. Who is second from right?

(a) Avi   (b) Vipul   (c) Aarav   (d) Atul

4. What is the position of Avi in sitting arrangement?
   (a) Second form left   (b) Second from right
   (c) Fourth from left   (d) In the middle

5. In a school, there were 5 teachers.
   - A and B were teaching Hindi and English.
   - C and B were teaching English and Geography.
   - D and A were teaching Mathematics and Hindi.
   - E and B were teaching History and French.

   Who among the teachers was teaching maximum number of subjects?
   (a) B   (b) A   (c) D   (d) E

6. There are five different houses A to E in a row. A is right of B and E is to the left of C and right to A, B is to the right of D. Which of the houses is in the middle?
   (a) C   (b) B   (c) A   (d) E

7. Compare the knowledge of persons X, Y, Z, A, B and C in relation to each other. X knows more than A, Y knows as much as B. Z know less than C. A knows more than Y. The best knowledgeable person amongst all is:
   (a) C   (b) X
   (c) A   (d) Cannot be determined

8. Five men A, B, C, D and E read newspaper. The one who reads first gives it to C. The one who reads last had taken from A. E was not the first or last to read. There were two readers between B and A.

   Who read the newspaper last?
   (a) A   (b) D   (c) E   (d) C

9. Five boys took part in a race. Raj finished before Mehul but behind Garv. Ashish finished before Shabd but behind Mehul. Who won the race?
   (a) Raj   (b) Mehul   (c) Garv   (d) Shabd

10. On a trip there are 11 children and 1 adult per boat. If a total of 96 people went on this boat trip, how many children were there?
    (a) 85   (b) 86   (c) 88   (d) 90

11. I-Gmail runs faster than Yahoo.

    II-Hotmail runs faster than Gmail.

    III-Yahoo runs faster than Hotmail.

    If the first two statements are true, the third statement is __________ ?
    (a) True   (b) False   (c) Uncertain   (d) None of these

12. Meeta has to read 12 books over the summer. If each book has 260 pages, how many pages does Meeta have to read in all?

(a) 3120   (b) 3220   (c) 3520   (d) 3820

Direction (Qs. 13-16): Read the given information carefully and answer the following questions carefully.

Six students A, B, C, D, E and F are sitting in the field. A and B are from Delhi while the rest are from Bangaluru. D and F are tall while others are short. A, C and D are girls while others are boys.

13. Which is the tall girl from Bangaluru?

(a) C   (b) E   (c) F   (d) D

14. Which tall boy does not belong to Delhi?

(a) B   (b) E   (c) F   (d) A

15. How many girls belong to Bangaluru?

(a) 1   (b) 2   (c) 3   (d) 4

16. How many students from Delhi are short?

(a) 2   (b) 1   (c) 4   (d) 4

17. I. Preeti is taller than Megha.   II. Meet is taller than Megha.

III. Preeti is taller than Meet.

If the first two statements are true, the third statement is?

(a) True   (b) False   (c) Uncertain   (d) None of these

18. Daya has a brother Anil, Daya is the son of Chandra. Devesh is Chandra's father. In term of relationship, what is Anil to Devesh?

(a) Son   (b) Brother   (c) Grandson   (d) Grandfather

19. Rahul's mother is the only daughter of Monika's father. How is Monika's husband related to Rahul?

(a) Father   (b) Uncle   (c) Brother   (d) Grandfather

20. Deepak is brother of Ravi, Rekha is sister of Atul. Ravi is son of Rekha. How is Deepak related to Rekha?

(a) Father   (b) Son   (c) Nephew   (d) Brother

Direction (Qs. 21-25): Read the given statements carefully and answer the following questions.

Seven boys A, B, C, D, E, F, and G live on seven floors. Ground, 1st, 2nd, 3rd, 4th, 5th and 6th (Top), not necessarily in that order. A lives just above B's floor.

F lives at top floor. E lives in between B's and C's floor. D lives just above the A's floor. G lives on the ground floor and E lives on the second floor.

21. Who lives on the first floor?

    (a) B   (b) C   (c) E   (d) D

22. Who lives on the second floor?

    (a) F   (b) C   (c) E   (d) A

23. Who lives on the third floor?

    (a) B   (b) C   (c) F   (d) G

24. Who lives on the fourth floor?

    (a) D   (b) F   (c) A   (d) E

25. Who lives on the fifth floor?

    (a) G   (b) E   (c) A   (d) D

26. Tom has more toys than Jonny and Bill. Albert has more toys than Tom. Which statement is true?

    (a) Jonny has more toys than Tom.   (b) Bill has more toys than Albert.

    (c) Jonny has more toys than Albert.   (d) Albert has more toys than Bill.

27. Sara, Juhi and Messy all have different jobs. One is engineer, one is a librarian and one is a doctor. Juhi loves to read books. Sara helps sick people. Who is engineer?

    (a) Sara   (b) Juhi

    (c) Messy   (d) Cannot be determined

Direction (Qs. 28-30): Read the given information carefully and answer the following questions.

- Four people ate pizza. One person had two slices, one person had three slices, one person had seven slices, one person had eight slices.
- Atul ate more than seven slices of pizza.
- Vasu ate fewer than seven slices of pizza.
- Abhay ate more than three slices of pizza.
- Dev ate the least slices of pizza.

28. Who ate two slices of pizza?

    (a) Atul   (b) Vasu   (c) Abhay   (d) Dev

29. Who ate more than seven slices of pizza?

    (a) Atul   (b) Vasu   (c) Abhay   (d) Dev

30. How many slices of pizza have been eaten by Vasu?

(a) 2   (b) 3   (c) 7   (d) 8

31. Take  as one cube and then count the number of cubes in the given soli(d)

(2022)

(a) 17   (b) 19   (c) 18   (d) 20

32. If X represents the average distance between the Earth and its Moon, while Y represents the average distance between the Earth and the Sun, then find the correct combination of statements with respect to X and Y.

1. Y is greater than X.   **(2022)**

2. Sum of X and Y is greater than five hundred thousands kilometres.

3. Difference of Y and X is greater than five hundred thousands kilometres.

(a) Only 1 and 2   (b) Only 3   (c) Only 1   (d) All 1, 2, 3

Answers and Explanations

Level-1

1. (d) Number of balloons broken by Ritika and Tanni = 18

   Number of balloons broken by Tanni = $12 \times \dfrac{1}{2} = 6$

2. (b)

Friends	Games
A	Badminton

B	Cricket
C	Volleyball
D	Hockey

B plays cricket.

3. (d) C plays volleyball.

4. (c) Descending order of weight is

   $$A > C > B$$

5. (a) Vijay and Saurabh are of the same age and Reena is younger than Saurabh.

Solutions (Qs. 6-7)

Gaurav > Raj > Mohit > Ashish

   (I)   (II)   (III)   (IV)

6. (c) Gaurav won the race.

7. (a) Raj was on the second position.

8. (a)

Total number of baseball cards = 32

Number of cards sold = 8

Number of cards after selling = 32 – 8 = 24

Number of cards Paresh bought = 12

Total number of cards Paresh has now = 24 + 12 = 36.

9. (b)

1	2	3
2		
3			→Rani's Desk
Left 4			Right

Hence, there are 12 desks in the classroom.

10. (b) 6 is more than 4 and less than 7.

11. (b) 2 Pineapples produce 3 glasses of juices.

We need $\frac{6}{3}$ = 2 times as many glasses

We need twice as many Pineapples: $2 \times 2 = 4$.

12. (a)

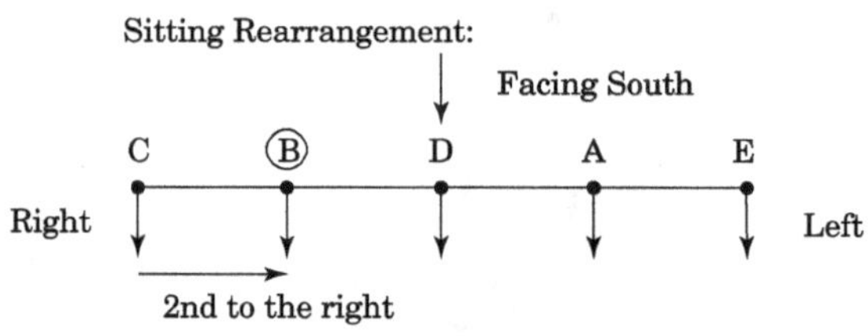

13. (a)

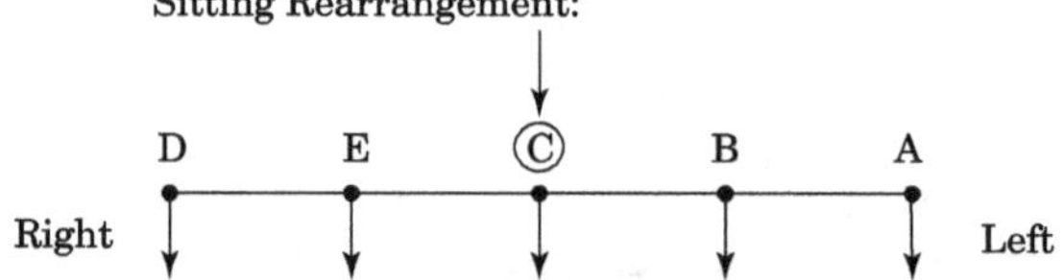

C will be second to the right of A.

14. (b) The information can be represented as:

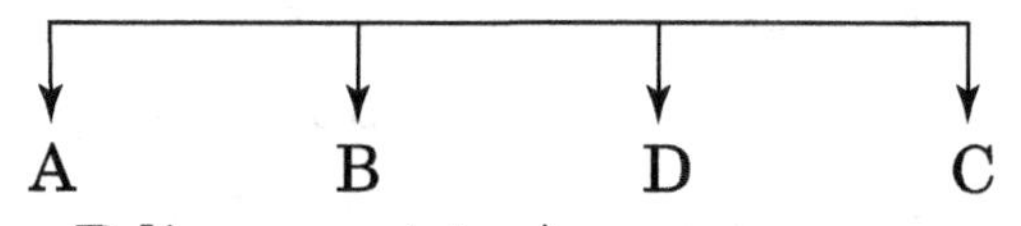

B lives next to A.

15. (d)

Number of boats = 35

Number of people held by 1 boat = 49

Total people in all boats = 35 × 49

$$= 1715.$$

Solutions: (16-18)

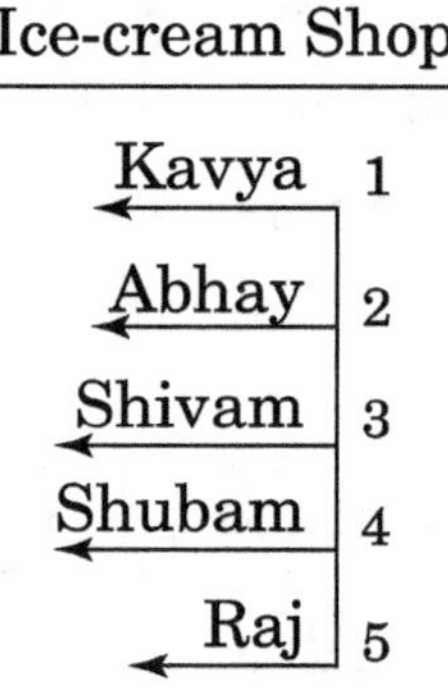

16. (b) Raj is standing at last.

17. (c) Shubam is standing between Shivam and Raj.

18. (b) Option (b) is the correct order.

19. (b) The see-saw tilts towards Riya's side because Riya is heavier than Neha and Radhika is heavier than Tara. Both are heavier. Neha and Tara are lighter. That is why see-saw tilts towards Riya and Radhika.

Solutions: (20 and 21)

Friends	Sports
Raj	Football
Amit	Cricket
Manav	Hockey
Raghav	Tennis

20. (d) Raj plays Football.

21. (d) Tennis is Raghav's favourite sport.

Solutions: (22-24)

Persons	House Number
Mukul	2
Mayank	1
Anshul	3

22. (c) Mayank lives in house number 1.

23. (b) Mukul lives in house number 2.

24. (c) Anshul lives in house number 3.

25. (c) 3 + 6 + 6 = 15

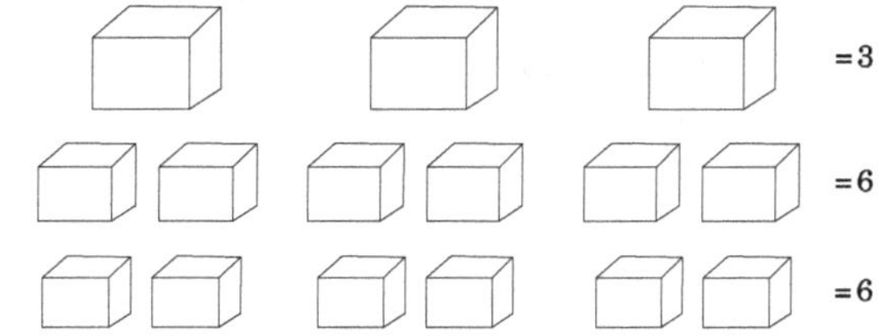

Solutions (Q 26-27)

Girls	Gifts
Mayra	Shirt
Antra	Scooter
Sanya	Radio
Neha	Nintendo
Sapna	Computer

26. (c) Sanya receives radio as a gift.

27. (d) Sapna receives computer as a gift.

28. (c) Four people in a queue

So, Anita is at third place counting from front.

29. (d) The number of cookies baked is needed to determine how many cookies each person could get.

30. (a) Option (a) is correct.

31. (c) 15. The relationship is: number of sides of inner figure × number of sides of outer figure.

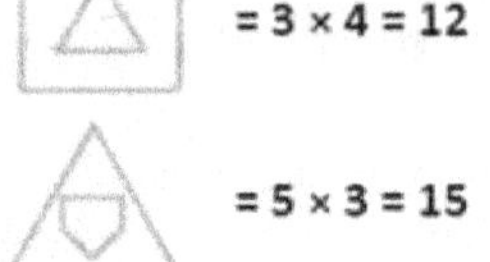

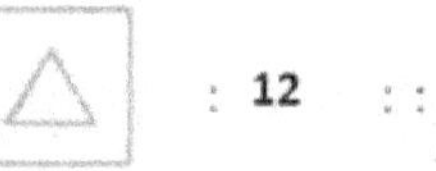

Level-2

1. (d) Team 1 : Ansh, Dev, Amit

Team 2 : Raj, Vinay, Raghav.

Solutions: (2-4)

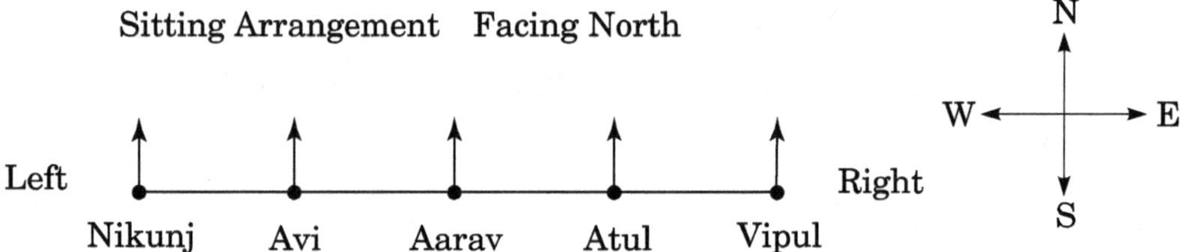

2. (b)   **3.** (d)   **4.** (a)

5. (a)

Teachers	English	Hindi	Maths	Geography	History	French
A	✓	✓	✓			
B	✓	✓		✓	✓	✓
C	✓			✓		
D		✓	✓			
E					✓	✓

Therefore, Teacher B teaches maximum number of subjects i.e. 4.

6. (c) Houses' sequence in a row:

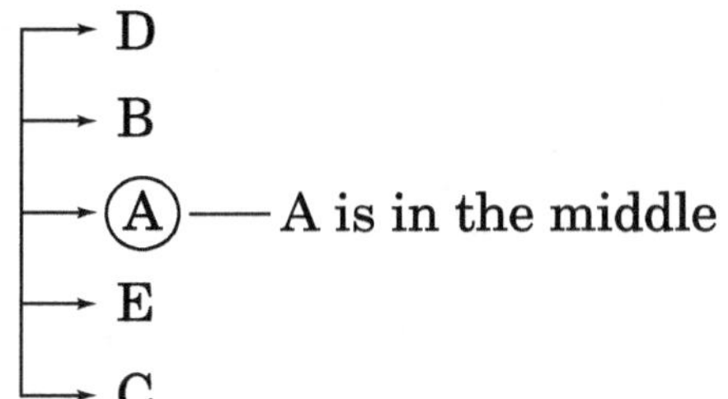

7. (d) X > A, Y = B

C > Z, X > A > Y = B

But we do not know the position of C and Z in relation to others . So, (d) is the answer.

8. (b) Readers Position

Position	Readers
I	B
II	C
III	E
IV	A
V	D

So, D reads the newspaper last.

9. (c)

Garv > Raj > Mehul > Ashish > Shabd.

(1)   (2)   (3)   (4)   (5)

So, Garv won the race.

10. (c) Total people per boat = 11 + 1
= 12
Total people on trip = 96
Boats required for 96 people
= 96 ÷ 12 = 8
There were 8 adults
96 − 8 = 88 children.

11. (b) Statement I:
Gmail > Yahoo,
Statement II:
Hotmail > Gmail
Statement III:
Hotmail > Gmail > Yahoo.
Therefore, the third statement is false.

12. (a) Number of books = 12

Number of pages in 1 book = 260

Total Number of pages Meeta have to read in all= 12 × 260

= 3120 pages.

Solutions (13-16)

Students	Delhi	Bangaluru	Tall	Short	Girls	Boys
A	√			√	√	
B	√			√		√
C		√		√	√	
D		√	√		√	
E		√		√		√
F		√	√			√

13. (d) Clearly, D is the tall girl from Bangaluru.

14. (c) F is the tall boy who does not belong to Delhi.

15. (b) Only 2 girls belong to Bangaluru.

16. (a) Only 2 students from Delhi are short.

17. (c) Statement I :

Preeti > Megha

Statement II :

Meet > Megha

Statement III :

Preeti > Meet (uncertain).

18. (c) Anil is the brother of Daya and Daya is the son of Chandra. So, Anil is the son of Chandra. Now Devesh is the father of Chandra. So, Anil is the grandson of Devesh.

19. (a) Clearly, the only daughter of Monika's father is Monika herself. So, Rahul's mother is Monika. Thus, Monika's husband is the father of Rahul.

20. (b) Deepak is the brother of Ravi, who is the son of Rekha. Therefore, Deepak is the son of Rekha.

Solutions: (21-25).

Floor Arrangement

Floor	Owner
6th (Top)	F
5th	D
4th	A

3rd	B
2nd	E
1st	C
Ground	G

21. (b) C lives on the first floor.

22. (c) E lives on the second floor.

23. (a) B lives on the third floor.

24. (c) A lives on the fourth floor.

25. (d) D lives on the fifth floor.

26. (d) Albert > Tom > Jonny and Bill.

Albert has the most number of toys.

27. (c)

Juhi → Librarian as she loves to read books

Sara → Doctor as he helps sick people

Messy → Engineer

Solutions: (Qs 28-30)

Persons ↓	2 Slices	3 Slices	7 Slices	8 Slices
Abhay	×	×	√	×
Vasu	×	√	×	×
Atul	×	×	×	√
Dev	√	×	×	×

28. (d) Dev ate two slices of pizza.

29. (a) Atul ate more than seven slices of pizza.

30. (b) Vasu ate three slices of pizza.

31. (d)

32. (d)

Estimation

- Students will be able to generate a range of possible outcomes.
- They will be able to judge the size, amount and cost of something.

INTRODUCTION

Estimation is a rough calculation of the value, number, quantity, or extent of something.

Example 1:

2 litres is most likely the amount of liquid in a ___________.

(a) Bathtub   (b) Pond

(c) Large bottle of soda   (d) Swimming pool

Ans. (c)

Explanation: 2 litres is most likely the amount in a large bottle of soda.

Example 2:

What is the closest estimate of how much longer the back of truck is than the front?

(a) 60 feet (b) 70 feet (c) 50 feet (d) 40 feet

Ans. (c)

Explanation: Nearest Estimation is $70 - 20 = 50$ feet.

Example 3:

How many 250 ml cartons of milk would it take to fill the 1 l carton?

(a) 2 (b) 3 (c) 4 (d) 5

Ans. (c)

Explanation:

$$250 \text{ ml} + 250 \text{ ml} \quad 250 \text{ ml} + 250 \text{ ml}$$
$$500 \text{ ml} \quad + \quad 500 \text{ ml}$$
$$1000 \text{ ml} = 1\,l$$

Example 4:

The amount of water in a bath tub is about 50 __________.

(a) mililitres (b) litres (c) centilitres (d) kilograms

Ans. (b)

Explanation: The amount of water in a bath tub is about 50 litres.

Example 5:

Ben had 2 boxes of blocks

- Each box had 50 blocks

- He built a tower with $\dfrac{1}{5}$ of the blocks out of each of the boxes.

How many blocks did Ben use to build the tower?

(a) 50 (b) 40 (c) 30 (d) 20

Ans. (d)

Explanation: Each box had = 50 blocks

$$2 \text{ boxes had} = 50 \times 2 = 100 \text{ blocks}$$

$$\text{Ben used } \dfrac{1}{5} \text{ of blocks} = 100 \times \dfrac{1}{5} = 20 \text{ blocks.}$$

1. Mridula has written following statements about the metric unit she would use to measure the same objects. Find the incorrect sentence among the following sentences:

   P : Centimetre is used to measure the length of a pencil.

   Q : Kilometer is used to measure distance from one city to another.

   R : Kilogram is used to measure depth of a bucket.

   S : Metre is used to measure height of a tree.

   (a) Q   (b) R   (c) S   (d) P

Direction (Qs. 2-4): Estimate the total capacity of the following.

2. 25 L and 19L

   (a) 42L   (b) 50L

   (c) 40L   (d) 45L

3. 37L and 63L

   (a) 90L   (b) 91L

   (c) 99L   (d) 96L

4. 75L and 12L

   (a) 80L   (b) 85L

   (c) 88L   (d) 84L

5. A container has 2550 ml of water. How many litres and Millilitres of water is in the container?

   (a) 2L500 ml   (b) 2L525 ml

   (c) 2L505 ml   (d) 2L550 ml

6. Nimisha is learning metric unit of length. She wrote following sentences in her notebook. Write True/false (T/F) for the following sentences.

   • There are 100 centimeters in a metre.

   • There are 100 metres in a kilometre.

- Centimetre is larger unit than kilometre.
- Metre is smaller unit than centimetre.

(a) TFTF   (b) FFFT   (c) TFFF   (d) FTFT

7. If the cost of 1 litre of a cough syrup is Rs. 480.40, find the cost of 500 ml?

(a) ₹ 240.40   (b) ₹ 280.40   (c) ₹ 240.10   (d) ₹ 240.20

Direction (Qs. 8-10): Balance the equation by choosing the correct estimated solution.

8. Each ☐ stands for 10g. Find the mass of three ☐.

(a) 10g   (b) 30g   (c) 60g   (d) 120g

9.

(a) 1kg   (b) 2kg   (c) 1500g   (d) 1000g

10.

He bought _______ more apples than strawberries.

(a) 2   (b) 4   (c) 6   (d) 8

11. Which ball is the lightest in the given three figures?

(a) P   (b) Q   (c) R   (d) S

Direction (Qs. 12-15): Choose the correct option. What is the correct estimation of water in the given jugs?

12.

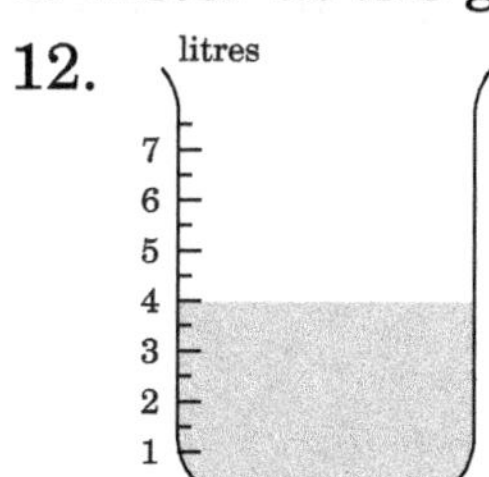

(a) 6 litres   (b) 4 litres   (c) 3 litres   (d) 200 ml

13.

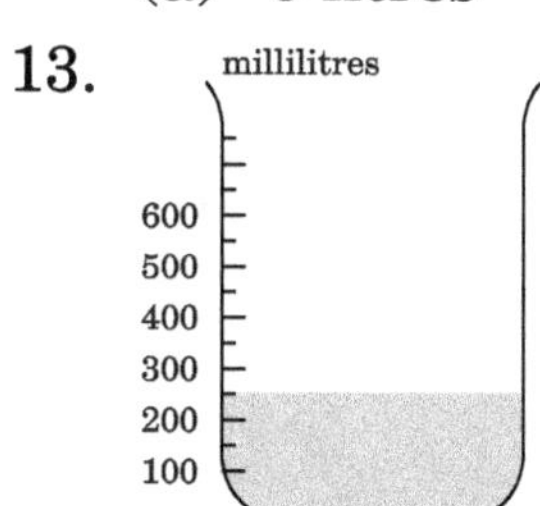

(a) 300 ml   (b) 200 ml   (c) 250 ml   (d) None of these

14.

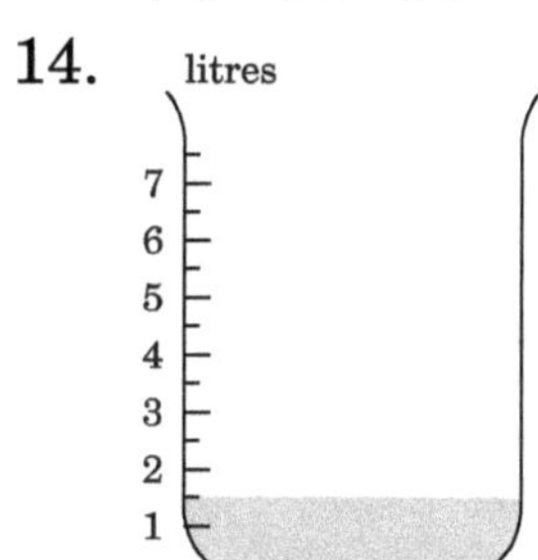

(a) 1 litre   (b) 1.5 litres   (c) 2.5 litres   (d) 0.5 litre

15.

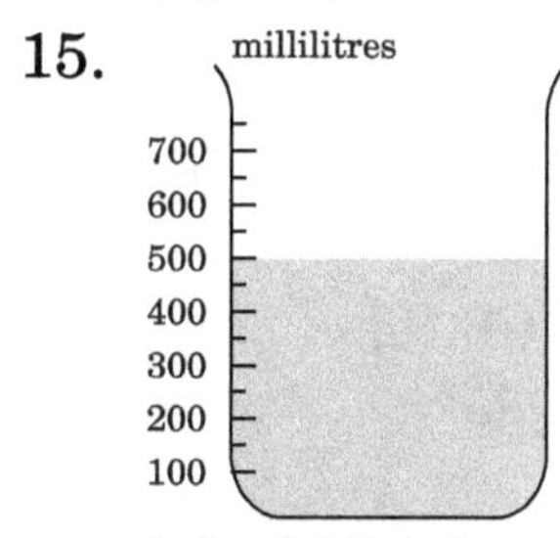

(a) 100 ml   (b) 500 ml   (c) 300 ml   (d) 700 ml

16.

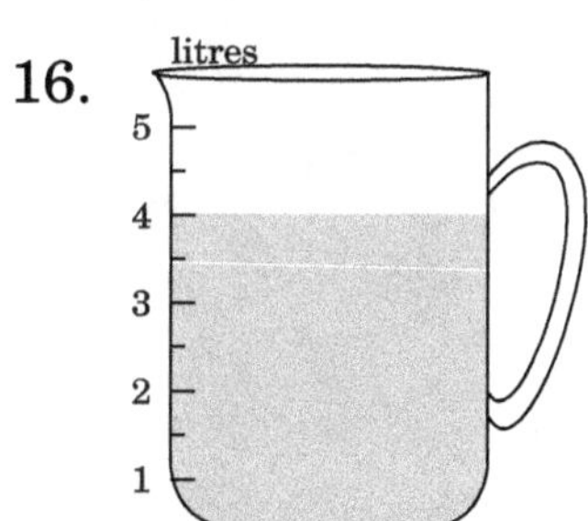

The jug is filled with _______________ of water.

(a) 4 litres   (b) 3 litres   (c) 5 litres   (d) None of these

17. 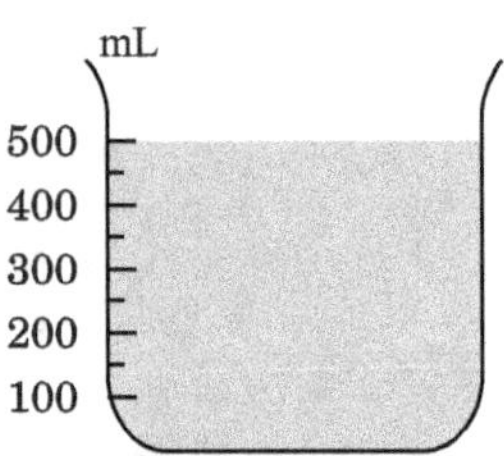

The jug is filled with __________ of water.

(a) 100 ml   (b) 400 ml   (c) 500 ml   (d) 0 ml

18. Rohit is comparing some objects. He wrote some sentences. Write true/false (T/F) for them.

M : Sofa is heavier than chair.

N : Towel is lighter than paper.

O : Shoe box is heavier than shoes.

P : Gas stove is lighter than gas cylinder.

(a) TFFT   (b) FTTF   (c) TFFF   (d) FFTF

19. Estimate the correct weight to balance the scale.

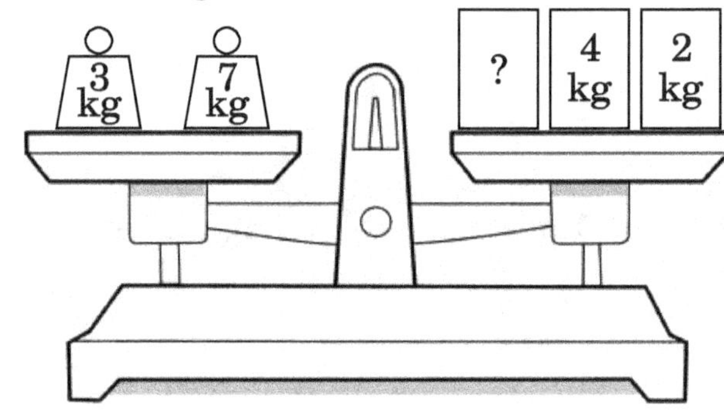

(a) 5 kg   (b) 4 kg   (c) 6 kg   (d) 2 kg

20. Estimate the correct weight for balancing the weight/scale.

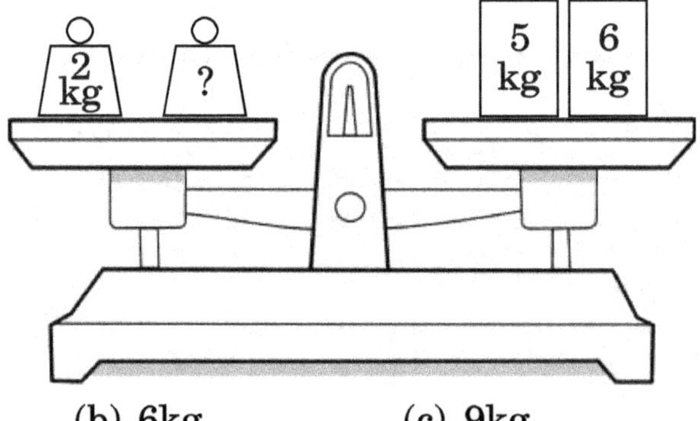

(a) 8kg   (b) 6kg   (c) 9kg   (d) None of these

Direction (Qs. 21-24): Read the thermometre and estimate the correct temperature.

21. In Delhi on 12th May 2016 the temperature was _________°C.

    (a) 30°C

    (b) 32°C

    (c) 28°C

    (d) None of these

22. December 14th the temperature was recorded _________°C.

    (a) 15°C

    (b) 9°C

    (c) 20°C

    (d) None of these

23. On November 15th the temperature was _________°F

    (a) 0°F

    (b) 25°F

    (c) 30°F

    (d) 70°F

24. Highest temperature of the month till today is _________?

    (a) 59°C

    (b) 35°C

    (c) 28°C

    (d) 21°C

25. There are 53 flowers on each quilt. About how many flowers are there on 62 quilts? Choose the better estimate.

    (a) 2500   (b) 3300   (c) 3800   (d) 4000

26. Which is a better estimate for the weight of a slice of pizza?

    (a) 22 kg   (b) 22 l   (c) 22 g   (d) 22 ml

Direction (Qs. 27-30): Balance the scales by correct estimation.

27.

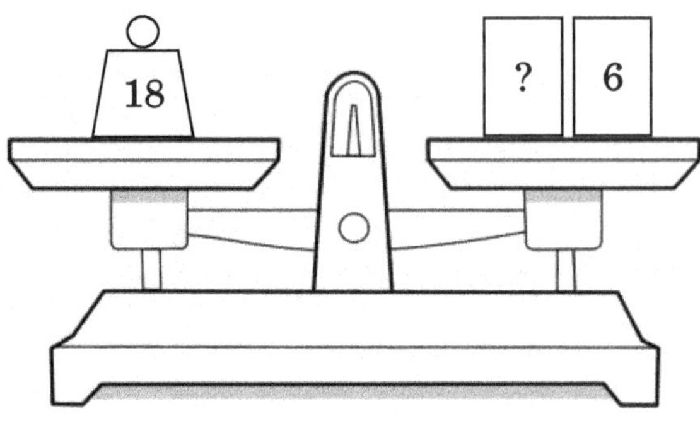

    (a) 11   (b) 12   (c) 10   (d) 16

28.

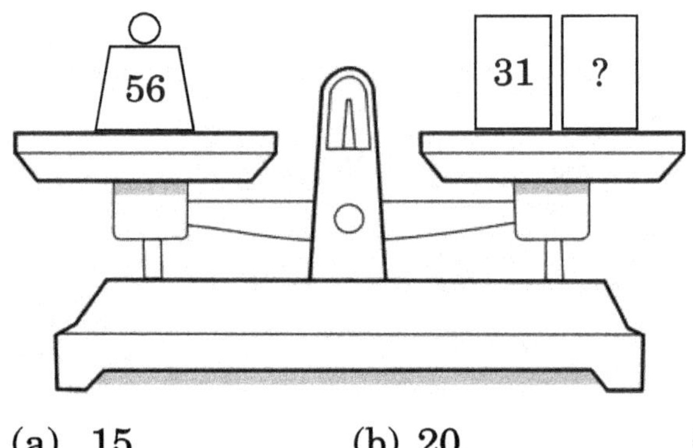

    (a) 15   (b) 20   (c) 25   (d) 30

29. Which is a better estimate for the weight of a butterfly?

    (a) 60 kg   (b) 20 kg   (c) 30 g   (d) 10 g

30. How many oranges (◯) can balance the weight of one cube (◻) ?

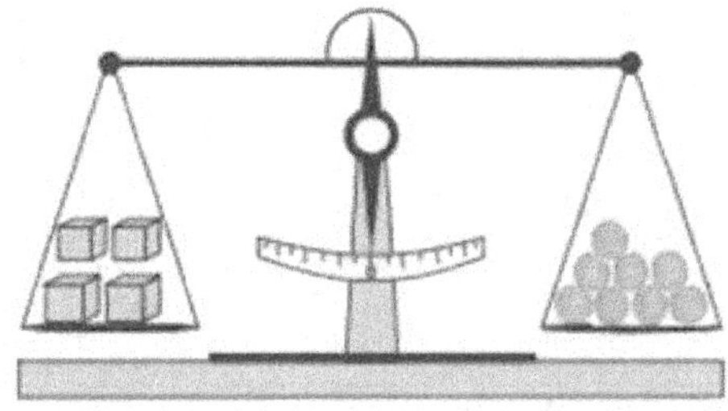

    (a) 8 oranges   (b) 2 oranges   (c) 4 oranges   (d) 16 oranges

LEVEL-2

1. Estimate the product. Read each number to its greatest place value, then multiply 9.8×43

   (a) 242.4 (b) 421.4 (c) 400 (d) None of these

2. Estimate the sum by remaining each number to the nearest whole number and then adding.

   $$7.73 + 8.86$$

   (a) 20 (b) 19 (c) 17 (d) 15

3. Estimate $2{,}342 + 637$. Round to the hundred place.

   (a) 2000 (b) 2900 (c) 2500 (d) None of these

4. Which of the following has capacity of 1 litre water?

   (a) Tea-cup (b) Spoon (c) Bowl (d) Bottle

5. Ramesh walks the following distance each day of the week. Estimate the total distance that he walks?

Monday	Tuesday	Wednesday	Thursday	Friday	Saturday	Sunday
3.5 km	2.5 km	0.5 km	1 km	3 km	4 km	5.5 km

   (a) 10 km (b) 15 km (c) 20 km (d) 25 km

6. List objects whose length would not be measured using centimetre unit.

   (a) (b) (c) (d)

7. Mitali bought a 50 litre container of oil. She used 44 litres 300 ml of it. How much oil is left?

   (a) 5L 700 ml (b) 6L 700 ml (c) 5L 300 ml (d) None of these

8. We can estimate our heights in ___________ and ___________

   (a) cm and m (b) inches and feet
   (c) kg and g (d) litres and millilitres

9. We can estimate the weight of any object in ___________ and ___________

   (a) cm and m (b) km and m (c) kg and g (d) None of these

10. Ratnakar has written some statements about length and height of some objects. Write true/false (T/F) for the sentences.

    M : Length of a bed is more than 1 metre.

    N : Height of a new born baby is more than 1 metre.

O : Height of a sofa is less than 1 metre.

P : Height of a school is less than 1 km.

(a) FTTF   (b) TFFT   (c) FFFT   (d) FFTF

Direction (Qs. 11-13): Look at the diagram and answer the following questions.

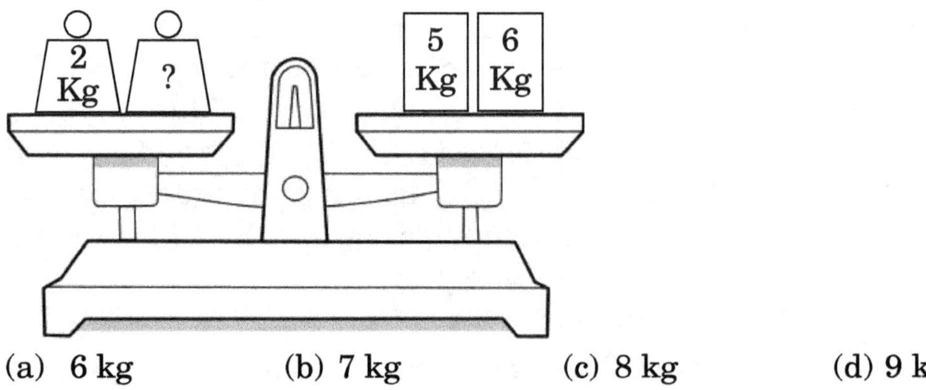

11. Which is the shortest wire?

    (a) Q   (b) R   (c) S   (d) P

12. Which is the largest wire?

    (a) Q   (b) R   (c) S   (d) P

13. Which wire has more curves than others?

    (a) Q   (b) R   (c) S   (d) P

14. If pin : grams :: ? : kilograms

    (a) Paper   (b) Pencil   (c) Book   (d) None of these

15. If water : litres :: ? : kilograms

    (a) Feather   (b) Paper   (c) Fruits   (d) Distance

16. Diya's aunty has made a list of objects with their weights. Find the incorrect statement of the following:

    P : Weight of a mug full of coffee is about 450 gm.

    Q : Weight of a thread roll is about 2 kg

    R : Weight of a letter is about 5 g.

    S : Weight of a pair of Chappals is about 200 gm.

    (a) S   (b) R   (c) Q   (d) P

17. Estimate the weight to balance the scale.

    (a) 6 kg   (b) 7 kg   (c) 8 kg   (d) 9 kg

18. 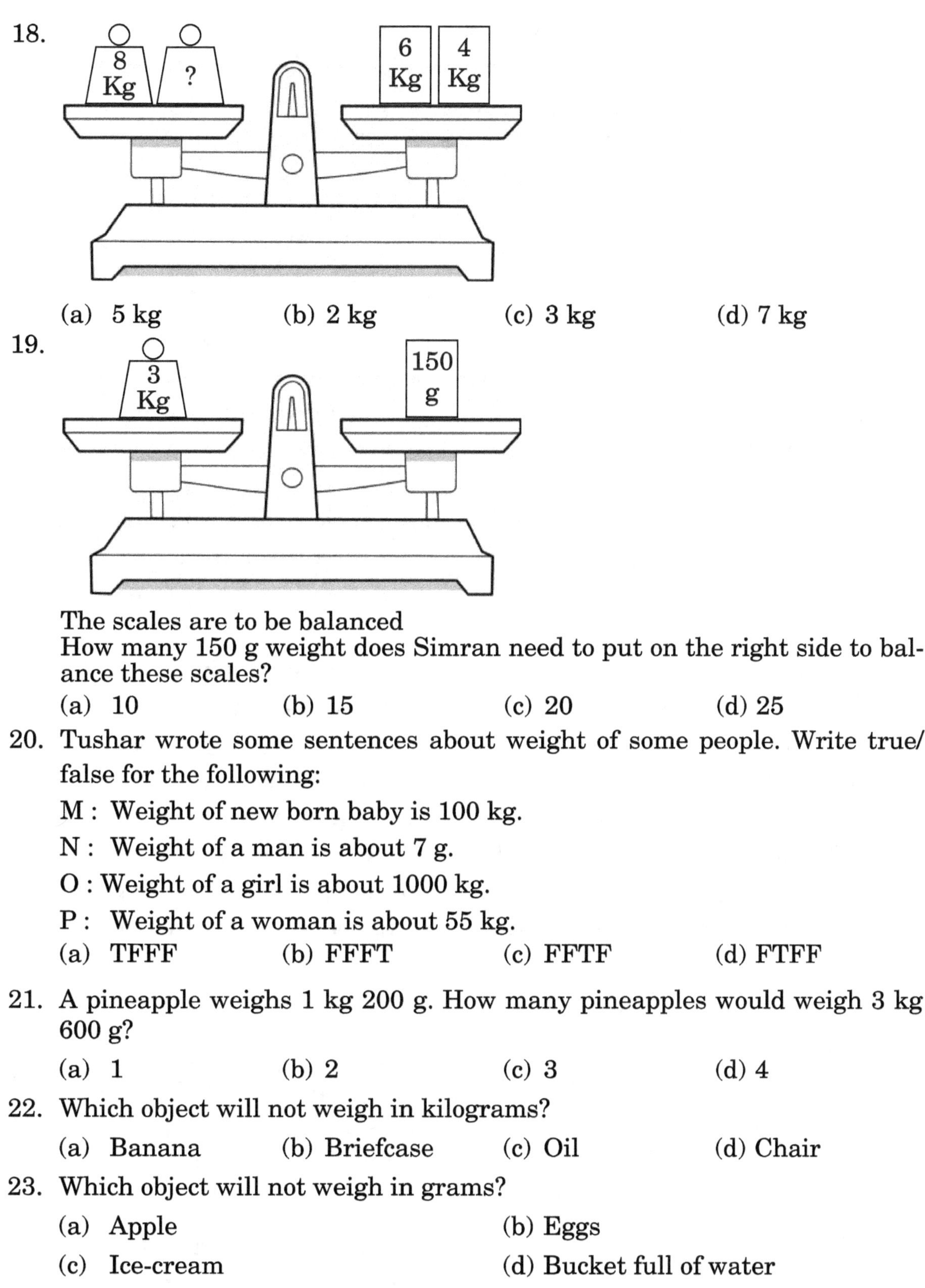

(a) 5 kg   (b) 2 kg   (c) 3 kg   (d) 7 kg

19.

The scales are to be balanced

How many 150 g weight does Simran need to put on the right side to balance these scales?

(a) 10   (b) 15   (c) 20   (d) 25

20. Tushar wrote some sentences about weight of some people. Write true/false for the following:

M : Weight of new born baby is 100 kg.

N : Weight of a man is about 7 g.

O : Weight of a girl is about 1000 kg.

P : Weight of a woman is about 55 kg.

(a) TFFF   (b) FFFT   (c) FFTF   (d) FTFF

21. A pineapple weighs 1 kg 200 g. How many pineapples would weigh 3 kg 600 g?

(a) 1   (b) 2   (c) 3   (d) 4

22. Which object will not weigh in kilograms?

(a) Banana   (b) Briefcase   (c) Oil   (d) Chair

23. Which object will not weigh in grams?

(a) Apple   (b) Eggs

(c) Ice-cream   (d) Bucket full of water

24. Estimate the weight and balance the scale?

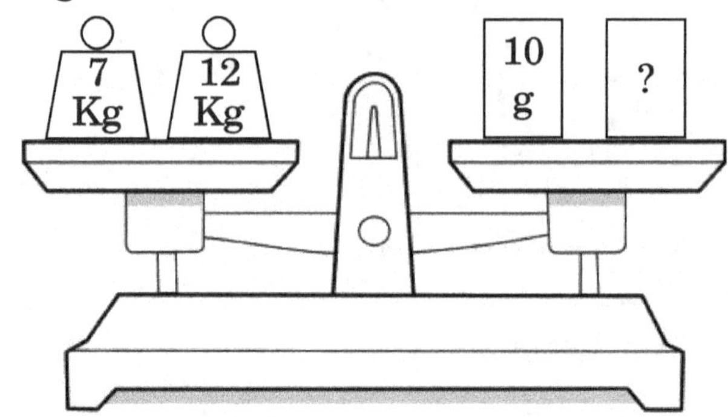

(a) 6 kg   (b) 8 kg   (c) 9 kg   (d) None of these

25. Gram is used to weigh ______________ objects?

(a) heavier   (b) lighter   (c) both (a) and (b) (d) None of these

26. 100 centimetres = 1 metre

   1 kilogram = ?

(a) 100 g   (b) 1001 g   (c) 1000 g   (d) None of these

27. Millilitre is used to measure ______________ quantity of liquids.

(a) more   (b) less   (c) greater   (d) None of these

28. Meaning of BMI?

(a) Body Mass Index   (b) Big Mass Inquiry

(c) Bio Mass Index   (d) None of these

29. The adult human brain weighs ______________ to ______________ gm?

(a) 100 to 1000 gm   (b) 1300 to 1400 gm

(c) 110 to 140 gm   (d) None of these

30. If football : 1 kg :: Cricket ball : ?

(a) 1 kg   (b) 1 gm   (c) 20 kg   (d) 200 gm

31. About how many beads would you have if you bought small and large sizes?

139 beads   275 beads   399 beads   650 beads

(a) 675   (b) 725   (c) 925   (d) 900

32. What is the weight of big strawberry?

(a) 3 g   (b) 4 gm   (c) 6 gm   (d) 8 g

33. Which of the following options is NOT exactly embedded or hidden in the given figure? **(2018)**

(a)    (b) 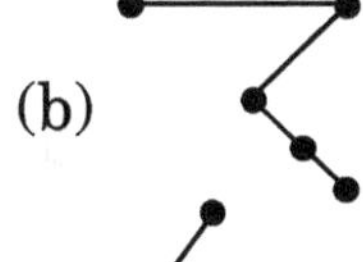

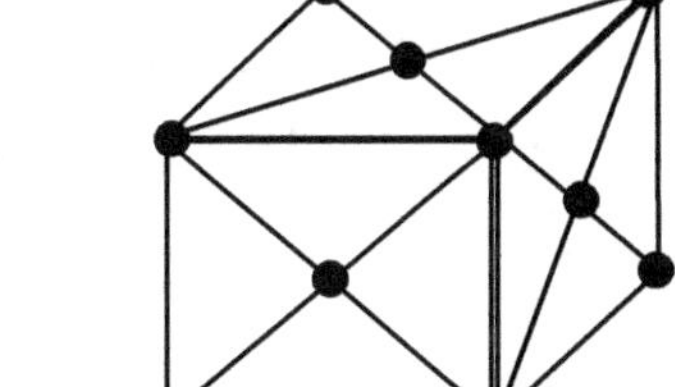

(c) 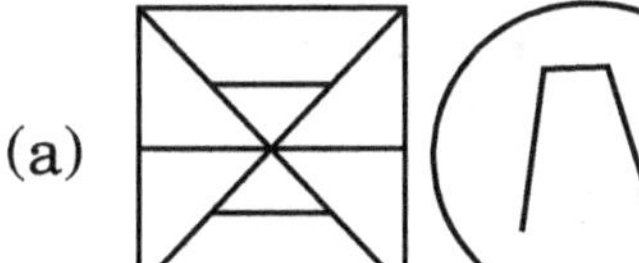   (d) 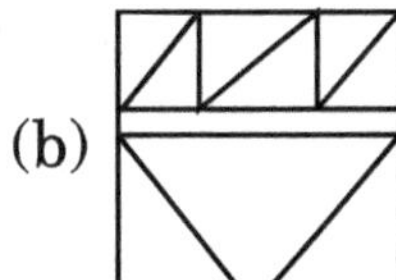

34. In which of the following options, the given figure is exactly embedded as one of it parts? **(2022)**

(a) 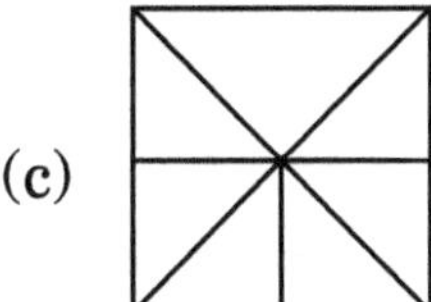   (b) 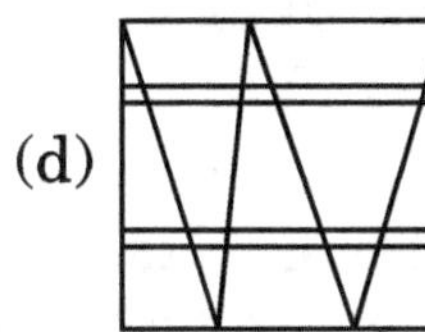

(c)   (d)

35. In which of the following options, the given figure is exactly embedded as one of its parts? **(2022)**

(a) 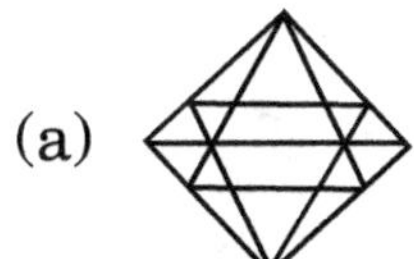   (b) 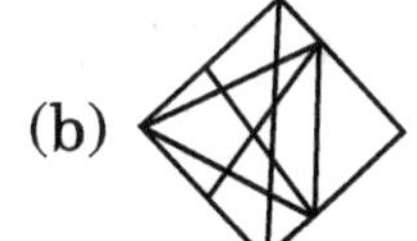   (c) 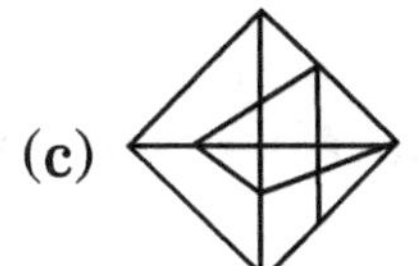   (d) 

Level-1

1. (b) The incorrect statement is, kilogram is used to measure depth of a bucket.
2. (d) 45
3. (c) 99L
4. (c) 88L
5. (d) 2L550 ml
6. (c) TFFF
7. (d) Cost of 500 ml of a cough syrup = 480.40/2
   = Rs. 240.20.

8. (b) Each ▯ stands for = 10gm

   Three ▯ stands for = 10 × gm

   As = ▯ = ▯

   Then; three ▯ stands for = 30g

9. (c) 1kg = 1000g
   4kg = 4 × 1000 = 4000g
   To balance the equance
   4000 − 2500 = 1500g

10. (c) Step 1
    The first statement tells us that one box contains 4 apples
    Step 2
    Therefore, 3 boxes = 3 × 4 = 12 apples
    Step 3
    The second statement tells us that one jar contains 2 strawberries.

    Step 4
    Therefore, 3 jars = 3 × 2 = 6 strawberries
    Step 5
    Thus, the difference between the number of apples and strawberries
    = 12 − 6 = 6

11. (c) Arranging balls from lighter to heavier:
    R < S < Q < P
    So, ball R is the lightest.

12. (b) 4 litres
13. (c) 250 ml
14. (b) 1.5 litres
15. (b) 500 ml
16. (a) The jug is filled with 4 litres of water.
17. (c) The jug is filled with 500 ml of water.
18. (a) TFFT
19. (b) 4 kg
20. (c) 9 kg
21. (b) 32°C
22. (b) 9°C
23. (b) 25°F
24. (b) 35°C
25. (b) 3300.
26. (c) 22 g.
27. (b) 6 + 12 = 18.
28. (c) 56 = 31 + 25 ; 56 = 56 (Balanced).
29. (d) 10 g.
30. (b) 1 cube (▱) = 20 oranges.

1. (c) Round 9.8 to the nearest whole number

   Round 43 to the nearest ten

   $9.8 \times 43 = ?$

   $10 \times 40 = 400.$

2. (c) Round off each number to the nearest whole number

   $7.73 + 8.86 = ?$

   $8 + 9 = 17$

   The sum is about 17

3. (b) Round each number to the nearest hundreds

   $2,342 \longrightarrow 2,300$

   $+ 637 \longrightarrow + 600$

   $2,900$

4. (d) Bottle

5. (c) Total distance = 3.5 + 2.5 + 0.5 + 1.0 + 3.0 + 4.0 + 5.5

   $= 20.$

6. (a) Door

7. (a) 5L 700 ml

8. (b) inches and feet

9. (c) kg and g

10. (c) FFFT

11. (c) S

12. (a) Q

13. (b) R

14. (c) Book

15. (c) Fruits

16. (c) Q

17. (d) 5 kg + 6 kg = 11

   2 kg + ? = 11, ? = 9

   2 kg + 9 kg = 11.

18. (b) (6 + 4)kg = 10 kg

   (8 + ?)kg = 10 kg, = ? = 2

   (8 + 2)kg = 10 kg.

19. (c) 3 kg = 3000 gm

   Number of 150 g weight require $= \dfrac{3000}{150} = 20.$

20. (b) FFFT

21. (c) Weight of 1 Pineapple = 1 kg 200 g

   $= 1200$ g

   $\therefore$ Weight of 3 Pineapples = 3 × 1200 g = 3600 g

   = 3 kg 600 g.

22. (c) Oil

23. (d) Bucket full of water

24. (c) 7 + 12 = 19 kg

10 + ? = 19 kg, ? = 9

10 + 9 = 19 kg.

25. (b) lighter

26. (c) 1000 g

27. (b) less

28. (a) Body Mass Index

29. (b) 1300 to 1400 gm

30. (d) 200 gm.

31. (c) Beads in large sizes = 275

Beads in small sizes = 050

Total beads = 275 + 650 = 925.

32. (c)

Total weight of 4 strawberries = 8 gm

Weight of a strawberry = 8/4 = 2 gm

Weight of 5 strawberries = 5 × 2 = 10 gm

Weight of a big strawberry = 16 − 10 = 6 gm.

33. (d) Figure shown in option (d) is not exactly embedded in the given figure.

34. (d) The given image is embedded in option (d).

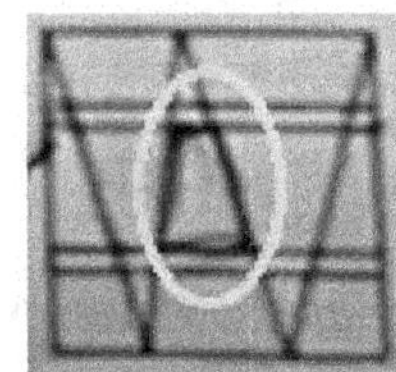

35. (d) The given figure is exactly embedded in option (d).

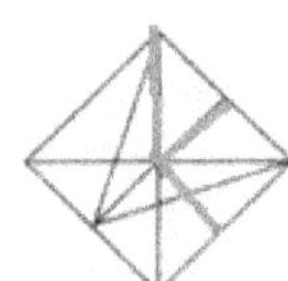

Logical Venn Diagram

INTRODUCTION

A Venn Diagram is a visual brainstorming tool used to compare and contrast two (sometimes three) different things. Comparing is looking at traits that things have in common, while contrasting is looking at how they differ from each other.

A Venn Diagram is made up of two large circles that intersect with each other to form a space in the middle. Each circle represents something that you want to compare and contrast. Where the two circles intersect, you would write traits that the two things have in common. In either side of the intersecting space, you would write the differences among the two things.

TYPE-I : Different Types of Questions Based on Venn Diagrams

CASE 1:

When one group of items is completely included in the second group of items and the second, again completely belongs to the third group, they are represented as shown.

Examples 1

Tree, Forest, Leaf
Explanation:

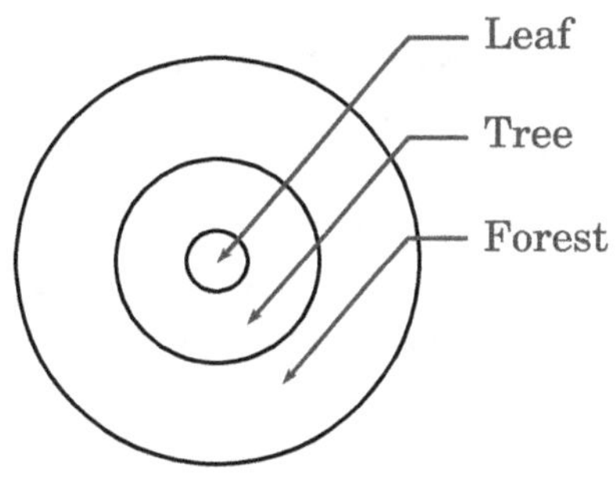

Venn diagram would be as follows : Clearly, leaf is apart of tree and tree is a part of forest.

CASE 2:

If the items evidently belong to three different groups, i.e., they are not corelated with each other in any way. They are represented as shown.

Example 2

Whale, Crocodile, Bird

Explanation:

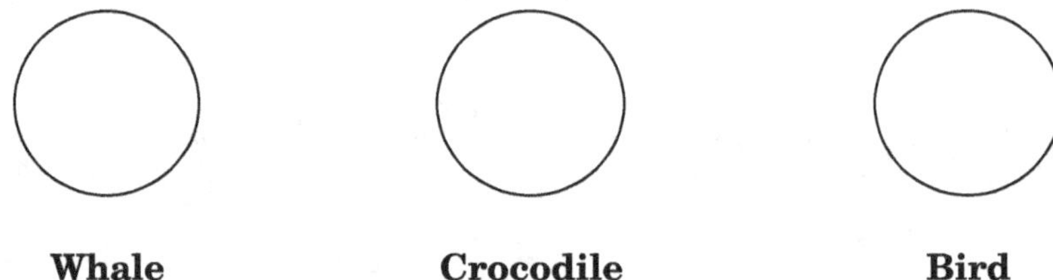

They all belong to different categories.

CASE 3:

If the three items are partly related to each other, they are represented as shown.

Example 3

Teachers, Authors, men

Explanation:

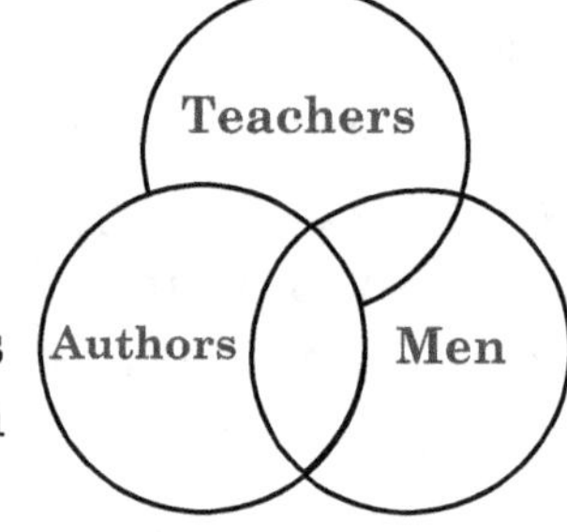

Here, some Teachers may be Authors and some Teachers may be Men. Also some Authors may be Men. So, the given items are partly related to each other.

Case 4:

If two separate groups of items are completely unrelated to each other, but they are completely included in the third group, then the relationships can be diagrammatically shown as:

Example 4

Hospital, Nurse, Patient

Explanation:
Nurse and Patient are entirely different. But both are parts of Hospital.

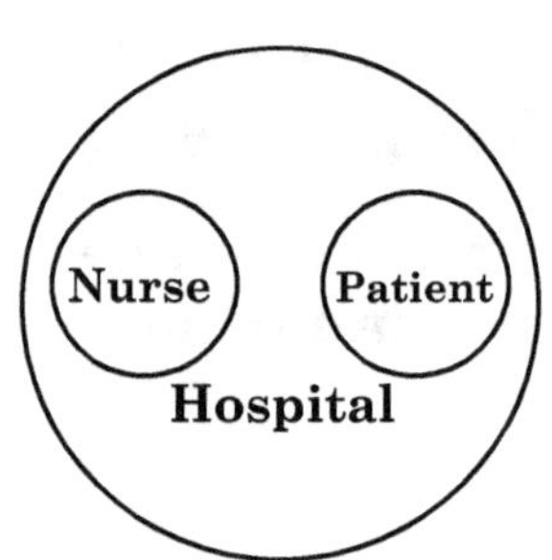

Case 5:

When two groups of items have some common relationship and both of them are completely included in the third group, the relationship is shown by two smaller intersecting circles in a third large circle.

Example 5

Animal, Cat, Pet

Explanation:
Some Cats are Pets and some pets are cats but all Cats and Pets are Animals.

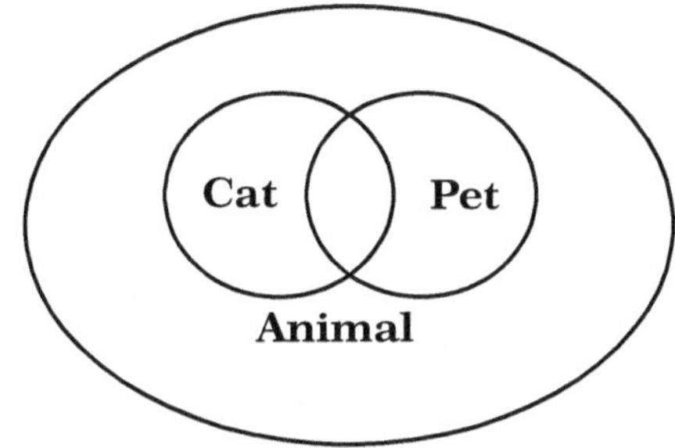

Case 6:

If one item belongs to the class of second while, third item is entirely different from the two and they may be represented by the following diagram.

Example 6

Doctors, Human, Ducks

Explanation:

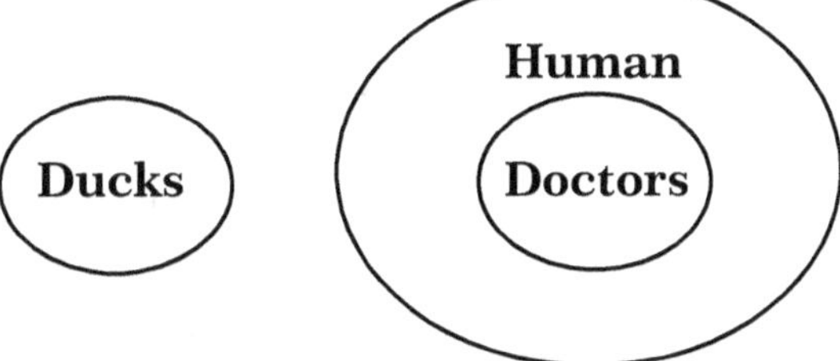

We know all Doctors are Humans but Ducks are entirely different to both of them.

Case 7:

If one group of items is partly included in the second group of items and the third group is completely unrelated to these two groups, their relationship is diagrammatically shown as:

Example 7

Wire, Copper, Rubber

Explanation:

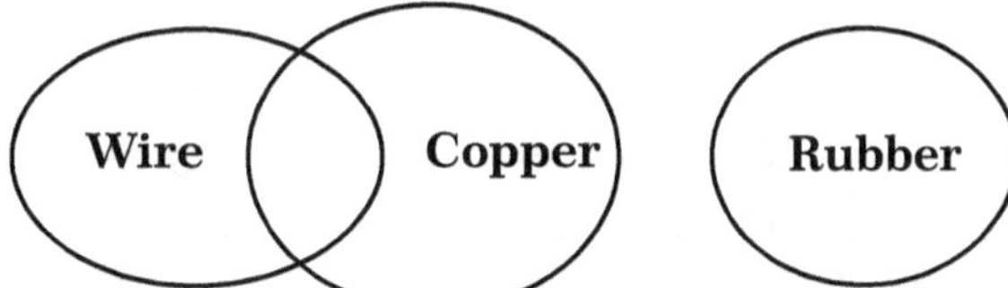

Some Wires are made of Copper but Rubber is entirely different.

Case 8:

If one item belongs to the class of second and the third item is partly related to these two, they are represented as shown:

Males, Fathers, Doctors

Explanation:

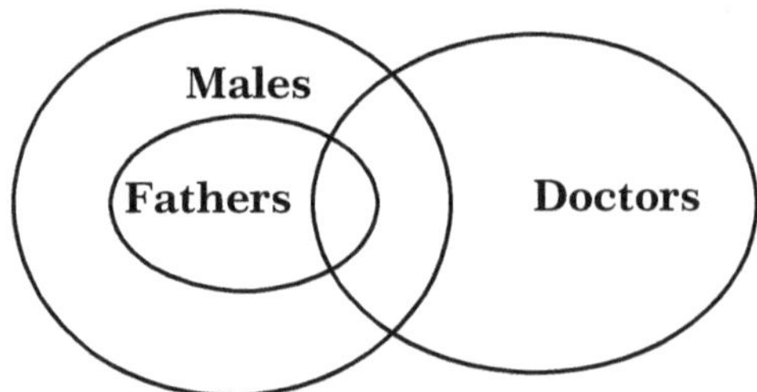

All Fathers are Males but some Males and some Fathers can be Doctors. So, the circles representing Doctors would intersect both of the two concentric circles.

Case 9:

If one item belongs to the class of second and the third item is partly related to the second, they are represented as shown.

Example 9

Females, Mothers, Children

Explanation:

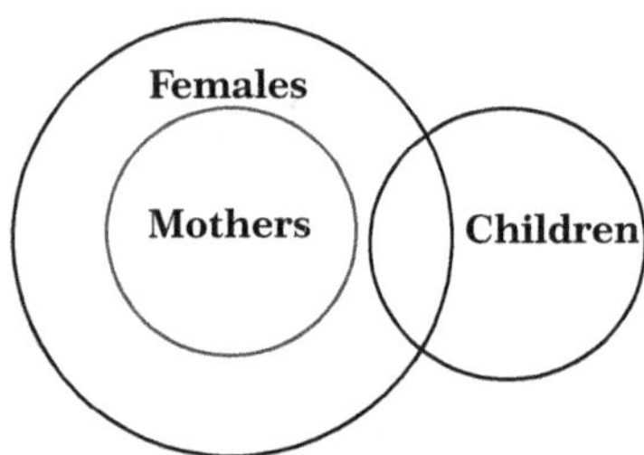

All Mothers are Females. This would be represented by two concentric circles but some females are Children but Children cannot be Mothers.

TYPE–II : Venn Diagrams formed by using different Geometrical Figures

We have used only circles to represent different relationships. Here, we will use different figures to show different relationships.

Example 10

Directions: Study the figure given below carefully and answer the questions that follow:

Which part (number) shows Males, who are neither Teacher nor Literate?

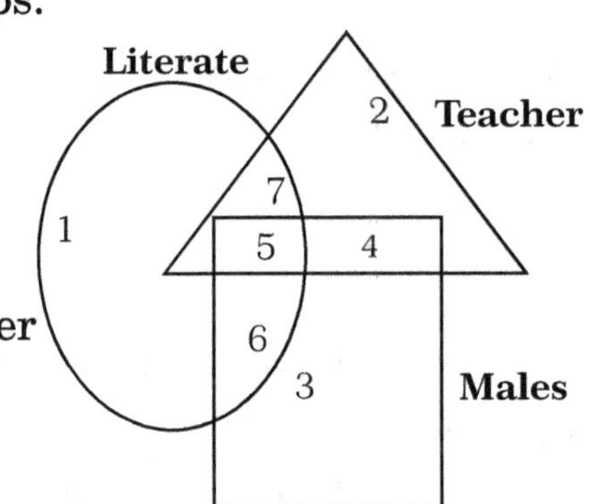

    (a) 1   (b) 2
    (c) 3   (d) 4

Ans: (c)

Explanation: To depict the required part, the figure should show only males, i.e., 3. 3 belongs to only Males.

Direction (Examples 11 and 12): Study the diagram given below and answer each of the following questions.

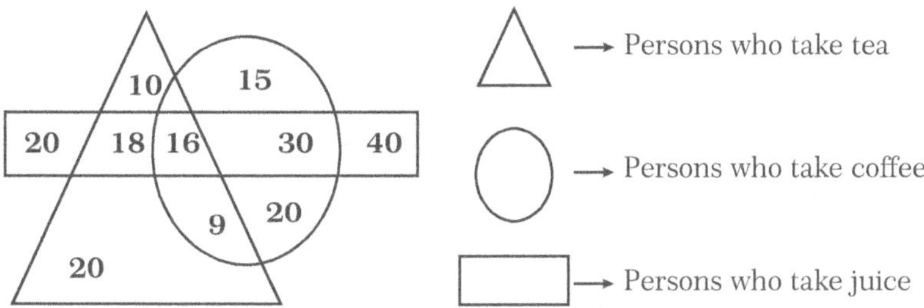

Example 11

How many persons who take both tea and juice but not coffee?

    (a) 20   (b) 18   (c) 25   (d) 15

Ans: (b)

Explanation: 18 persons take both tea and juice but not coffee.

Example 12

How many persons are there who take both tea and coffee but not juice?

    (a) 22   (b) 17   (c) 9   (d) 20

Ans: (c)

Explanation: Number of persons who take both tea and coffee but not juice is 9.

LEVEL-1

1. Which of the following diagrams indicates the best relation between Travellers, Bus and Train?

    (a) 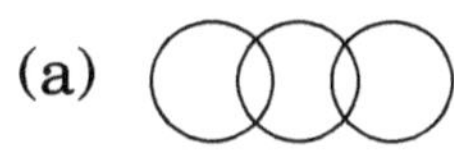   (b) 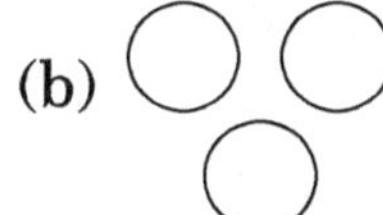   (c) 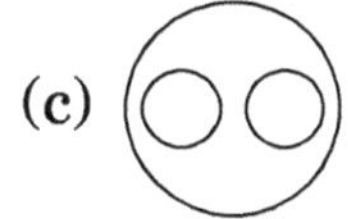   (d) 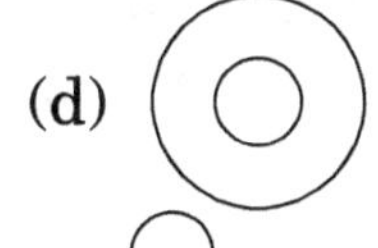

2. Which Venn diagram indicates the best relation between Vegetable, Potato and Brinjal?

    (a)    (b)    (c) 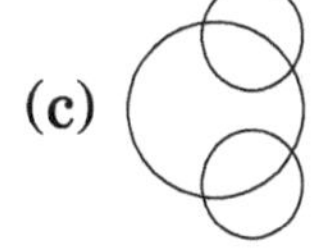   (d) 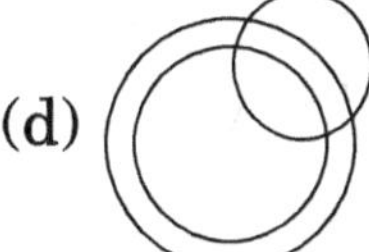

Direction (Qs. 3-5): Study the diagram given below and answer the following questions.

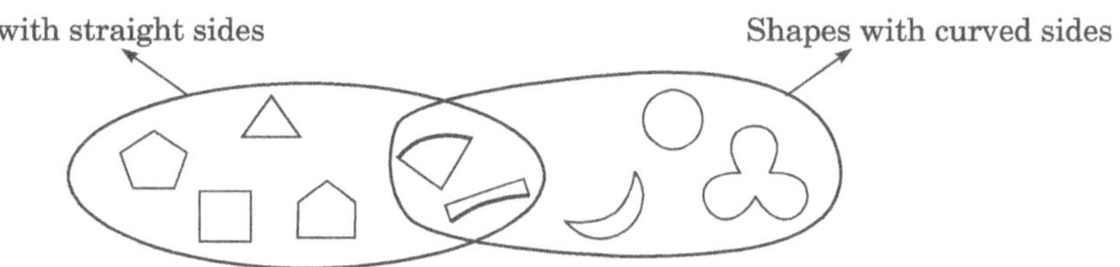

3. How many shapes have only straight sides?
    (a) 4   (b) 6   (c) 7   (d) 9

4. How many shapes have curved sides?
    (a) 3   (b) 5   (c) 4   (d) 6

5. How many shape have both straight and curved sides?
    (a) 4   (b) 3   (c) 2   (d) None

6. Which Venn diagram represents the relation between Boys, Students, Athletes?

    (a)    (b)    (c) 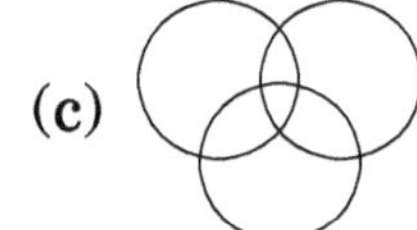   (d) 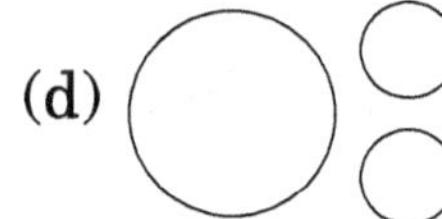

Direction (Qs. 7 and 8): Choose the correct option / diagram which represents the correct relation.

7. Which Venn Diagram correctly shows the relationship between A and B?

    Whereas:
    A = (even numbers less than 10),

    B = (odd numbers less than 10)

    (a) 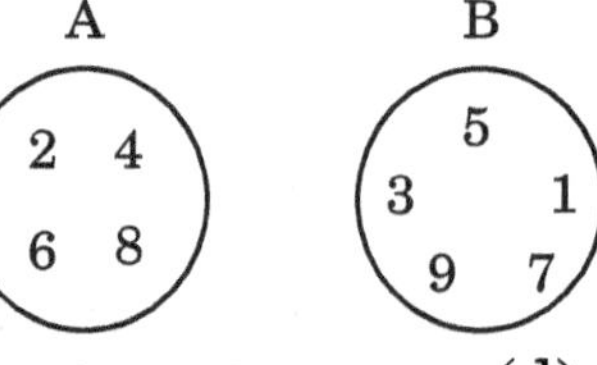   (b) 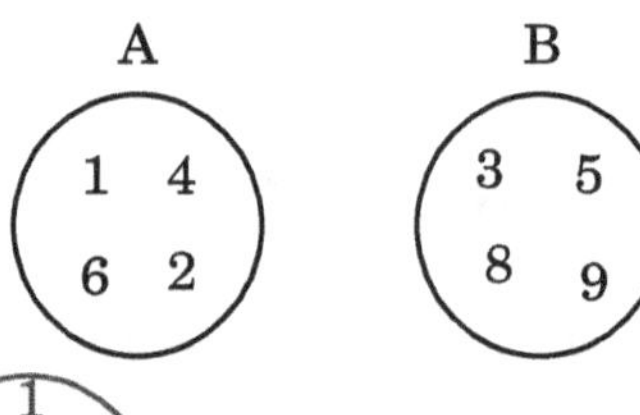

    (c) 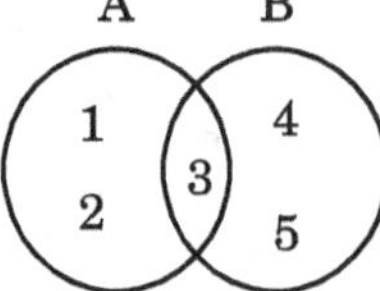   (d) 

8. Elephants, Wolves, Animals.

    (a) 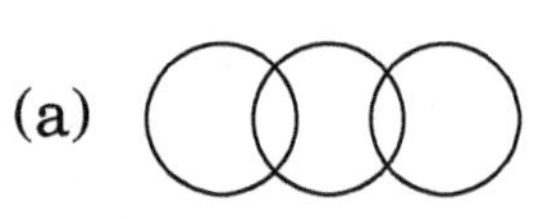   (b) 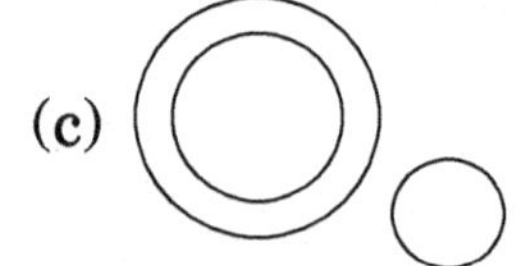   (c)   (d) 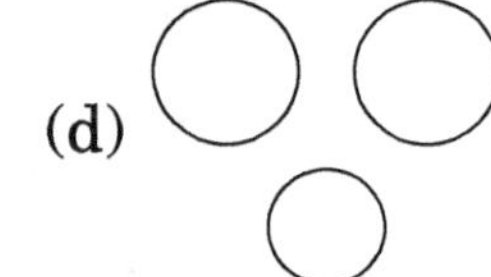

Direction (Qs. 9-11): Shivam asked a group of students which brand of cola they like: Lime and Pepsi. The results can be seen in the following Venn Diagram. Use the diagram to answer the questions.

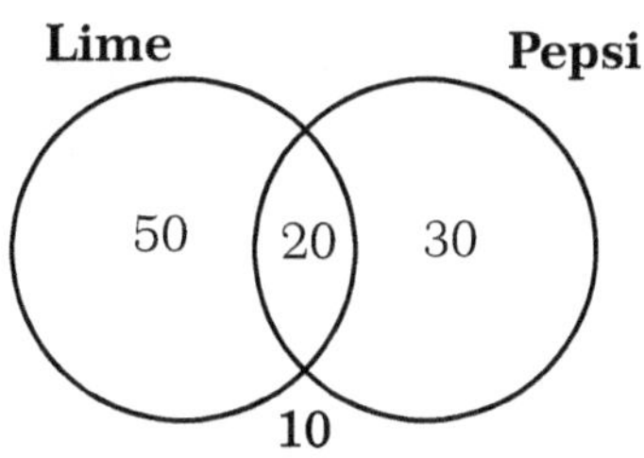

9. How many students like only Lime?

    (a) 50   (b) 20   (c) 30   (d) 10

10. How many students like both Lime and Pepsi?

    (a) 50   (b) 30   (c) 20   (d) 10

11. How many students like neither Lime nor Pepsi?

    (a) 20   (b) 10   (c) 50   (d) 30

Direction (Qs. 12 and 13): Study the diagram given below carefully and answer the following questions.

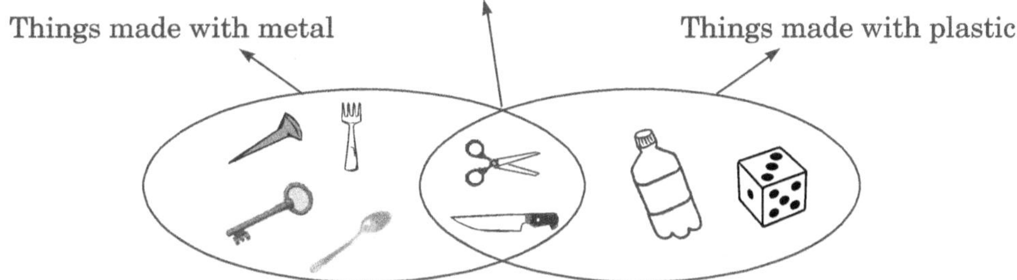

12. How many things are made of only metal?

    (a) 2   (b) 4   (c) 3   (d) 5

13. How many things are made of plastic?

    (a) 2   (b) 5   (c) 4   (d) 3

14. In the following figure, triangle represents Boys, square represents Players and circle represents Coach. Which part of the diagram represents the Boys who are Players but not Coach?

    (a) P

    (b) R

    (c) Q

    (d) T

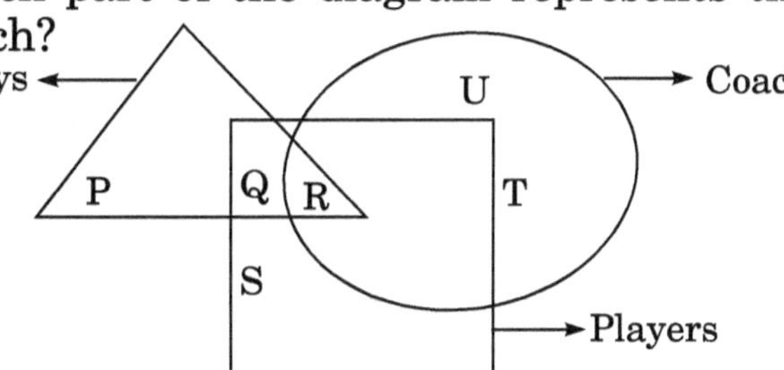

15. The diagram given below represents those students who play Basketball, Kho-Kho and Cricket. Study the diagram and identify the students who play all the three games.

(a) T

(b) S

(c) V

(d) S + T + V

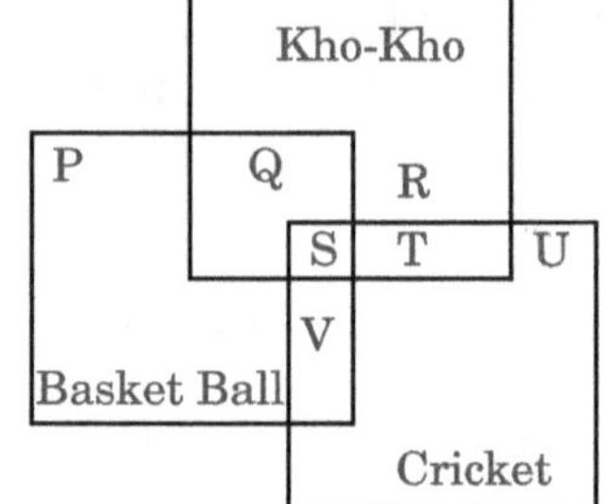

16. Study the diagram and identify the people who can speak only one language.

(a) L + M + O

(b) K

(c) K + J + I

(d) I

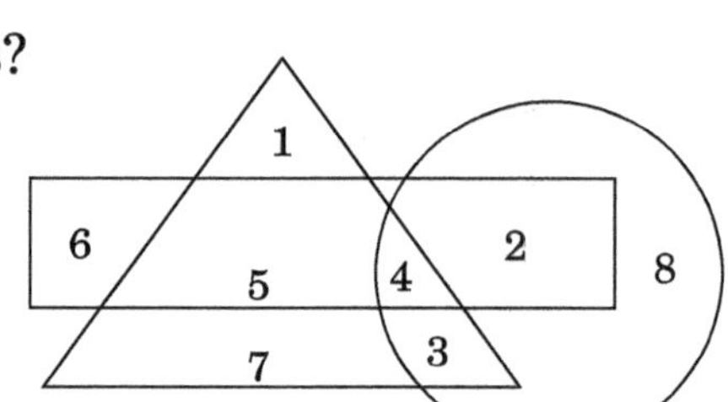

17. Which number is in all geometrical figures?

(a) 6

(b) 5

(c) 4

(d) 8

18. Read the clues to find the secret number.

- It is not an even number
- It is in the triangle
- It is in the rectangle

What number is it?

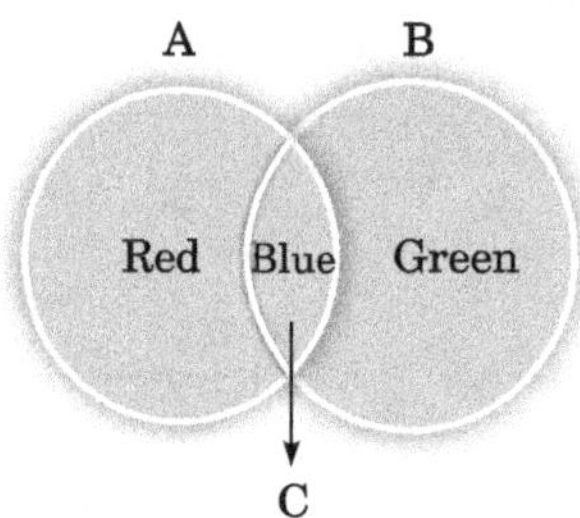

(a) 2   (b) 4   (c) 3   (d) 5

19. In the given Venn-diagram, what does the red circle represent?

(a) Set A   (b) Set B   (c) Set C   (d) None of these

20. Which one of the following Venn-diagrams best illustrates the relationship among: Crows, Birds, Dogs.

(a) 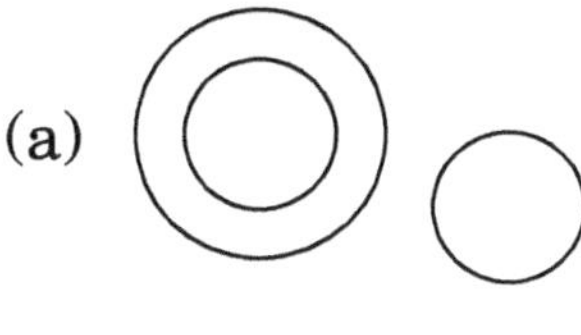

(b) 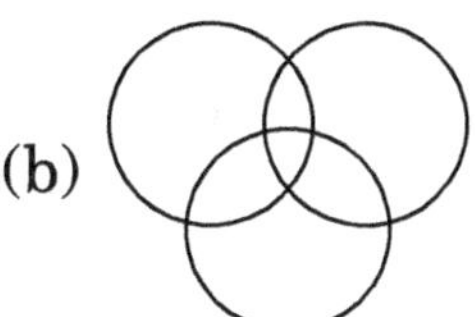

(c) 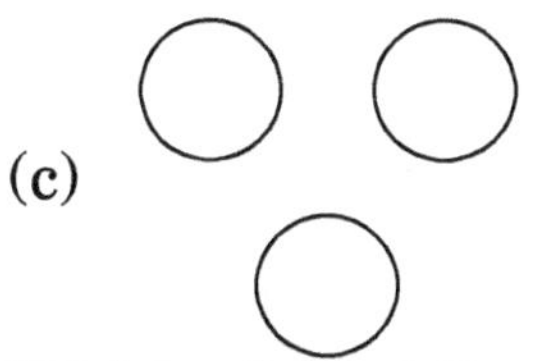

(d) 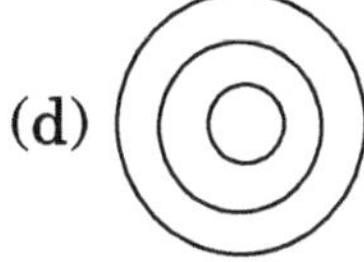

21. Which of the following statements is correct with regard to the given figure?

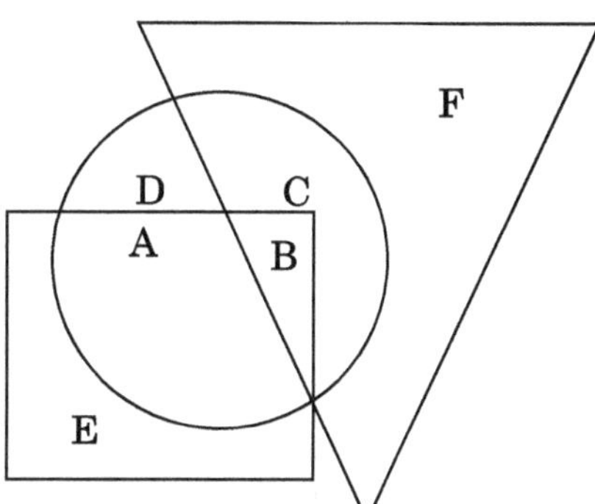

(a) A and B are all in three shapes

(b) E, A, B, C are all in three shapes

(c) F, C, D, B, A are all in three shapes.

(d) Only B is in all three shapes

Direction (Qs. 22-24): Study the following diagram to answer these questions.

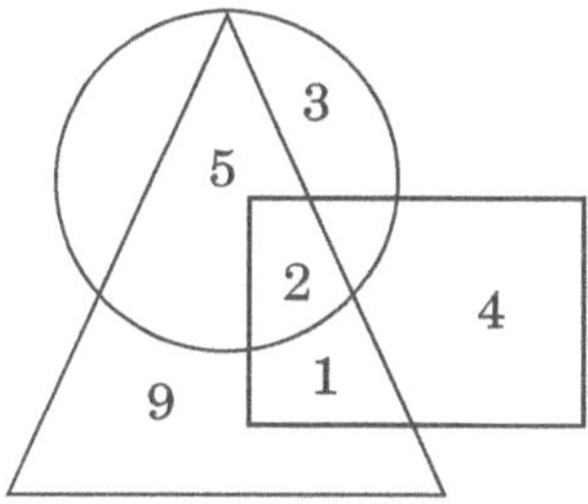

22. Find out the number that lies inside all the figures?
    (a) 2   (b) 5
    (c) 4   (d) 9

23. What are the numbers that lie inside any two figures?
    (a) 2, 1   (b) 5, 1
    (c) 9, 1   (d) 5, 9

24. Find out the number that lies only inside the triangle?

    (a) 5   (b) 2   (c) 9   (d) 3

25. Which Venn diagram is best illustrate the relationship among Sea, Island, Mountain.

    (a)   (b)   (c)   (d)

Direction (Qs. 26-30): In a birthday party, pizzas, burgers and cakes are served and it is represented by a Venn-diagram given below. Study the given diagram carefully and answer the following questions based on it.

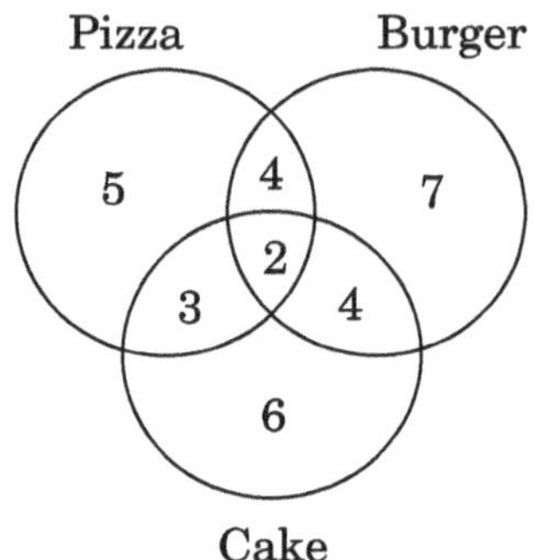

26. How many persons had cakes?

    (a) 6   (b) 6 + 3   (c) 6 + 4   (d) 6 + 2 + 3 + 4

27. How many persons had only pizzas?

    (a) 3   (b) 2   (c) 5   (d) 5 + 4

28. How many persons had both pizzas and burgers but not cakes.

    (a) 2   (b) 4   (c) 5   (d) 7

29. How many persons had cakes and pizzas but not burgers?

    (a) 3   (b) 2   (c) 4   (d) 6

30. How many persons had at least two items?

    (a) 2   (b) 3 + 2   (c) 3 + 4 + 2   (d) 3 + 4 + 2 + 4

LEVEL-2

1. How many squares are shaded?

    (a) 2

    (b) 3

    (c) 4

    (d) 5

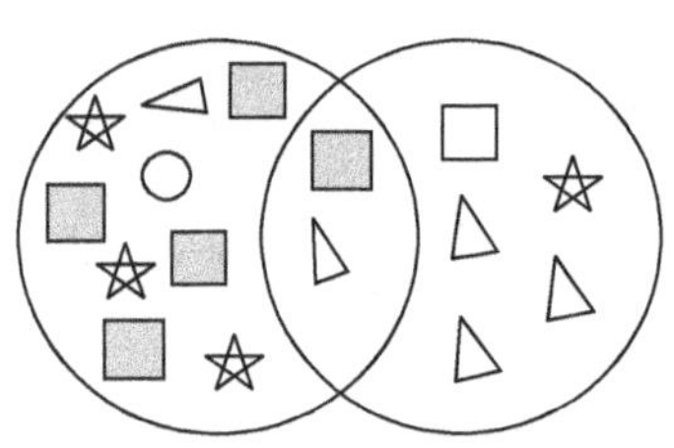

2. How many students are taking Dance Classes in Summer Camp?

(a) 11

(b) 15

(c) 20

(d) 30

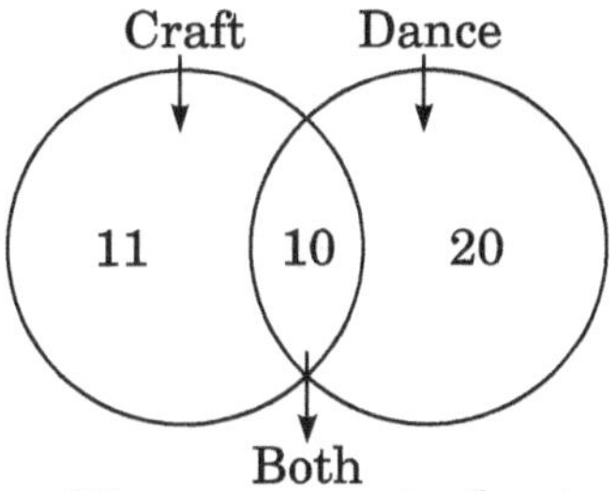

3. The diagram below shows the pet of students in a class. How many students had a dog?

(a) 28

(b) 32

(c) 38

(d) 42

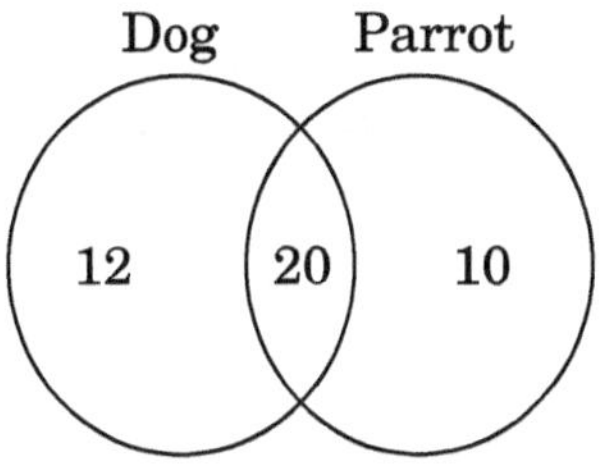

4. The diagram below shows the drinks people consumed at the hockey match. How many people did not drink water?

(a) 13

(b) 16

(c) 10

(d) 29

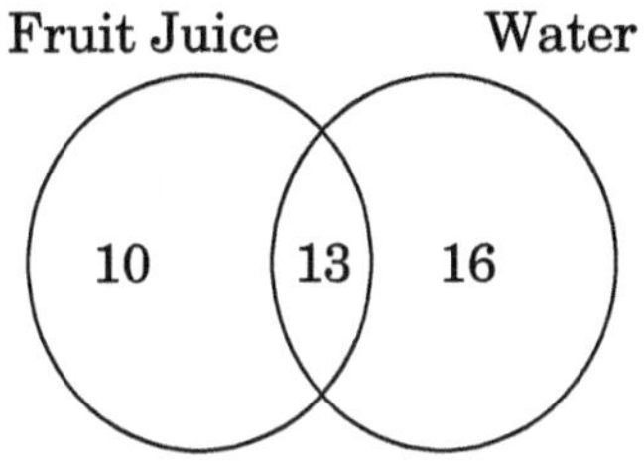

5. The diagram below shows the Cakes and Candies taken by children from a bakery shop. How many children have only cakes?

(a) 16

(b) 19

(c) 22

(d) 26

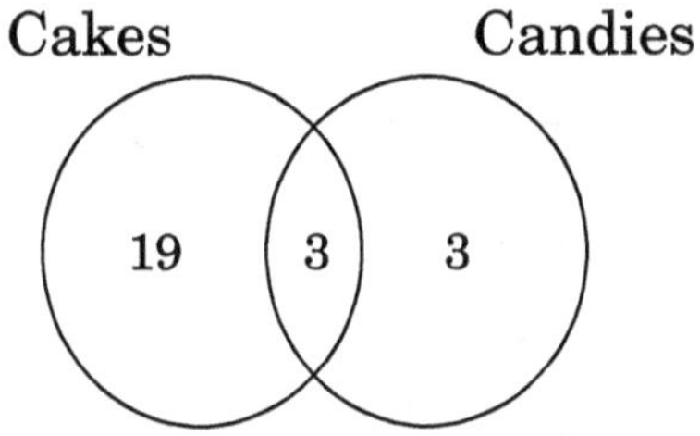

6. The diagram below shows the sports people watched. How many people watched Tennis match?

(a) 10

(b) 15

(c) 20

(d) 25

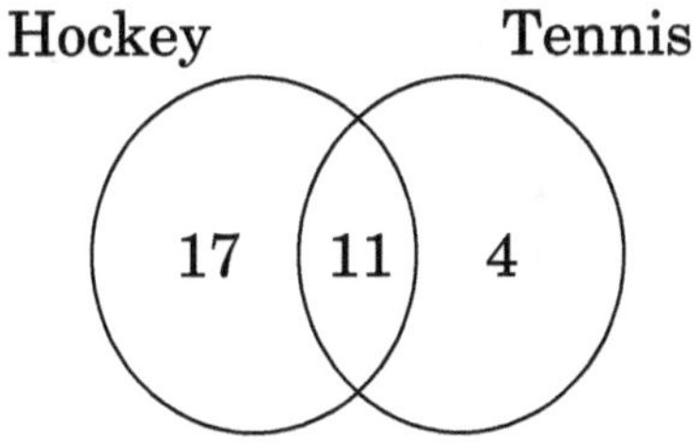

7. The diagram below shows number of men and women watching a Cricket match. How many persons are watching cricket match?

(a) 8

(b) 19

(c) 18

(d) 15

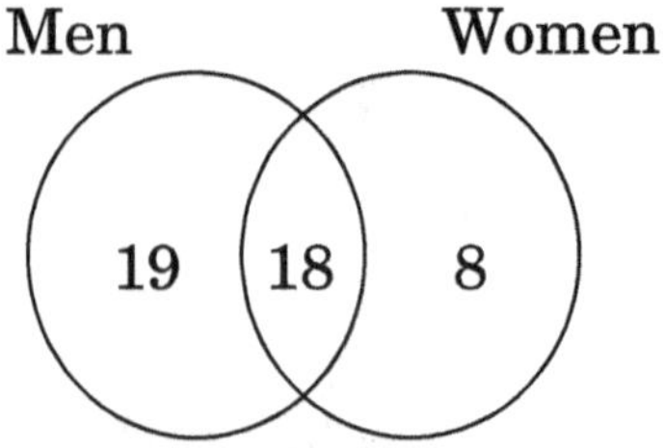

8. The diagram below shows the number of chocolates and pizza. How many children like only pizza?

(a) 5

(b) 6

(c) 8

(d) 9

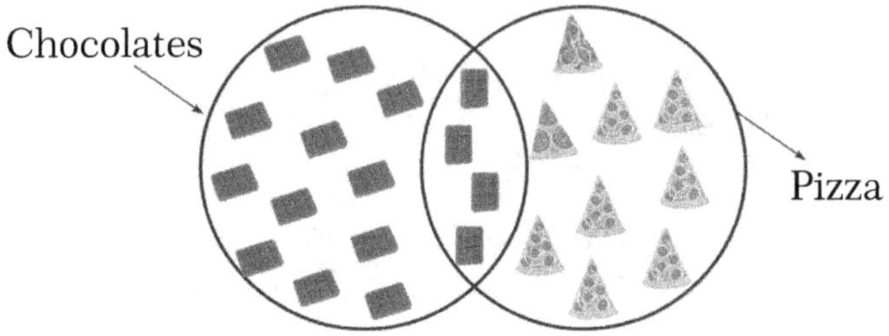

9. How many flowers are only Pink?

(a) 3

(b) 4

(c) 5

(d) 1

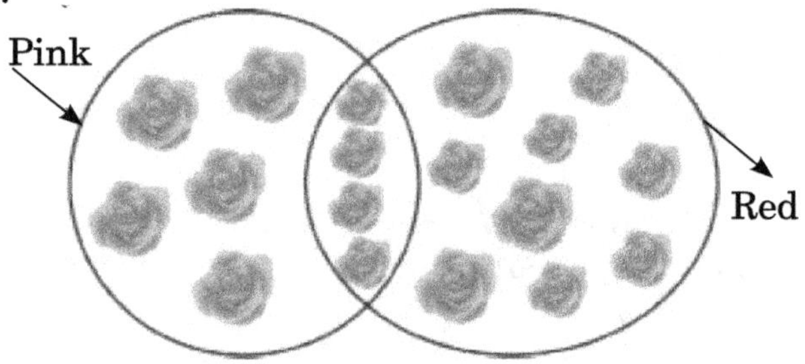

10. How many shapes are heart?

(a) 4

(b) 7

(c) 10

(d) 14

11. The diagram below shows the number of people watching sports at J.L.N. Stadium. How many people watched only Baseball?

(a) 11

(b) 10

(c) 19

(d) 29

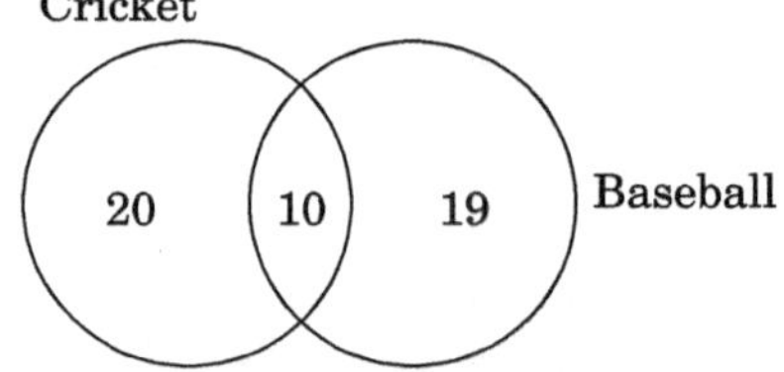

12. How many students are not taking both Dance and Drama classes?

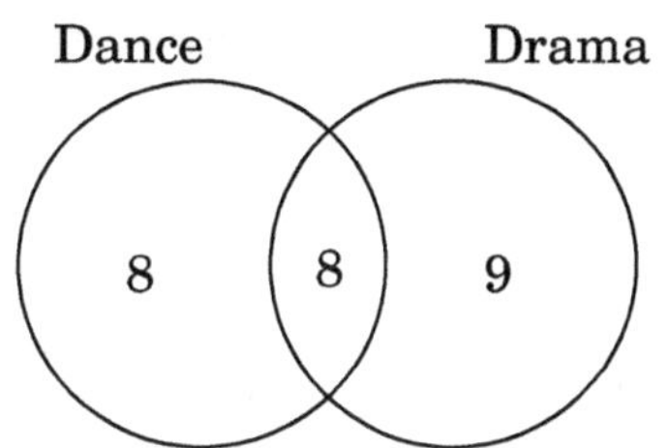

(a) 8

(b) 9

(c) 12

(d) 17

Direction (Qs. 13 and 14): Observe the diagram carefully and answer the questions.

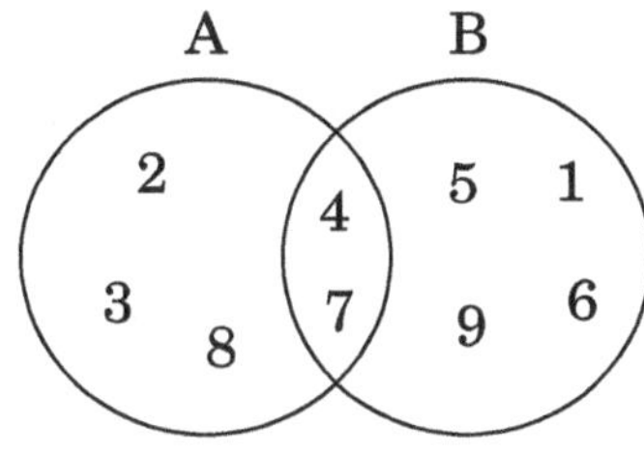

13. What are the elements of Set A?

(a) (2, 3, 8)

(b) (2, 3, 8, 4)

(c) (2, 3, 8, 4, 7)

(d) (5, 1, 9, 6)

14. What are the elements of both Set A and Set B?

(a) (2, 3, 8, 4)

(b) (4, 7)

(c) (5, 1, 9, 6, 4, 7)

(d) (2, 3, 8, 4, 7)

15. How many students like apples as well as mangoes?

(a) 12

(b) 11

(c) 8

(d) 4

16. The diagram below shows the attributes of flowers in a flower shop. How many flowers are only Yellow?

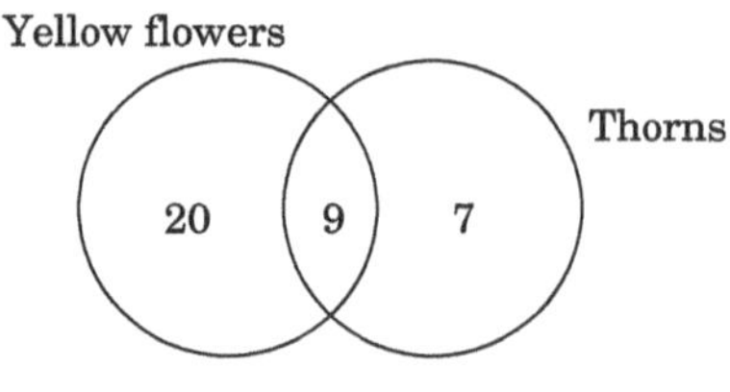

(a) 9   (b) 7   (c) 20   (d) 28

Direction (Qs. 17 and 18): The diagrams below represent a class of children. G is the set of girls and F is the set of children who like football.

(a) 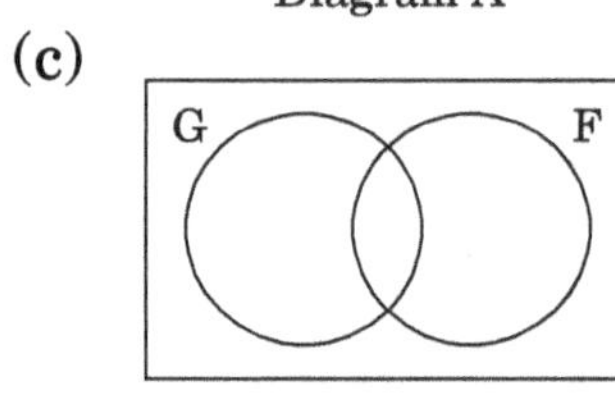

Diagram A

(b)

Diagram B

(c) 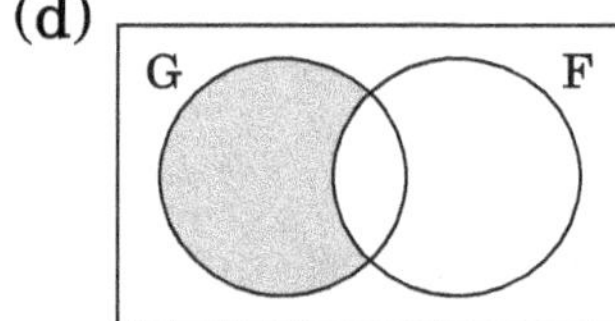

Diagram C

(d)

Diagram D

17. Which diagram has the shading which represents girls who like football?
    (a) Diagram A   (b) Diagram B   (c) Diagram C   (d) Diagram D

18. Which diagram represents girls who dislike football?
    (a) Diagram A   (b) Diagram B   (c) Diagram C   (d) Diagram D

19. The Triangle stands for Hindi, Circle for French, Square for English and Rectangle for German.

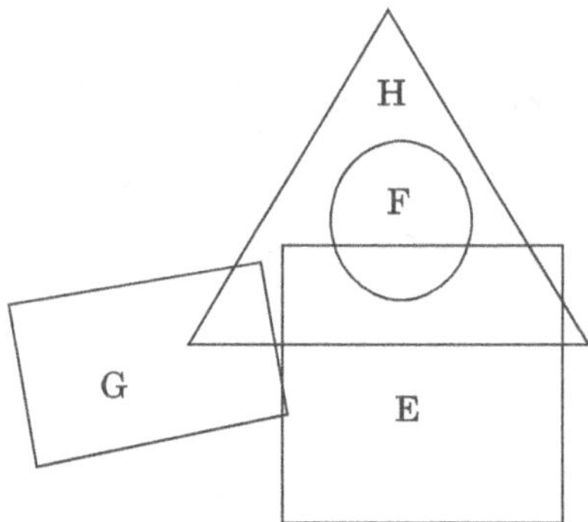

On the basis of above diagram, which of the following statements is true?

(a) All French speaking people speak German

(b) All French speaking people speak English

(c) All German speaking people speak English and Hindi

(d) All French speaking people speak Hindi also

20. Which Venn diagram is best to illustrate the relationship among Pigeon Birds and Parrot?

(a) 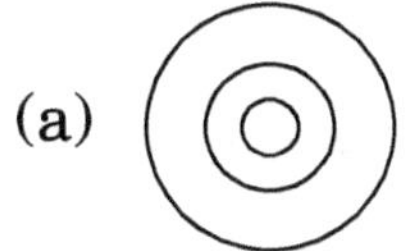 (b) 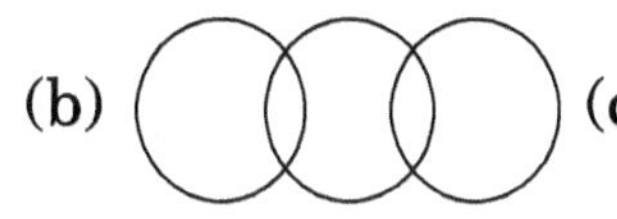 (c)  (d) 

21. Which Venn diagram is best to represent the relationship among Earth, Planets, Sun?

(a)  (b)  (c)  (d) 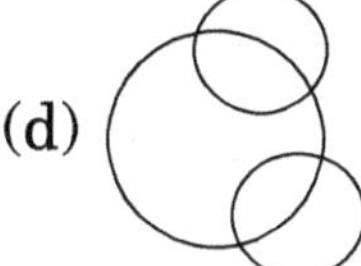

22. How many shapes are diamonds but not red?

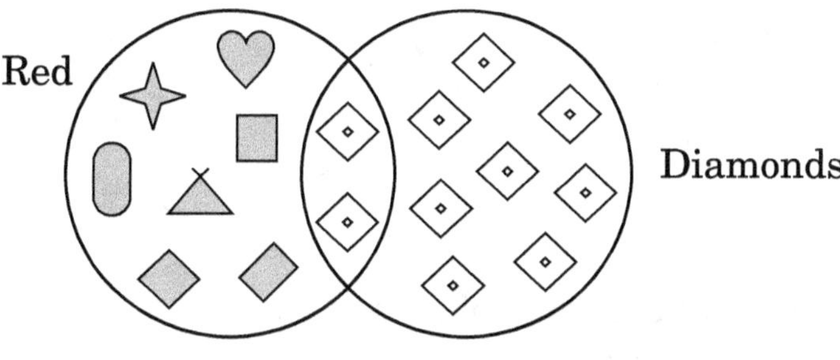

(a) 8 (b) 9 (c) 10 (d) 12

23. Which Venn diagram is best to represents the relationship among English, German, Latin.

(a) 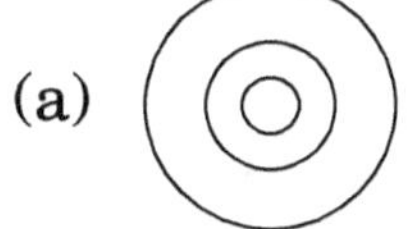 (b)  (c) 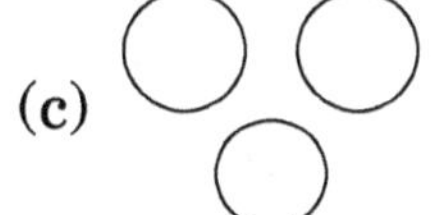 (d) 

24. Which number is in all the geometrical figures?

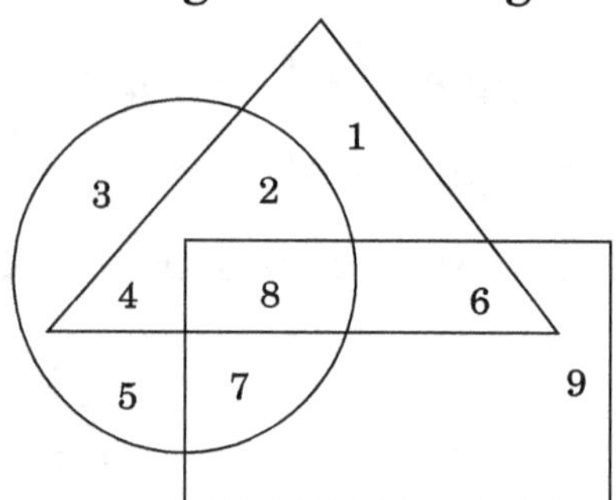

(a) 2　　　　　(b) 4　　　　　(c) 8　　　　　(d) 9

25. Which Venn diagram represents the best relation among Paper, Stationery, Ink?

(a) 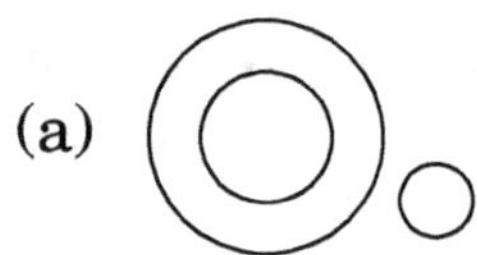　　　(b) 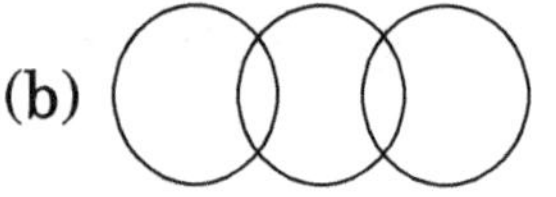　　　(c) 　　　(d)

Direction (Qs. 26-30): Study the diagram given below and answer the following questions.

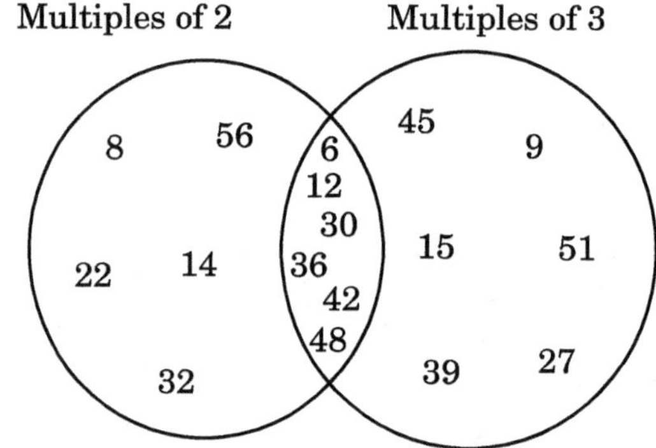

26. How many Numbers are multiple of 2 only?
　　(a) 5　　　　　(b) 11　　　　　(c) 6　　　　　(d) 4

27. How many numbers are multiple of 3?
　　(a) 6　　　　　(b) 5　　　　　(c) 12　　　　　(d) 11

28. How many numbers are multiple of 2 and 3 both?
　　(a) 5　　　　　(b) 6　　　　　(c) 11　　　　　(d) 4

29. How many numbers are not multiples of both 2 and 3?
　　(a) 5　　　　　(b) 6　　　　　(c) 10　　　　　(d) 11

30. How many numbers are multiple of only 3?
　　(a) 11　　　　　(b) 12　　　　　(c) 5　　　　　(d) 6

Level-1

1. **(a)** Bus and Train are different from each other but some travellers travel by Bus and Train both.

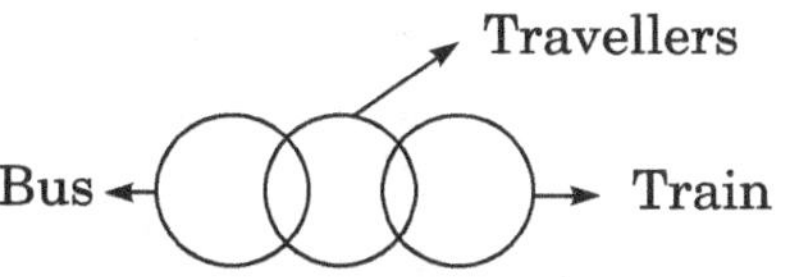

2. **(b)** Potato and Brinjal are entirely different but both are vegetables.

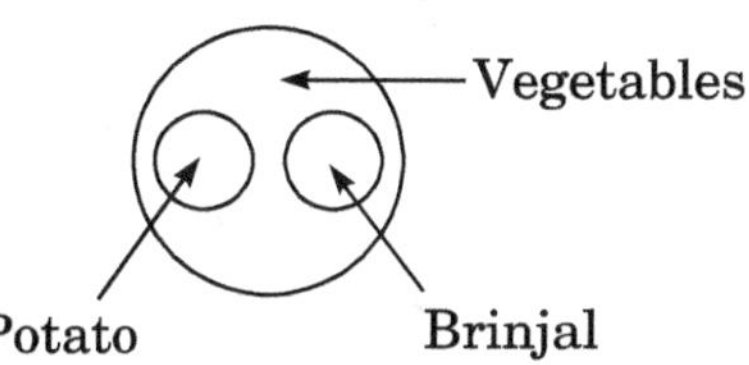

3. **(a)** Only four shapes have straight sides. These shapes are △, □, ⬠ and ⬠.

4. **(b)** Five shapes (▽, ▭, ⌣, ○, ♧) have curved sides.

5. **(c)** Only 2 shapes (△ and ▭) have both straight and curved sides.

6. **(c)**

Some boys are students.

Some students are athletes.

Some athletes are boys.

7. **(a)** In option (a) A represents even Numbers less than 10 and B represents odd numbers less than 10. But both are entirely different.

8. **(b)**

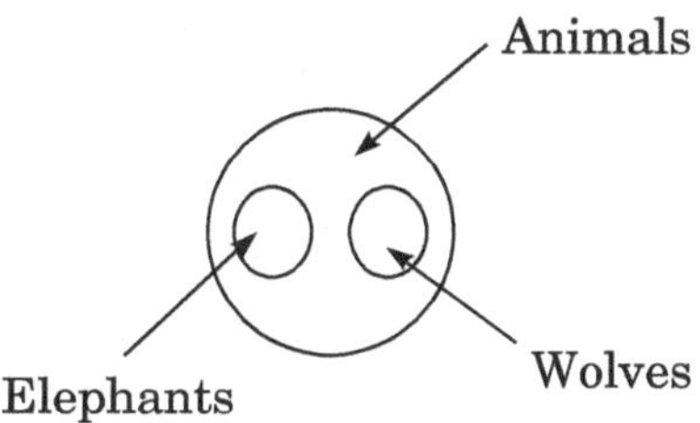

Elephants and Wolves are entirely different. But both are animals.

9. **(a)** 50 students like only lime.

10. **(c)** 20 students like both lime and Pepsi.

11. **(b)** 10 students like neither Lime nor Pepsi.

12. **(b)** 4 things are made of only metal.

13. **(c)** 4 things are made of plastic.

14. **(c)** Q is the part of the figure represents those boys who are players but not coach.

15. **(b)** S indicates those students who play all three games.

16. **(c)** The regions represented by the letters K, J and I denote such people who can speak only one language.

17. (c) Number 4 lies inside all geometrical figures.

18. (c) Number 3 is an odd number which lies inside both triangle and rectangle.

19. (a) Set A represents the red circle.

20. (a) All Crows are Birds. But, Dogs are entirely different.

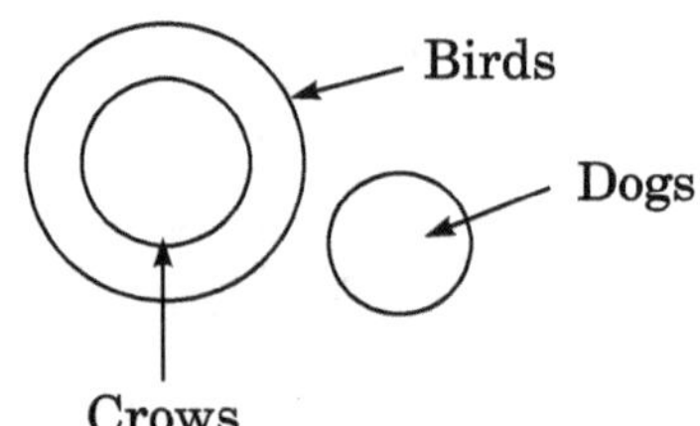

21. (d) Only B is in all three shapes.

22. (a) 2 Number lies inside all the figures.

23. (b) Numbers 5 and 1 lie inside two figures.

Number 5 lie inside triangle and circle.

Number 1 lie inside triangle and rectangle.

24. (c) Number 9 lies only inside the triangle.

25. (d)

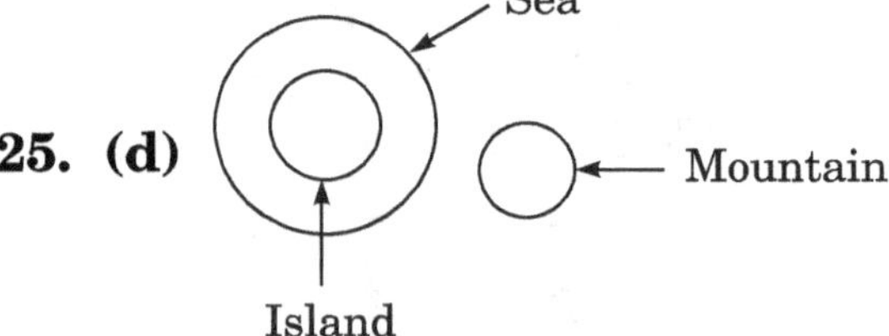

Island is a part of sea. But Mountain is entirely different.

26. (d) 6 + 2 + 3 + 4 = 15 persons had cakes.

27. (c) 5 persons had only pizzas.

28. (b) 4 persons had both pizzas and burgers but not cakes.

29. (a) 3 persons had cakes and pizzas but not burgers.

30. (d) 3 + 4 + 2 + 4 = 13 persons had at least two items.

Level-2

1. (d) 5 Squares are shaded.

2. (d) (10 + 20) = 30 students are taking Dance Classes in Summer Camp.

3. (b) 12 + 20 = 32 students have dog.

4. (c) 10 people did not drink water.

5. (b) 19 children have only cakes.

6. (b) 11 + 4 = 15 people watched Tennis Match.

7. (c) 45 persons are watching cricket match.

8. (d) 9 children like only pizza.

9. (c) 5 flowers are only pink.

10. (b) 7 shapes are heart shaped.

11. (c) 19 watched only Baseball.

12. (d) (8 + 9) = 17 (Dance + Drama) students are not taking both Dance and Drama

13. (c) 2, 3, 8, 4, 7 are the elements of Set A.

14. (b) 4, 7 are the elements of both Set A and Set B.

15. (d) 4 students like apples as well as mangoes.

16. (c) 20.

17. (b) In diagram shading region represents girls who like football.

18. (d) Diagram D represents girls who dislike football.

19. (d) Since the circle lies inside the triangle, so, all the French speaking people speak Hindi also.

20. (c)

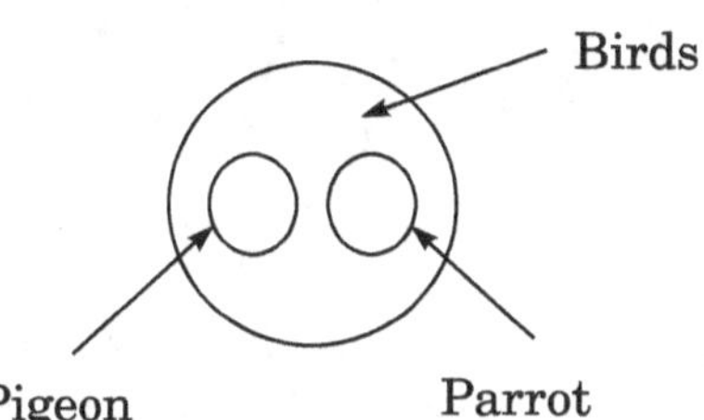

All Pigeons and Parrots are birds. Both come in the same class of Birds.

21. (c)

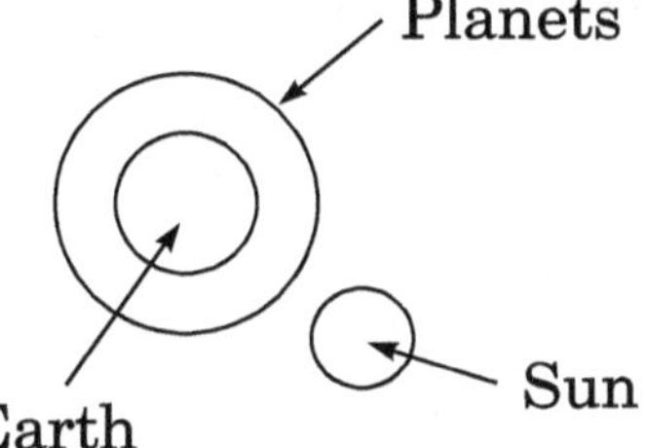

Earth is a planet. But, sun is entirely different.

22. (a) 10 shapes are diamond but not red.

23. (c)

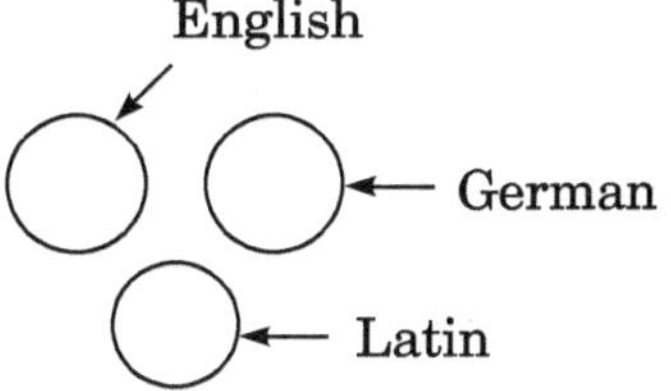

English, German and Latin are entirely different from each other.

24. (c) Number 8 lies in all three shapes.

25. (d)

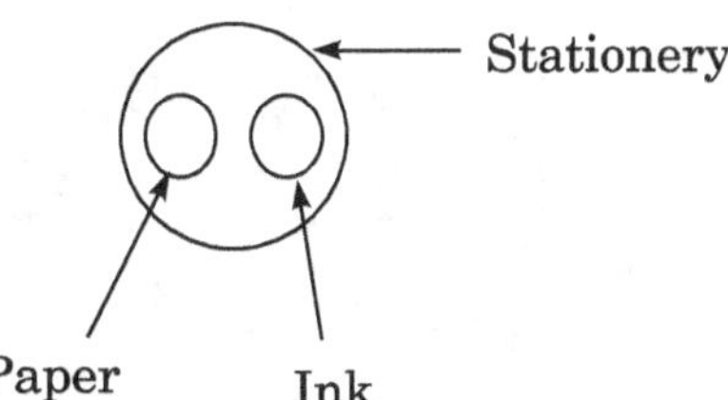

Paper and Ink are entirely different. But both are items of stationery.

26. (a) 5 numbers (8, 56, 14, 22, 32) are multiples of 2.

27. (c) 12 numbers are multiple of 3.

12 numbers are 6, 12, 30, 36, 42, 48, 45, 9, 15, 51, 39, 27.

28. (b) 6 numbers (6, 12, 30, 36, 42, 48) are multiple of 2 and 3 both.

29. (d) Multiple of 2 only = 5 numbers (8, 14, 22, 32, 56)

Multiple of 3 only = 6 numbers (9, 15, 27, 39, 45, 51)

5 + 6 = 11 numbers are not multiples of both 2 and 3.

30. (d) 6 numbers are multiple of only 3.

Geometrical Shapes

OBJECTIVES

- To identify different objects which represent some kind of geometrical shapes which we are coming across in our day to day life. (Both 2D and 3D)
- To recognise different parts of various geometrical shapes such as vertex and sides of a particular geometrical pattern.
- Use of different geometrical shapes for creating Tangrams.
- Knowledge of line of symmetry. (horizontal and vertical)

GEOMETRIC SHAPE

Geometric Shape is defined as a set of points or vertices and sides connecting to the point to form a closed entry. There are various kinds of geometrical shapes. Basing upon the number of vertices and sides they are identified.

2d Geometric Shapes

Triangle	• Triangle has three sides. • It has three vertices.
Square	• Squares have 4 equal sides and 4 right angles. • They have 4 lines of symmetry. • All squares belong to the rectangle family. • All squares belong to the rhombus family. • All squares are also parallelograms.

Rectangle	• Rectangles have 4 sides and 4 right angles.
	• They all have 2 lines of symmetry (4 lines if they are also a square!)
	• All rectangles belong to the parallelogram family.
Rhombus	• Rhombuses (rhombii) have 4 equal sides.
	• Both pairs of opposite sides are parallel.
	• They all have 2 lines of symmetry (4 lines if they are a square)
	• All rhombuses belong to the parallelogram family.
Parallelogram	• Parallelograms have 2 pairs of parallel sides.
	• Some parallelograms have lines of symmetry (depending on whether they are also squares, rectangles or rhombuses), but most do not.
Circle	• Circles have a point in the centre from which each point on the diameter is equidistant.
	• They have infinite lines of symmetry.
Ellipse	• Ellipses are like circles which have been squashed or stretched.
	• They have 2 lines of symmetry.
	• They are also a special type of oval.
	• The longest and shortest diameters of the ellipses are called the major and minor axes. These axes are also the lines of symmetry.
Crescent	• Crescent shapes are made when two circles overlap, or when one circle is removed from another circle.
	• The perimeter of crescents made from two circular arcs.
	• They have one line of symmetry.
	• Our moon forms crescent shapes during its phases.

Pentagon	• 5 sided polygon
Hexagon	• 6 sided polyon
Heptagon	• 7 sided polygon
Octagon	• 8 sided polygon

3D Geometrical Shapes

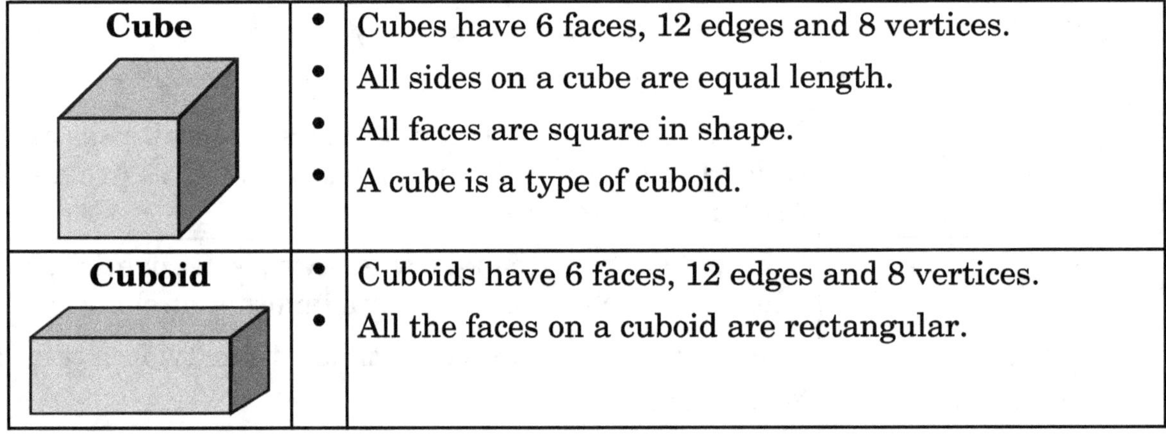

Cube	• Cubes have 6 faces, 12 edges and 8 vertices. • All sides on a cube are equal length. • All faces are square in shape. • A cube is a type of cuboid.
Cuboid	• Cuboids have 6 faces, 12 edges and 8 vertices. • All the faces on a cuboid are rectangular.

Sphere	•	Spheres have either 0 or 1 faces, 0 edges and 0 vertices.
Cylinder	•	Cylinders have either 2 or 3 faces, 0 or 2 edges, and 0 vertices.
Cone	•	Cones have either 1 or 2 faces, 0 or 1 edges, and 1 apex (which is described by some mathematicians as a vertex).

REGULAR GEOMETRIC SHAPE

The geometric shapes whose all sides are equal sides and equal interior angles are known as regular geometric shape.

 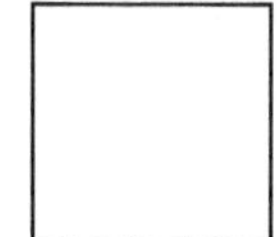 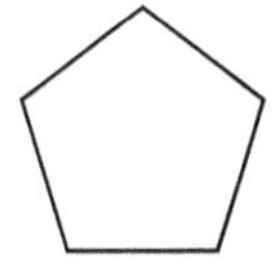 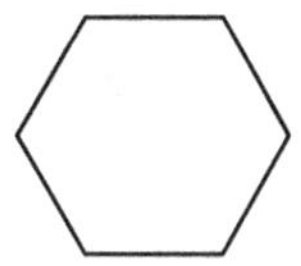 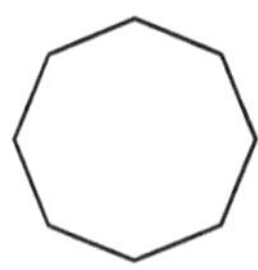

IRREGULAR GEOMETRIC SHAPES

The geometric shapes which have sides and angles of any length and size.

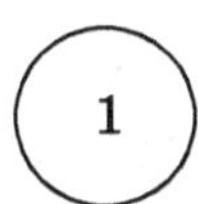 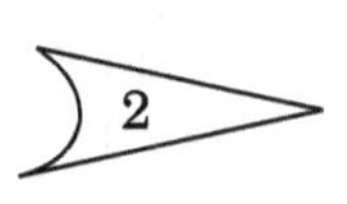 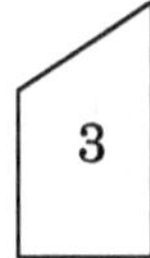 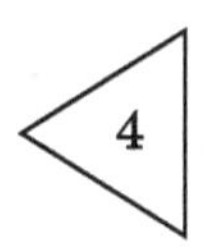 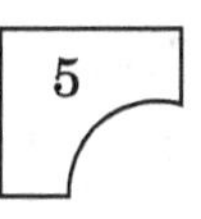

Direction (Examples 1 and 2): Answer the questions based on given figure (X).

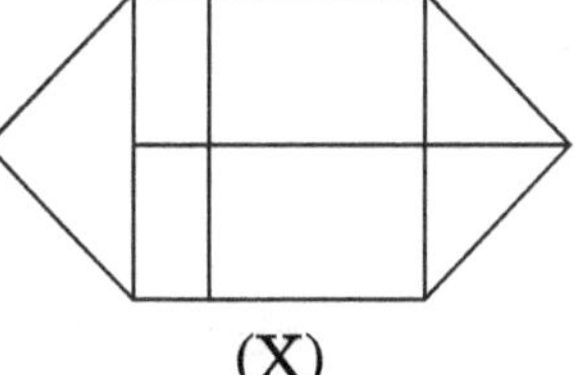

(X)

Example 1:

How many rectangles are three in the given figure (X)?

   (a) 10   (b) 9   (c) 8   (d) 7

(1-2) The figure may be labelled as shown.

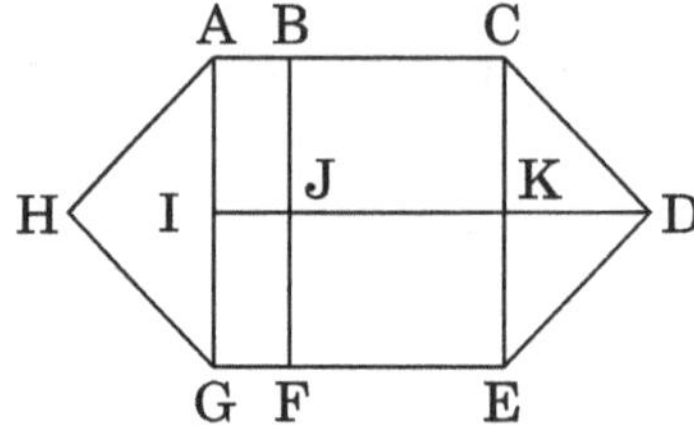

Ans. (b)

The simplest rectangles are ABJI, BCKJ, IJFG and JKEF i.e. 4 in number.

The rectangles composed of two components each are ACKI, BCEF, IKEG and ABFG i.e. 4 in number.

The only rectangle composed of four components is ACEG.

Thus, there are 4 + 4 + 1 = 9 rectangles in the given figure.

Example 2:

How many triangles are there in the given figure (X).

   (a) 1   (b) 2   (c) 3   (d) 4

Ans. (d)

Triangles are :

    $\triangle$ AHG, $\triangle$CKD, $\triangle$KED and $\triangle$CDE i.e. 4 in number.

Example 3:

In the four alternatives a, b, c and d given below there are four different geometric shapes. Which among these is an irregular geometric shape?

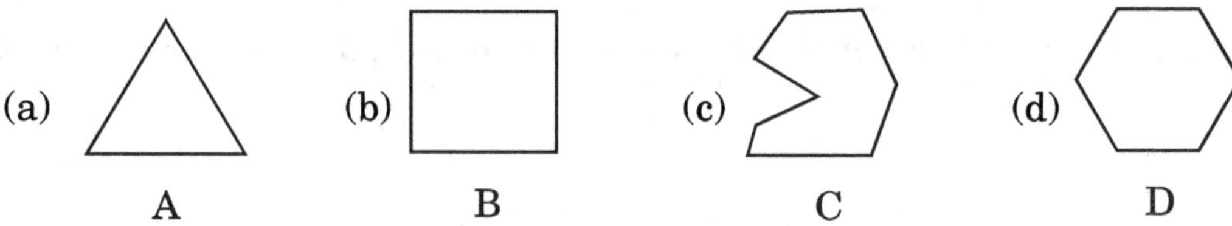

Ans. (c)

The figure C is an irregular geometry shape.

These are the dissection puzzles which have seven different pieces of three geometrical shapes placed in specific numbers. The pieces are arranged in such manner that it reflects various features of real life like houses, people, animals, fruits etc. They are made in such a way that they are easily identifiable.

Here three tangram images are given below. Identify each one of them.

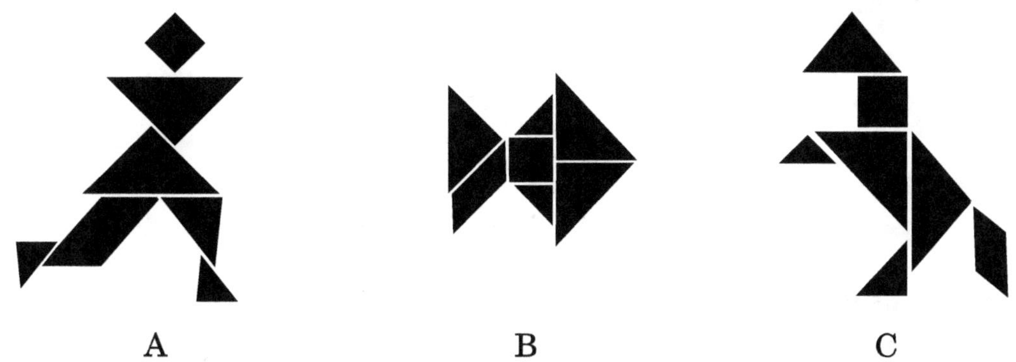

| A | B | C |

The three images serially are

(A) A person in a running posture

(B) A fish

(C) A horse

Example 4:

Which of the three images given above is having square in place of its head?

(a) A   (b) B   (c) C   (d) None of these

Ans. (a)

The man in running posture in image A is having a square in place of its head.

SYMMETRY

When an object is cut from the middle gives two equal parts of the main item then it is known as symmetrical object. On the other hand when the sub divided parts are not at all equal to each other it is called as asymmetric object.

There are some symmetrical objects which are given below:

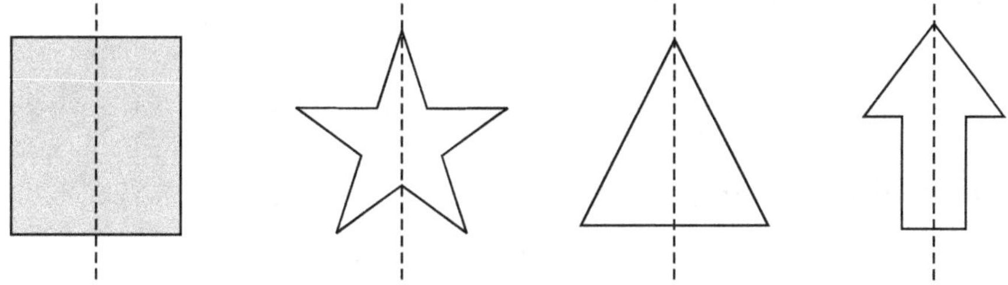

The line from which the image is cut into two equal parts is known as Line of symmetry which can be further divided into horizontal line of symmetry and vertical line of symmetry.

HORIZONTAL LINE OF SYMMETRY

When a line divides an object in such a way that both the upper and lower parts of the image will be equally opposite to each other, it is known as horizontal line of Symmetry.

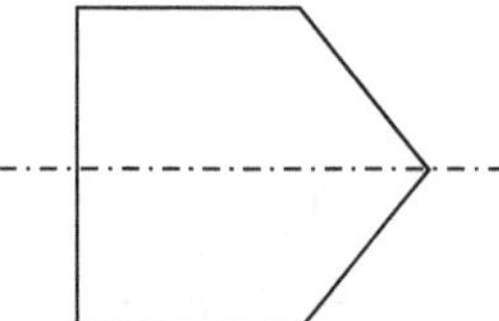

Horizontal Line of Symmetry

VERTICAL LINE OF SYMMETRY

When a line divides an object in such a way the image in the right hand side is equally opposite to the image of the left hand side, it is known as vertical line of Symmetry.

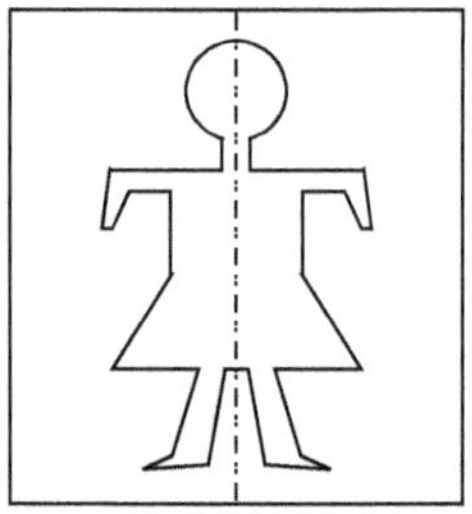

Vertical line of symmetry

Example 5:

How many letters given below have at least one line of symmetry?

CPTIOHS

(a) 5   (b) 6   (c) 7   (d) None

Ans. (a)

Dotted lines are lines of symmetry.

1. 

Carefully observe the picture given above and count how may quadrilateral surround the only hexagon in the image.

(a) 3 (b) 4 (c) 5 (d) 6

Direction (Qs. 2–5): Observe the given geometrical shapes based scenario carefully and answer the following questions carefully.

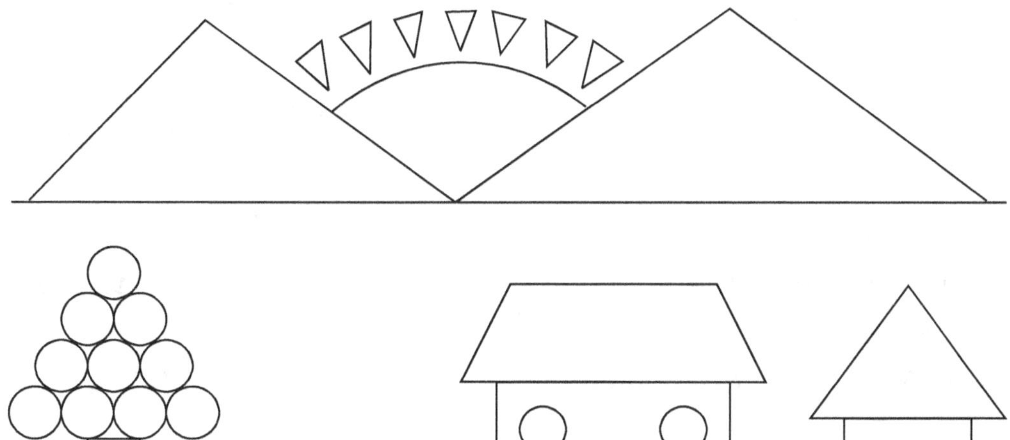

2. How many circles are there in the given image?

(a) 15 (b) 10 (c) 12 (d) 18

3. Which shape appears for maximum times?

(a) Square (b) Circles (c) Triangle (d) Rectangle

4. Which shape has appeared for the least number of times?

(a) ☐   (b) 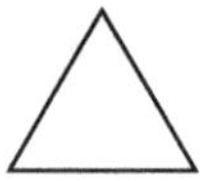 △   (c) 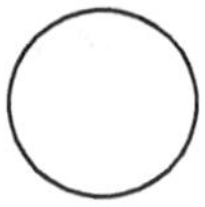 ◯   (d) 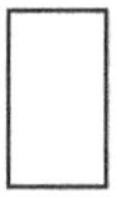 ▯

5. How many different types of shapes are there in the given image?

(a) 8   (b) 8   (c) 4   (d) 2

Direction (Qs. 6–10): Given below some tangrams which represent some animals. Now carefully observe each one of them and give answer to the following question.

(a)

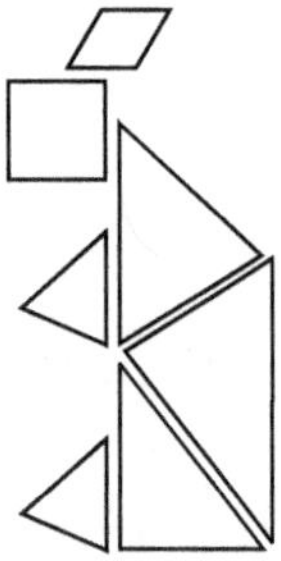

Rabbit

(b)

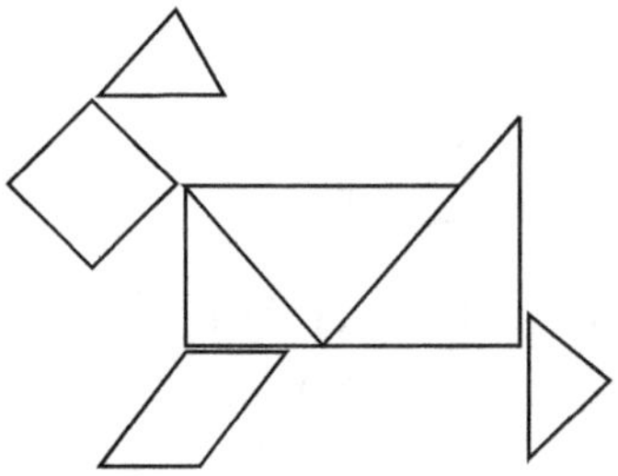

Dog

(b)

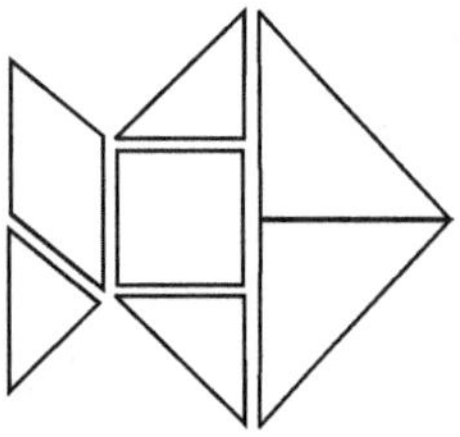

Fish

(d)

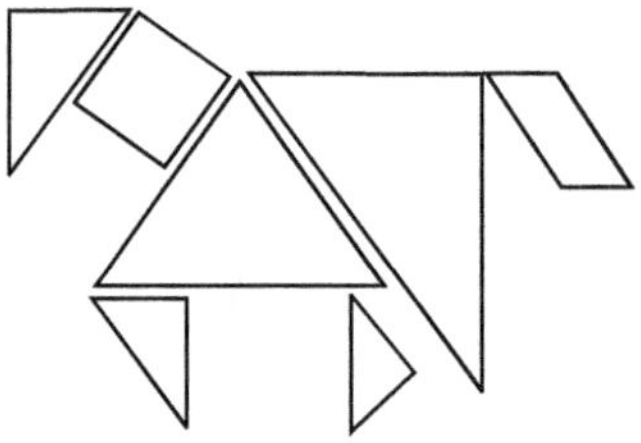

Horse

6. In which of the above figure square is surrounded by the triangles and parallelogram

(a) Fish   (b) Rabbit   (c) Horse   (d) Dog

7. Which animal has a tail made up of only a parallelogram?

(a) Rabbit   (b) Horse   (c) Fish   (d) Dog

8. Which animal has an ear in the shape of triangle?

(a) Fish   (b) Horse   (c) Rabbit   (d) Dog

9. Whose face is made up of 2 triangles?

(a) Rabbit   (b) Dog   (c) Fish   (d) Horse

10. Which of the following statements is correct?

    (a) Fish has 2 triangles in its tail

    (b) Horse has 2 squares in its legs

    (c) All animals are made us of seven tangrams

    (d) All are correct.

11. Shivam used a crayon to draw a shape on a piece of paper. The shape has 6 angles which shape could Shivam have drawn?

    (a) 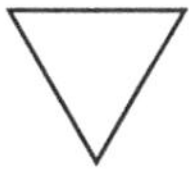   (b) 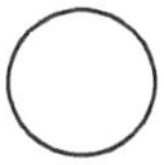   (c) 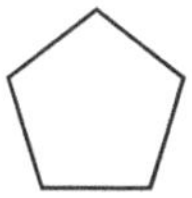   (d)

12. Which shape can be depicted from the following figure?

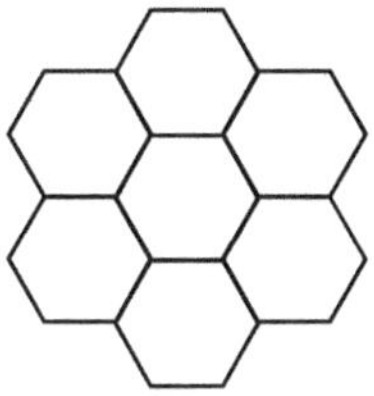

    (a) Square   (b) Pentagon   (c) Square   (d) Hexagon

13. Which shape is depicted by the figure (X).

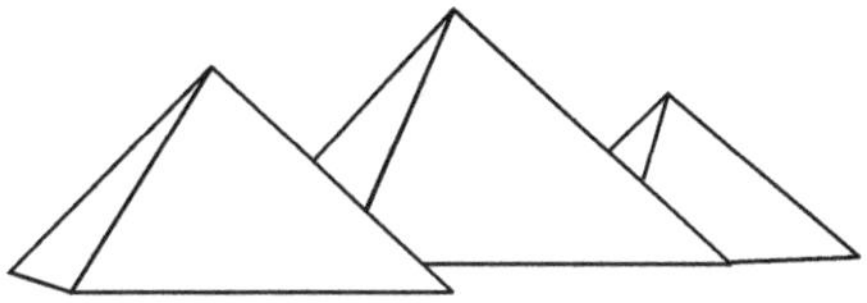

    (X)

    (a) Triangle   (b) Rectangle   (c) Square   (d) Circle

14. A hexagon can be divided into how many triangles?

    (a) 3   (b) 2   (c) 6   (d) 4

15. Which of the following shape is identical to the figure (X)

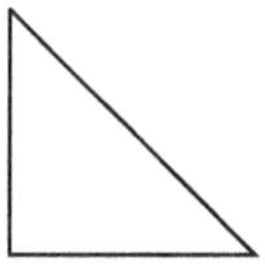

    (X)

    (a)    (b)    (c) 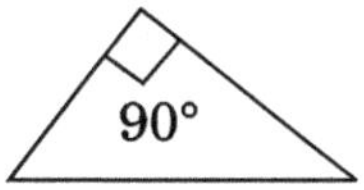 90°   (d)

16. Which of the following figures correctly shows a line of symmetry?

(a) 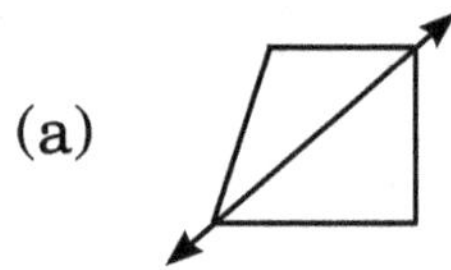

(b) 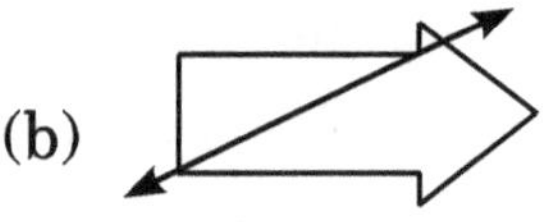

(c) 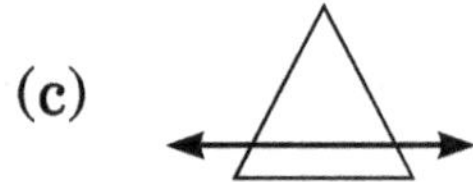

(d) 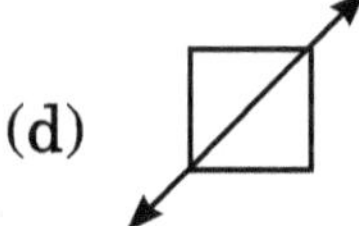

17. Which of the following shapes is regular shape.

(a) 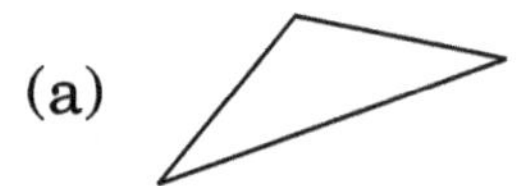 (b)  (c) 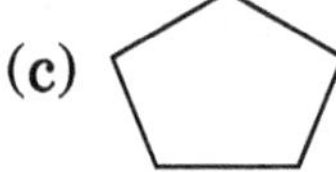 (d) 

18.

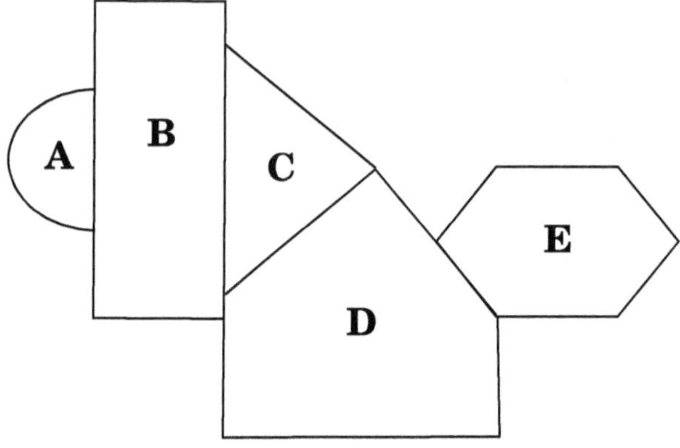

Which among the above shapes shares a common border?

(a) Half circle, Rectangle, Pentagon

(b) Hexagon, Pentagon, Half circle

(c) Rectangle, Triangle, Pentagon

(d) Hexagon, Triangle, Half circle

19. How many faces does a cube have?

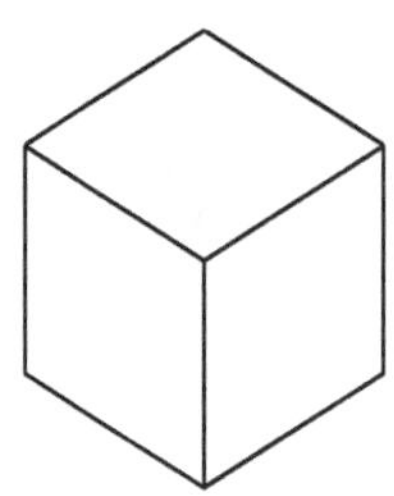

(a) 12 (b) 10 (c) 6 (d) 8

20. 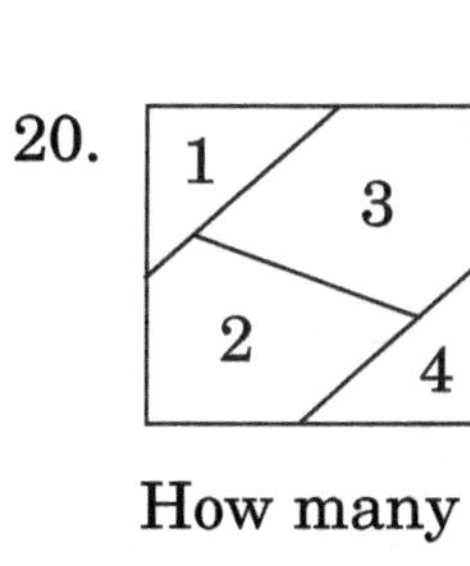

How many pairs of identical shapes are there in the above figure?

(a) 2   (b) 4   (c) 3   (d) 5

21. How many vertical lines are there in the figure below?

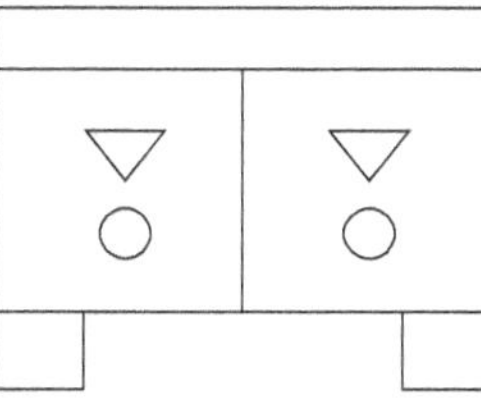

(a) 4   (b) 5   (c) 6   (d) 7

22. At least how many triangles can be formed of the figure given below

(a) 5   (b) 6   (c) 8   (d) 10

23. If the quadrilateral will be cut along AB then which shape would have more area

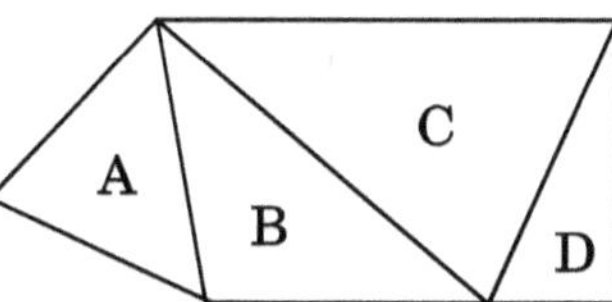

(a) 1

(b) 2

(c) Both will be equal

(d) None of these

24. 

Which of the above triangles has the largest area?

(a) B   (b) C   (c) A   (d) D

25. Which shape has as obtuse angle in it?

(a) 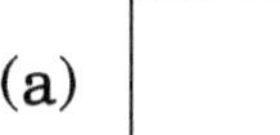   (b) 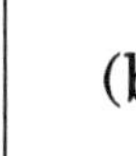   (c)    (d) 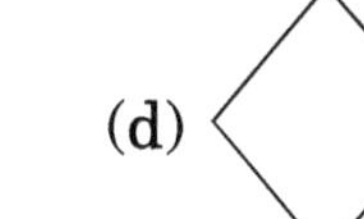

26. How many pieces do you form with 6 cuts of a pizza? All cuts go through the center.

(a) 7   (b) 10   (c) 11   (d) 12

27. Which of the following shapes has a maximum number of sides?

(a) 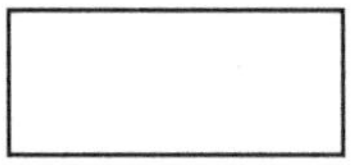   (b) 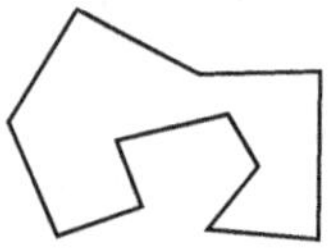   (c) 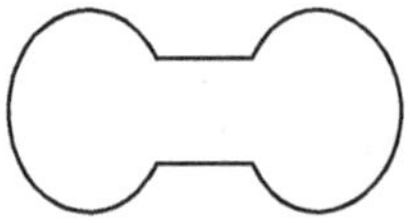   (d)

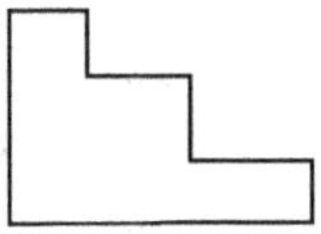

28. What is the intermediate shape of the given image (X)?

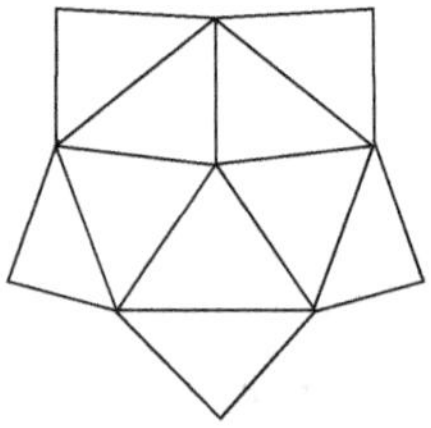

(X)

(a) 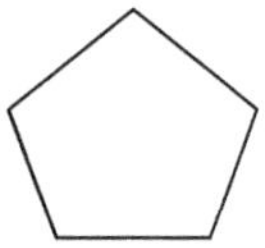   (b) 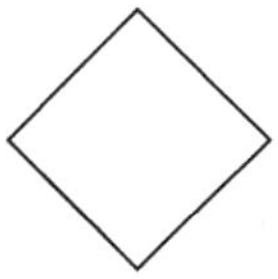   (c) 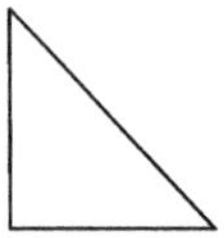   (d)

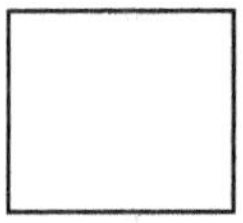

29. How many vertical lines are there in the figure (X)?

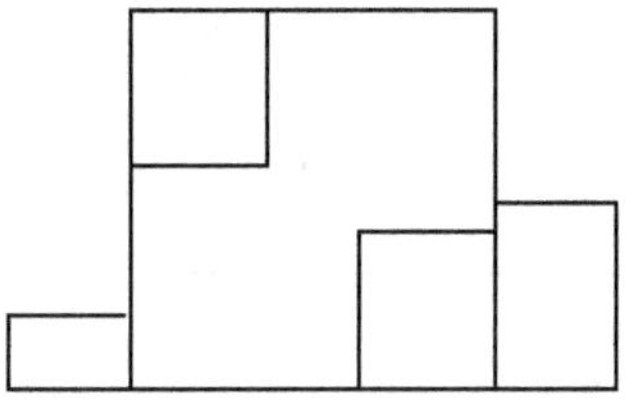

(X)

(a) 5   (b) 2   (c) 6   (d) 9

30. How many triangles are there in Figure (X)?

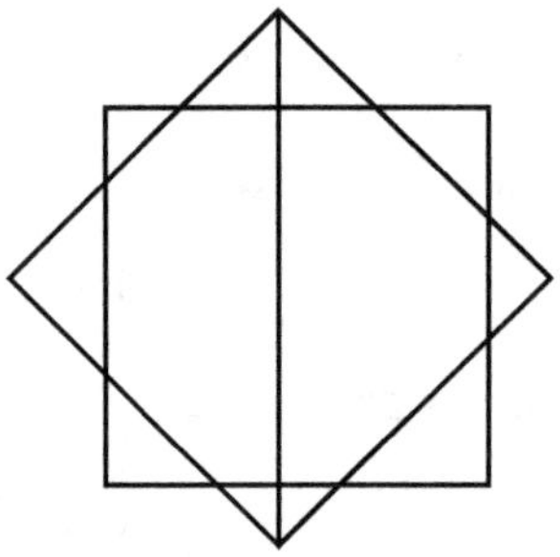

Figure (X)

(a) 12   (b) 16   (c) 14   (d) None of these

LEVEL-2

1. If you cut a pizza in six equal segments, then how many triangle-shaped pieces will you get out of it?

   (a) 8 (b) 6 (c) 7 (d) 5

2. How many more triangles are required to complete the shape of a hexagon in the given figure

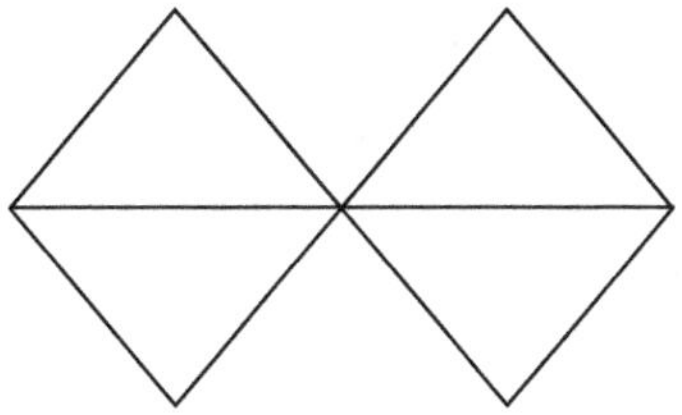

   (a) 1 (b) 3 (c) 2 (d) 4

3. Which part of the given shape has a minimum number of squares?

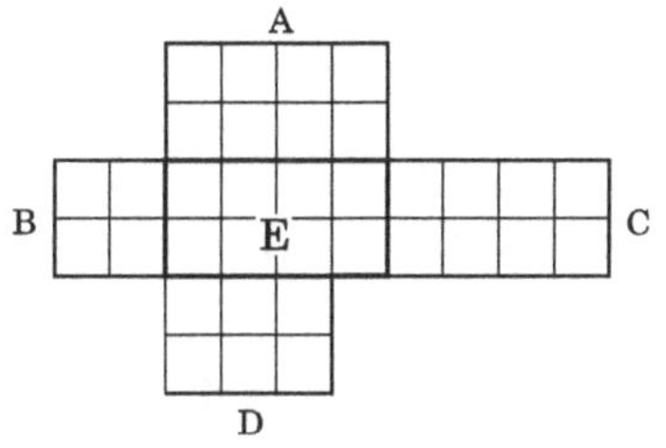

   (a) D (b) A (c) B (d) E

4. Find a shape with no line of symmetry.

   (a) 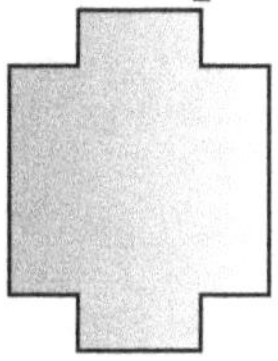 (b) 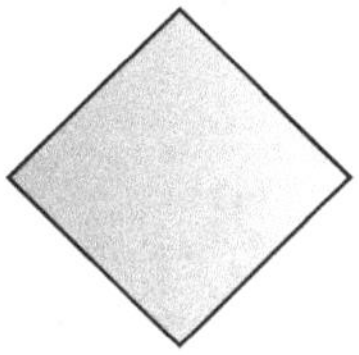 (c) 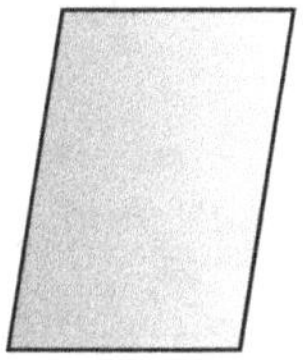 (d)

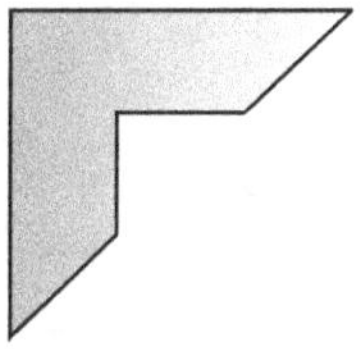

5. Which two shapes could be placed together to form the rectangle?

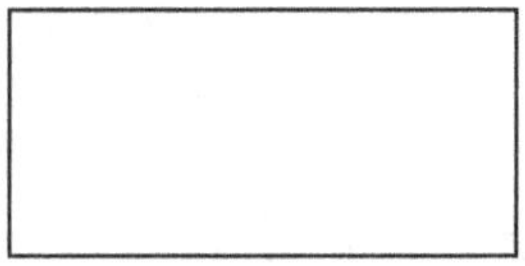

   (a) 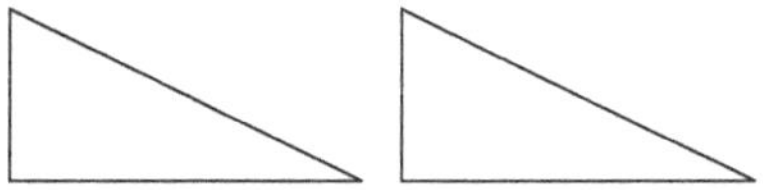 (b)

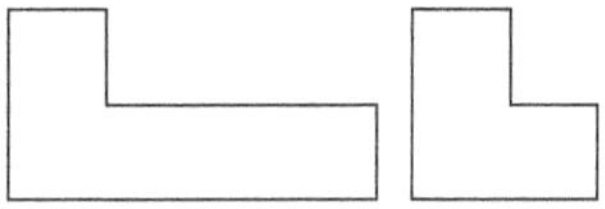

   (c) 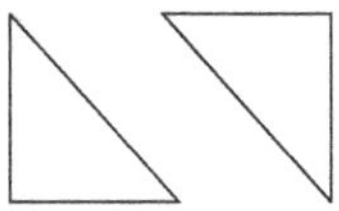 (d)

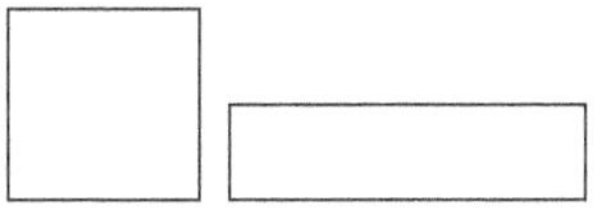

6. Sunita was making a border across her notebook paper. She used one shape and kept flipping it over a vertical axis (reflecting the shape). What did her border look like?

(a)

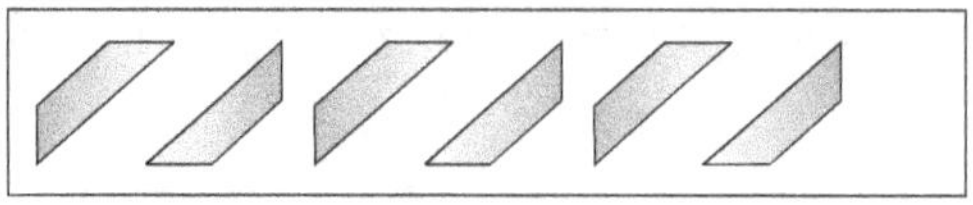

(b)

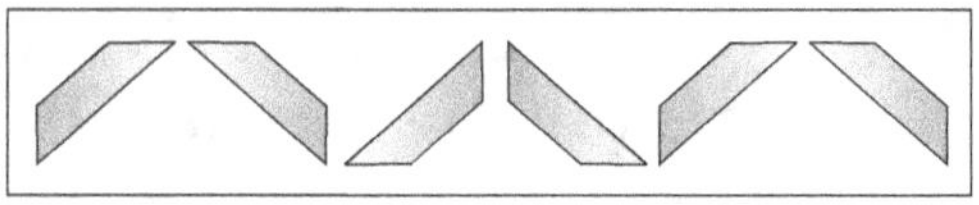

(c)

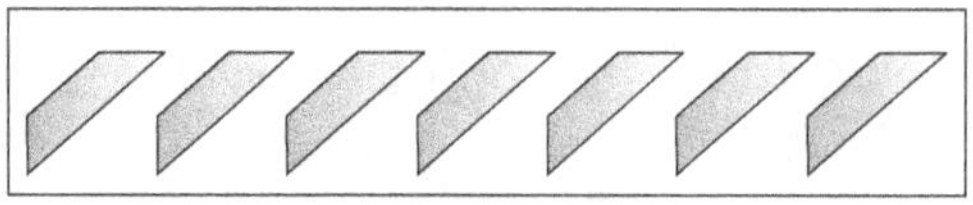

(d)

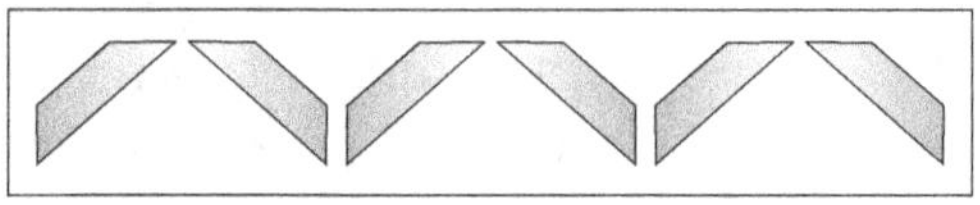

7. There have been given four pairs of shapes which can completely fit into one another. Choose the one which does not completely fit into one another.

(a)

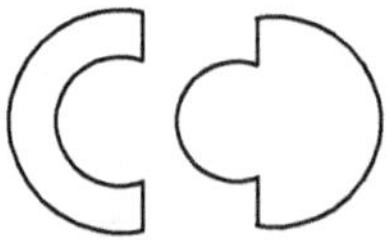

(b)

(c)

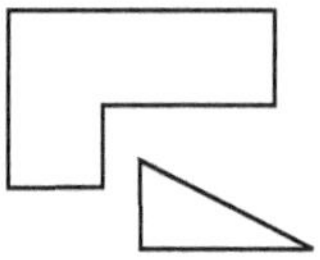

(d)

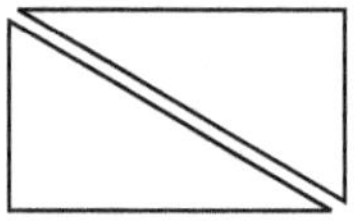

8. How many triangles are there in the given figure.
    (a) 8 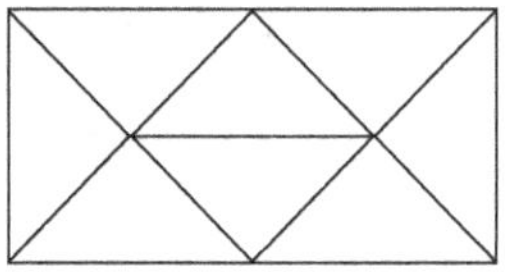
    (b) 10
    (c) 12
    (d) 14

9. At least how many regular rectangles can be formed from the figure given below. 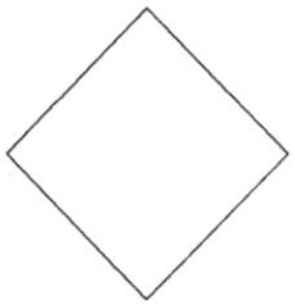
    (a) 4   (b) 3

    (c) 2   (d) 1

10. Which set has shapes with the same number of corners?

(a)

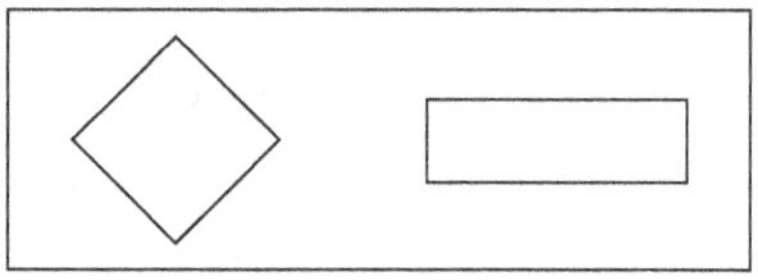

(b)

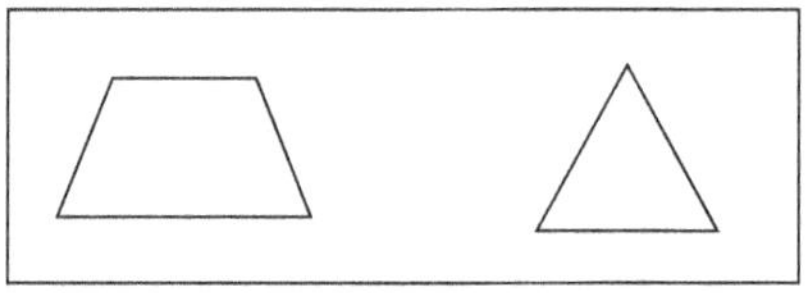

(c)

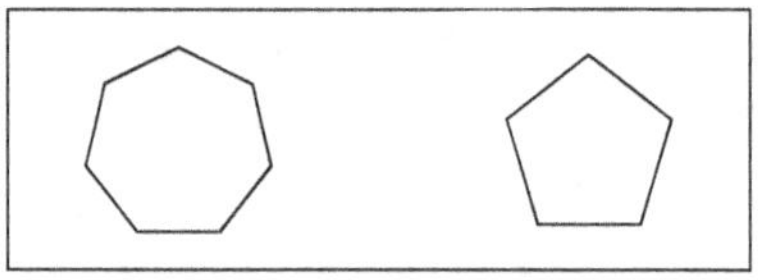

(d)

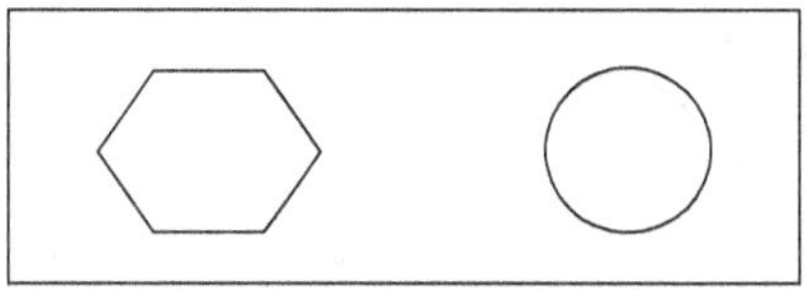

11. How many minimum number of circles have to be separated so as to free all the circles?
    (a) 5 
    (b) 3
    (c) 2
    (d) 9

12. Which shape has the maximum number of sides in the figure given below?

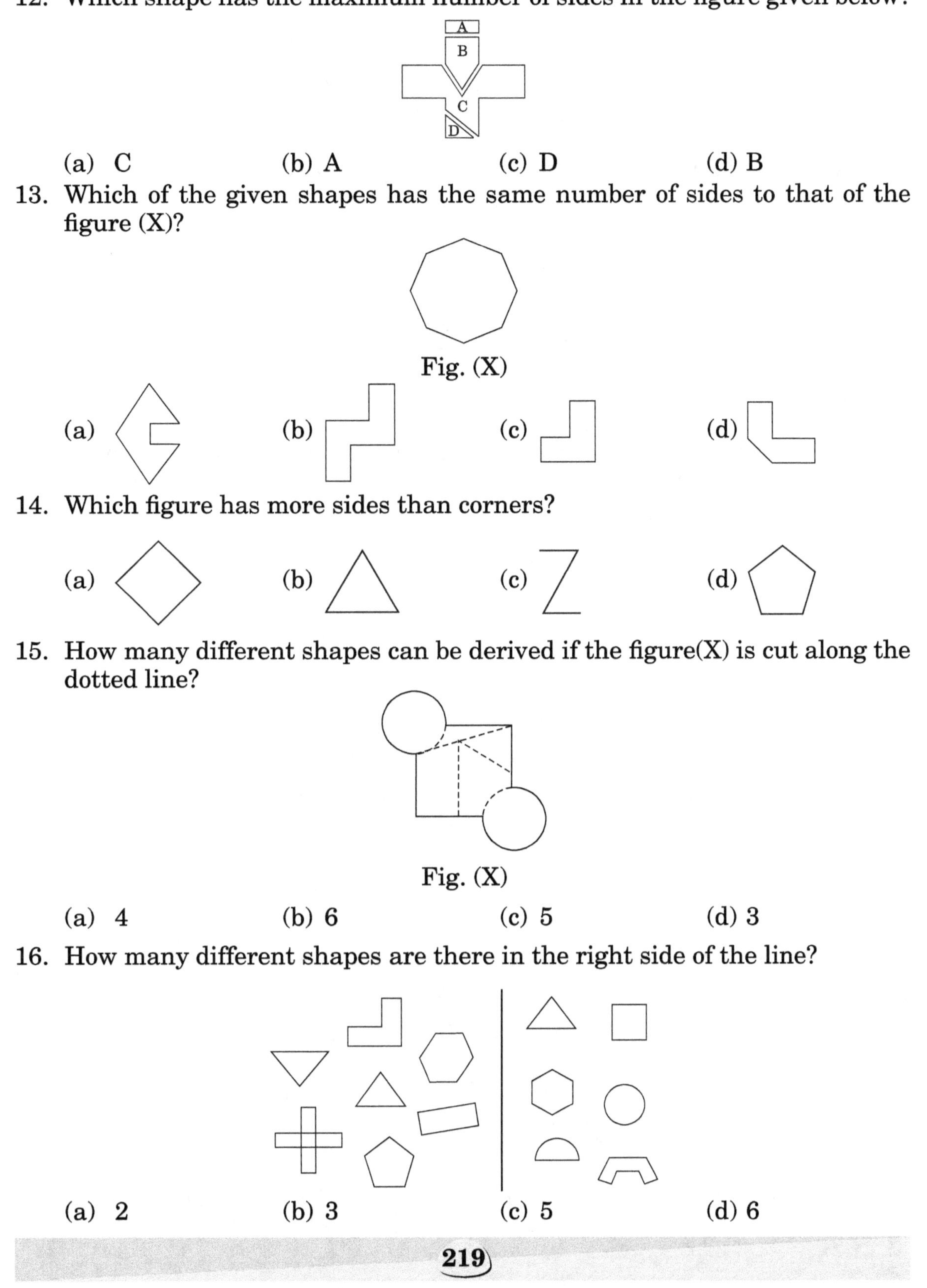

(a) C   (b) A   (c) D   (d) B

13. Which of the given shapes has the same number of sides to that of the figure (X)?

Fig. (X)

(a)   (b)   (c)   (d)

14. Which figure has more sides than corners?

(a)   (b)   (c)   (d)

15. How many different shapes can be derived if the figure(X) is cut along the dotted line?

Fig. (X)

(a) 4   (b) 6   (c) 5   (d) 3

16. How many different shapes are there in the right side of the line?

(a) 2   (b) 3   (c) 5   (d) 6

17. Which of the following shapes has 9 sides in it?

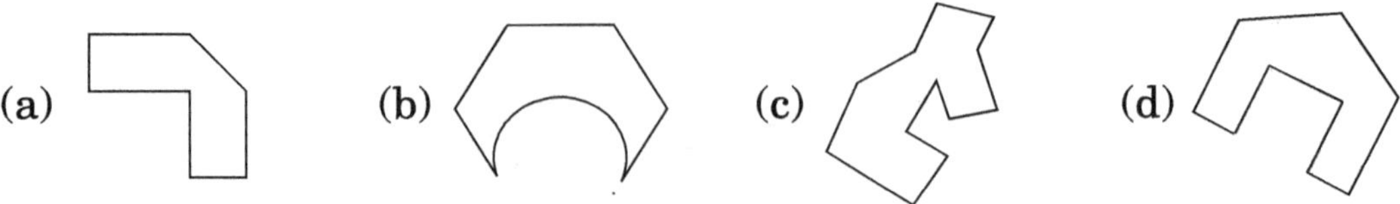

(a) (b) (c) (d)

18. In the figure (X) which of the shapes are identical?

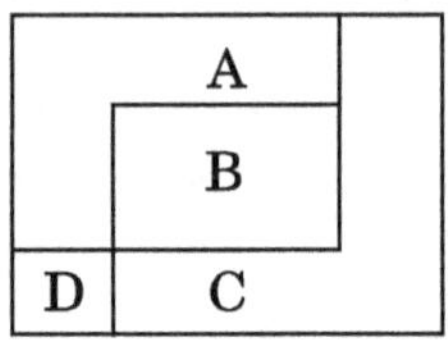

Fig. (X)

(a) A and C   (b) B and D   (c) D and A   (d) C and D

19. Which of the following would complete the figure so that it becomes a five-pointed star?

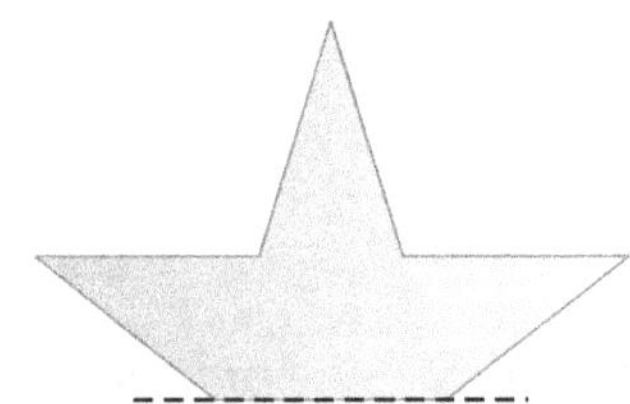

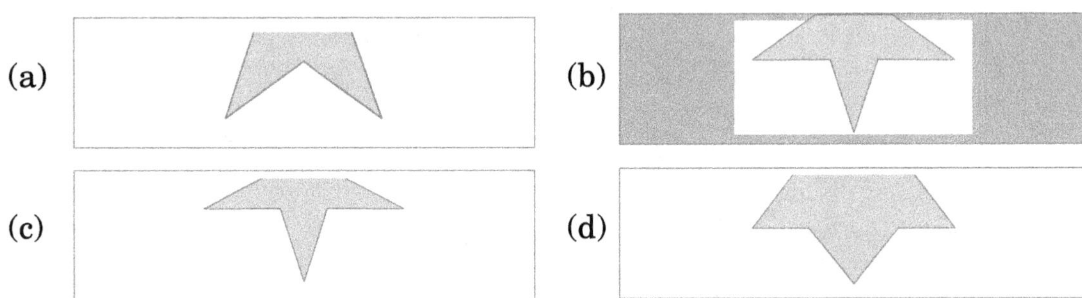

(a)   (b)

(c)   (d)

20. Which among the following shapes doesn't intersect each other?

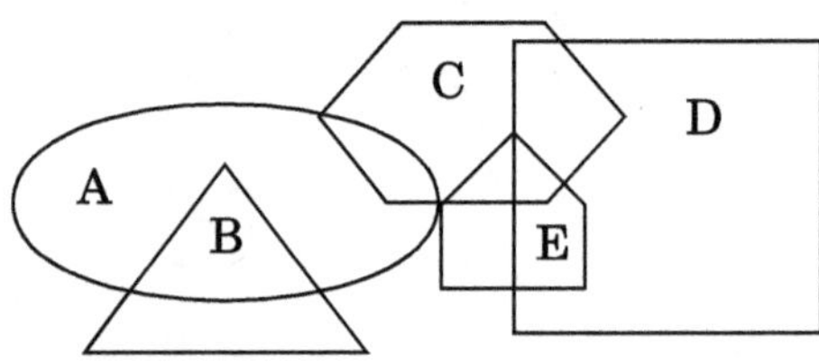

(a) A and C   (b) C and D   (c) C and E   (d) A and D

21. 4 sets of shapes are given below. Identify the set which has maximum number of identical images.

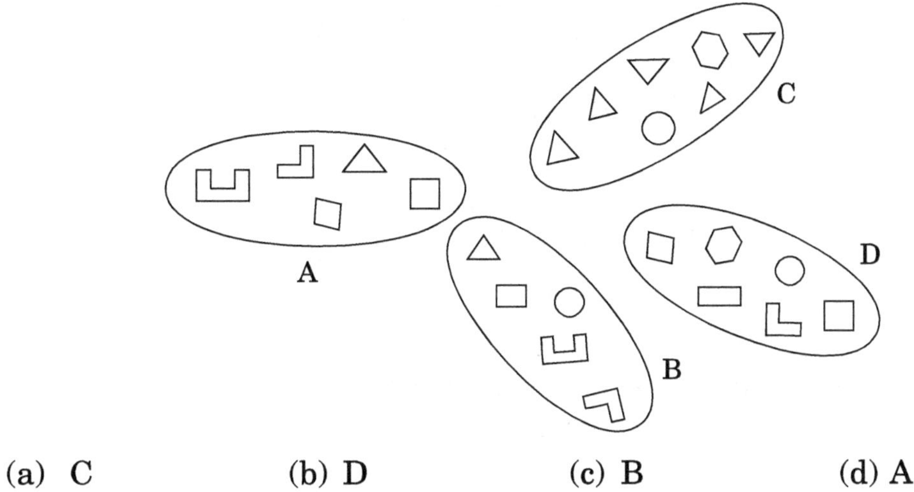

(a) C   (b) D   (c) B   (d) A

22. How many rectangular shapes are there in the figure given below?

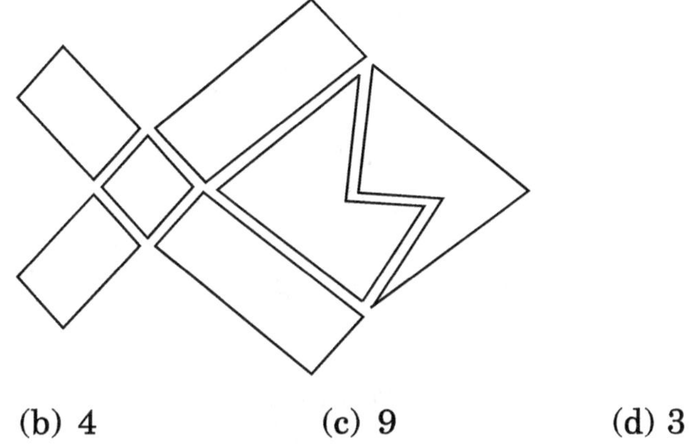

(a) 5   (b) 4   (c) 9   (d) 3

23. A sculptor cuts a corner of a cube. How many edges does the new shape have?

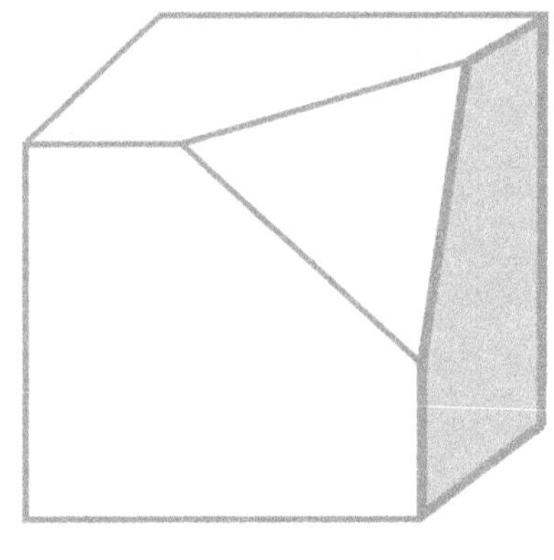

(a) 11   (b) 12   (c) 15   (d) 18

24. How many more triangles than squares are there in the figure (X)?

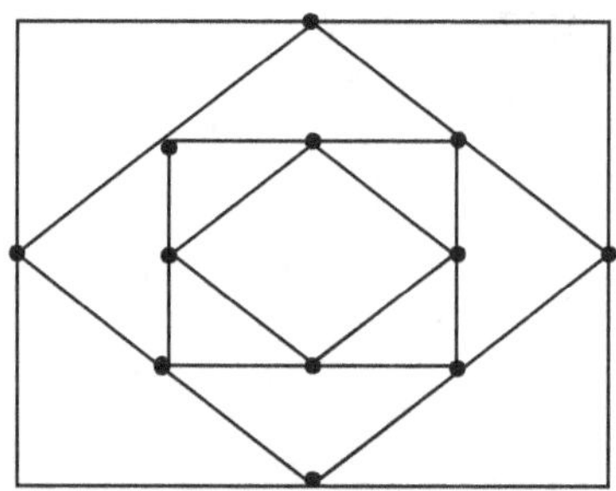

Fig. (X)

(a) 4   (b) 8   (c) 7   (d) 12

25. Name the part of the shape which is hidden.

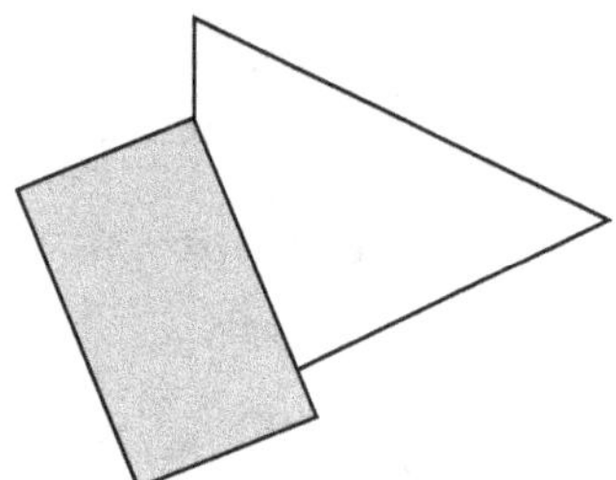

(a) Circle   (b) Triangle   (c) Hexagon   (d) Octagon

26. The letter A is symmetrical. A symmetrical figure can be folded in half and have both sides match exactly. Of the 26 capital letters of the alphabet, how many are symmetrical (vertical or horizontal)?

(a) 12   (b) 13   (c) 13   (d) 15

27. How many squares are there in Figure (X)?

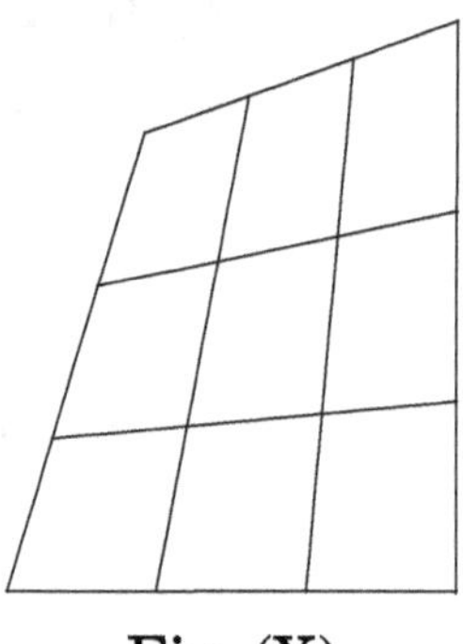

Fig. (X)

(a) 1

(b) 2

(c) 3

(d) There are no square in Figure (X).

28. How many vertical lines are there in the image given below?

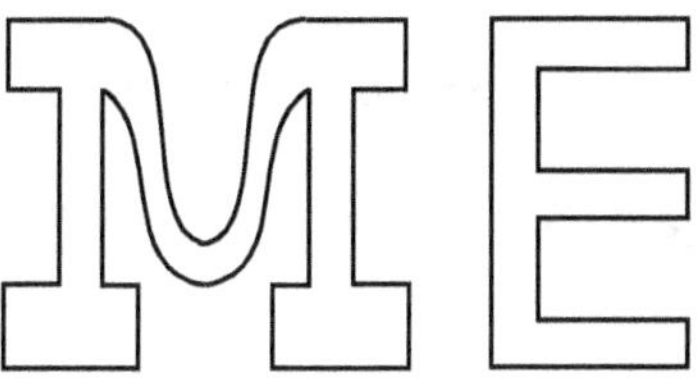

(a) 16   (b) 18   (c) 10   (d) 12

(Olympiad)

29. There are _______ number of cubes in the given figure.

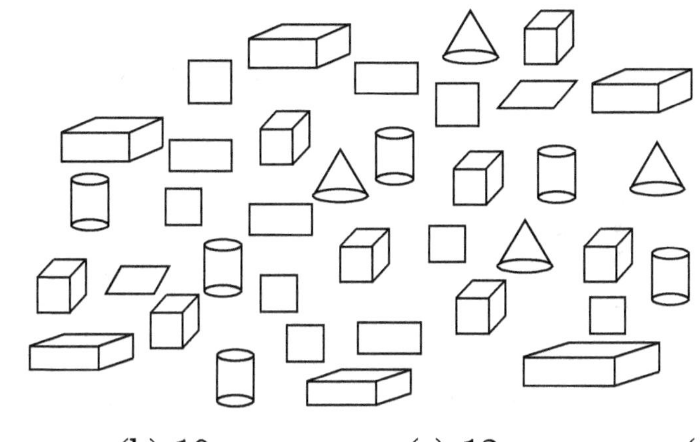

(a) 8   (b) 10   (c) 12   (d) 15

(Olympiad)

30. How many triangles are there in the given figure?

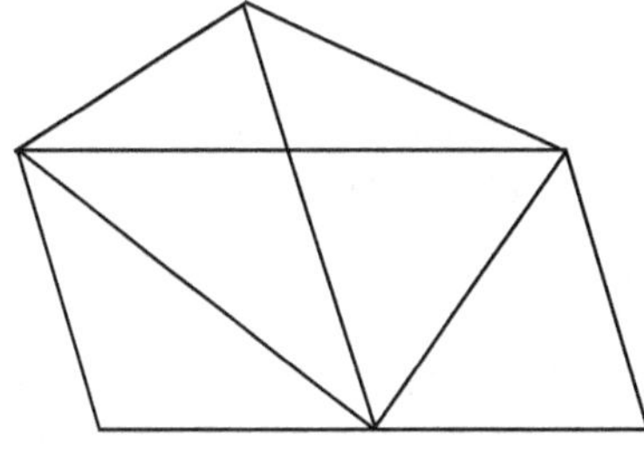

(a) 11   (b) 12   (c) 10   (d) 14

(Olympiad))

Level-1

1. (a) 3 quadrilaterals surround the only hexagon in the above image.

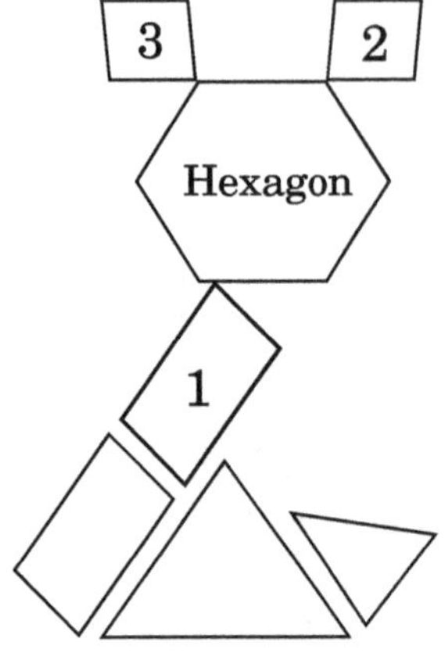

2. (c) Ten are in tree and two circles are in hut.

3. (c) The triangle appears for maximum times in the image and the number is 14.

4. (a) Square is the only shape which appears once in the given image.

5. (c) There are 4 types of shapes given in the image.

6. (a) The fish tangram has a square which is surrounded by triangle and parallelogram.

7. (b) Horse has a parallelogram in its tail.

8. (d) Dog has a triangle shape of ear.

9. (c) The face of fish is made up of two triangles.

10. (c) All animals are made up of seven tangrams.

11. (d) Shivam has drawn a hexagon.

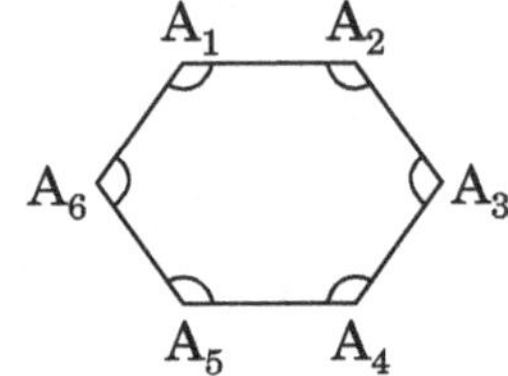

12. (d) Hexagon is a six sided polygon.

13. (a) Triangle is the shape that is depicted from the figure (X).

14. (c)

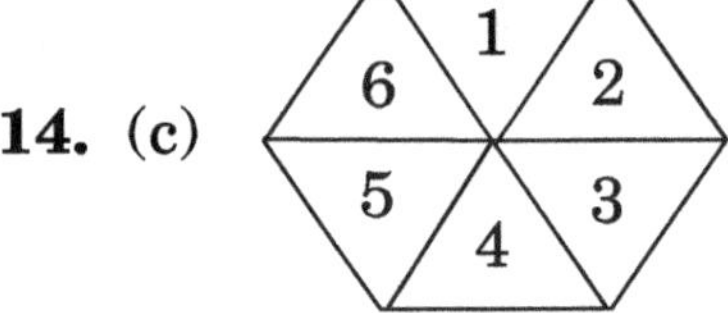

15. (c) The image given in option (c) is identical to figure (X) as both are right angle triangle.

16. (d)

17. (c) The pentagon has regular shape.

18. (c) B, C and D i.e. Rectangle, Triangle and Pentagon share the common boundary.

19. (c)

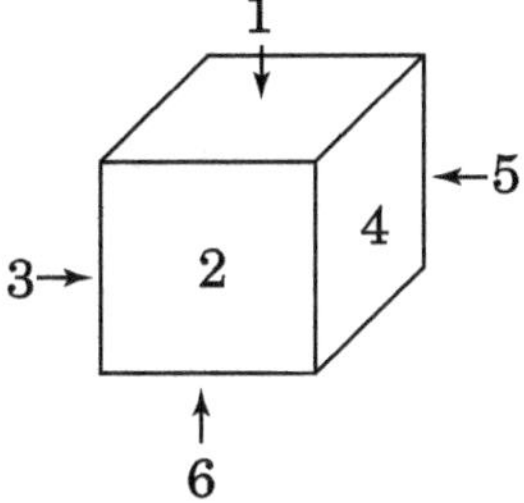

20. (a) Shape 1 is identical to shape 4.

Shape 2 is identical to shape 3.

21. (b)

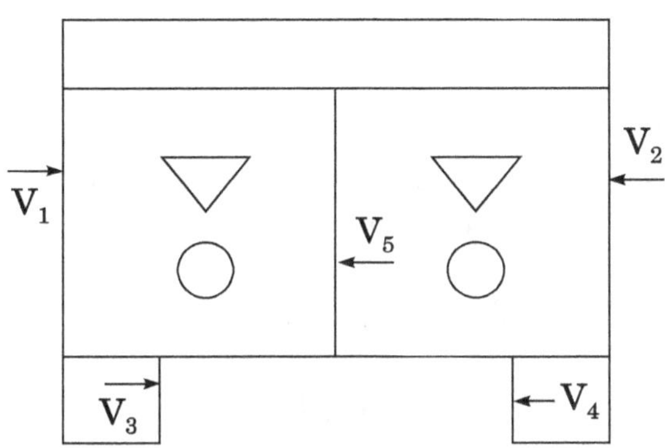

22. (a) 5

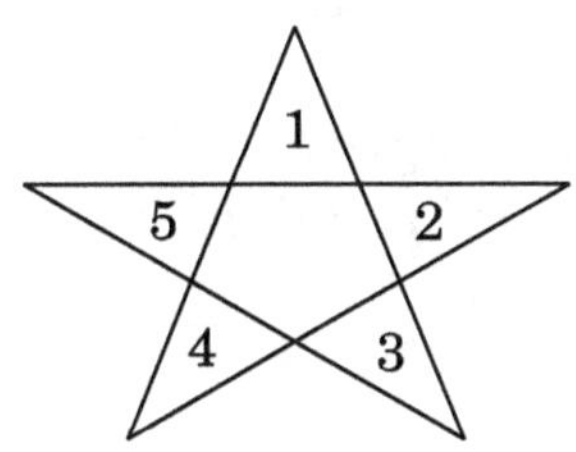

23. (b) The figure 2 will be of more area.

24. (b) The triangle C is of largest area.

25. (d) Option (d) has obtuse angle in it.

26. (d) Every cut forms two more pieces.

$6 \times 2 = 12$

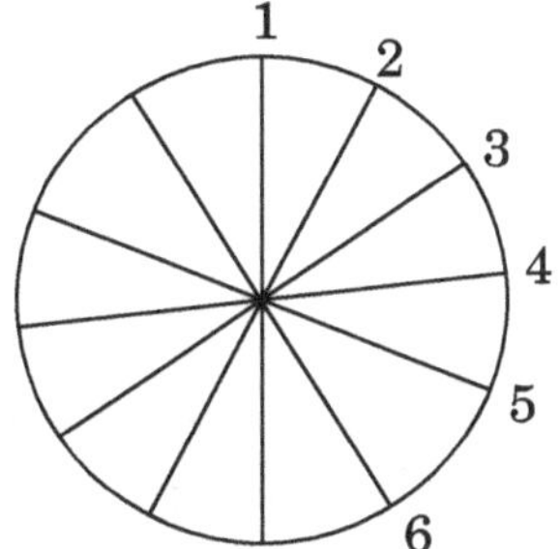

27. (b) There are 11 sides in the given figure.

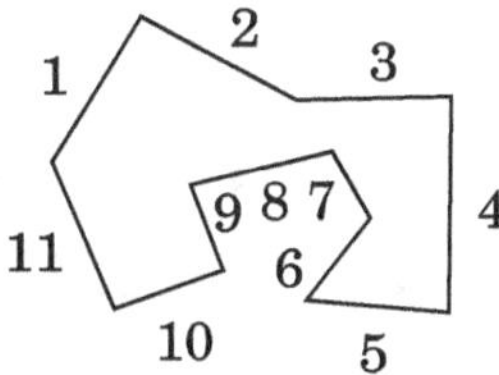

28. (a) The intermediate shape is a pentagon.

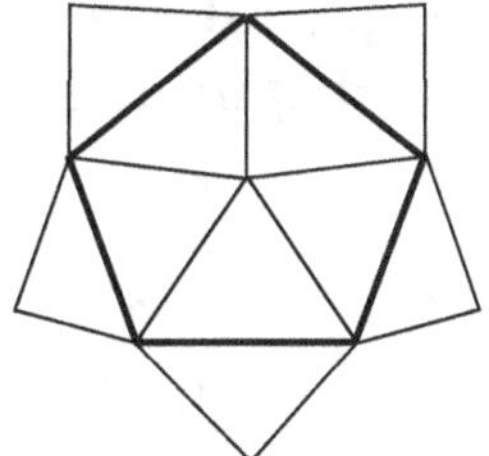

29. (c) There are six vertical lines in the figure (X).

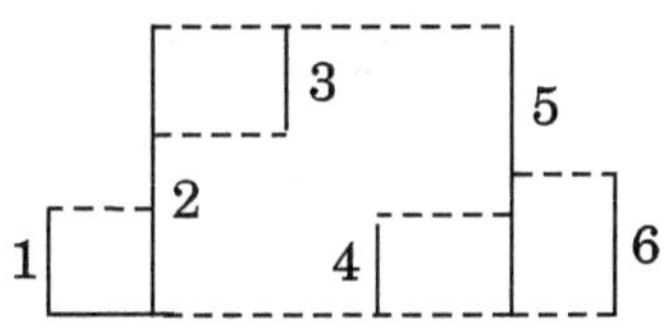

30. (c)

1. (b)

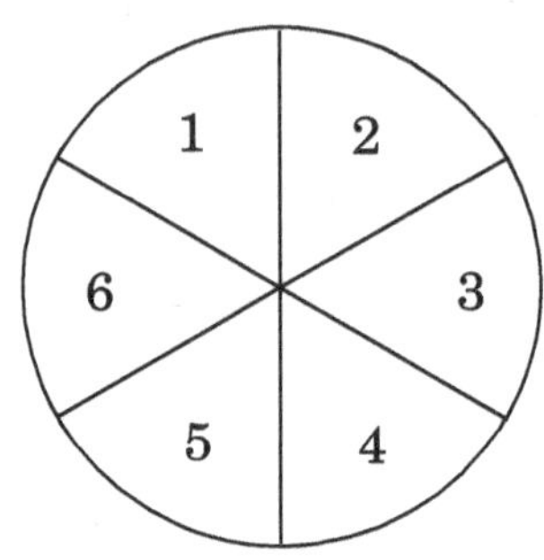

2. (c) 2 more triangles are required to make the figure a complete hexagon.

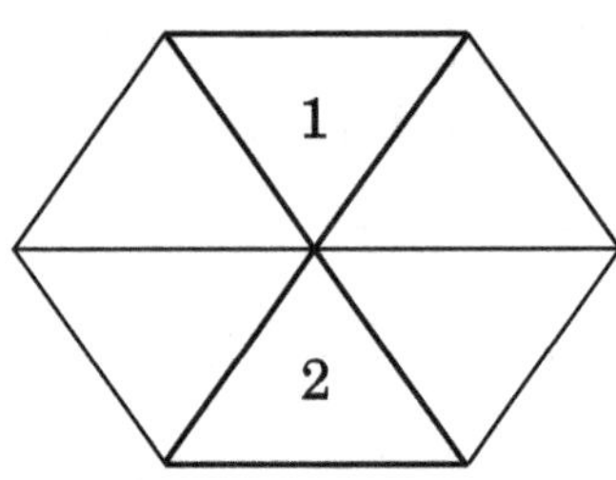

3. (c) The section "B" has the least number of squares i.e. 5.

4. (c) The parallelogram has no lines of symmetry.

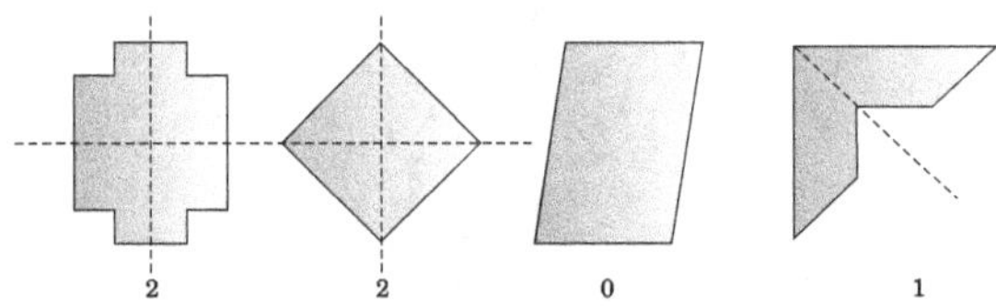

5. (a)

6. (d)

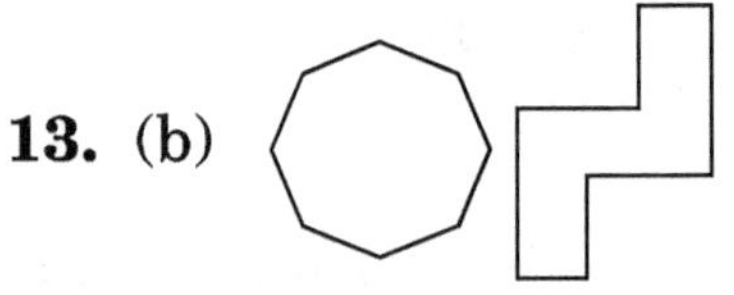

7. (c) The third pair does not fulfill the given criteria.

8. (d)

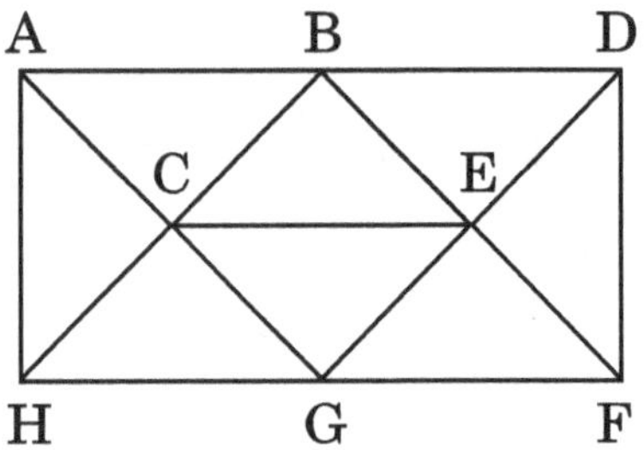

Δ ABC, ΔBCE, ΔBDE, ΔDFE, ΔEGF, ΔCHG, ΔCEG ΔACH, ΔABH, ΔDBF, ΔHAG, ΔFDG, ΔADG, ΔBHF

9. (c) At least two regular shape rectangles can be formed out of the image given.

10. (a) The rhombus and the rectangle have the same number of corners that is 4.

11. (b) At least three circles have to be separated so as to free all the circles.

12. (a) The figure "C" has maximum number of sides.

13. (b)

both has 8 sides.

14. (c) figure has 3 sides and 2 corners.

15. (c) 5

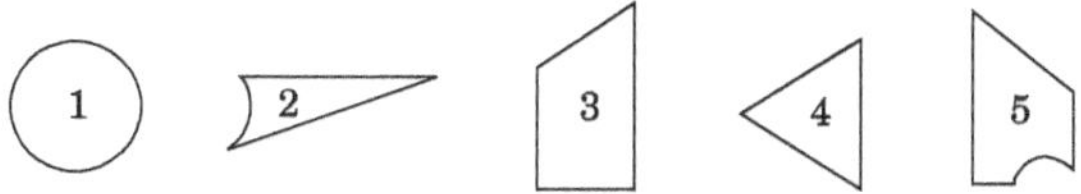

16. (d) There are six different types of shapes in the right side of the line.

17. (d)

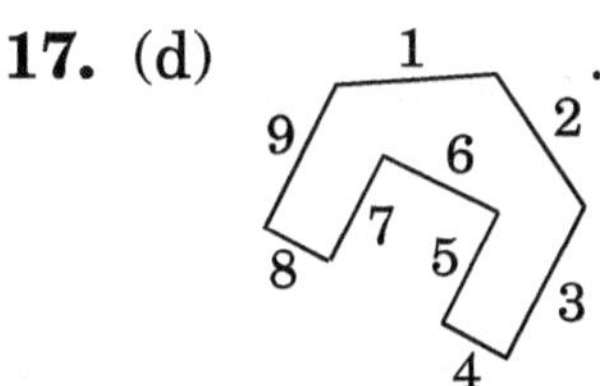

18. (a) A and C are identical.

19. (a)

20. (d) A and D didn't intersect with each other.

21. (a) The set C has maximum number of identical triangles.

22. (b) There are 4 rectangular-shapes in the figure.

23. (c) A cube has 8 vertexes, 6 rectangular faces, and 12 edges. There are 3 additional edges. $12 + 3 = 15$.

24. (b) Squares = 4

Triangles = 12

There are $12 - 4 = 8$ more triangles than squares.

25. (b) Hidden part of the shape is triangle.

26. (d) 15 letters are symmetrical, either along the vertical axis or along the horizontal axis.

Letters are:

A B C D E F G H I J K L M
N O P Q R S T U V W X Y Z

27. (d) A square has four right angles.

28. (a)

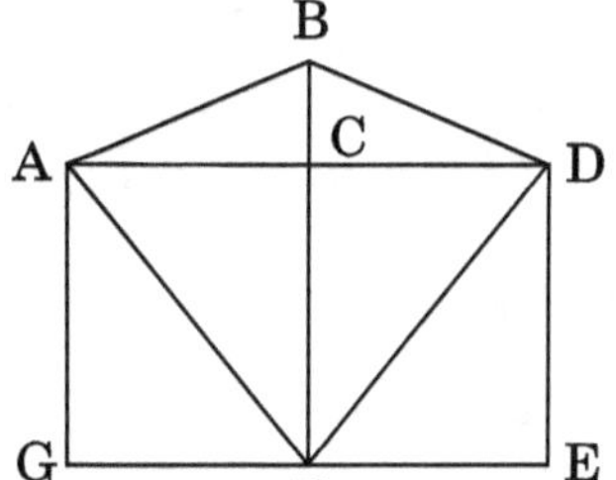

29. (a)

30. (c)

10 Triangles are:

$\triangle ABC, \triangle CBD, \triangle ABD$

$\triangle AFC, \triangle DFC, \triangle ADF$

$\triangle ABF, \triangle DBF, \triangle AGF, \triangle DFF$

Embedded Figure

OBJECTIVES

- It will measure cognitive functioning and style of students.
- Students will be able to find shapes within the large more complex image.

INTRODUCTION

A figure is said to be embedded in figure (X), if figure (X) contains a part of that figure.

Types of Questions

Type I: Identify the Small Part hidden in given figure:

In such type of problems, a figure (X) is given, followed by four parts, such that one of them is hidden in figure (X), students have to identify that part.

Example 1:

Identify which shape is hidden in the Figure (X).

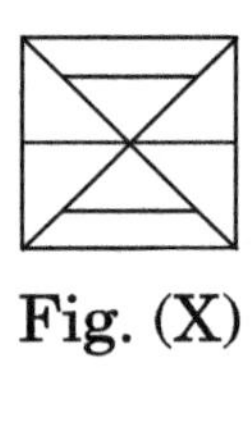

Fig. (X)

(a) 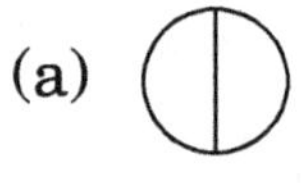   (b) 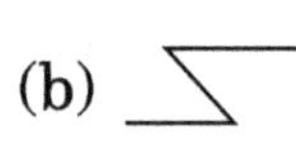   (c) 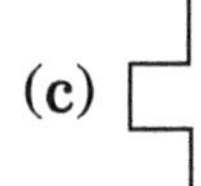   (d) 

Ans. (b) 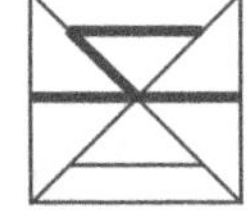

Type II: *Identify the Figure in Which Given Part is Hidden*

In such problems, a figure X is given which is followed by four alternative of complex figures in such a way that figure (X) is hidden or embedded in one and only one of them. Student have to identify that particular figure in which the figure (X) is hidden.

Example 2:

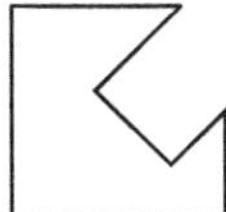

Fig. (X)

(a)   (b)   (c)   (d)

Ans. (a) 

LEVEL-1

Direction (Qs. 1-15): One problem figure is followed by four options. In one of the options, the figure similar to the problem figure is embedded/hidden. Find the option.

1. 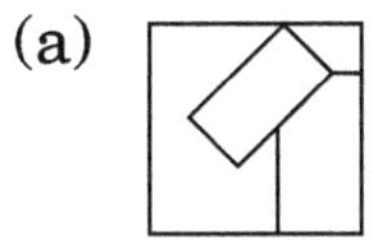   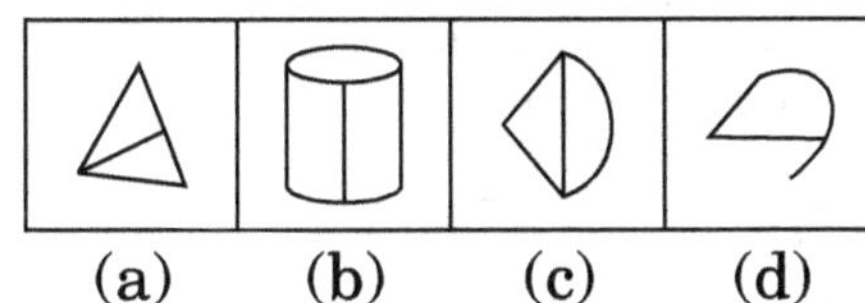
    (a)   (b)   (c)   (d)

2.    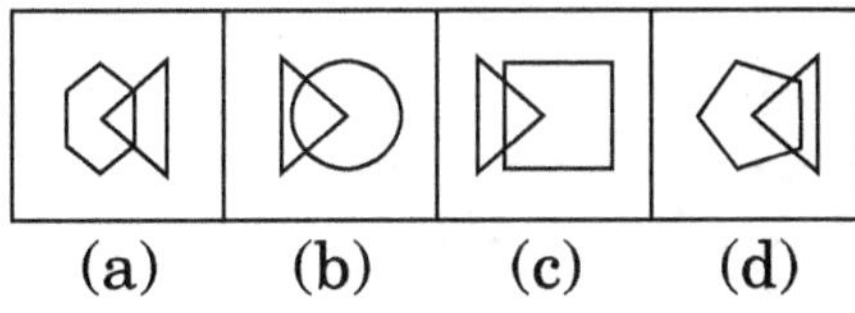
    (a)   (b)   (c)   (d)

3.

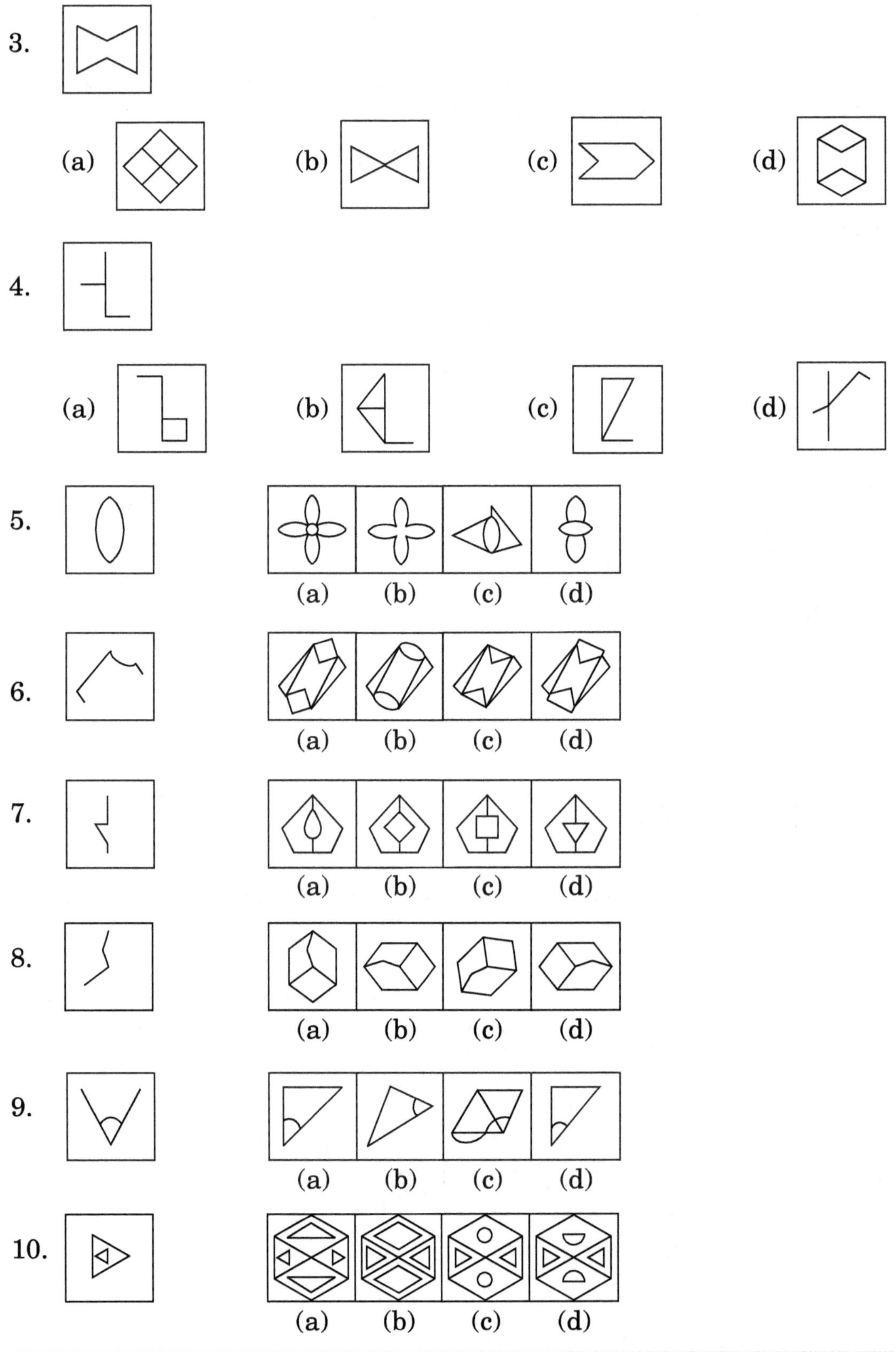

4.

5.   (a)   (b)   (c)   (d)

6.   (a)   (b)   (c)   (d)

7.   (a)   (b)   (c)   (d)

8.   (a)   (b)   (c)   (d)

9.   (a)   (b)   (c)   (d)

10.   (a)   (b)   (c)   (d)

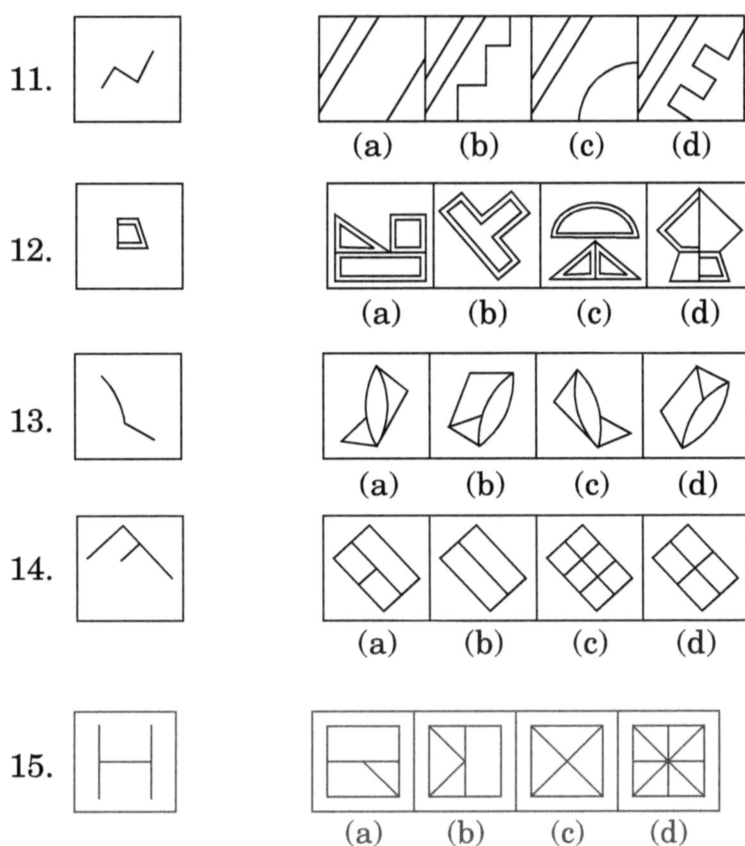

Direction (Qs. 16-30): Which of the following parts is exactly embedded or hidden in figure (X).

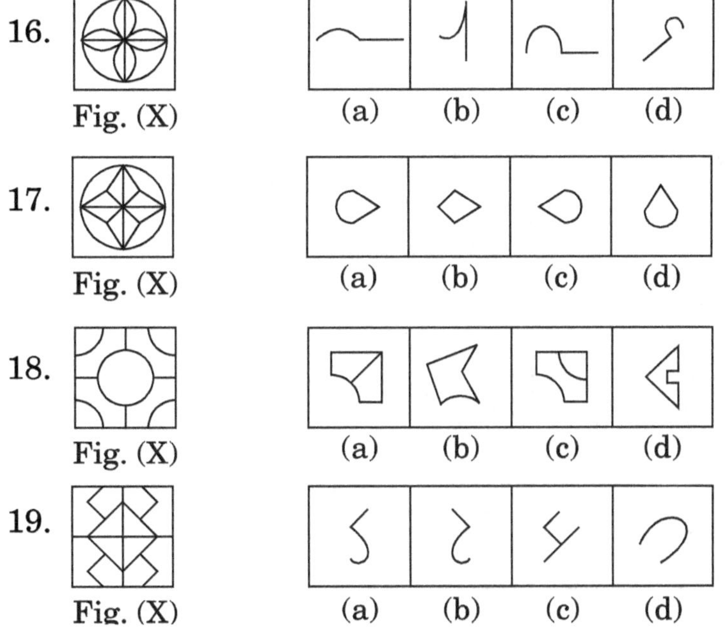

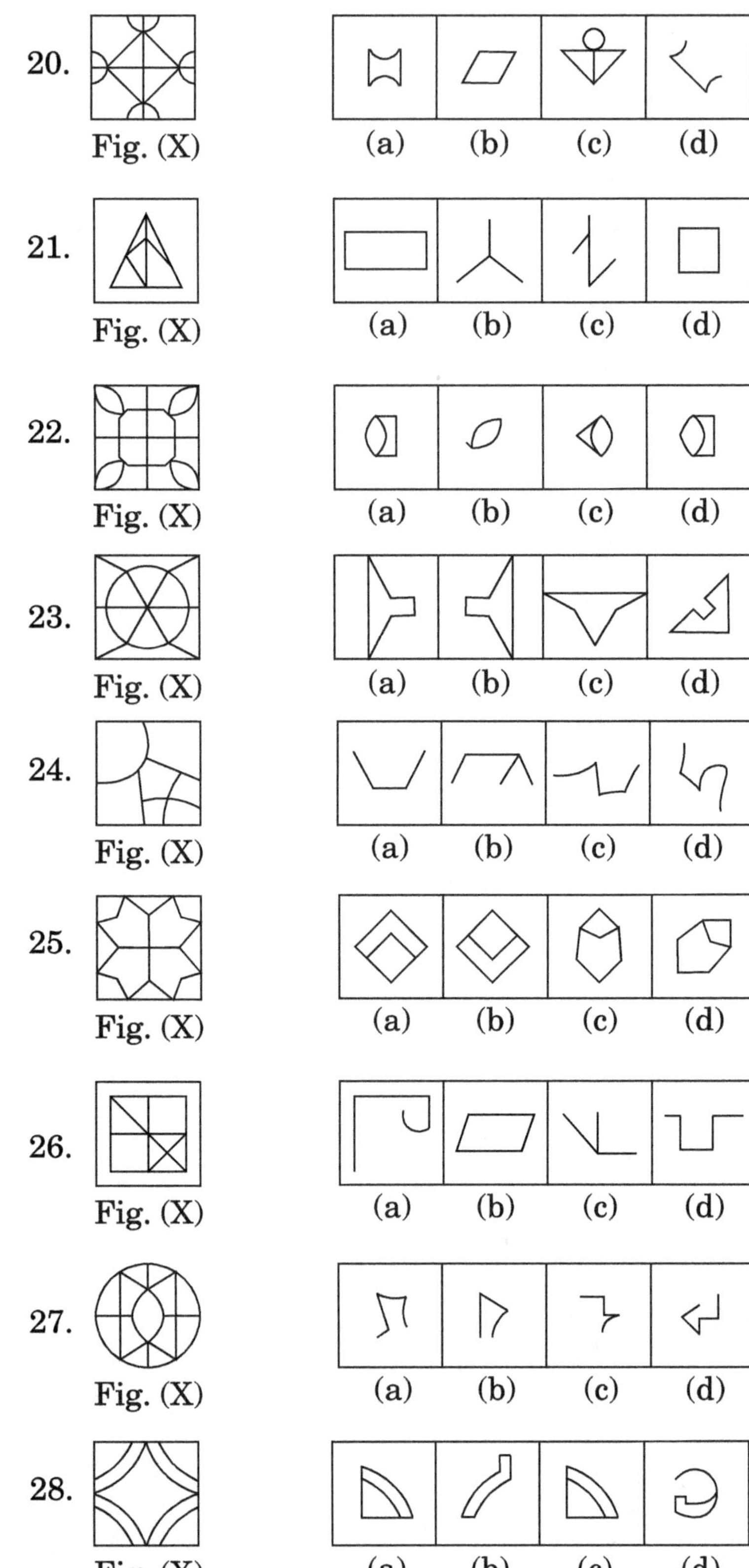

20. Fig. (X)   (a)   (b)   (c)   (d)

21. Fig. (X)   (a)   (b)   (c)   (d)

22. Fig. (X)   (a)   (b)   (c)   (d)

23. Fig. (X)   (a)   (b)   (c)   (d)

24. Fig. (X)   (a)   (b)   (c)   (d)

25. Fig. (X)   (a)   (b)   (c)   (d)

26. Fig. (X)   (a)   (b)   (c)   (d)

27. Fig. (X)   (a)   (b)   (c)   (d)

28. Fig. (X)   (a)   (b)   (c)   (d)

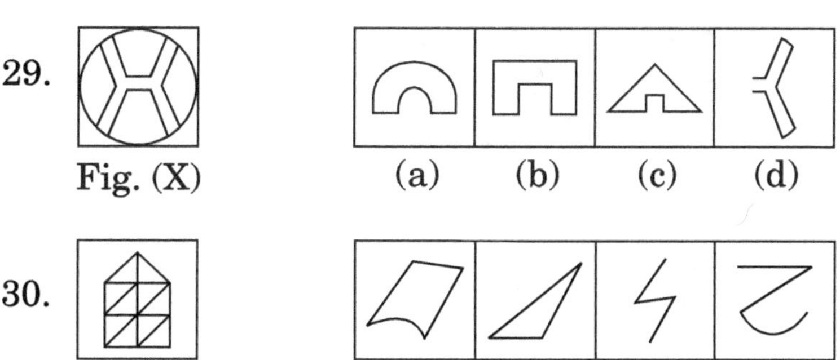

29. Fig. (X)   (a)   (b)   (c)   (d)

30. Fig. (X)   (a)   (b)   (c)   (d)

LEVEL-2

Direction (Qs. 1-9): One problem figure is followed by four options. In one of the options, the figure similar to the problem figure is exactly embedded/hidden. Find the option.

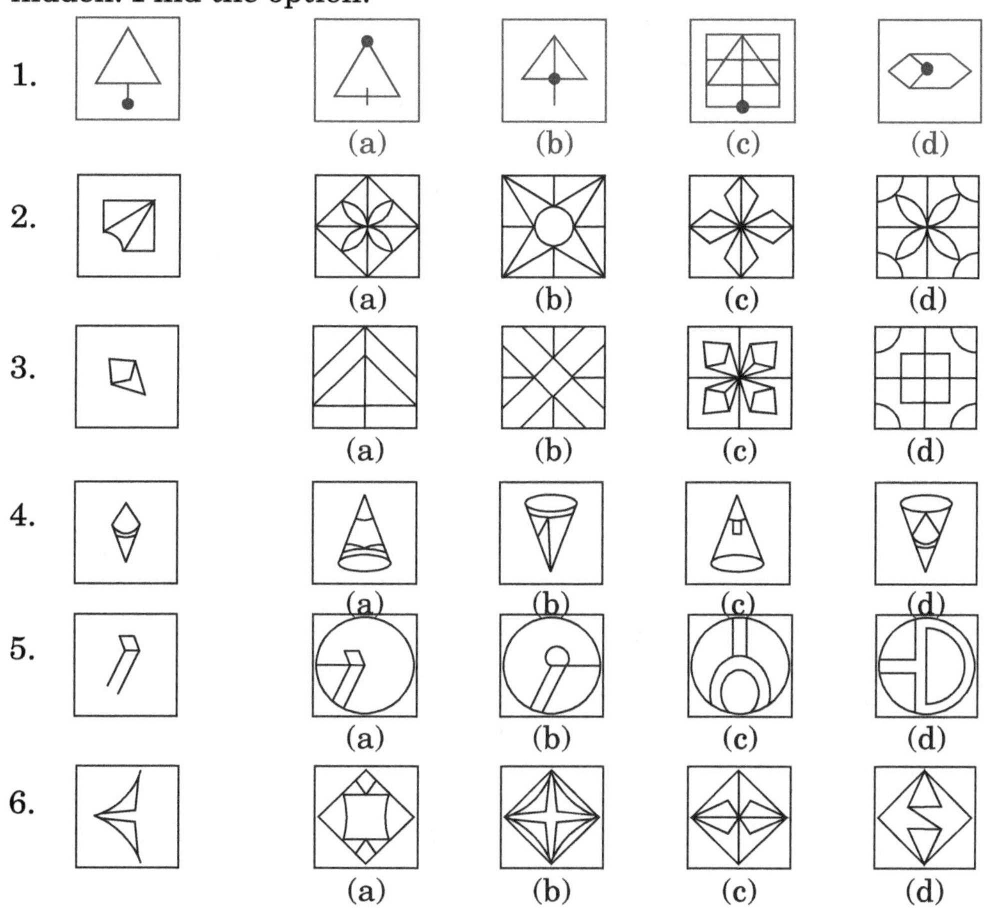

1. (a) (b) (c) (d)

2. (a) (b) (c) (d)

3. (a) (b) (c) (d)

4. (a) (b) (c) (d)

5. (a) (b) (c) (d)

6. (a) (b) (c) (d)

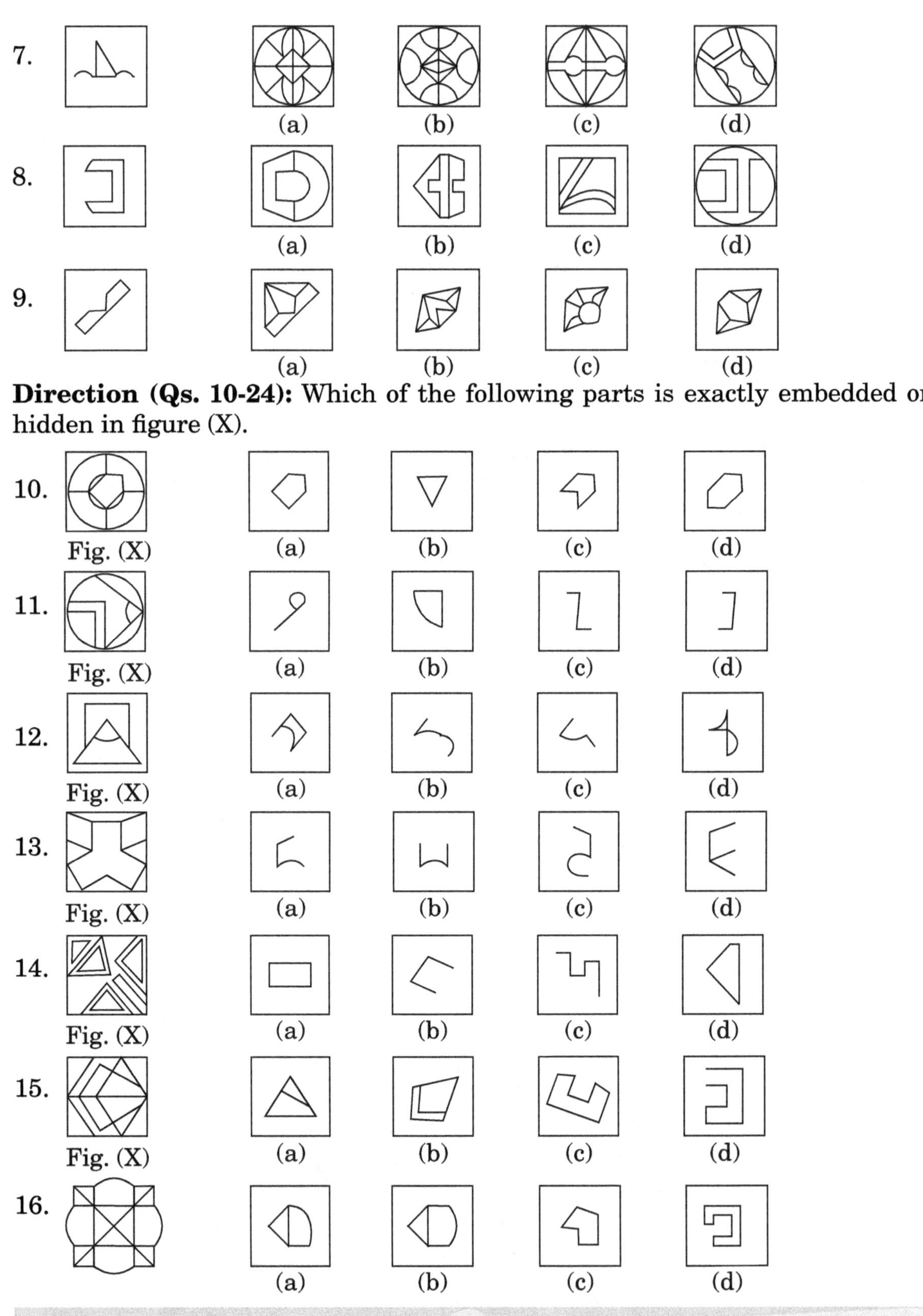

7. (a) (b) (c) (d)

8. (a) (b) (c) (d)

9. (a) (b) (c) (d)

Direction (Qs. 10-24): Which of the following parts is exactly embedded or hidden in figure (X).

10. Fig. (X) (a) (b) (c) (d)

11. Fig. (X) (a) (b) (c) (d)

12. Fig. (X) (a) (b) (c) (d)

13. Fig. (X) (a) (b) (c) (d)

14. Fig. (X) (a) (b) (c) (d)

15. Fig. (X) (a) (b) (c) (d)

16. (a) (b) (c) (d)

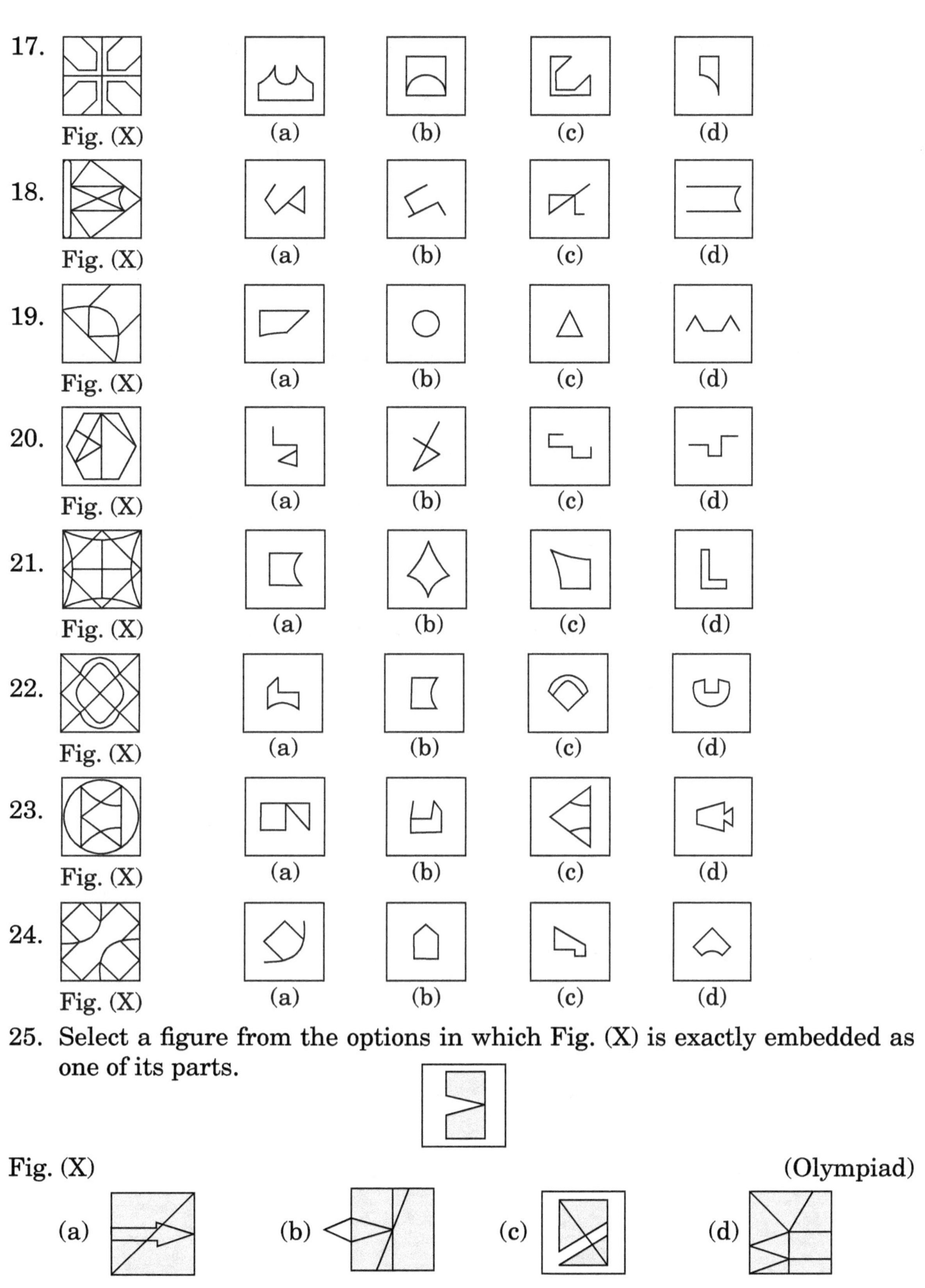

17. Fig. (X)   (a)   (b)   (c)   (d)

18. Fig. (X)   (a)   (b)   (c)   (d)

19. Fig. (X)   (a)   (b)   (c)   (d)

20. Fig. (X)   (a)   (b)   (c)   (d)

21. Fig. (X)   (a)   (b)   (c)   (d)

22. Fig. (X)   (a)   (b)   (c)   (d)

23. Fig. (X)   (a)   (b)   (c)   (d)

24. Fig. (X)   (a)   (b)   (c)   (d)

25. Select a figure from the options in which Fig. (X) is exactly embedded as one of its parts.

Fig. (X)   (Olympiad)

(a)   (b)   (c)   (d)

26. Which of the following parts is exactly embedded in Fig. (X)?

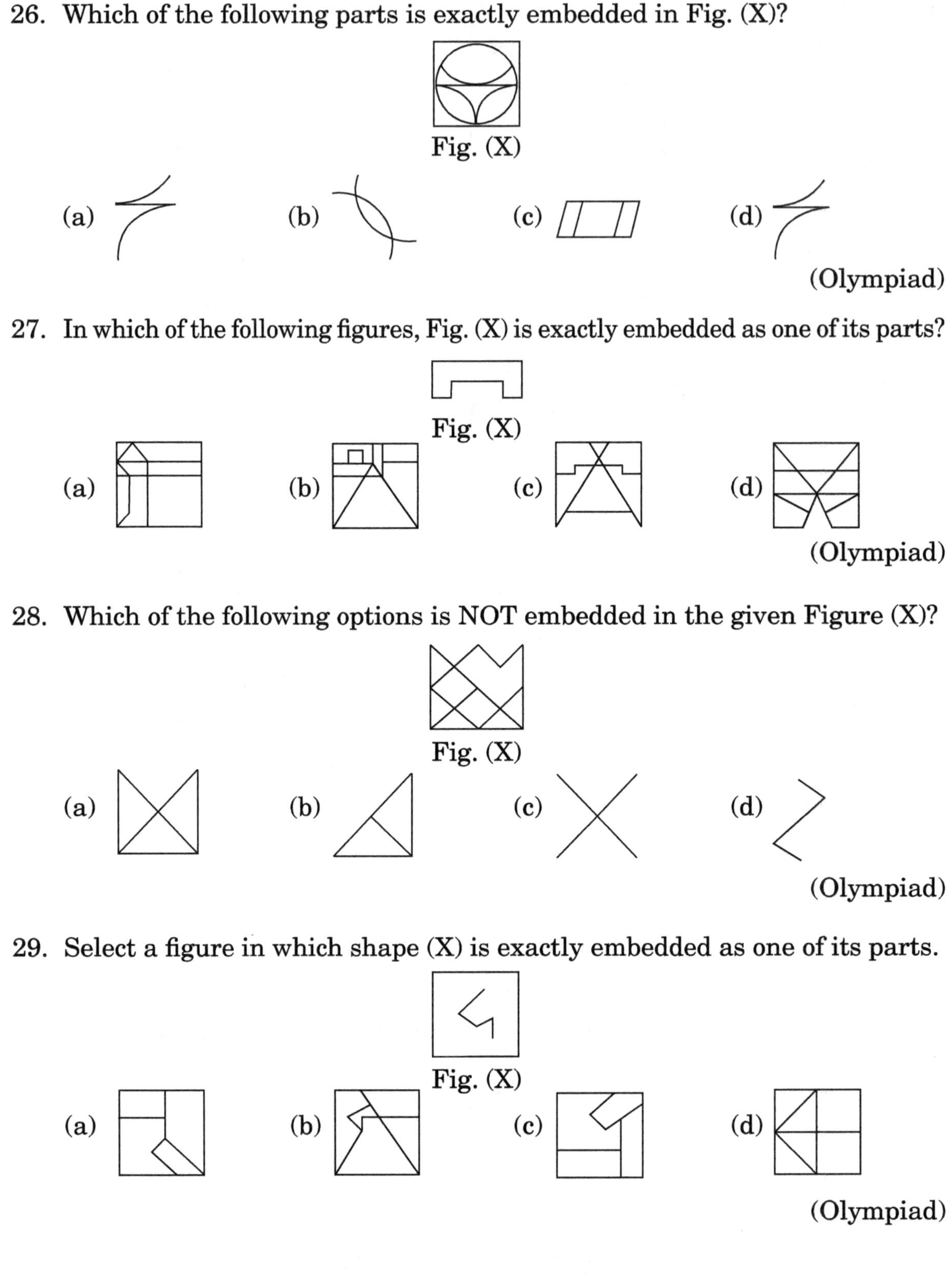

Fig. (X)

(a)   (b)   (c)   (d)

(Olympiad)

27. In which of the following figures, Fig. (X) is exactly embedded as one of its parts?

Fig. (X)

(a)   (b)   (c)   (d)

(Olympiad)

28. Which of the following options is NOT embedded in the given Figure (X)?

Fig. (X)

(a)   (b)   (c)   (d)

(Olympiad)

29. Select a figure in which shape (X) is exactly embedded as one of its parts.

Fig. (X)

(a)   (b)   (c)   (d)

(Olympiad)

30. In which of the following options, Shape (X) is exactly embedded as one of its parts?

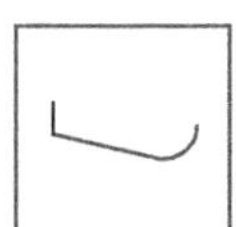

Shape (X)

(a)    (b) 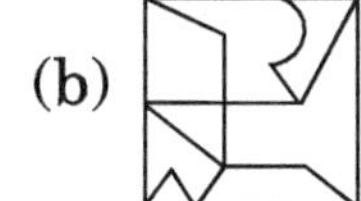   (c)    (d) 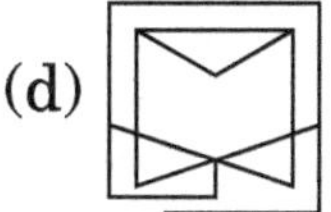

(Olympiad)

Answers and Explanations

Level-1

1. **(a)** 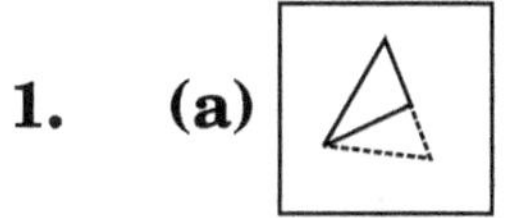	2. **(b)** 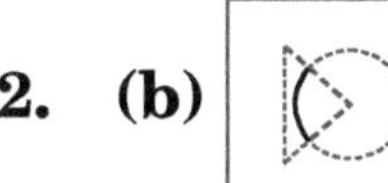	17. (b) 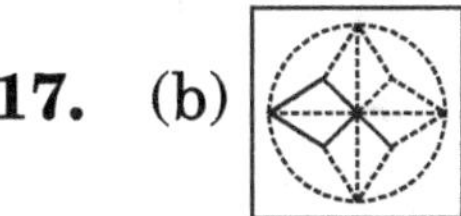	18. (c) 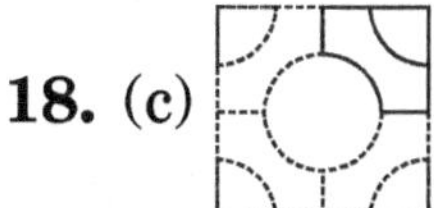
3. (d)	4. (b) 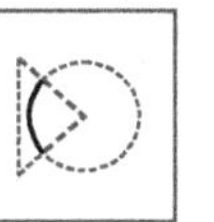	19. (c) 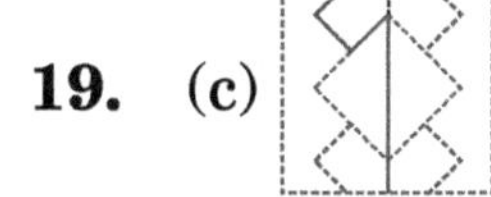	20. (d) 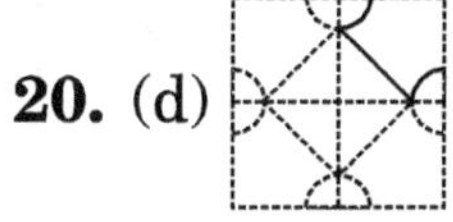
5. **(c)**	6. (b)	21. (b) 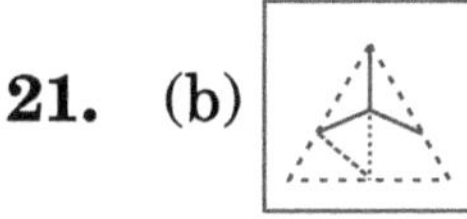	22. (b) 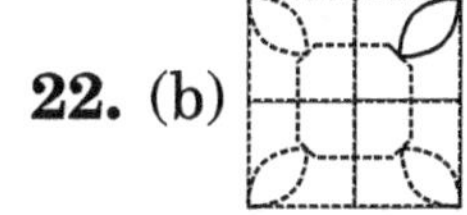
7. (d)	8. (a)	23. (c) 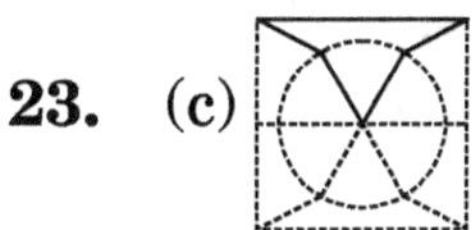	24. (c) 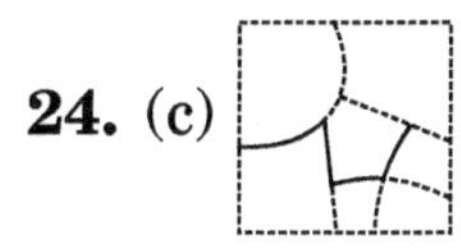
9. (c)	10. (a)	25. (d) 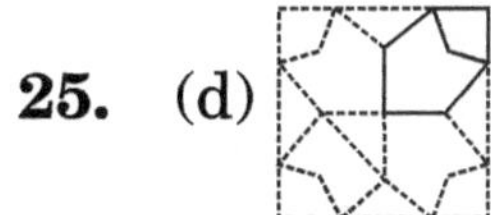	26. (c) 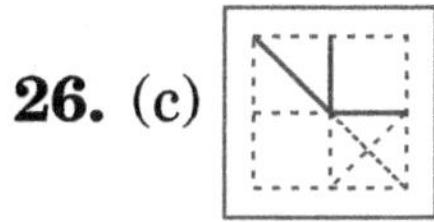
11. (d)	12. (d)	27. (b) 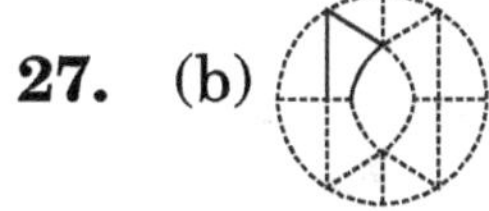	28. (c) 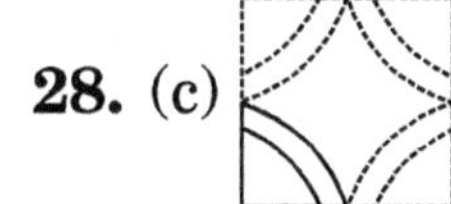
13. (c)	14. (d)	29. (d) 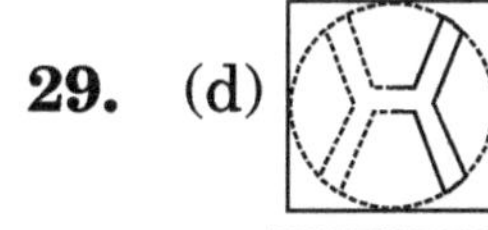	
15. (d)	16. (a)	30. (c)	

1. (c) 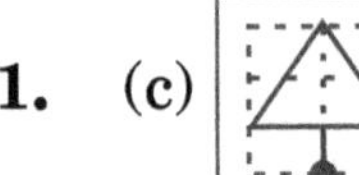   **2.** (b) 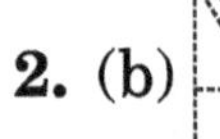   **21.** (c) 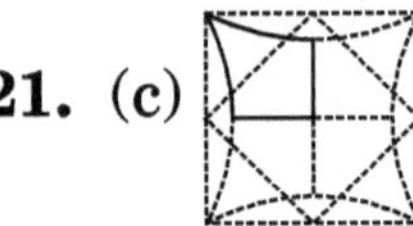   **22.** (c) 

3. (c) 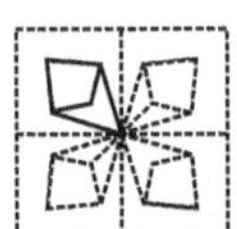   **4.** (d)    **23.** (c) 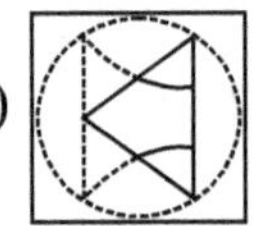   **24.** (a) 

5. (a) 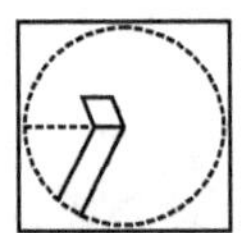   **6.** (b) 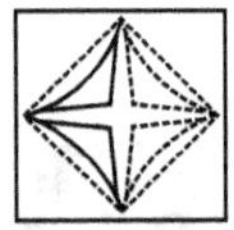   **25.** (b) 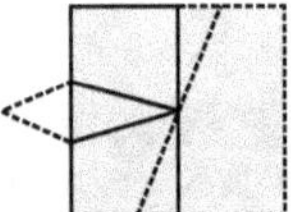   **26.** (a) 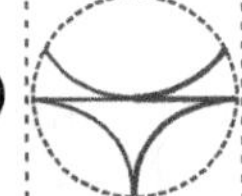

7. (c) 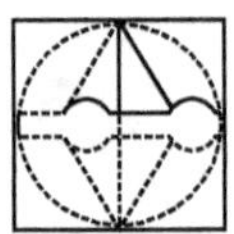   **8.** (d) 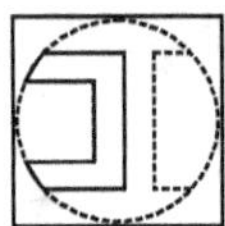   **27.** (c) 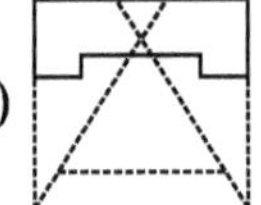

9. (a) 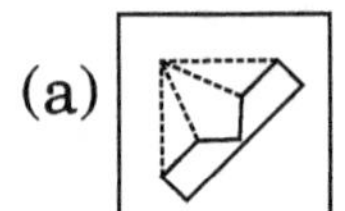   **10.** (a) 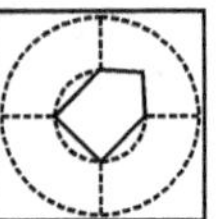   **28.** (a)

11. (b) 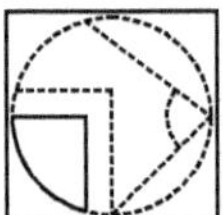   **12.** (c) 

Option (b) is embedded.

Option (c) is embedded.

Option (d) is embedded.

13. (d)    **14.** (d) 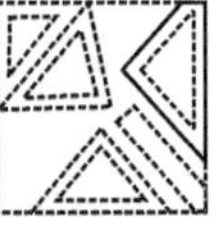

Hence, Option (a) is correct answer.

15. (a) 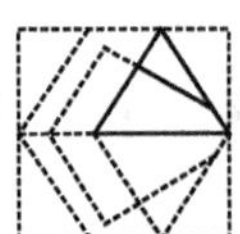   **16.** (b) 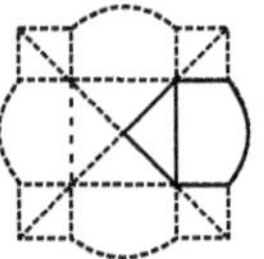

17. (c)    **18.** (d) 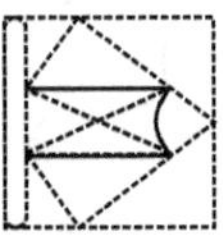

29. (c)    **30.** (a) 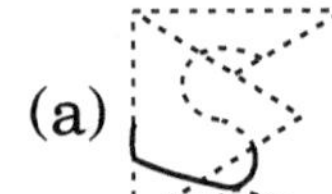

19. (a) 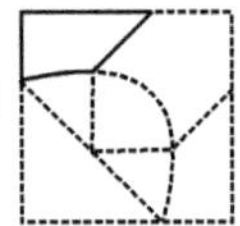   **20.** (b) 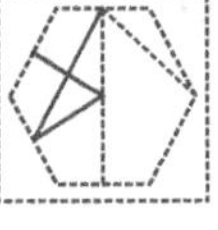

Mirror/Water Image

OBJECTIVE

- Students will learn how different objects are seen when they get reflected both in Mirror and in Water.

INTRODUCTION

The reflection of object into the mirror is called its mirror image. It is obtained by inverting an object laterally. If we combine the original figure and mirror image together they form symmetry.

MIRROR IMAGES

Mirror Images of Capital letters

A	A	H	H	O	O	V	V
B	ꓭ	I	I	P	ꟼ	W	W
C	Ɔ	J	Ⴑ	Q	Ọ	X	X
D	ꓷ	K	ꓘ	R	ꓤ	Y	Y
E	Ǝ	L	⅃	S	ꙅ	Z	Ƨ
F	ꟻ	M	M	T	T		
G	ꓨ	N	И	U	U		

- The capital letters which have the same mirror images are:

A, H, I, M, O, T, U, V, W, X, Y

Mirror Images of Small letters

a	ɒ	n	ᴎ
b	d	o	o
c	ɔ	p	q
d	b	q	p
e	ɘ	r	ɿ
f	ʇ	s	ƨ
g	ǫ	t	ɟ
h	ʜ	u	ᴝ
i	i	v	v
j	ʝ	w	w
k	ʞ	x	x
l	l	y	ʏ
m	ᴍ	z	ƹ

- The small letters which have the same mirror images are:

i, l, o, v, w, x

Mirror Images of Numbers

0	1	2	3	4	5	6	7	8	9	10	11	12	13	14	15
0	Ɩ	Ƨ	Ƹ	ᔭ	ट	∂	Ƚ	8	e	0Ɩ	ƖƖ	ƧƖ	ƸƖ	ᔭƖ	टƖ

- 0 and 8 numbers have the same mirror images.

Mirror Image of Clock Time

For mirror image of clock time, the given time shall be subtracted from 12.00 or 11.60.

Example 1:

What will be the mirror image of clock time 3:40?

Explanation:

By using simple trick

$$\begin{array}{r} 11:60 \\ -\ 3:40 \\ \hline 8:20 \end{array}$$

WATER IMAGES

INTRODUCTION

The reflection of an object into the water is called its water image. It is obtained by inverting an object vertically.

Technical Definition

In water image (horizontal), the LOWER and UPPER parts interchange positions and the LEFT and RIGHT parts remain constant.

Water Images of Capital Letters

Water	A B C D E F G H I J K L M N O P Q R S T U V W X Y Z
	Ɐ B C D E Ⅎ G H I ꓩ K Ⅼ M N O Ԁ Ꝺ ꓤ Ƨ ꓕ ꓵ Ʌ Ʌ M X ꓬ Z

Water Images of Small Letters

Water	a	b	c	d	e	f	g	h
	ɐ	p	c	q	ɘ	ɟ	ᵷ	ɥ

Water	i	j	k	l	m	n	o	p
	ı	ꞁ	ʞ	ʃ	ɯ	ɥ	o	b

Water	q	r	s	t	u	v	w	x
	d	ɹ	ꙅ	ʇ	ɥ	ʌ	ʍ	x

Water	y	z
	ʎ	ꙅ

Water Images of Numbers

Water	1	2	3	4	5	6	7	8	9
	⇂	ꙅ	Ɛ	ㄣ	ꙅ	℮	ㄥ	8	ϱ

Water Images of Clock Time

For water image of clock time, the given time shall be subtracted from 18 : 30.

Example 2:

What will be the water image of clock time 4 : 20?

Explanation:

By using simple trick

$$18 : 30$$
$$\underline{4 : 20}$$
$$14 : 10$$

14 : 10 means 2 : 10

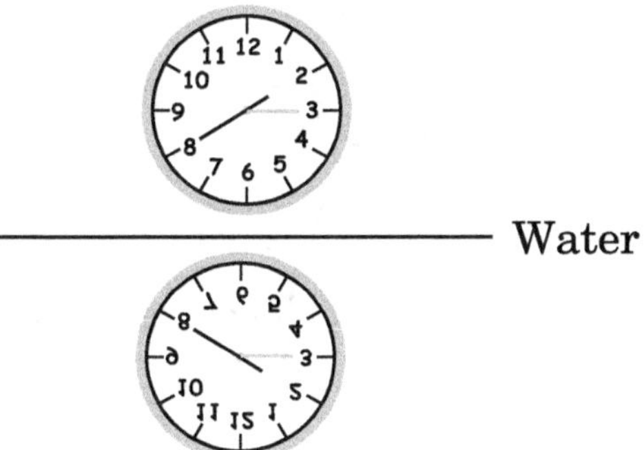

Water

There is a short trick which can be applied while doing this exercise.

- Certain alphabets in capital form have the mirror image as well as the water image the same.

  They are

  H   I   O   X

- Some alphabets have similar water reflection i.e.

  C   D   E   H   I   O   X

- Two number 0 and 8 have their water images exactly the same.
- The mirror image of number 6 is the same as the water image of number 9.

Example 1:

Choose the mirror image of the following combination of alphabets from the four alternatives given mirror below.

BFGFT

(a) TϾꟻꟼꓭ

(b) ꟻϽTꟻꓭ

(c) ꟻTꟼꓭϽ

(d) ꟻꓭTꟻG

Ans. (a)

Explanation:

BFGFT ꟻꟼϽTꓭB

Example 2:

Choose the correct mirror image for the given picture.

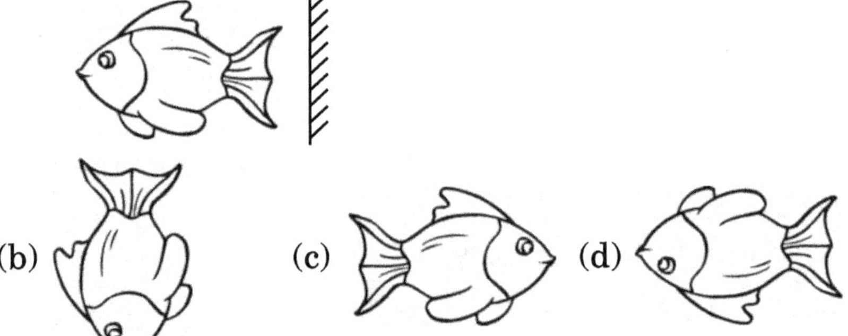

(a)   (b)   (c)   (d)

Ans. (c)

Explanation: The correct mirror image of the picture is

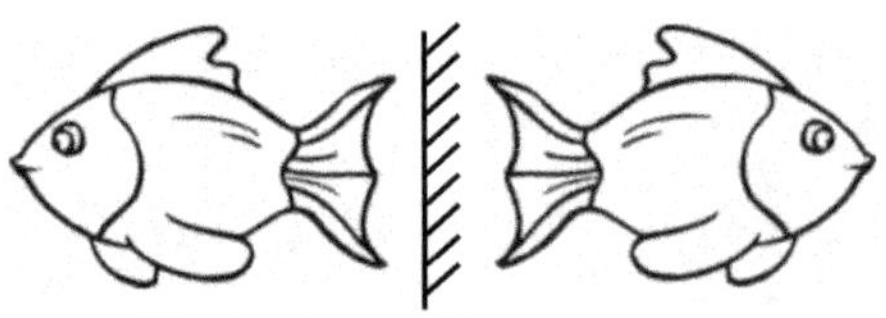

Example 3:

Given below is a set of alphabets along with its four alternatives. Now, identify the correct option which resembles the exact water image of the given combination.

$$\frac{\text{pynkrai}}{\text{water}}$$

(a) uqkɹɐʌ   (b) pʌuꞰɹɐi   (c) iɐuꞰɹʌp   (d) pʌuɹɐiu

Ans. (b)

Explanation:

$$\frac{\text{pynkrai}}{\text{pʌuꞰɹɐi}}$$

Example 4:

In the question given below, choose the correct option for the water image from the four given alternatives.

$$\frac{\text{FAB}}{\text{water}}$$

(a) ꟻBA   (b) ꟻAB   (c) ꟻAꓭ   (d) ꓭAꟻ

Ans. (c)

Explanation:

$$\frac{\text{FAB}}{\text{ꟻAꓭ}} \text{ Water}$$

Example 5:

In the question there is a combination of small letter alphabets and numbers. Choose the correct mirror image of the following combination.

apcr92d | mirror

(a) 2qᴐ9abɿ   (b) pꙄꟼɿɔqɒ   (c) apꙄ2obɿ   (d) cɿd29pɒ

Ans. (b)

Explanation:

The mirror image will be

apcr92d | pꙄꟼɿɔqɒ

Direction (Qs. 1-8): Choose the one from the alternatives which most closely resembles the mirror image.

1. PROVE
   (a) PROVE (mirrored)　(b) PYORE (mirrored)　(c) EVORP (mirrored)　(d) PRVEO (mirrored)

2. KNOW
   (a) NOWK (mirrored)　(b) KNOW (mirrored)　(c) WONK (mirrored)　(d) OKNW (mirrored)

3. D51P
   (a) P51D　(b) 51PD (mirrored)　(c) D51P (mirrored)　(d) P15D (mirrored)

4. ULTRA
   (a) ULTRA (mirrored)　(b) LURTA (mirrored)　(c) ULRTA (mirrored)　(d) ULTRA (mirrored)

5. BATTLE
   (a) BATTLE (mirrored)　(b) BATTLE (mirrored)　(c) BATTLE　(d) LEATTB (mirrored)

6. UNION
   (a) NIONU (mirrored)　(b) UNION (mirrored)　(c) UNNOI (mirrored)　(d) UNION (mirrored)

7. 5239
   (a) 5236 (mirrored)　(b) 5239 (mirrored)　(c) 5239 (mirrored)　(d) 6325 (mirrored)

8. % 9 ≠ ☆
   (a) ≠ % 9 ☆　(b) ☆ 9 % ≠　(c) % 9 ≠ ☆ (mirrored)　(d) ☆ ≠ 9 % (mirrored)

Direction (Qs. 9-15): Choose the one from the alternatives which most closely resembles the mirror image.

9.  | 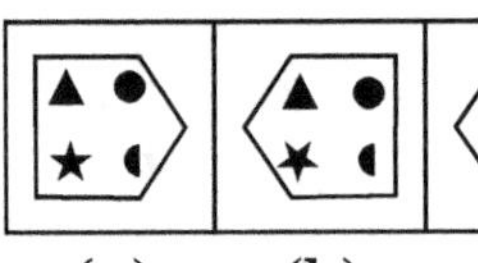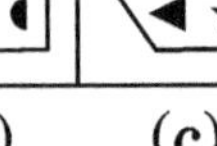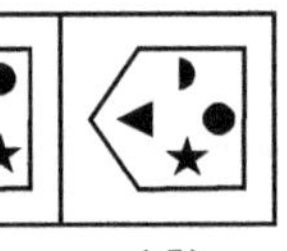
   (a)　　(b)　　(c)　　(d)

10.  | 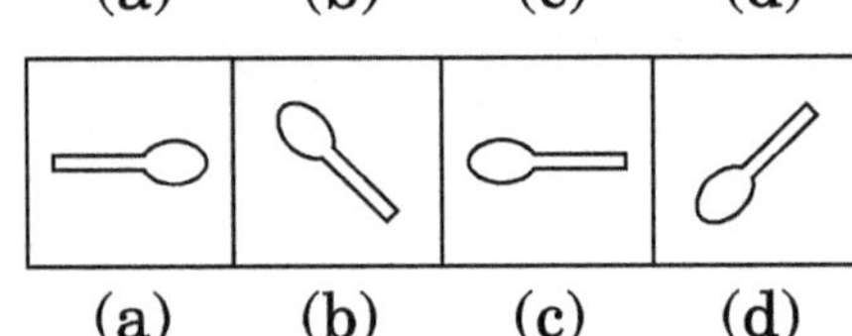
    (a)　　(b)　　(c)　　(d)

11. 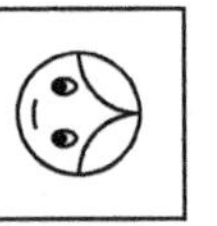 | 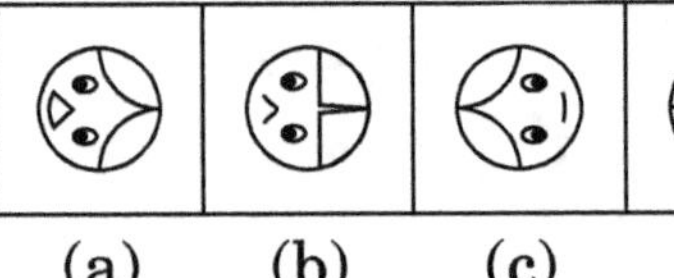
    (a)　　(b)　　(c)　　(d)

12. 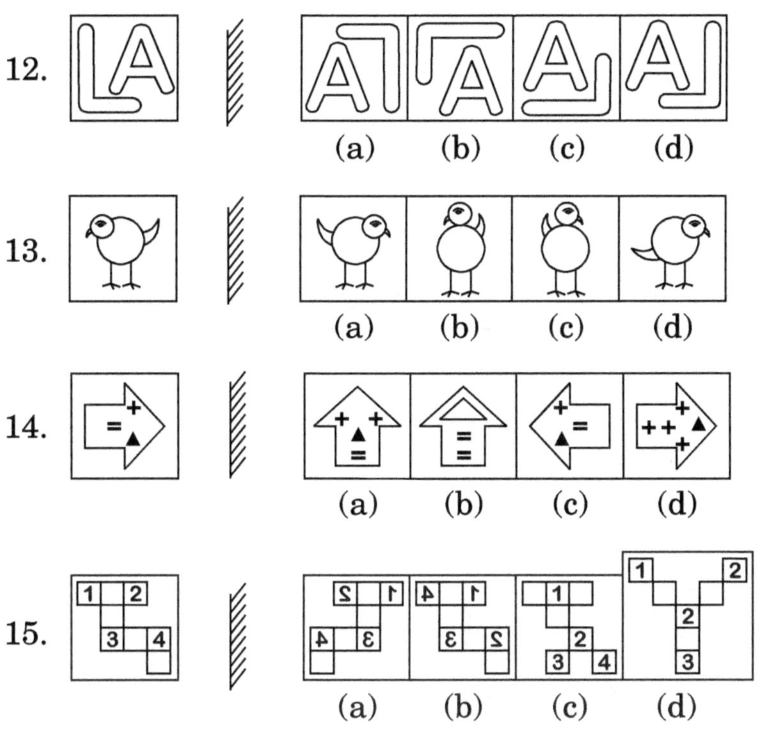

13.

14.

15.

Direction (Qs. 16-22): Choose the one from the alternatives which most closely resembles the water image.

16. PEACE

(a) ꟼEACE   (b) ꓒEACE   (c) ꟼEACE   (d) ECAEꟼ

17.  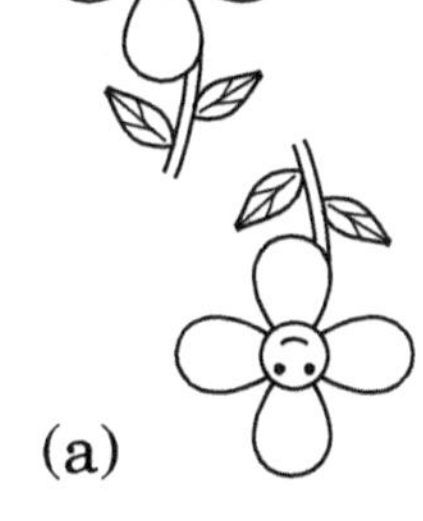

(a) 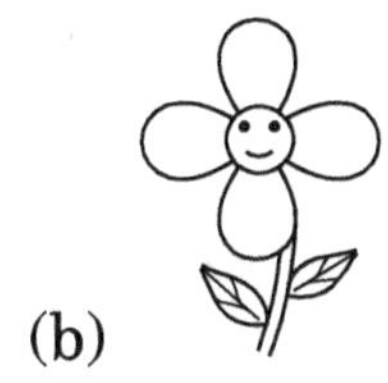   (b) 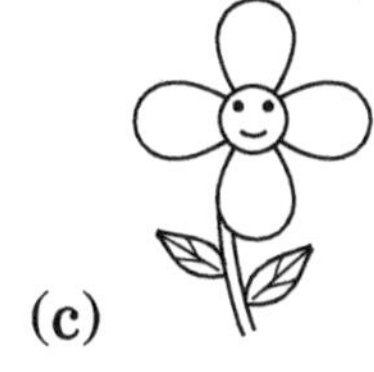   (c)   (d) 

18. INFER

(a) ꓤEꟼNI   (b) IꟼENꓤ   (c) INꟼEꓤ   (d) ꓤEꟼNI

19. SALE

(a) EASꓶ   (b) ꓱAꙄꓶ   (c) ꙄꓶAꓱ   (d) ꙄAꓶE

20. 2ᵃ58V

(a) V85ᵣɒ2   (b) Ƨ ᵃ85Λ   (c) Λ85ɒ2   (d) 2a58Λ

21. 5432

    (a) 5432 (reflected)   (b) 5432 (reflected)   (c) 5432 (reflected)   (d) 5325

22. 275%1

    (a) 275%1 (reflected)   (b) 275%1 (reflected)   (c) %5√51 (reflected)   (d) 1%5√5 (reflected)

Direction (Qs. 23-27): Choose the one from the alternatives which most closely resembles the water reflection of the image given below.

23. 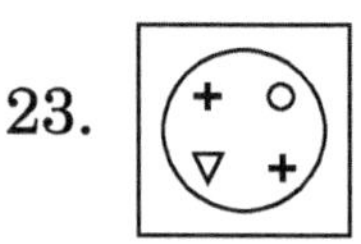 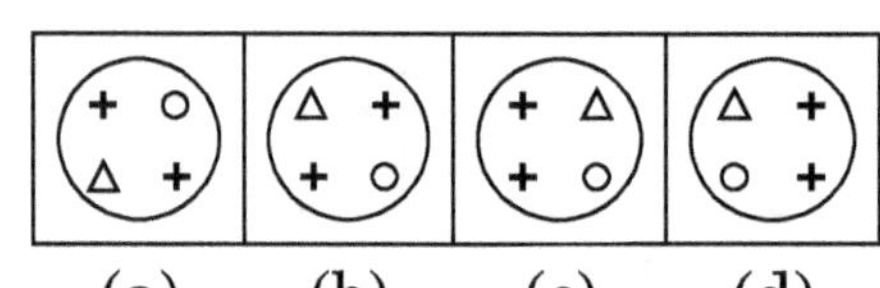

        (a)   (b)   (c)   (d)

24.  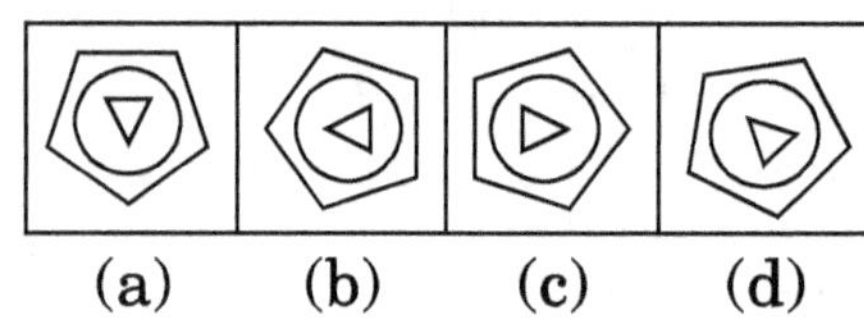

        (a)   (b)   (c)   (d)

25. 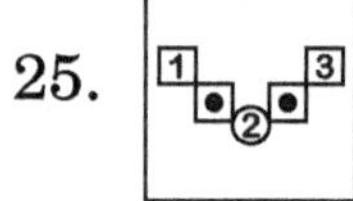 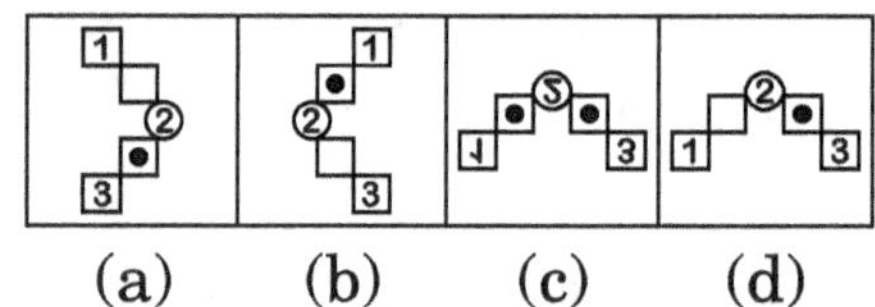

        (a)   (b)   (c)   (d)

26.  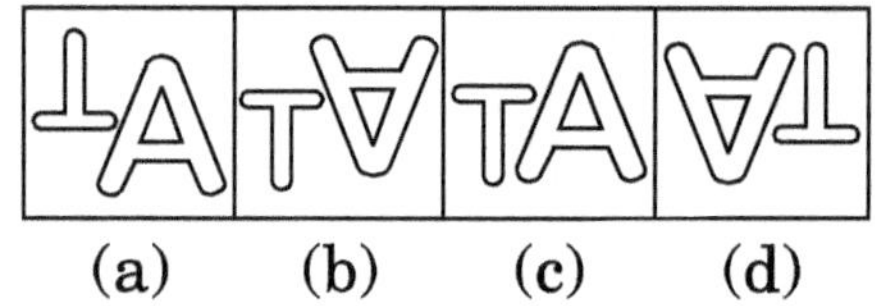

        (a)   (b)   (c)   (d)

27. 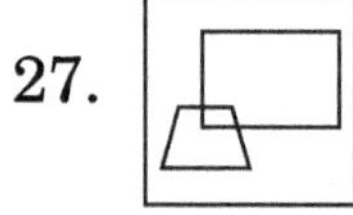 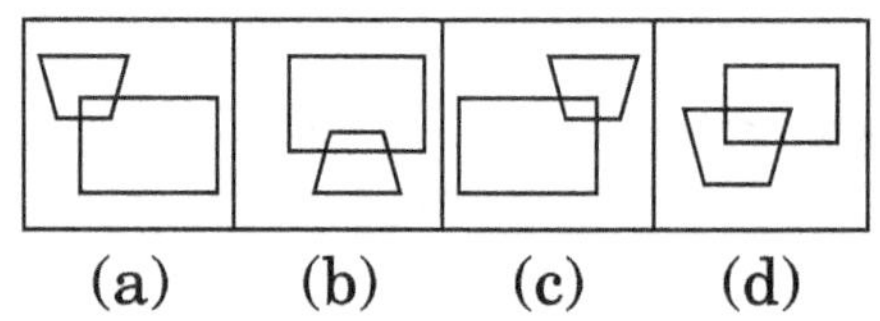

        (a)   (b)   (c)   (d)

28. 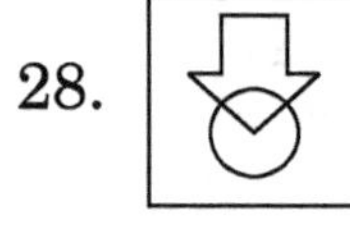 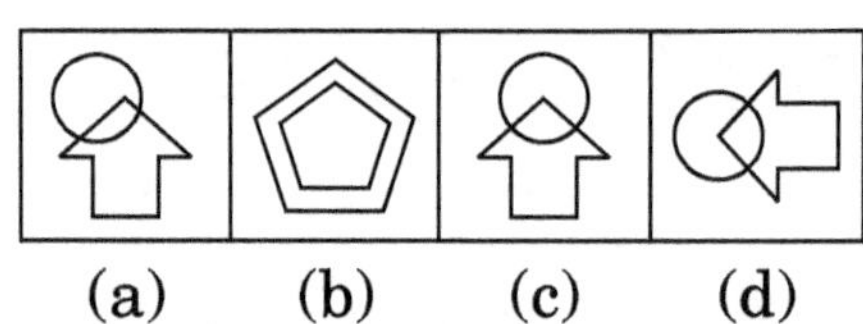

        (a)   (b)   (c)   (d)

29. Given below are some combination of images, numbers, symbols and their associated mirror images in two columns. Match the columns as per appropriate mirror image.

<table>
<tr><th>Group A</th><th>Group B</th></tr>
</table>

Group A		Group B	
A. 		1 	
B. 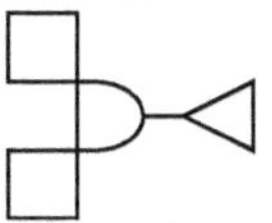		2 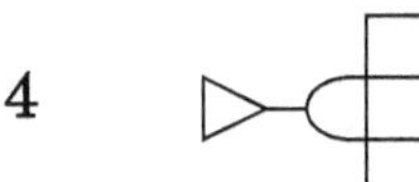	
C. AMAZE		3	
D. 19625%		4	

CODES:

	A	B	C	D		A	B	C	D
(a)	1	2	4	3	(b)	3	4	2	1
(c)	4	3	1	2	(d)	3	4	2	3

30. Given below are some combination of images, numbers symbols and their associated water images in two columns. Match the column A with column B on the basis of appropriate water reflection.

Group A   **Group B**

Group A		Group B	
A. 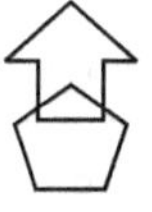		1 	
B. 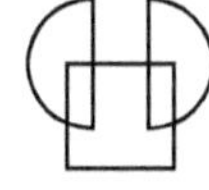		2 	
C. 		3 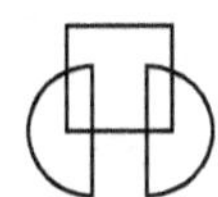	
D. 		4 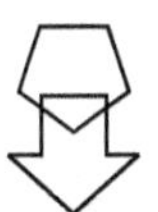	

CODES:

	A	B	C	D		A	B	C	D
(a)	4	2	1	3	(b)	2	3	1	4
(c)	4	3	2	1	(d)	3	1	4	2

31. Which of the following figures is symmetrical along the dotted line? **(2018)**

(a) 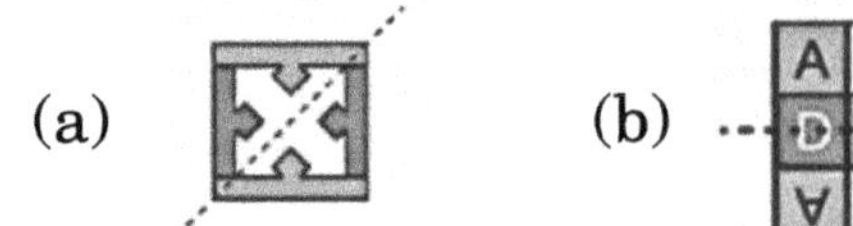 (b) 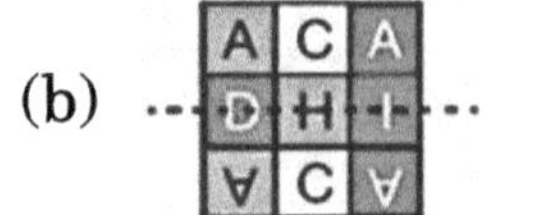 (c) 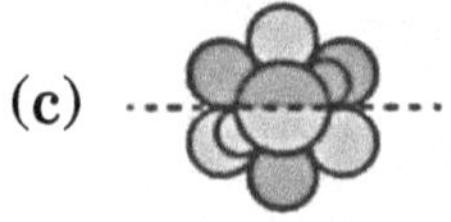 (d) 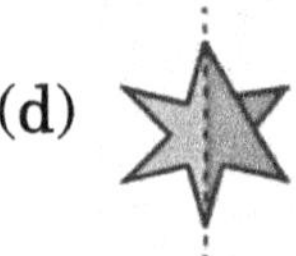

32. Which of the given figure has a line of symmetry? **(2019)**

(a) Only P

(b) Only Q

(c) Both P and Q

(d) Neither P nor Q

33. Find the correct mirror image of the giver figure. **(2021)**

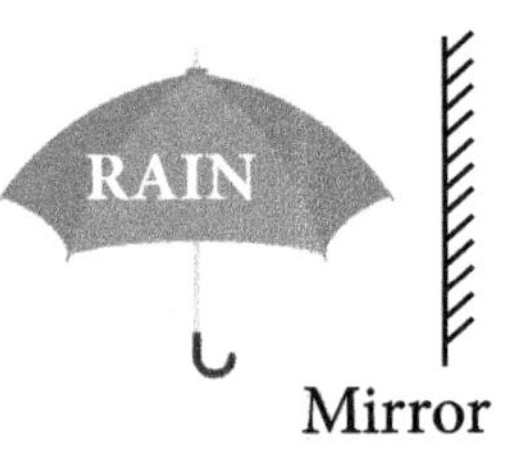

(a) 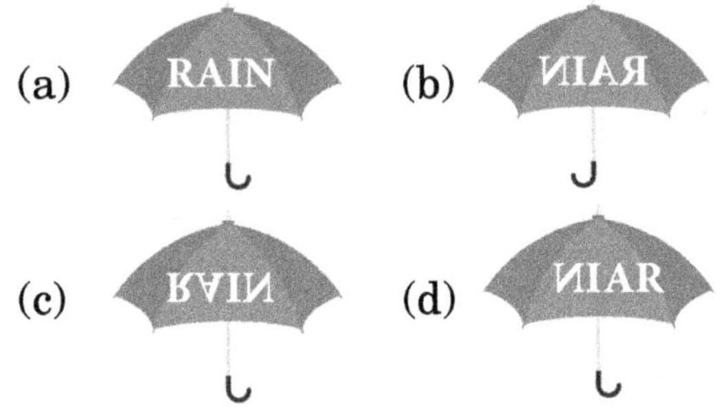

34. Find the CORRECT mirror image of the given figure. **(2021)**

(a) 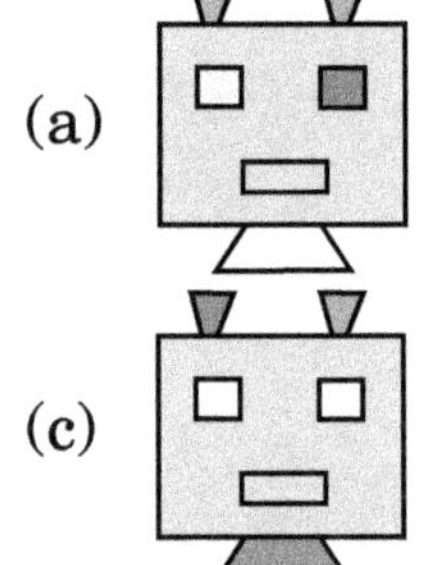   (b) 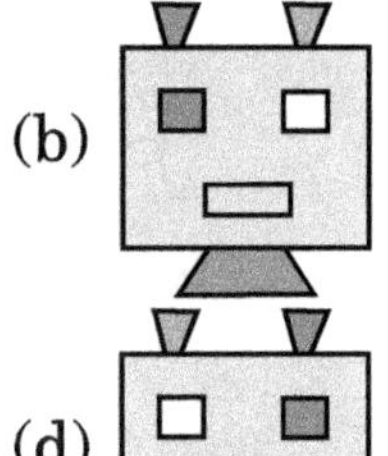

(c) 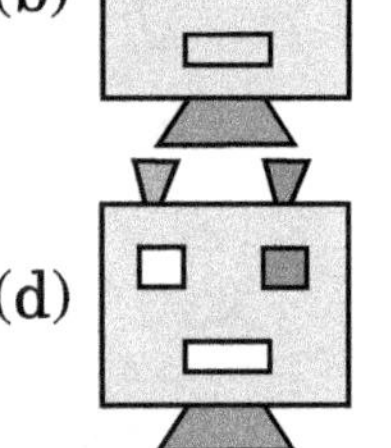   (d)

35. Find the mirror image of the given figure. **(2022)**

(a) 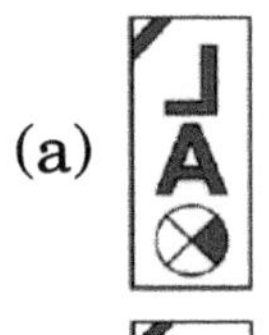   (b) 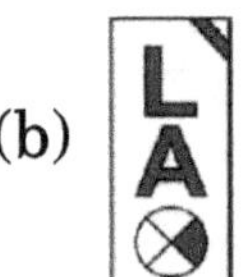

(c) 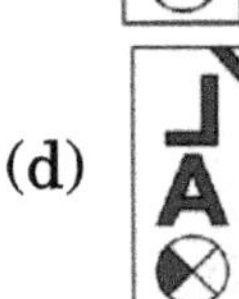   (d)

Direction (Qs. 1-8): Choose the one from the alternatives which most closely resembles the mirror image of the given combination.

1. ALLOW

WOLLA	ALLOW	AOWLL	AWLLO
(a)	(b)	(c)	(d)

2. BENIGN

BEGIEN	BENIGN	ENIGEB	BEGINE
(a)	(b)	(c)	(d)

3. CLOCK

CLOCK	COLCK	CLOCK	CLOKC
(a)	(b)	(c)	(d)

4. ORDER

ORDRE	ODERR	OEDOR	ORDER
(a)	(b)	(c)	(d)

5. CURRENT

CURRENT	CURRENT	CURREBNT	CURREBNT
(a)	(b)	(c)	(d)

6. GULF

GULF	FLUG	LGUF	GUFL
(a)	(b)	(c)	(d)

7. CAMP

CAMP	PCMA	CAMP	CMAP
(a)	(b)	(c)	(d)

8. % A ≠ 4 $

% A ≠ 4 $	$ ≠ A 4 %	% A 4 ≠ $	$ 4 ≠ A %
(a)	(b)	(c)	(d)

Direction (Qs. 9-15): In each of the questions there is a picture which is followed by four alternatives (a), (b), (c), (d). Identify the option which most closely resembles the mirror reflection of the given image.

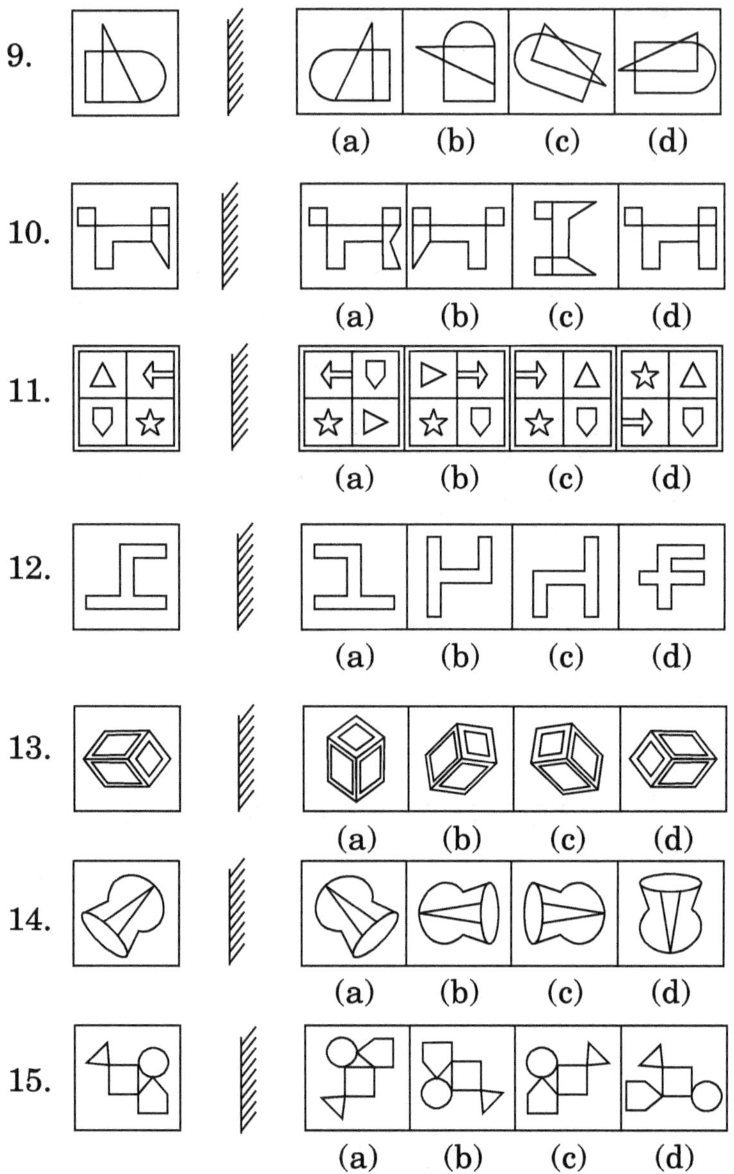

9.

    (a)   (b)   (c)   (d)

10.

    (a)   (b)   (c)   (d)

11.

    (a)   (b)   (c)   (d)

12.

    (a)   (b)   (c)   (d)

13.

    (a)   (b)   (c)   (d)

14.

    (a)   (b)   (c)   (d)

15.

    (a)   (b)   (c)   (d)

Direction (Qs. 16-22): Choose the one from the alternatives which most closely resembles the water image of the given combination.

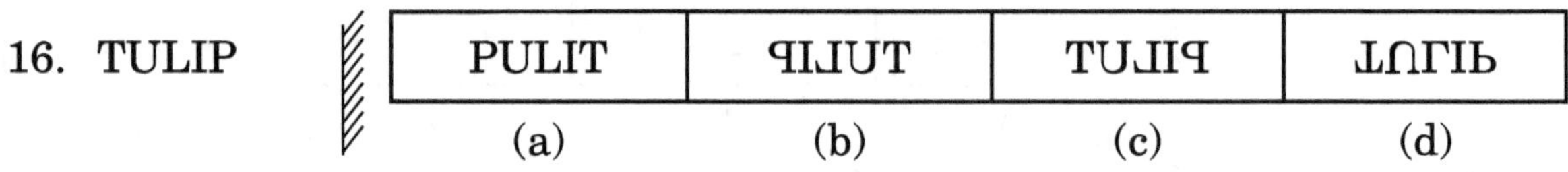

16. TULIP

PULIT	ꟻIꞀUT	TUꞀIꟼ	ꟼUꞀIT
(a)	(b)	(c)	(d)

17. PARKING

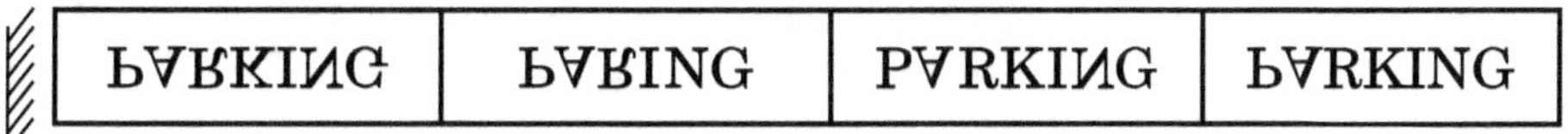

18. LUMINOUS

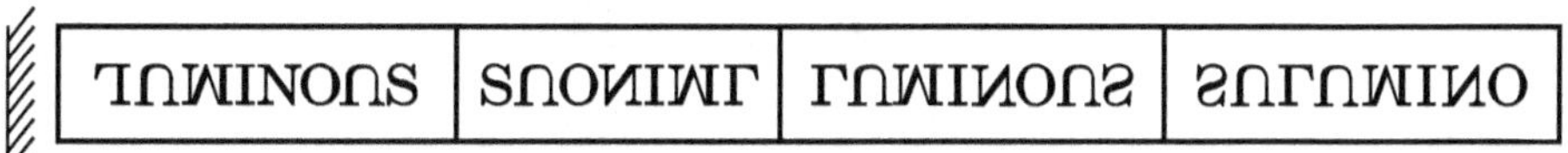

19. 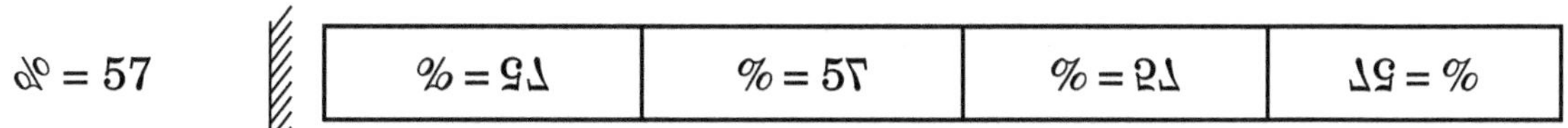 % = 57

20.

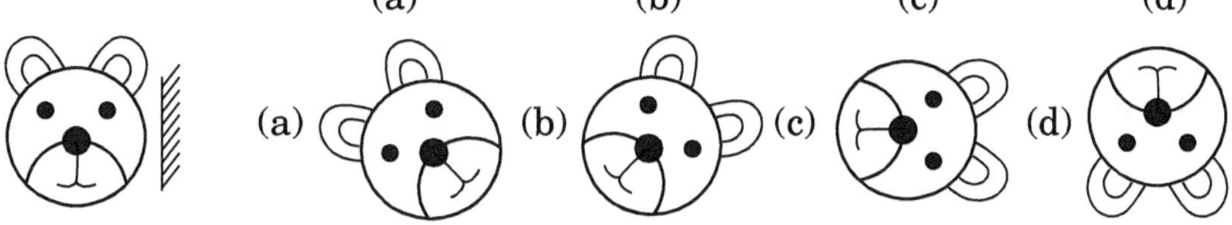

21.

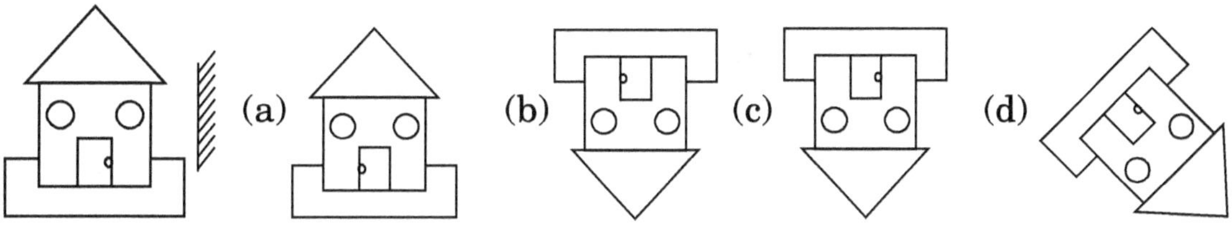

22.

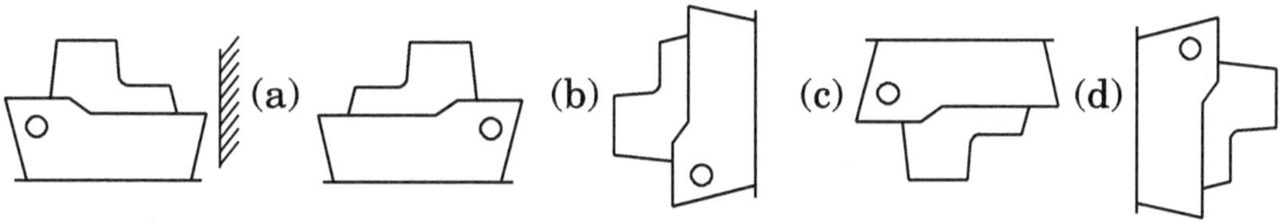

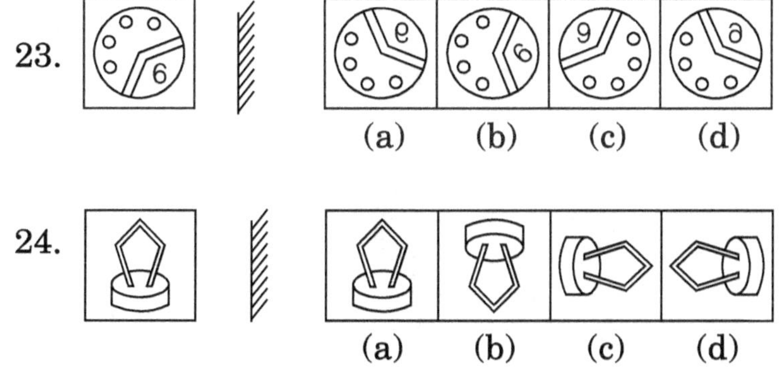

Direction (Qs. 23-30): Choose the one from the alternatives which most closely resembles the water image of the given image.

23.

24.

25. Find the mirror image of Fig. (X), if mirror is placed along MN.

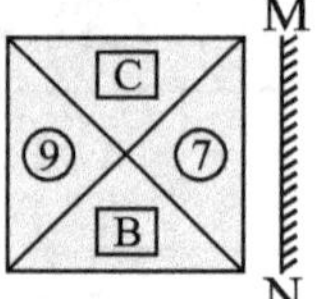

Fig. (X)

(a) 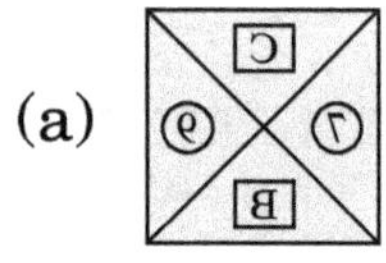 (b) 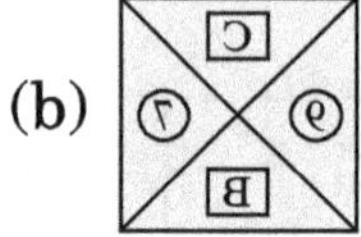 (c) 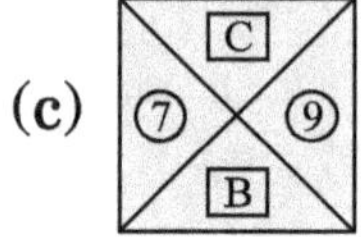 (d) 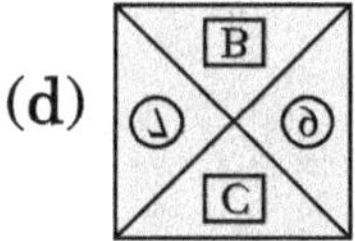

(Olympiad)

26. Which of the following options shows the correct mirror image of the given combination?

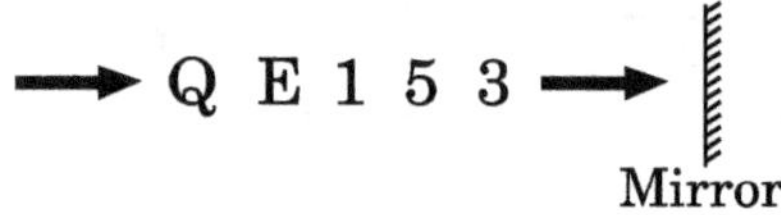

(a) → ℺ E Ɩ ꙅ 3 →   (b) ← Ɛ ꙅ Ɩ E ℺ ←

(c) ← Ɛ ꙅ Ɩ E ℺ ←   (d) → Q EƖ ꙅ 3 →

(Olympiad)

27. Which of the following options shows the correct mirror image of the given combination?

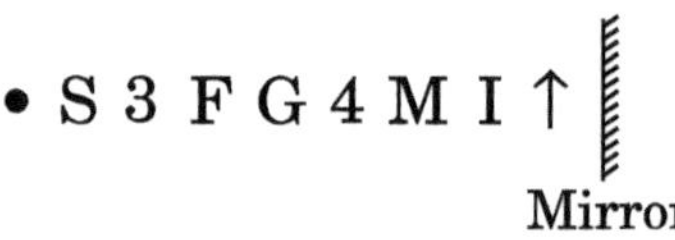

(a) • ꙅ 3 Ⅎ G ꟻ M I ↓   (b) ↑ I M ꟻ G Ⅎ Ɛ ꙅ •

(c) ↑ I M ꟻ Ð Ⅎ 3 ꙅ •   (d) ↑ I M ꟻ G Ⅎ Ɛ ꙅ •

(Olympiad)

28. Which of the following is the correct mirror image of Figure (X), if a mirror is placed along MN?

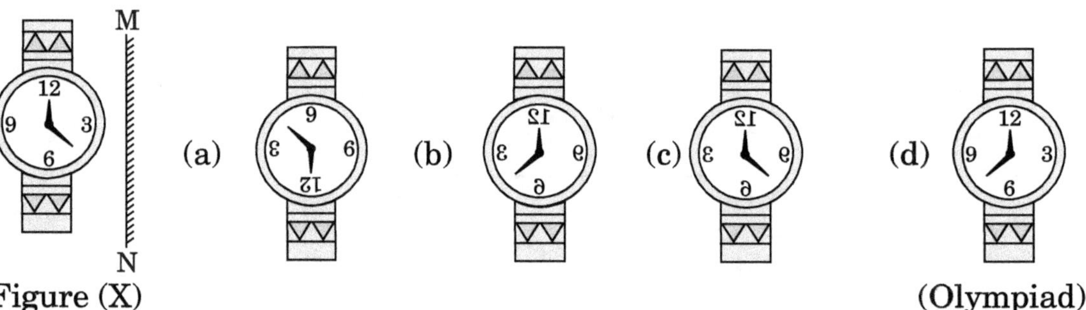

Figure (X)

(a) (b) (c) (d)

(Olympiad)

29. Find the mirror image of Figure (X), if the mirror is placed along the dotted line MN.

Figure (X)

(a) 

(b) 

(c) 

(d) 

(Olympiad))

30. Select the correct mirror image of Fig. (X).

Fig. (X)

(a) 

(b) 

(c) $T3\_|\heartsuit$

(d) $T\&L|\heartsuit$

(Olympiad)

31. Select the correct mirror image of the given figure. **(2020)**

(a) SC120

(b) SC120

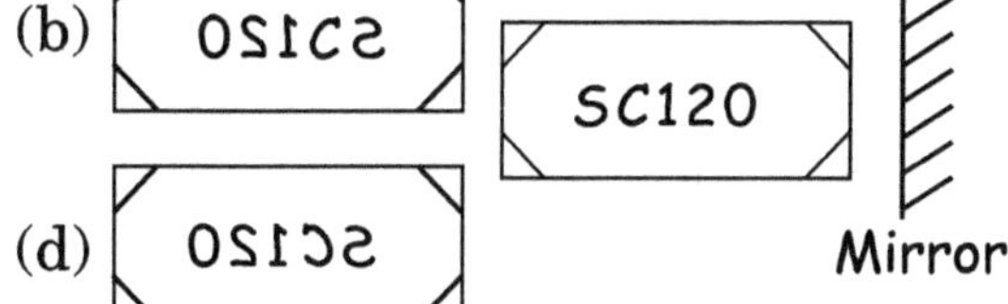

(c) 02120

(d) SC120

32. Which of the following figures is symmetrical along the dotted line?

(2021)

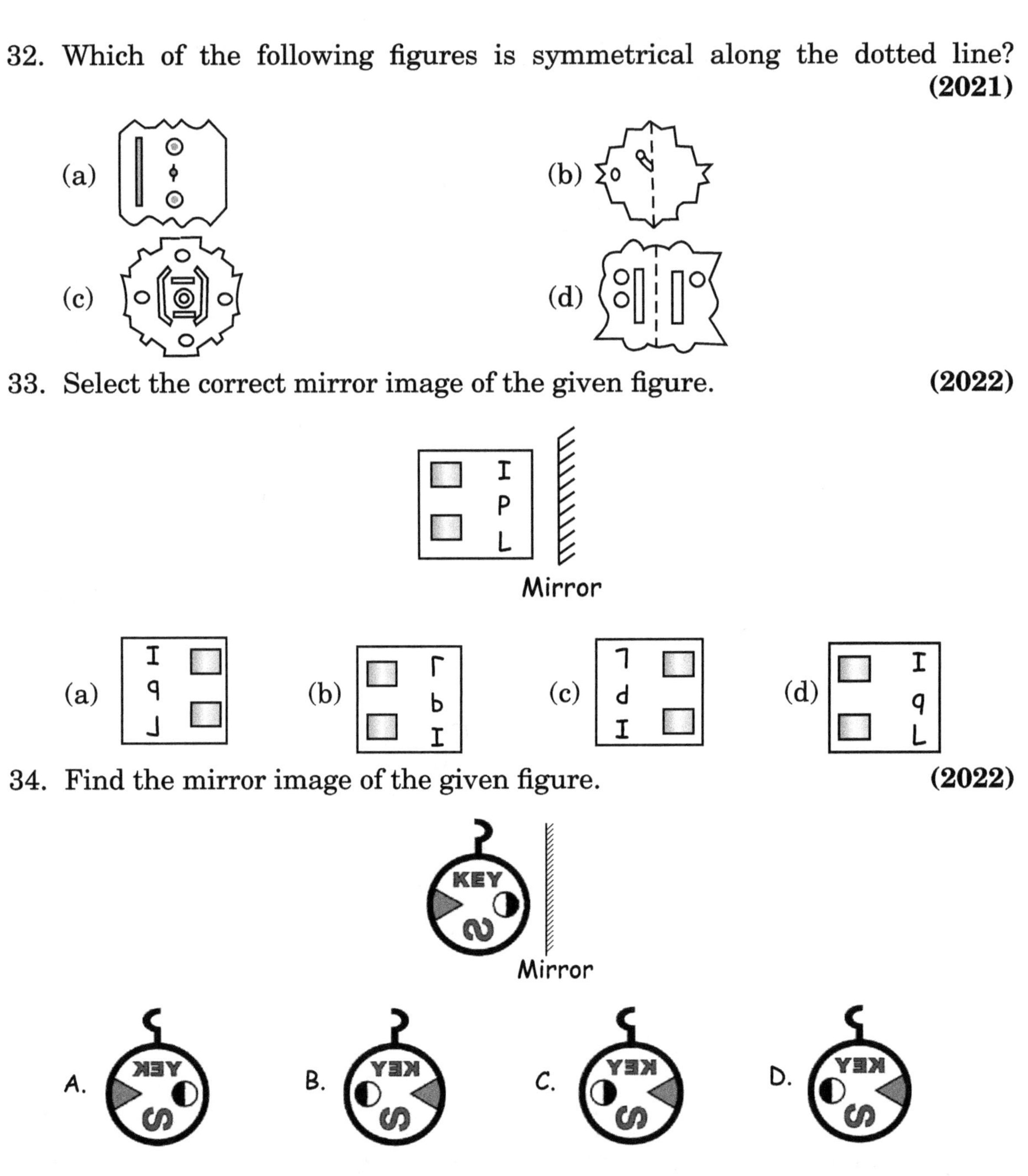

(a)

(b)

(c)

(d)

33. Select the correct mirror image of the given figure.

(2022)

(a)

(b)

(c)

(d)

34. Find the mirror image of the given figure.

(2022)

A.

B.

C.

D.

Level-1

1. (a) PROVE │ ƎVOЯꟼ

2. (b) KNOW │ WOИꓘ

3. (c) D51P │ ꟼ1ꝰꓷ

4. (d) ULTRA │ AЯTⱢU

5. (a) BATTLE │ ƎⱢTTAꓭ

6. (b) UNION │ ИOIИU

7. (c) 5239 │ ꝰƐꙄꙄ

8. (d) % 9 ≠ ☆ │ ☆ ≠ 6 %

9. (b)

10. (b)

11. (c)

12. (d) 

13. (a)

14. (c)

15. (a)

16. (a) $\dfrac{\text{PEACE}}{\text{ꟼEᴧCE}}$

17. (a) Option (a) is correct water image.

18. (c) $\dfrac{\text{INFER}}{\text{IИꟻEЯ}}$

19. (d) $\dfrac{\text{SALE}}{\text{ƧA⅃Ǝ}}$

20. (b) $\dfrac{\text{2a58V}}{\text{Ʌ82ɒƧ}}$

21. (b) $\dfrac{5432}{Ƨ4ƏⱾ}$

22. (b) $\dfrac{275\%1}{Ȿ⅄Ƨ\%⅃}$

23. (b)

24. (a)

25. (c)

26. (d)

27. (a)

28. (c)

29. (b) A-3, B-4, C-2, D-1

30. (c) A-4, B-3, C-2, D-1.

31. (b) Figure B is symmetrical along the dotted line.

32. (c) Both P and Q

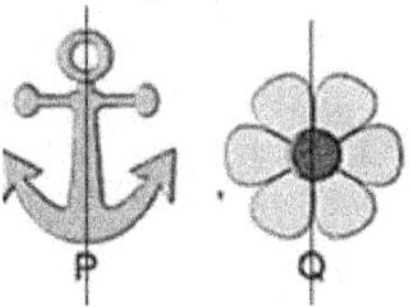

33. (b)

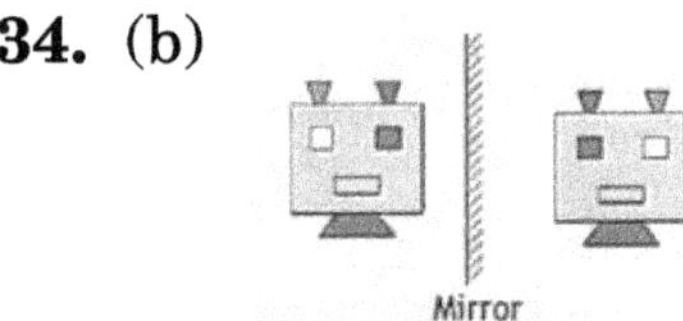

34. (b)

35. (d)

1. (a) ALLOW | ᴡOⱵⱵA
2. (b) BENIGN | ᴎ⅁ɪᴎƎᗺ
3. (c) CLOCK | ᴋↃOⱵↃ
4. (d) ORDER | ᴙƎᗡᴙO
5. (a) CURRENT | ⊤ᴎƎᴙᴙUↃ
6. (a) GULF | ⅎⱵU⅁
7. (c) CAMP | ⱯMⱯↃ
8. (d) % A ≠ 4 $ | $ 4 ≠ A %

9. (a) 

10. (b)

11. (c)

12. (a)

13. (d)

14. (a)

15. (c)

16. (d) $\dfrac{\text{TULIP}}{\text{ꓕ∩Ⱶ|ꓕ}}$

17. (a) $\dfrac{\text{PARKING}}{\text{ⱣⱯᴚᴋɪᴎ⅁}}$

18. (c) $\dfrac{\text{LUMINOUS}}{\text{Ⱶ∩ꟽɪᴎO∩Ꙅ}}$

19. (c) % = 57
% = ꓌ϛ

20. (d) 

21. (c) 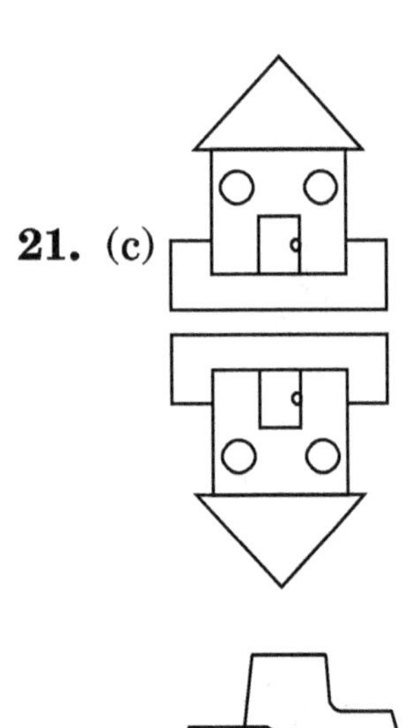

22. (c) 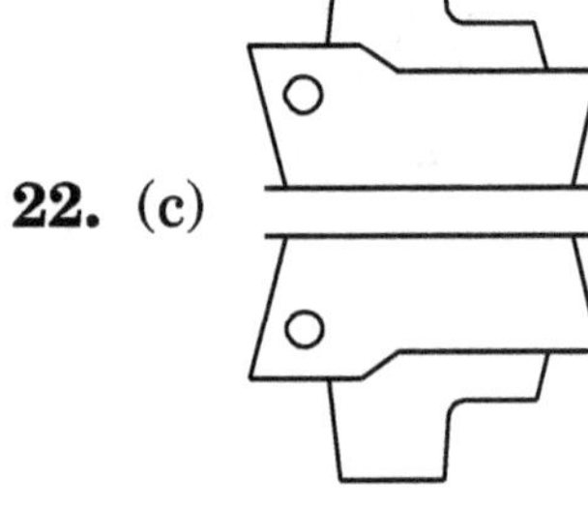

23. (a) 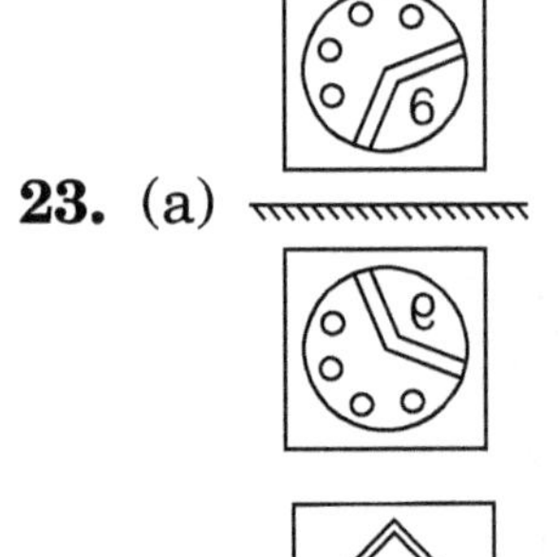

24. (b) 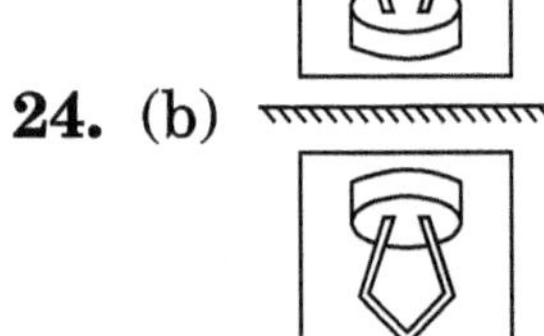

25. (b) 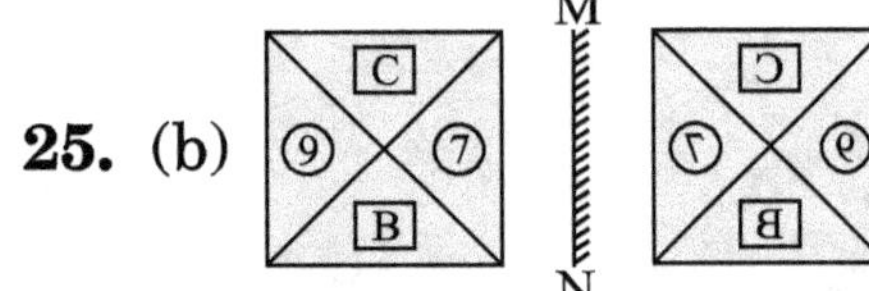

26. (b) 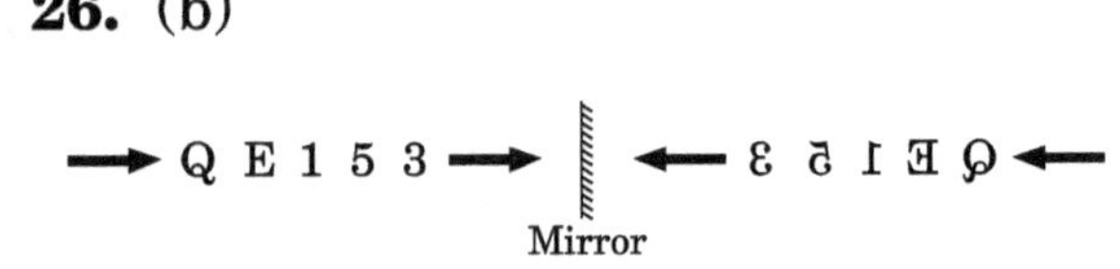

27. (b) 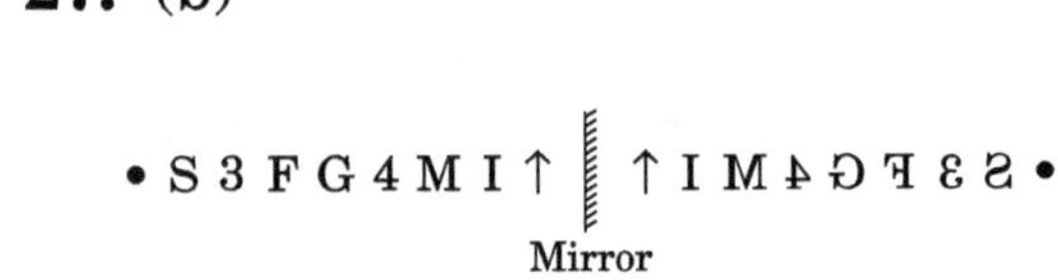

28. (b) 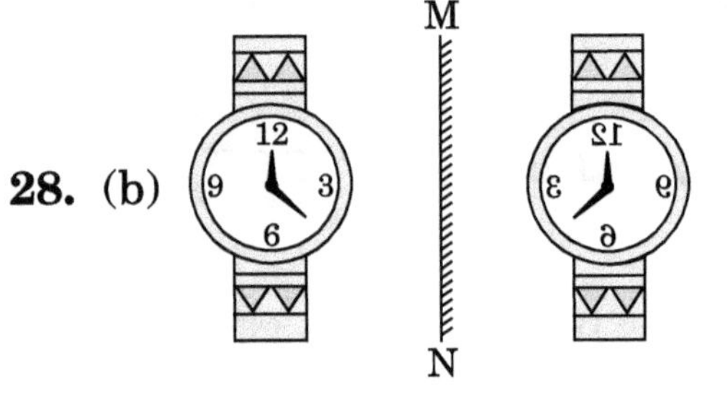

29. (c) 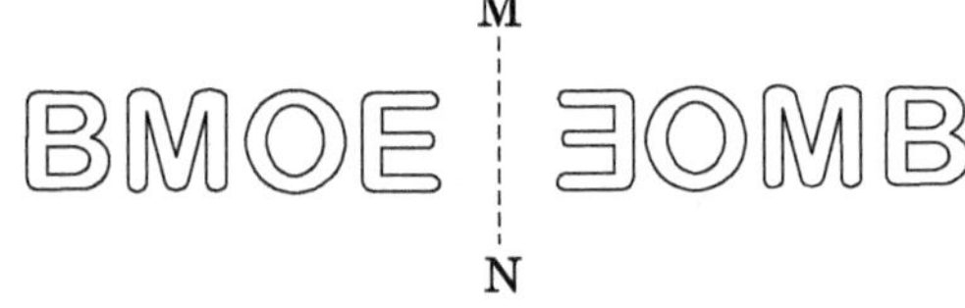

30. (b) 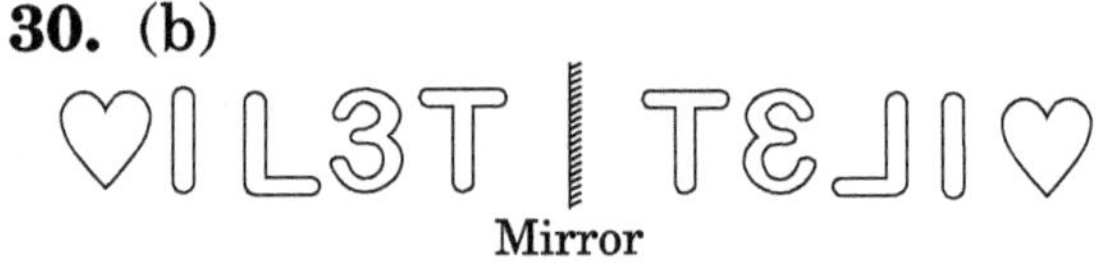

31. (a) 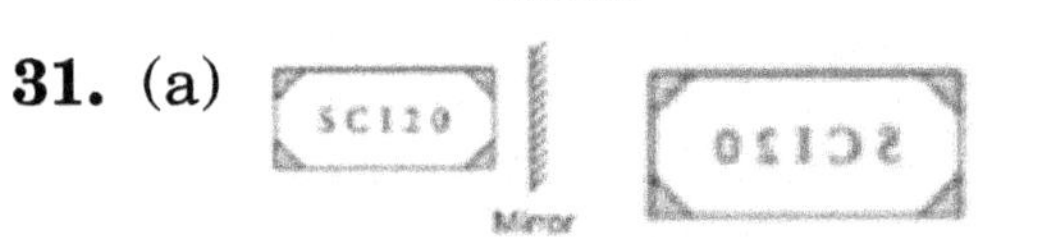

32. (c) 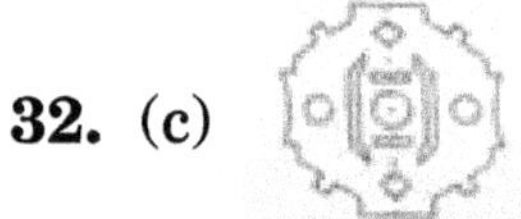

33. (a)

34. (d)

Logical Reasoning

OBJECTIVES

- To identify relationships, similarities and differences between shapes and patterns.
- To recognise visual sequences and relationships between objects and remembering these.

INTRODUCTION

Visual reasoning is the process of manipulating one's mental image of an object to reach a certain conclusion.

Types of Questions

The chapter includes:

1. Grouping of figures.
2. Paper folding and cutting.
3. Merging and splitting of images.
4. Finding difference between two images.
5. Clock wise and anticlock wise rotation of objects.
6. Tessellation puzzle.
7. Completion of image.
8. Corresponding image.
9. Different sections of image.
10. Symmetry
11. Rule detection

1. Paper Folding and Cutting

In this type of questions, there are three or four figures given in one line. Each figure followed a pattern. Each figure consists of a dotted line along which it is to be folded and the arrow shows the side which it is to be folded.

After folding, the paper is cut or punched and then students have to visualize the correct figure that will be produced when the paper is unfolded.

Direction (Example 1): In the following example, a piece of paper is folded and cut and then unfolded. One of the four options resembles the unfolded paper. Select the correct option.

Example 1:

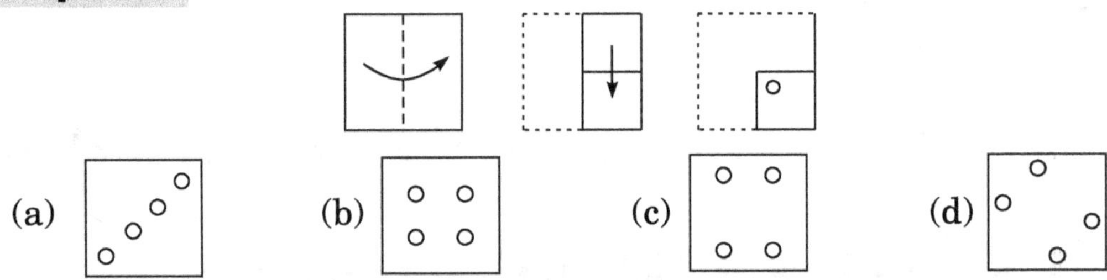

Ans. (b) The punch is made at the corner of the folded paper near the top of the left end. So, the unfolded paper shows equidistance punches.

2. *Merging and Splitting of Images*

Merging of images: In this segment, there are two different images. The student has to visualize the resulting image which will be produced by merging these two images.

Direction (Example 2): Two different images (x) and (y) are given which will be merged to form an image which appears in one of the options given below. Identify the correct option.

Example 2:

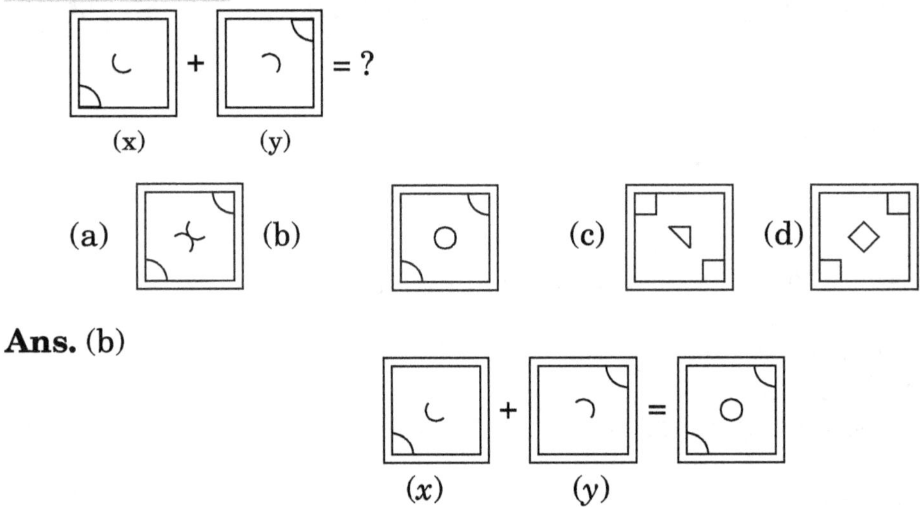

Ans. (b)

Splitting of Image

In this activity, a student will be given an image which can give two different images after splitting in some particular manner. The student has to identify which two images will appear from the given image.

Direction (Example 3): Which two images from the Figure (X) will appear after splitting. Choose the correct option.

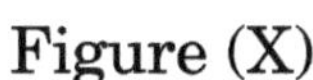

(a) 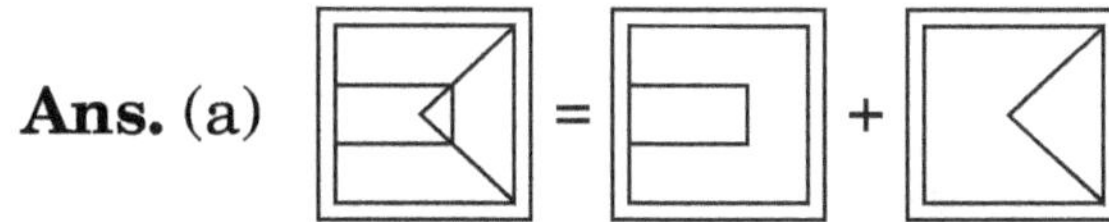 (b) (c) (d)

Figure (X)

Ans. (a) 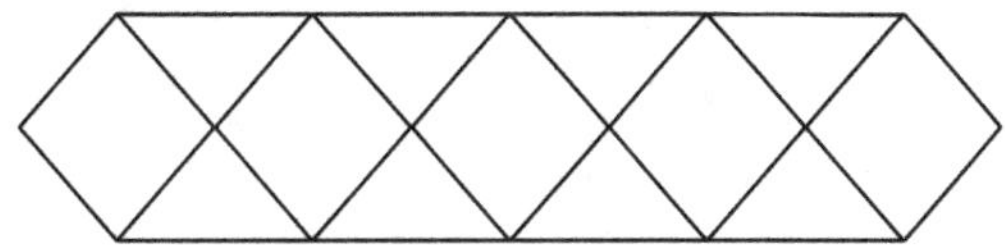 = +

3. Tessellation

A tessellation is created when a shape is repeated over and over again covering a plane without any gaps or overlaps. Here are examples of

- A tessellation of triangles:

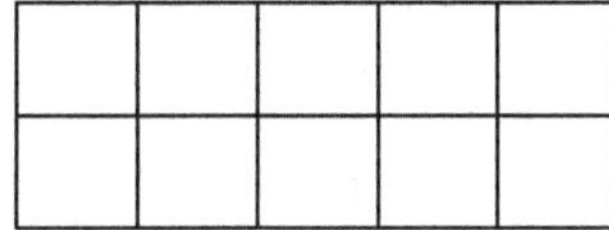

- A tessellation of squares:

Direction (Example 4): In the below given tessellation, some part is missing. Identify the correct shape which will correctly fit into the missing part. 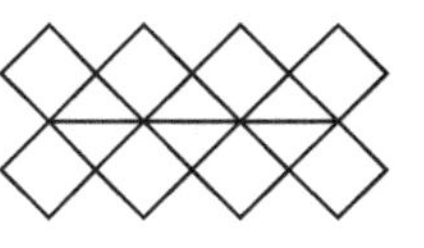

(a) (b) (c) (d)

Ans. (a) Option (a) will be correctly fit into the missing part.

4. Completion of Image

In this type of questions, a particular matrix or a set of figures follows a particular pattern, out of which one part, generally a quarter, is left blank. Now, the student has to identify the missing part out of four alternatives that follow the pattern.

Direction (Example 5): Complete the given figure.

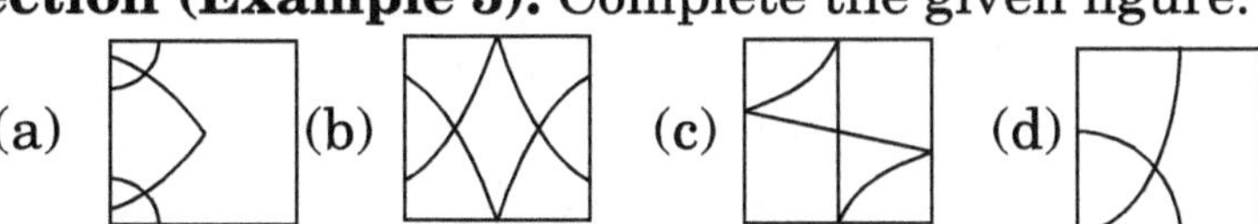

(a) (b) (c) (d)

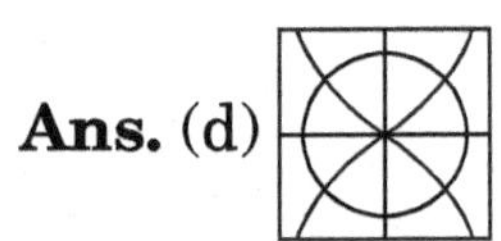

Ans. (d)

Example 6. Complete the given figure.

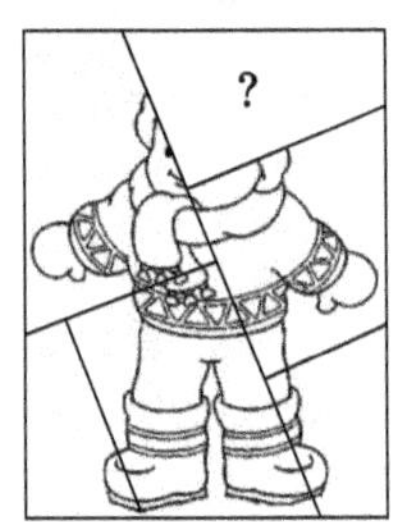

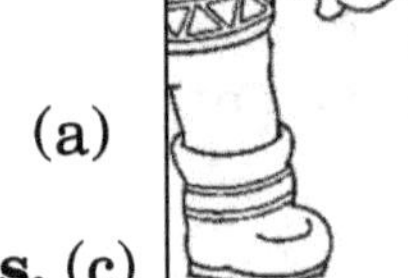
(a)

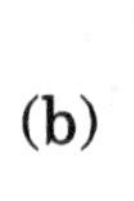
(b)

(c)

(d)

Ans. (c)

Solution: From the given four alternatives, figure (c) will correctly fit into the missing section.

5. Rule Detection

In these type of questions, there is a series of four figures which are related to each other in terms of certain rule. The student has to identify the rule and complete the given series.

Direction (Example 7): On the basis of the given rule, choose the correct option.

Rule: The inside figure is increasing by its sides.

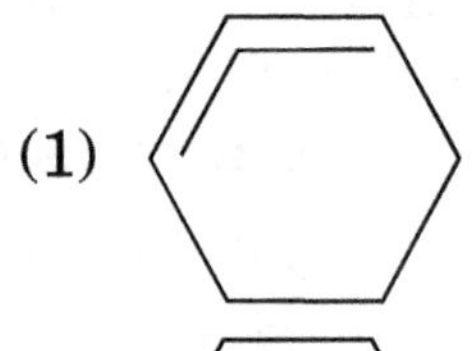
(1)

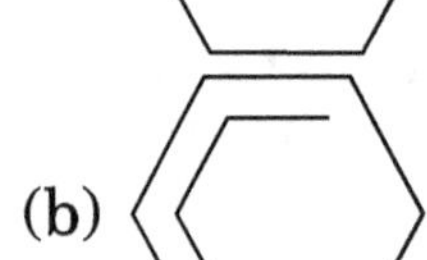
(2)

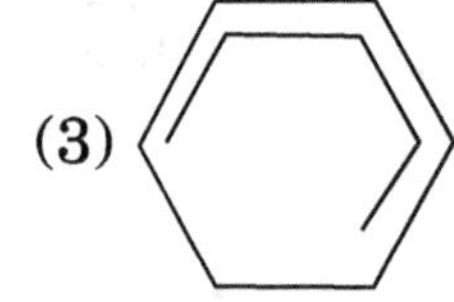
(3)

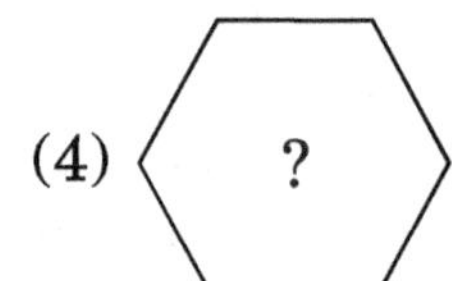
(4)

(a)

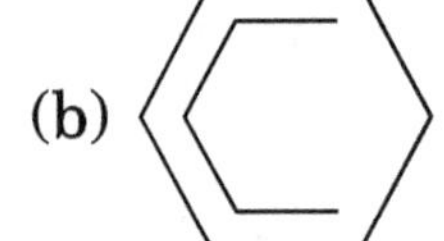
(b)

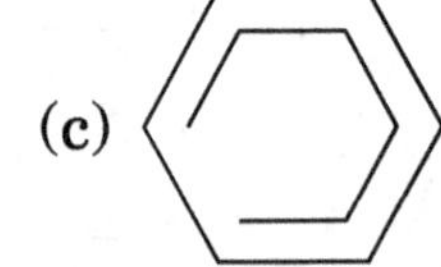
(c)

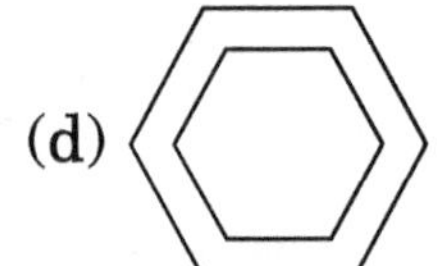
(d)

LEVEL-1

Direction (Qs. 1-5): In each of the following questions, group the given figures into three classes using each figure only once.

1.

(a) 1, 4, 8; 3, 5, 7; 2, 6, 9
(b) 1, 6, 9; 2, 4, 3; 5, 7, 8
(c) 2, 5, 6; 1, 3, 7; 4, 8, 9
(d) 1, 3, 5; 2, 4, 6; 7, 8, 9

2.

(a) 1, 2, 4; 5, 7, 9; 3, 6, 8
(b) 1, 3, 5; 2, 6, 8; 4, 7, 9
(c) 1, 2, 7; 3, 8, 9; 4, 5, 6
(d) 1, 5, 7; 4, 6, 9; 2, 3, 8

3.

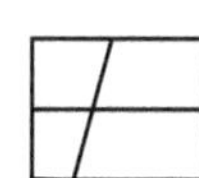

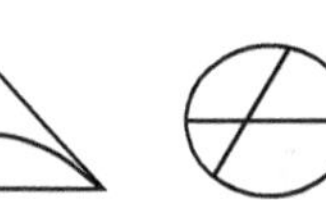

(a) 1, 2, 9; 6, 7, 8; 3, 4, 5
(b) 1, 6, 9; 3, 5, 7; 2, 4, 8
(c) 2, 7, 9; 4, 5, 6; 1, 2, 3
(d) 1, 5, 9; 3, 6, 8; 2, 4, 7

4. 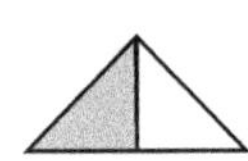

(a) 1, 3, 5; 2, 7; 4, 6   (b) 2, 4, 5; 3, 7; 1, 6

(c) 1, 6, 7; 2, 3; 4, 5   (d) 1, 5; 2, 4, 7; 3, 6

5.  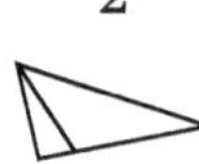 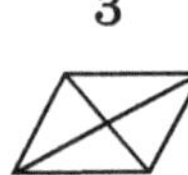 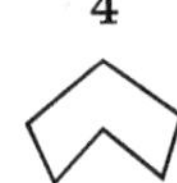    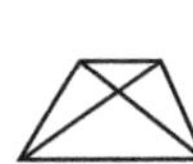 

(a) 1, 4, 7; 2, 6, 9; 3, 5, 8   (b) 1, 5, 9; 2, 6, 7; 3, 4, 8

(c) 1, 2, 9; 3, 4, 7; 5, 6, 8   (d) 3, 4, 5; 1, 6, 7; 2, 8, 9

Direction (Qs. 6 and 7):

6. Given below is the folded form of paper. Which of the following shows the correct figure when the paper is unfolded along the dotted line?

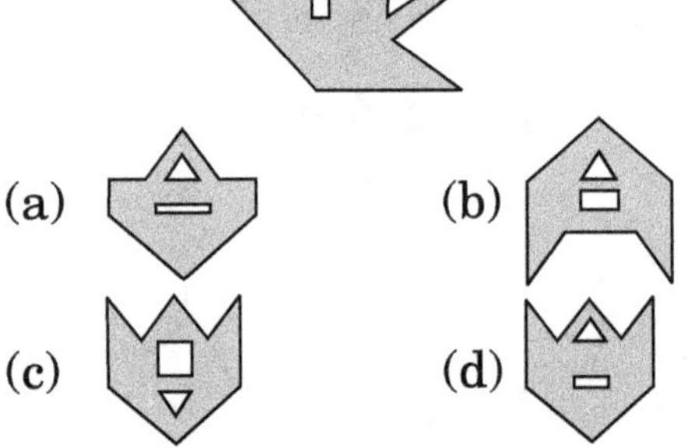

(a)   (b)   (c)   (d)

7. Which of the following shows the correct figure when the paper given below is unfolded along the dotted line?

Direction (Qs. 8-12): Given below are some questions in which two different parts of an image are given. Identify the image after merging the two parts.

8. 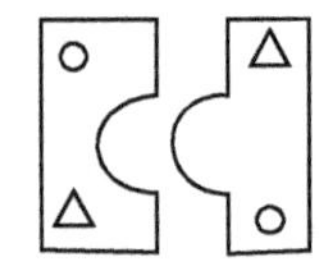

(a) 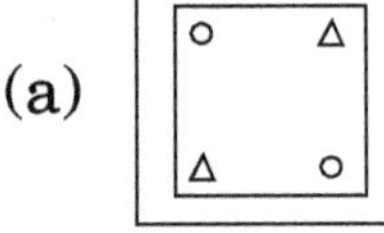   (b) 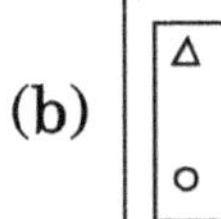

(c) 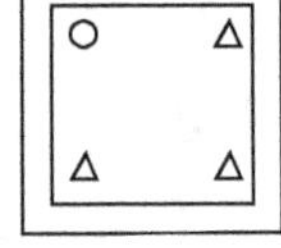   (d) 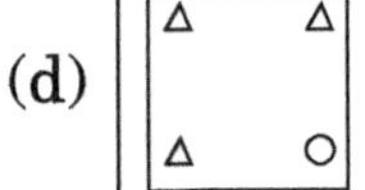

9. 

(a) 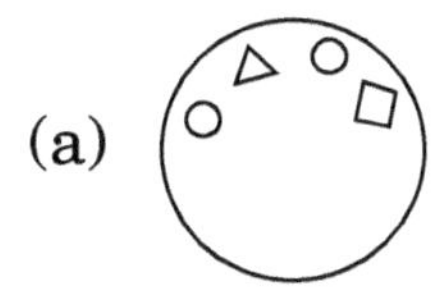   (b) 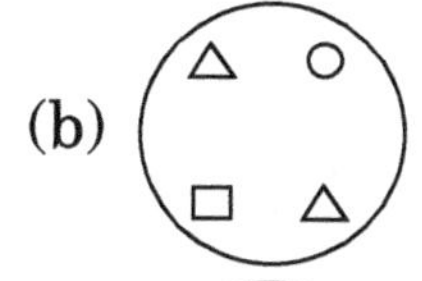

(c) 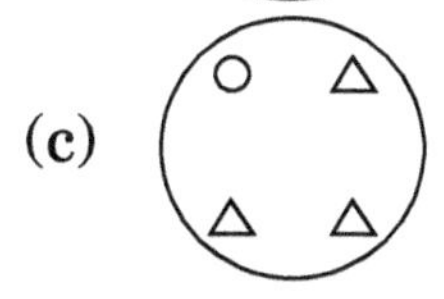   (d) 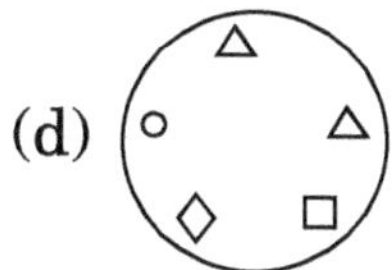

(c) 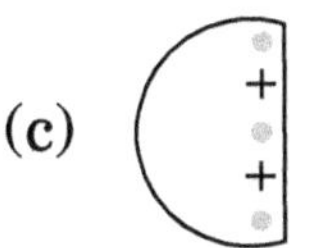   (d) 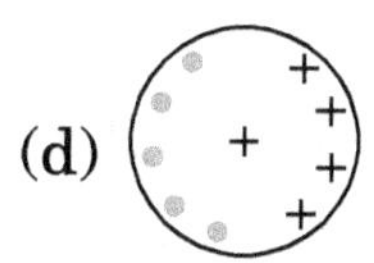

Direction (Qs. 13-17): In the questions given below, there is an image which is the combination two different figures. Choose the best combination for the given image.

10. 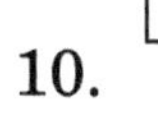 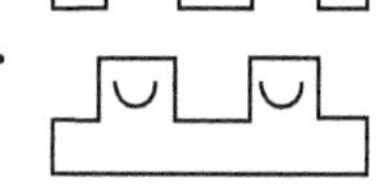

(a) 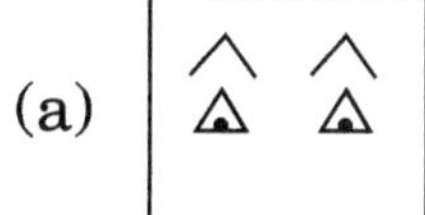   (b) 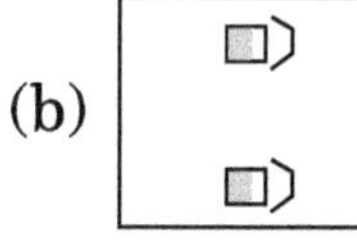

(c)    (d) 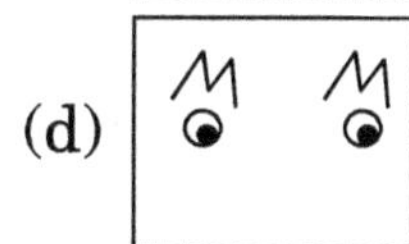

13. 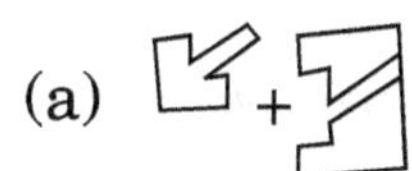 = ?

(a) 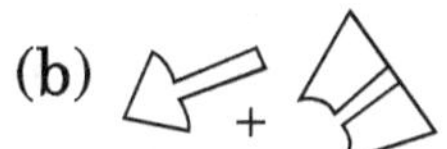

(b) 

(c)

(d)

11. 

(a) 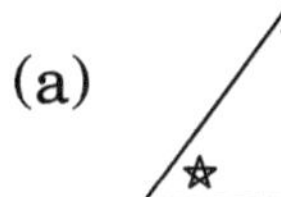   (b) 

(c)    (d) 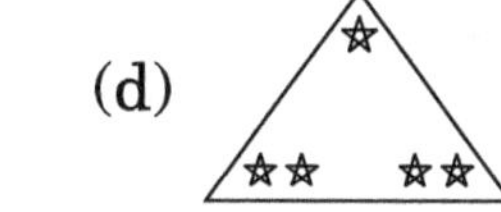

14. = ?

(a)   (b)

(c)   (d)

12. 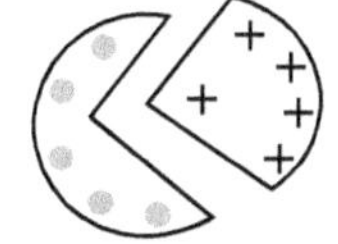

15. = ?

(a) 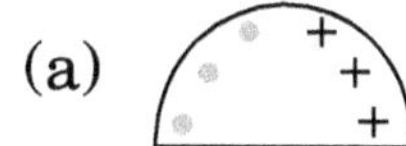   (b) 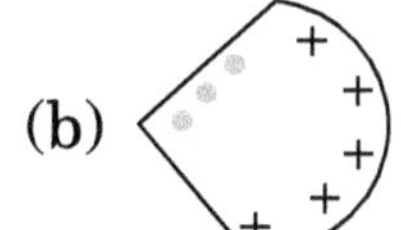

(a)   (b)

(c)   (d) 

16.  = ?

(a) 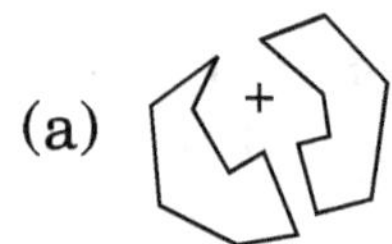

(b) 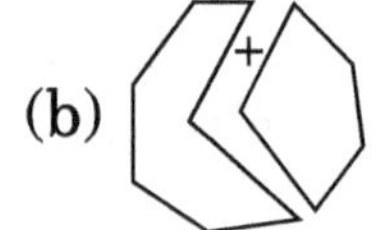

(c) 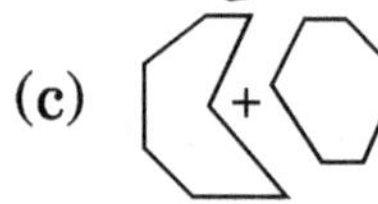

17.  = ?

(a) 

(b) 

(c) 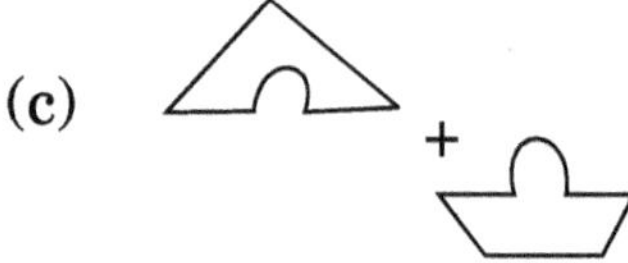

(d)

Direction (Qs. 18-22): In each of the questions given below, a tessellation pattern is given. Carefully observe each pattern and identify which shape is missing in each figure?

18. 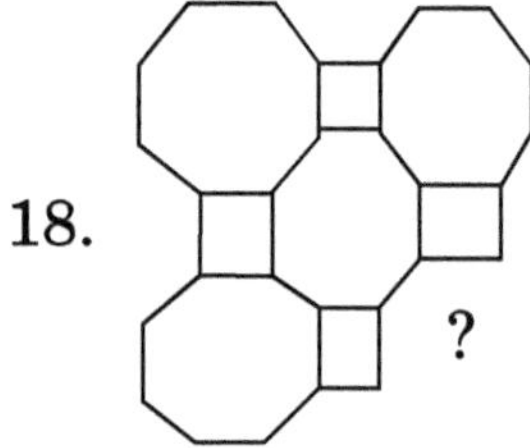

(a) ⬡
(b) ▭
(c) △
(d) ⬠

19.

(a) □
(b) △
(c) ⬡
(d) ⬠

20. 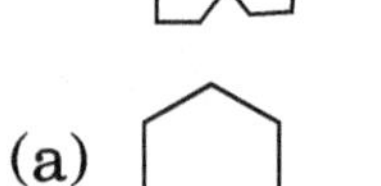 

(a) ⬡
(b) ✡
(c) ✪
(d) ◈

21. ? 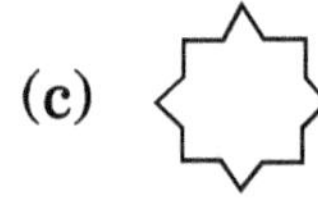 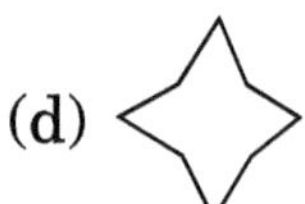

(a)
(b)
(c)
(d)

22. 

(a)
(b)
(c)
(d)

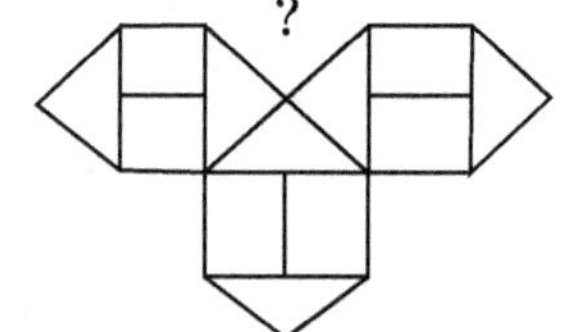

Direction (Qs. 23-25): In each of the questions given below, there is a set of images which are linked by certain rules. Carefully observe the set in each question and the rule associated with it. Find the missing image in the set.

23. **Rule:** The sides of the figure are reducing from 1 to 4.

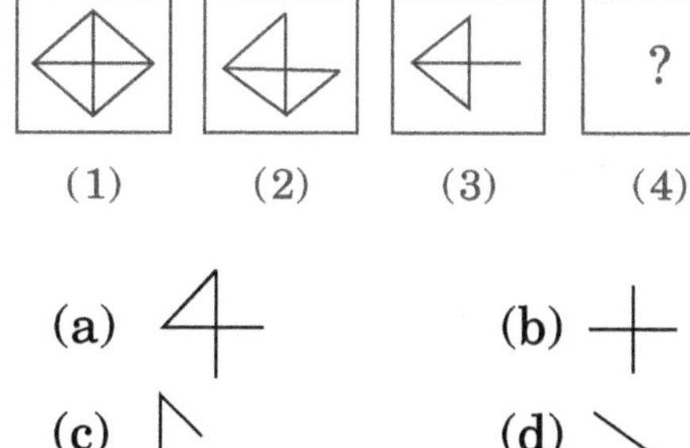

   (1)   (2)   (3)   (4)

(a)   (b)

(c)   (d)

24. **Rule:** As the series continues, the inside image reduces in its sides and the outside image increases in its size.

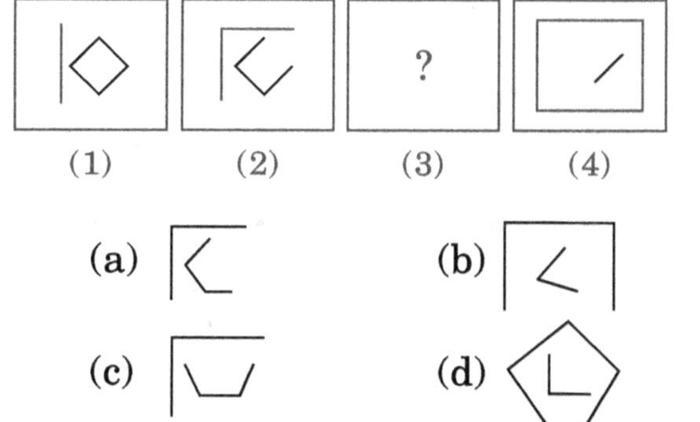

   (1)   (2)   (3)   (4)

(a)   (b)

(c)   (d)

25. **Rule:** As the series proceeds, one extra leaf is added to the flower.

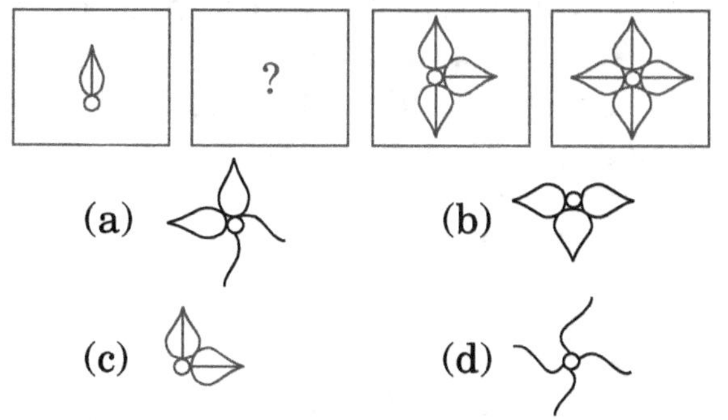

(a)   (b)

(c)   (d)

26. If all the numbers are removed from the given arrangement, then how many elements are left in the series? **(2020)**

P M 4 @ 2 L 1 T U X V $ 9 © N X 7 & A G Z ● 6 #

(a) 24   (b) 10
(c) 16   (d) 18

27. If 'Monkey' is called 'Lion', 'Lion' is called 'Tiger' and 'Tiger' is called 'Deer', then _______ is the king of jngle. **(2021)**

(a) Lion   (b) Tiger
(c) Monkey   (d) Deer

28. How many possible combinations of 1 teacher and 1 student each can be formed from the given teachers and students? **(2022)**

(a) 12

(b) 8

(c) 14

(d) 15

Teachers	Students
Kamal	Varun
Anand	Shreya
Krishna	Shruti
	Arjun
	Karan

29. Pointing to a man in the photograph, Meena said, "He is the brother of my father". How is Meena related to man? **(2022)**

(a) Sister   (b) Daughter
(c) Niece   (d) Nephew

30. Take  as one cube and then count the number of cubes in the given soli(d) **(2022)**

(a) 17

(b) 19

(c) 18

(d) 20

LEVEL-2

Direction (Qs. 1-5): In each of the questions given below, there is a box with six sections which are occupied by segments of a complete image. One of the four alternatives is not a part of the complete image. Now, identify which alternative is not a part of the complete image.

1.

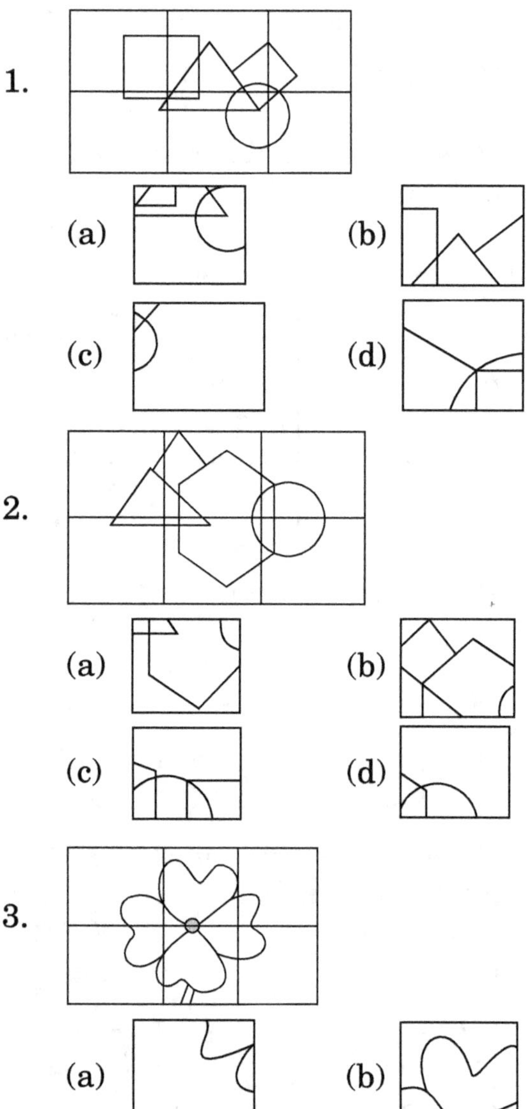

(a)

(b)

(c)

(d)

2.

(a)

(b)

(c)

(d)

3.

(a)

(b)

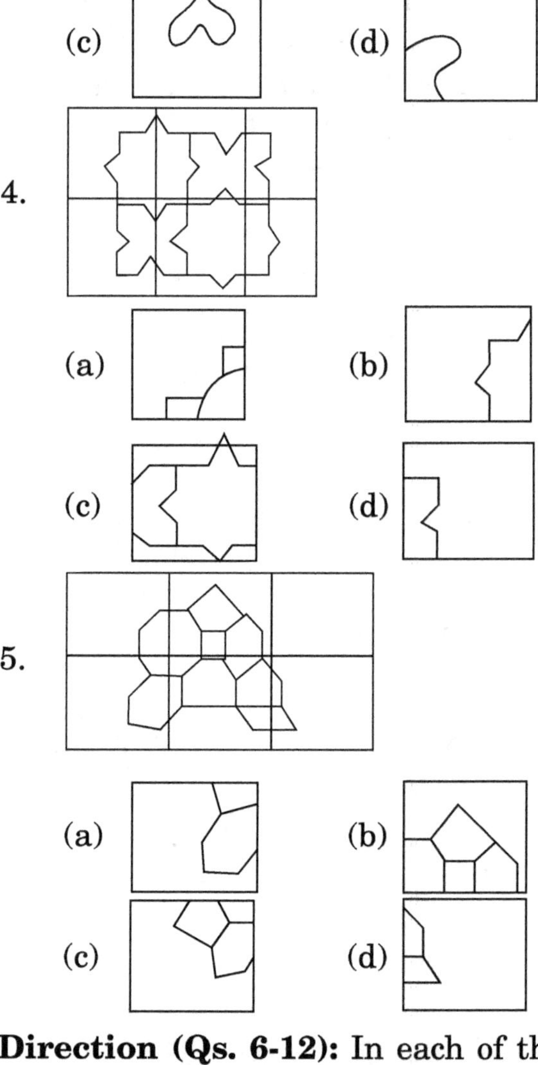

4.

(a)

(b)

(c)

(d)

5.

(a)

(b)

(c)

(d)

Direction (Qs. 6-12): In each of the questions given below, there are four alternatives, which when placed in the blank spaced would complete the pattern. Identify the correct alternative that complete the image.

6.

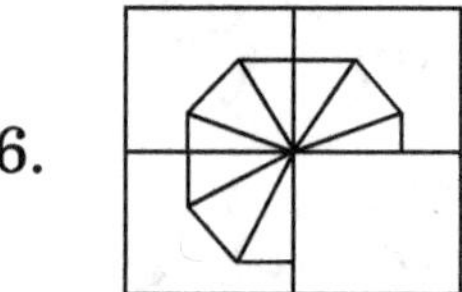

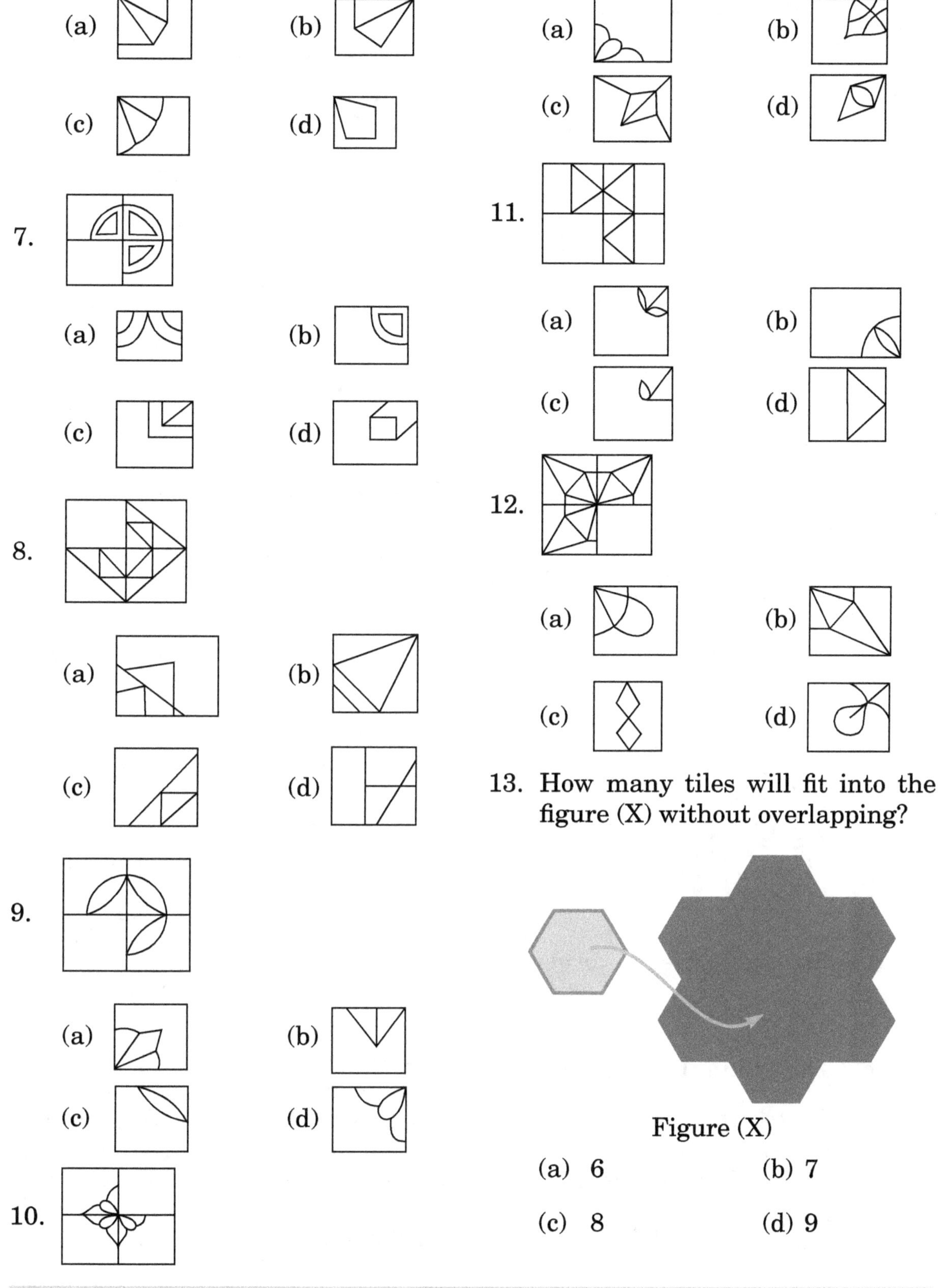

13. How many tiles will fit into the figure (X) without overlapping?

(a) 6 (b) 7

(c) 8 (d) 9

14. Which two shapes do not intersect?

(a) 1 and 2

(b) 1 and 3

(c) 2 and 4

(d) 2 and 3

15. Which ball is farthest from the
centre of the triangle?

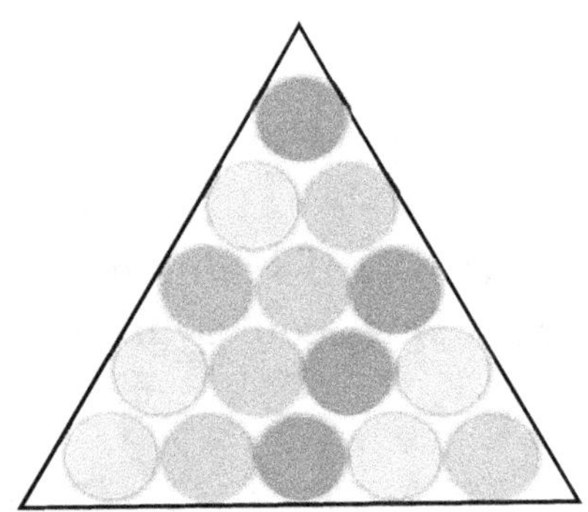

(a) The ball in the top corner

(b) The ball in the left corner

(c) The ball in the right corner

(d) These three balls are at
the same distance from the
centre of the triangle.

16. Which option completes the figure (X)?

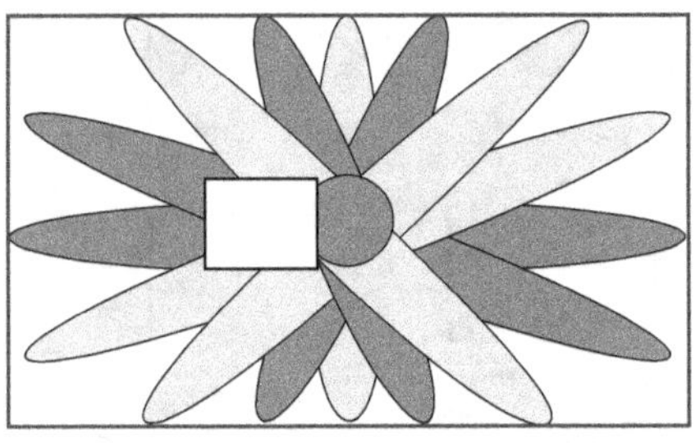

Figure (X)

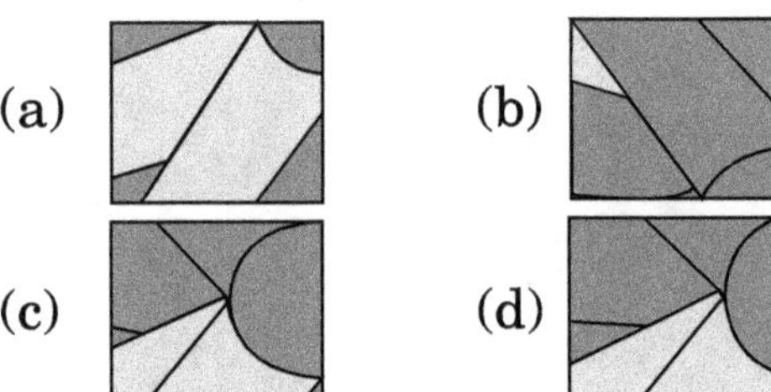

17. Which option completes the figure (X)?

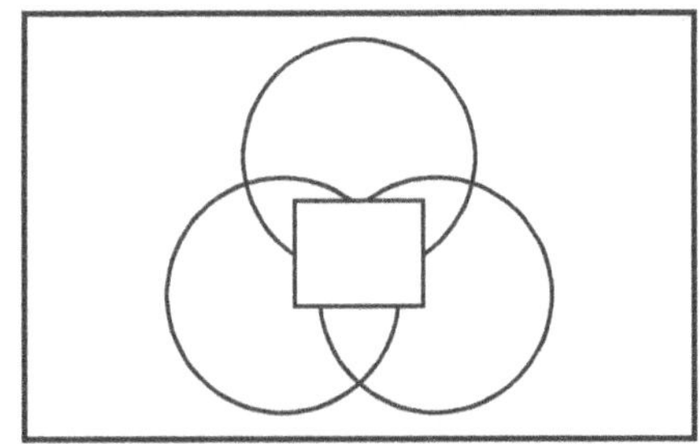

Figure (X)

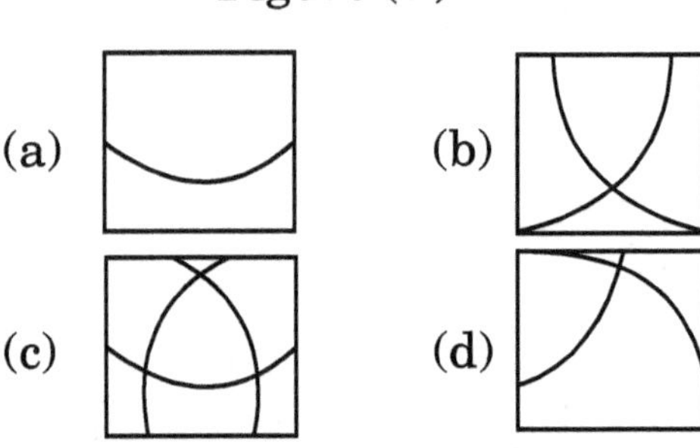

Directions (Qs. 18 and 19): In each
of the following questions, a square
transparent sheet (X) with a pattern
is given. Figure out from amongst the
four options how the pattern would
appear when the transparent sheet is
folded along the dotted line.

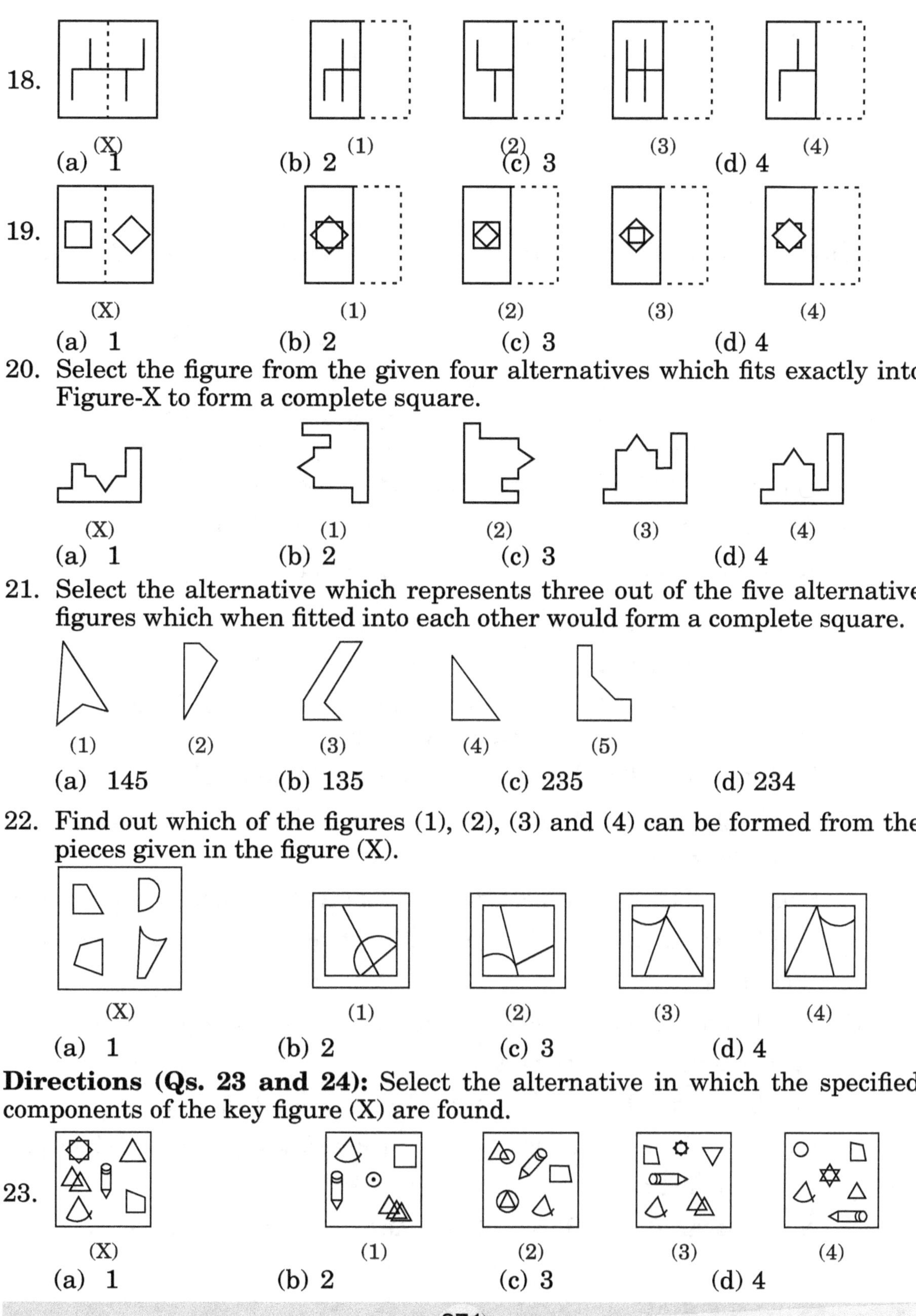

18.
(a) 1 (X)(1)   (b) 2 (1)   (c) 3 (2)   (3)   (d) 4 (4)

19.
(X)   (1)   (2)   (3)   (4)
(a) 1   (b) 2   (c) 3   (d) 4

20. Select the figure from the given four alternatives which fits exactly into Figure-X to form a complete square.

(X)   (1)   (2)   (3)   (4)
(a) 1   (b) 2   (c) 3   (d) 4

21. Select the alternative which represents three out of the five alternative figures which when fitted into each other would form a complete square.

(1)   (2)   (3)   (4)   (5)
(a) 145   (b) 135   (c) 235   (d) 234

22. Find out which of the figures (1), (2), (3) and (4) can be formed from the pieces given in the figure (X).

(X)   (1)   (2)   (3)   (4)
(a) 1   (b) 2   (c) 3   (d) 4

Directions (Qs. 23 and 24): Select the alternative in which the specified components of the key figure (X) are found.

23.
(X)   (1)   (2)   (3)   (4)
(a) 1   (b) 2   (c) 3   (d) 4

24. 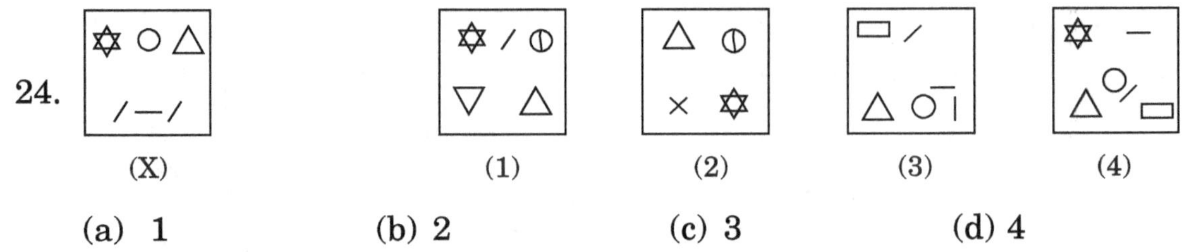

    (X)   (1)   (2)   (3)   (4)

(a) 1   (b) 2   (c) 3   (d) 4

25. Select the alternative which represents three out of the five alternative figures which when fitted into each other would form an equilateral triangle.

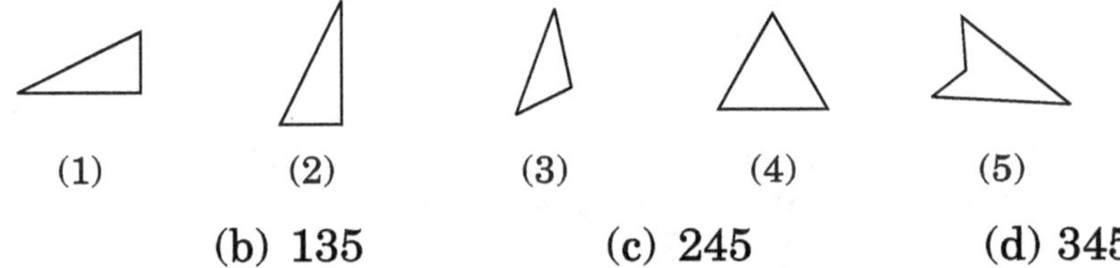

    (1)   (2)   (3)   (4)   (5)

(a) 123   (b) 135   (c) 245   (d) 345

26. P is the son of E while E is the mother of Q. F is the father of P and Q. L is the brother of F and Q is the sister of P. How is L related to Q? **(2022)**

(a) Grandfather   (b) Maternal Uncle

(c) Paternal Uncle   (d) Brother

27. Names of a few types of wastes are given below. **(2022)**

Classify them as biodegradable and non-biodegradable.

Glass bottles, Vegetable peels, Metal cans, Plastic bags, Seeds of fruits, Used cotton, Waste papers, Used matchsticks

(a) Biodegradable: Glass bottles, Used matchsticks, Plastic bags, Used cotton

    Non-biodegradable: Metal cans, Seeds of fruits, Waste papers, Vegetable peels

(b) Biodegradable: Metal cans, Used matchsticks, Plastic bags, Used cotton

    Non-biodegradable: Seeds of fruits, Waste papers, Vegetable peels, Glass bottles

(c) Biodegradable: Vegetable peels, Seeds of fruits, Waste papers, Used cotton, Used matchsticks

    Non-biodegradable: Glass bottles, Metal cans, Plastic bags

(d) Biodegradable: Plastic bags, Seeds of fruits, Waste papers, Used cotton, Used matchsticks

    Non-biodegradable: Glass bottles, Metal cans, Vegetable peels

Level-1

1. (a) 1, 4, 8; 3, 5, 7; 2, 6, 9
2. (c) 1, 2, 7; 3, 8, 9; 4, 5, 6
3. (b) 1, 6, 9; 3, 5, 7; 2, 4, 8
4. (d) 1, 5; 2, 4, 7; 3, 6
5. (a) 1, 4, 7; 2, 6, 9; 3, 5, 8
6. (d) 7. (b) 8. (a)
9. (b) 10. (c) 11. (a)
12. (d) 13. (a) 14. (b)
15. (c) 16. (d) 17. (a)
18. (a)  19. (b)
20. (c)
21. (d)
22. (b) 23. (a)

24. (b) 25. (c)
26. (d)

PM4@2L1TUXV$9©NX7&AGZ·6#

If all the numbers are removed, there will be 18 elements left in the series.

27. (b) Lion is the king of Jungle. Since, lion is called tiger. So, tiger is the answer.

28. (d) There are 3 teachers for 5 students. Possible combinations will be:

Teacher Kamal with each of the 5 students = 5

Teacher Anand with each of the 5 students = 5

Teacher Krishna with each of the 5 students = 5

Total combinations = 15

29. (c) 30. (b)

Level-2

1. (d) 2. (c) 3. (c) 4. (a)
5. (c)
6. (a)
7. (b)
8. (c)
9. (c)
10. (a)
11. (d)
12. (b)
13. (b)

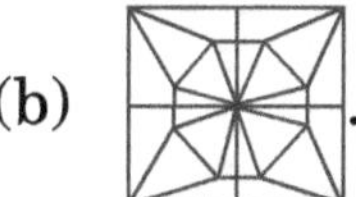
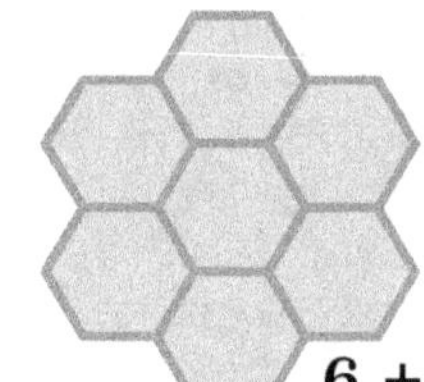

14. (d) Shapes 2 and 3 do not intersect.

15. (d) These three balls are at the same distance from the center of the triangle.

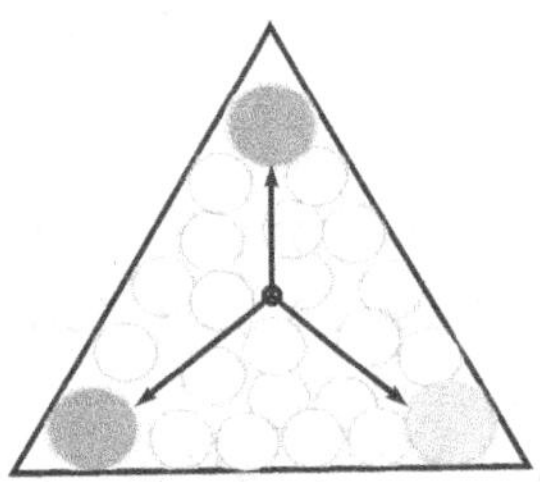

16. (d)

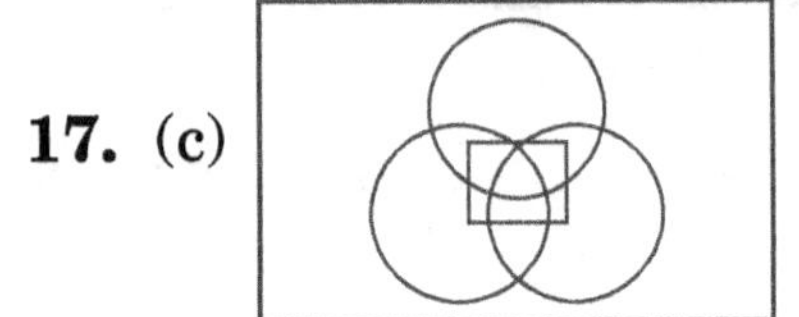

17. (c)

18. (c)

19. (a)

20. (c) 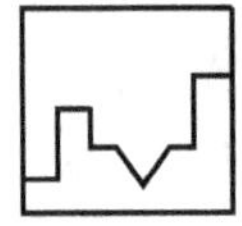

21. (d) 

22. (b)

23. (c)

24. (b)

25. (b) 

26. (c)

27. (c)